Regulating Reproductive Donation

The emergence of new empirical evidence and ethical debate about families created by assisted reproduction has called into question the current regulatory frameworks that govern reproductive donation in many countries. In this multidisciplinary book, social scientists, ethicists and lawyers offer fresh perspectives on the current challenges facing the regulation of reproductive donation, and suggest possible ways forward. They address questions such as: what might people want to know about the circumstances of their conception? Should we limit the number of children donors can produce? Is it wrong to pay donors or to reward them with cut-price fertility treatments? Is overseas surrogacy exploitative of women from poor communities? Combining the latest empirical research with analysis of ethics, policy and legislation, the book focuses on the regulation of gamete and embryo donation and surrogacy at a time when more people are considering assisted reproduction and when new techniques and policies are underway.

SUSAN GOLOMBOK is Professor of Family Research and Director of the Centre for Family Research at the University of Cambridge.

ROSAMUND SCOTT is Professor of Medical Law and Ethics and Co-Director of the Centre of Medical Law and Ethics in the Dickson Poon School of Law, King's College London.

JOHN B. APPLEBY is Research Associate at the Centre of Medical Law and Ethics in the Dickson Poon School of Law, King's College London.

MARTIN RICHARDS is Emeritus Professor of Family Research in the Centre for Family Research at the University of Cambridge.

STEPHEN WILKINSON is Professor of Bioethics in the Department of Politics, Philosophy and Religion at Lancaster University.

Regulating Reproductive Donation

Edited by

Susan Golombok

Rosamund Scott

John B. Appleby

Martin Richards

Stephen Wilkinson

CAMBRIDGE
UNIVERSITY PRESS

CAMBRIDGE
UNIVERSITY PRESS

University Printing House, Cambridge CB2 8BS, United Kingdom

Cambridge University Press is part of the University of Cambridge.

It furthers the University's mission by disseminating knowledge in the pursuit of education, learning and research at the highest international levels of excellence.

www.cambridge.org
Information on this title: www.cambridge.org/9781107090965

First published 2016

A catalogue record for this publication is available from the British Library

Library of Congress Cataloguing in Publication data
Regulating reproductive donation / edited by Susan Golombok, Rosamund Scott, John B. Appleby, Martin Richards, Stephen Wilkinson.
pages cm
Includes index.
ISBN 978-1-107-09096-5 (hardback)
1. Human reproductive technology. 2. Human reproductive technology – Law and legislation. 3. Ovum donors. 4. Sperm donors. 5. Reproductive rights. 6. Family planning. I. Golombok, Susan.
RG133.5.R383 2016
618.1′7806 – dc23 2015021712

ISBN 978-1-107-09096-5 Hardback

Contents

Editors, contributors and discussants

Editors

Susan Golombok, Professor of Family Research and Director, Centre for Family Research, University of Cambridge

Rosamund Scott, Professor of Medical Law and Ethics and Co-Director, Centre of Medical Law and Ethics, King's College London

John B. Appleby, Research Associate, Centre of Medical Law and Ethics, King's College London

Martin Richards, Emeritus Professor of Family Research, Centre for Family Research, University of Cambridge

Stephen Wilkinson, Professor of Bioethics, Department of Politics, Philosophy and Religion, Lancaster University

Contributors

John B. Appleby, Centre of Medical Law and Ethics, King's College London

Lucy Blake, Centre for Family Research, University of Cambridge

Kate Bourne, Victorian Assisted Reproductive Treatment Authority, Australia

Andrea M. Braverman, Department of Obstetrics and Gynecology, Thomas Jefferson University, USA

Bobbie Farsides, Brighton and Sussex Medical School, University of Sussex

Tabitha Freeman, Centre for Family Research, University of Cambridge

Natalie Gamble, Natalie Gamble Associates, Salisbury

Theresa Glennon, Beasley School of Law, Temple University, USA

Susan Golombok, Centre for Family Research, University of Cambridge

Susanna Graham, Centre for Family Research, University of Cambridge

Elena Ilioi, Centre for Family Research, University of Cambridge

Susan Imrie, Centre for Family Research, University of Cambridge

Mattias Iser, Binghamton University, State University of New York, USA

Vasanti Jadva, Centre for Family Research, University of Cambridge

Anja J. Karnein, Binghamton University, State University of New York, USA

Robert Klitzman, College of Physicians and Surgeons, Columbia University, USA

Sebastian Mohr, Aarhus University, Copenhagen, Denmark

Guido Pennings, Bioethics Institute, Ghent University, Belgium

Martin Richards, Centre for Family Research, University of Cambridge

Rosamund Scott, Centre of Medical Law and Ethics, King's College London

Jenna Slutsky, Center for Attachment Research, The New School for Social Research, New York, USA

Stephen Wilkinson, Department of Politics, Philosophy and Religion, Lancaster University

Katharine Wright, Nuffield Council on Bioethics, London

Sophie Zadeh, Centre for Family Research, University of Cambridge

Fernando Zegers-Hochschild, University Diego Portales, Santiago, Chile

Discussants

Kamal Ahuja, The London Women's Clinic

Joanne Anton, Human Fertilisation and Embryology Authority, London

David Archard, School of Politics, International Studies and Philosophy, Queen's University Belfast

Irenee Daly, School of Applied Social Sciences, De Montfort University, Leicester

Yolanda García-Ruiz, Faculty of Law, University of Valencia, Spain

Danielle Griffiths, Institute for Science, Ethics and Innovation, University of Manchester

Zeynep Gürtin, Department of Sociology, University of Cambridge

Florencia Herrera, Sociology Department, University Diego Portales, Santiago, Chile

Martin Johnson, Department of Physiology, Development and Neuroscience, University of Cambridge

Hallvard Lillehammer, Department of Philosophy, Birkbeck, University of London

Carol Smart, The Morgan Centre, University of Manchester

Venessa Smith, The London Women's Clinic

Helen Statham, Centre for Family Research, University of Cambridge

Effy Vayena, Institute of Biomedical Ethics, University of Zurich, Switzerland

Laura Witjens, National Gamete Donation Trust, London

Paul Woodgate, The Wellcome Trust, London

Acknowledgements

This book is the third and final volume in the series on 'Bioethics, Assisted Reproduction and the Family' produced through a Wellcome Trust Enhancement Award in Biomedical Ethics held by Professor Susan Golombok and colleagues at the University of Cambridge Centre for Family Research and, for this volume, in collaboration with Professor Rosamund Scott from the Centre of Medical Law and Ethics, Dickson Poon School of Law, King's College London and Professor Stephen Wilkinson from the Department of Politics, Philosophy and Religion at Lancaster University through their Wellcome Trust Senior Investigator Award, 'The Donation and Transfer of Human Reproductive Materials'. We are extremely grateful to the Wellcome Trust for supporting the workshop that led to the present volume.

The editors greatly appreciate the involvement of everyone who took part in this project throughout its many stages. Thanks are due to the authors for their lively contributions to the workshop, their insightful chapters and their tolerance during the editing process. We would also like to thank the discussants for their stimulating and invaluable input.

Workshop dinner at King's College, Cambridge

The workshop would not have been possible without the administrative genius of Abby Scott and Kathy Oswald who made everything run like clockwork. We are also indebted to Kathy Oswald for nurturing the book to fruition.

Introduction

Susan Golombok, Rosamund Scott, John B. Appleby, Martin Richards and Stephen Wilkinson

This book brings together empirical research with ethical, legal and policy analyses of key issues in the regulation of reproductive donation. The collection is primarily motivated by the thought that such analyses should be informed by relevant empirical data and that regulation should take account of this where possible. It is also shaped by the belief that empirical work which purports to have normative implications should be underpinned by a rigorous grasp of ethical and legal concepts and principles. The contributions have been chosen with an awareness of the importance of attending to the history of regulation, to social contexts, to the diversity of approaches in different jurisdictions and to the increasingly global nature of reproductive donation practices. Sometimes people, gametes or embryos cross borders and families are thereby formed.

In attending to the relationship between the empirical evidence, normative analysis and legal and regulatory responses, the work in this volume illustrates the complexity of the issues and hence the need for fine-tuned and sensitive law, regulation and policy. It also demonstrates the importance of challenging and 'unpacking' a range of assumptions, of identifying the diversity of the interests at stake and the ways in which these may or may not be aligned, and the scope for further empirical and empirically informed normative work, all of which are crucial for the development of appropriate legal, regulatory and policy responses.

The collection is the fruit of an international workshop held at the Centre for Family Research in Cambridge in April 2014. In addition to the contributing authors, there was a wide range of invited discussants, enabling discussion of pre-circulated chapters to be informed not just by a range of academics (from law, philosophy and the social sciences), but also by clinicians, fertility counsellors, practising lawyers, as well as members of regulatory and policy bodies.

Following an introductory chapter by Richards on 'The development of governance and regulation of donor conception in the UK', the book is divided into four parts.

Part I – 'International, cross-border and global issues' – attempts to reveal something of the diversity of approaches in different jurisdictions, coupled with the complexity of cross-border donation and surrogacy practices. The remaining three sections each address a key issue or related issues, with a mix of empirical, ethical and regulatory analysis.

Part II – 'How many children per donor?' – addresses the under-considered question of regulatory approaches to the number of offspring from any one donor; it also considers the question of donation as an aspect of global justice.

Part III – 'Donors: experiences, motivations and consent' – considers a cluster of issues relating to the experience of donors and conceptions of what makes a 'good donor', their reasons for donation and the possible effect of certain reasons, notably financial ones, on future donor-conceived people, and the relationship between reasons for and consent to donation in the context of egg-sharing.

In Part IV – 'Information about donors: the interests at stake' – four chapters address the complex question of the provision of information in relation to genetic parenthood, considering the interests of donor-conceived individuals, prospective and actual parents, as well as donors.

Turning now to the chapters themselves, in Chapter 1, 'The development of governance and regulation of donor conception in the UK', Richards reflects on the history underlying the UK's current system of regulating reproductive donation. The history of the governance of sperm donor conception in the UK is the story of a shift from self-regulated professional practice, developed in the face of much condemnation from church, public and fellow professionals to a legally regulated system set up in the wake of the coming of in vitro fertilisation (IVF) and the development of the commercial and National Health Service (NHS) practice of assisted reproduction. Though the practice of AIH (artificial insemination by husband) was much older, AID (artificial insemination by donor) began alongside AIH largely in the context of specialist infertility clinics in the late 1930s. While AIH was deemed to be acceptable by a Church Commission (The Wand Report) in 1948, this called for the criminalisation of AID on the grounds that it involved adultery, defrauded the begotten children and deceived both kin and society at large about ancestral heritage and bloodlines. In the 1950s and 1960s, the practice of AID developed slowly with increasing demand and growing public and professional acceptance. But without proper legal basis, the children born were regarded as illegitimate. The practice was carried out in secret by parents and clinicians so that the offspring would be protected from knowledge of their illegitimate status. A little over a decade after the birth of the first IVF baby (Louise Brown) in 1978, a legally regulated system of established limits for assisted reproduction was created under the Human Fertilisation and Embryology Act (HFE) 1990, ending professional autonomy for much infertility practice. In this system, the parental rights and duties of sperm and egg donors were transferred from donors to recipients. The law was amended in an important respect in 2004 to require the donor's identity to be made available to offspring at 18, thus ending anonymous donation.

This historical account of the development of regulation in the UK, a leader in the regulation of assisted reproduction in general and reproductive donation in particular, is followed by consideration of regulatory developments in a range of other jurisdictions, and of cross-border reproductive health care.

Part I – International, cross-border and global issues

Taking an international approach, in Chapter 2, 'International regulation and cross-country comparisons', Pennings, Klitzman and Zegers-Hochschild reveal and discuss trends in the evolving regulation of medically assisted reproduction across three continents: Europe, North America and Latin America. Three different types of regulation are considered in this investigation: legislation (national and international), court decisions and professional guidelines. Although regulation is very different in each of the continents, three similarities are highlighted. First, tensions exist between the nation-state level and the supranational level. Second, the courts are increasingly influential in the field of reproductive donation. Third, a plurality of different regulations exists in the three continents. The challenge of having such a variety of regulations, at both national and international levels, is that these regulatory systems are frequently found to be incoherent, contradictory and complex. It is unclear how these regulations will evolve over time, especially as reproductive technologies evolve. The differences in regulation between these continents highlight the extent to which assisted reproductive technologies (ARTs) continue to raise controversial and competing ethical concerns that can manifest in a wide variety of ways in our increasingly globalised world.

In Chapter 3, 'Legal regulation of family creation through gamete donation: access, identity and parentage', Glennon makes in-depth international legal comparisons between the United States, UK, Canada and Europe with regard to three major regulatory issues: access to assisted reproduction, challenges to donor anonymity and disputes regarding parentage. Issues about access to donated gametes arise based on status – age, sexual orientation and relationship status – as well as financial ability. In addition, donor-conceived individuals have asserted human rights claims that they are entitled to know the identity of all those involved in their conception. Finally, contests have arisen regarding the legal status of families formed through gamete donation. Disputes are especially common when gamete donation occurs outside licensed clinics or when parenting roles are unclear or those involved have conflicting views regarding their roles. Parentage disputes have also challenged the assumption that a child can have no more than two parents. Glennon's chapter surveys the varied responses of these jurisdictions to the rapidly changing landscape of gamete donation, and looks at the sharply conflicting values that support these differences. Overall, she notes that the regulatory trend is towards increasing access to assisted reproduction and the provision of information about genetic heritage to donor-conceived individuals. While some states have greater certainty regarding parentage than others, all face the need to review and revise their rules as societal views of parenting roles and the technology used in gamete donation continue to change.

Debates about population and the ethics of climate change are also of significance in the international context of regulating reproductive donation. In Chapter 4, 'Reproductive donation in the context of environmental and global justice', Karnein and Iser critically assess an argument in favour of restricting access to ARTs in westernised nations in order to help reduce human influence on climate change. The argument in question consists of two steps. First, it is suggested that members of western industrialised countries generally create more emissions that contribute to climate change than do members of less industrialised nations. Second, it is argued that in order to help curb the impact of the human population on climate change, society should not provide ARTs to help prospective parents have children in western industrialised countries. Karnein and Iser reject this argument and instead argue that society should not specifically burden prospective parents who need ARTs with the issue of reducing population for the sake of curbing climate change. Instead, they suggest that the burden of population reduction should be assumed by everyone, and a fair way to do this would be to directly tax persons based on the emissions they produce rather than the number of offspring they create.

Regardless of the legal and broader regulatory position in any one jurisdiction, where individuals or couples wish to have a child or children, they may seek to have some or all of their treatment needs fulfilled in another jurisdiction, either because of need (e.g. arising from a shortage of donor eggs), or because of certain restrictions in domestic regulation. In Chapter 5, 'Normative and regulatory issues in cross-border reproductive health care', Pennings addresses a number of issues that arise in relation to cross-border treatment. The first concerns the responsibility of the doctors involved. In this regard, Pennings raises two important questions related to the complicity of doctors in their patients' cross-border treatment activities. First, is a doctor responsible for the end result of cross-border treatment even if he/she did not know the goal of the patient and had no intention of participating in the medical intervention? For instance, this question may arise when patients transfer their embryos to another country to perform a selection that is considered immoral or illegal in the home country of the physician. Second, to what extent is a physician complicit when she either refers a patient abroad or provides information about treatment abroad that is forbidden at home? The primary issue here is whether or not such actions conflict with a physician's duty to act in the best interests of the patient. A secondary issue results from the introduction of restrictions on foreign patients in the destination countries that offer treatment. For example, some countries limit the number of foreign patients (for instance for donor eggs), or demand prior legal approval at home (for instance for surrogacy). Pennings discusses three reasons for introducing such measures and reveals the ethical complexity behind allowing cross-border reproduction to take place while also attempting to regulate it.

In recent years, the prevalence of surrogacy as a means to family building has increased, offering a route to parenthood for infertile heterosexual couples, same sex couples and single men. This increased need for surrogacy has been met with a ready supply of surrogates from countries where commercial surrogacy is widely practised. In Chapter 6, 'Surrogacy: issues, concerns and complexities', Jadva summarises the available findings from research carried out with intending parents, surrogates and children born using surrogacy and highlights the shortcomings in our understanding of the impact of surrogacy. Legislation and practice differ from one country to the next, making surrogacy difficult to evaluate; further, surrogacy needs to be assessed at a global level. Surrogates from diverse cultures conceptualise their 'connection' to the child differently, perhaps in a way which optimises their ability to give the child to the intending parents. It is apparent from the available literature that what motivates many women to become surrogates is a sense of altruism. Even in countries where commercial surrogacy is allowed, financial motivations in themselves are often mentioned in combination with other motivations, such as wanting to help a childless couple, and enjoyment of pregnancy. Regulation (either real or perceived) can have immediate consequences for those involved, with changes in law leading to people finding themselves in difficult situations. Jadva also highlights that we know very little about the consequences of surrogacy for the resulting child. Ten-year-old children have been reported to feel positive or neutral about their birth; however, this may change as they grow older and gain a more sophisticated understanding of surrogacy. It is vital that more is understood from the child's perspective in order to fully evaluate the impact of surrogacy.

The UK is among many countries in the world grappling with a sharp rise in the numbers of children being born through surrogacy, both domestically and via international surrogacy arrangements. In the final contribution, Chapter 7, 'A better legal framework for United Kingdom surrogacy?', Gamble examines the development of the law governing surrogacy in the UK, including the restrictions in the Surrogacy Arrangements Act 1985, and the rules on parenthood created by the HFE Act 1990 and subsequently amended by the HFE Act 2008. She tracks the original policy underpinning the law and how this policy has been applied (and stretched) via the UK court decisions which have applied the law over the past thirty years. The chapter also considers the impact of the law on the current landscape for surrogacy, both with regard to how it has fuelled the development of informal and unregulated surrogacy arrangement in the UK, and with regard to how it has driven the demand of UK parents for overseas surrogacy. Highlighting the problems that the current law creates, Gamble's chapter considers how we could implement a better UK legal framework for surrogacy. Considering legal, practical and ethical issues, the case is made for a more structured legal framework in the UK (including written agreements, pre-birth orders and a more transparent approach to compensating surrogates for their inconvenience) in order to protect parents, surrogates and children. Overall, this collection reveals the complexity of the bioethical, empirical and regulatory picture. It also highlights the amount of important work that still needs to be done in this field, including with regard to issues – such as information disclosure and surrogacy – that have already been the subject of significant research to date. The global and rapidly changing nature of donation practices is particularly evident and the challenges this presents should not be underestimated.

Part II – How many children per donor?

The question of what limit, if any, should be placed on how many children can be created with gametes from any given donor has been an important one since the start of regulation, but has received little in-depth consideration.

In Chapter 8, 'Sperm donors limited: psychosocial aspects of genetic connections and the regulation of offspring numbers', Freeman, Jadva and Slutsky address empirical questions raised by the regulation of donor offspring numbers. The chapter opens by outlining central ethical and regulatory debates about limiting the number of offspring conceived from any one sperm donor. Two key concerns are identified: the risk of unintentional consanguinity between half-siblings and the psychosocial impact of the discovery of large numbers of half-siblings. Freeman, Jadva and Slutsky suggest that arguments that respond to such concerns about limiting donor offspring numbers contain implicit assumptions about the meaning and significance of the 'genetic connections' created through donor conception, particularly with regard to donor-conceived individuals who share the same donor (referred to in this chapter as 'same-donor offspring'). In order to shed light on how these connections are perceived and managed by those involved, Freeman, Jadva and Slutsky present new data from an exploratory study of 'donor sibling' groups in the United States, comprising the first in-depth interviews with mothers of young donor-conceived children about their experiences of seeking and finding families who share the same gamete donor. Key findings include: the close link between interest in same-donor offspring and interest in the donor (e.g. parents may use connections with same-donor families to counter lack of knowledge, especially medical knowledge, about their donor); the diverse, decentralised process by which connections are being established, including initiating contact at the 'pre-conception' stage as well as the occurrence of 'unwitting' meetings between same-donor offspring families; the complexities of relationships between same-donor family members, including similarities to other forms of interpersonal and family relationships as well as specific qualities of voluntary commitment, agency and choice (referred to as 'elastic kinship'). The significance (or not) of these connections – and the number of same-donor offspring that one has – depends on the cultural and psychological meanings attributed to genetic relatedness. Freeman, Jadva and Slutsky propose a cautious approach to donor-offspring limits that recognises the way in which regulation is itself part of the cultural, social and personal framework in which people navigate the relationships that may be created through assisted reproduction.

The ethical concerns that underpin the perceived need to limit the number of people who may be born as a result of donations from a single donor also require analysis. In Chapter 9, 'Limiting offspring numbers: can we justify regulation?', Wright examines the potential harms that such limits are thought to prevent, and considers how the reasons behind these limits are changing. Limits were originally thought to be important in order to restrict the likelihood of donor-conceived people entering inadvertently into taboo relationships with unknown half-siblings (a fear that is real for many, regardless of the actual likelihood of it happening). As policy and practice has shifted towards more open attitudes to donor conception, and some donor-conceived people (and their parents) have attempted to make connections with their 'donor-siblings', a very different rationale has emerged: that of limiting the number of such connections in order to allow for the possibility of meaningful relationships with them all. The chapter explores assumptions about the significance of 'pure' genetic connection in the absence of any pre-existing social relationships that underpin these claims, and suggests that, where positive social relationships do subsequently develop, the genetic connection might better be seen as a 'trigger' for the initial encounter, rather than as a necessary element of the relationship that ensues. Wright concludes with an analysis of the role of regulation, suggesting that the evidence base for any specific limit on same-donor offspring is weak, and that further regulatory change (in either direction) would be unnecessary and would also send unwanted messages about the weight that ought to be given to genetic connection.

Part III – Donors: experiences, motivations and consent

Chapters 10, 11 and 12 consider a range of issues relating to the experiences of donors and their motivations for donation, conceptions of the 'good donor', the relationship between different motivations and the welfare of the future child on the one hand, and between motivations for donation and consent on the other.

In the first of these, Chapter 10, 'Regulating the "good" donor: the expectations and experiences of sperm donors in Denmark and Victoria, Australia', Graham, Mohr and Bourne cross both international and disciplinary borders by drawing on an anthropologist's account of the practices and donor experiences within commercial sperm banks in Denmark, and a counsellor's interactions and interviews with past and current sperm donors in Victoria, Australia. The result is a chapter that explores different modes of regulating the 'good donor' and examines how donors themselves think about and experience this regulation. The authors use the term 'regulation' quite broadly, encompassing: formal legislation; guidelines created by regulatory authorities such as the Danish Health Authority or the Australian Reproductive Technology Accreditation Committee; the organisational practices of sperm banks and the interactions between sperm bank staff and donors, through which sperm donors' compliance is enforced. Two case studies illustrate how the sperm donor as a person and a stakeholder with his own interests remains largely invisible in the regulatory and organisational contexts of sperm donation. Regulation is involved in making the 'good donor', as defined by other stakeholders – policymakers, sperm bank staff, recipients, as well as donor-conceived individuals. Donors are constructed as fulfilling a need and regulation ensures that they fulfil this need. However, it is argued that with a changing landscape of donation whereby identity-release donation is becoming more common and parents are encouraged to disclose their use of donor gametes, viewing sperm donors as a 'means to an end' is no longer feasible. Men who donate semen are themselves stakeholders and partners in donor conception and have their own perceptions and expectations of what being a 'good donor' entails. In regulating donor conception, whether formally or informally, the chapter concludes that it is important to ascertain the interests of all stakeholders: not only the recipients of, and offspring conceived through, donor sperm, but also the men who donate their semen.

Still attending to the question of motivations for donation, in Chapter 11, 'Gamete donor motives, payment and child-welfare', Wilkinson considers the issue of financial reasons for donation and the possible impact on donor-conceived people. He asks what implications would (and should) there be for ethics and policy if we accept a particular empirical premise: the claim that, when donor-conceived people find out that their donors' motives were primarily financial, they are often psychologically distressed or damaged, and seriously so? His chapter argues that if this premise is true then, when they have a choice (and all other things being equal), prospective parents ought to use an altruistic donor in preference to a paid one. The basis for this, however, is not harm to the child created but rather an impersonal ethical principle: the Same Number Quality Claim. Is this ethical requirement one that ought to be legally enforced? Not obviously so. Given the absence of harm, political liberals probably should not attempt to translate it into law. However, public bodies such as the NHS may have good reason to facilitate and promote altruistic, rather than paid, donation, since they have a legitimate interest in the well-being of future populations, and in maximising the benefit created by the deployment of health service resources. Finally, and more controversially perhaps, it is argued that the ethics of shortage situations are quite different from that in non-shortage situations. If preventing payment to gamete donors will cause a reduction in the size of the donor-conceived population, arguments against payment which appeal solely to interests of future donor-conceived people are likely to fail. For to propose that payment should be restricted in such circumstances for the sake of the possible future children's welfare implies either that the world would be a better place with fewer donor-conceived people, or that the children resulting from paid donation would not have lives not worth living (or both). Wilkinson concludes that such implications are highly implausible and so child-welfare arguments for restricting payments to donors in shortage situations should be rejected.

In the final chapter to consider issues relating to motivations for donation, Chapter 12, 'Egg-sharing, motivation and consent: ethical, legal and policy issues', Scott draws on relevant empirical research on the practice of egg-sharing in order to consider a number of ethical, legal and policy questions concerning the relationship between the reasons for egg-sharing on the one hand and consent thereto on the other. The practice of egg-sharing, in which a woman may donate half her eggs in exchange for reduced-fee or free IVF treatment gives a woman who needs, wants and is unable to afford such treatment a very precious chance – namely that of having a genetically related child. With reference to the empirical evidence, Scott first considers the significance of different kinds of reasons for donation, including altruism and financial constraints, noting that the (limited) available evidence suggests that the latter are the dominant motive for egg-sharing in most cases. She then addresses the implications of this discussion for the quality and legal validity of consent to donation. She argues that while, legally speaking, a woman can give valid consent to an egg-sharing arrangement, ethically speaking, it is important to recognise the limited options a woman has when she may decide to donate, thus drawing attention to the importance of viewing her autonomy in a broader ethical context which includes the restricted availability of IVF treatment on the UK's NHS, coupled with the high costs of private treatment. Scott also considers the extent to which either permitting, or not permitting, egg-sharing may benefit or harm a woman's interests, suggesting that, on the basis of the limited evidence that we have so far, the indications are that it may be more beneficial than harmful. Finally, Scott turns to address the broader regulatory position, analysing aspects of current Human Fertilisation and Embryology Authority (HFEA) policy against the backdrop of the European Union Tissue and Cells Directive (EUTCD) – which requires voluntary, unpaid and altruistic donation – and considers whether, or to what extent, the UK position permitting compensated egg-sharing is compliant with the Directive.

Part IV – Information about donors: the interests at stake

In Part IV, the book's focus shifts to consider issues of information disclosure and sharing regarding genetic parenthood.

In Chapter 13, 'Thoughts and feelings about the donor: a family perspective', Blake, Ilioi and Golombok examine the thoughts, feelings and experiences of individuals who are aware that they were conceived by sperm or egg donation. Parents' feelings about the donor are also explored, and compared between those families in which the donor is anonymous, open-identity and known. For those who conceived with an anonymous donor, the donor appears to exist on the margins of parents' and children's minds, occasionally drifting to the fore. Whereas for those who conceived using an open-identity donor, parents and children may have more practical concerns and curiosities about the donor and what he or she is like and what it would be like if they were ever to meet. This chapter also explores similarities and differences between families headed by heterosexual couples, lesbian couples and single mothers. The donor appears to be a more important figure for parents and children in families of single mothers compared to families headed by heterosexual or lesbian couples, which is perhaps unsurprising due to the absence of a second parent in these families. The data on families in which children are aware of their origins are in many ways limited. Therefore, the authors also turn to the adoption literature in order to examine trends and patterns that may have relevance to families created by gamete donation. For most donor offspring and adopted adolescents alike, there is a curiosity about their origins which may, for some, result in searching behaviours of varying degrees. The vast majority of donor-conceived individuals who search for their donor do not do so out of a desire to establish a parent–child relationship with him, which may be comforting to parents who may be concerned about their child's level of interest in their origins.

The interests of donor-conceived offspring have received the most attention in debates about the release of donor information, whilst the interests of parents have received much less attention. In Chapter 14, '"Choosing" a donor: parents' perspectives on current and future donor information provision in clinically assisted reproduction', Zadeh, Imrie and Braverman address the issue of donor information and its provision, from the perspective of the recipients of donor gametes in a clinical setting. The authors review current and cross-cultural research on the information needs of recipients of donor gametes, and reflect on the way in which these needs vary both within and between family types. This chapter also addresses the extent to which current regulation on donor information adequately meets the needs of recipients. Using research from two ongoing studies at the Centre for Family Research, University of Cambridge, the authors present findings showing that the majority of donor sperm and donor egg recipients in the UK are either satisfied with the amount of information that they have about their donor, desire further information that falls within existing regulatory parameters (e.g. the pen portrait), or acknowledge that further information is not a possibility.

These findings reveal that the majority of information provided – and deemed important to know – about both egg and sperm donors, is information about characteristics perceived to be, and generally described by the clinical sector as, 'genetically heritable'. The evidence presented within the chapter illustrates that there may be some differences between couples and single recipients of donor sperm with regard to how much information is requested or required, and that there may be some within-couple variation, particularly with regard to information regarding egg donation. The needs of recipients may change over time, and in concert with a changing recognition of their children's need for information, both about the donor, and about themselves. The authors conclude by questioning the changing nature of gamete donation in the UK (i.e. increases in the use of donation outside regulated clinics), and whether and to what extent this increase may be attributable to recipients' attitudes towards current donor information provision.

Drawing on the body of evidence presented in Chapter 13 by Blake, Ilioi and Golombok, in Chapter 15, 'Regulating the provision of donor information to donor-conceived children: is there room for improvement?', Appleby discusses the question of what information about the donor should be available to donor-conceived persons and whether or not there is room for improvement with respect to how donor information is made available to donor offspring. A key tension exists in the debate regarding the accessibility of donor information: if too much information is released, donors may claim that this constitutes an invasion of their privacy; however, if too little information is made available, donor-conceived persons may argue that their interests in knowing about their donor(s) are frustrated. After carefully considering the current regulations (predominantly in the UK) surrounding the collection and release of donor information to donor-conceived persons, Appleby suggests that although current law, regulation and policy generally appear to be satisfactory, given the evidence that is available about the preferences and well-being of donor-conceived persons, there is a major issue with respect to the management and release of open-identity donor information in the UK that requires attention. Currently, the HFE Act 1990 (as amended by the HFE Act 2008) only permits identifying information about open-identity donors to be released to donor-conceived offspring when those offspring reach the age of 18. Appleby argues that this age requirement lacks justification and that there is no convincing evidence available to suggest that this is in the interests of donor offspring (let alone their parents or the donors themselves). Rather, he argues that Parliament should reconsider the current legal requirement that a donor-conceived person must be 18 before he or she can access identifying information about open-identity donors; and that the amended HFE Act should instead provide that identifying donor information should be available to the parents of donor-conceived children at the time at which the donor is chosen by prospective parents.

In Chapter 16, 'The informational needs of prospective parents: an ethical perspective', Farsides discusses the informational needs and wants of recipient parents and the ethical issues that these raise. What level and what kind of information about gamete donors is it reasonable for recipient parents to expect? How does this relate to the parenting models that they have in mind, including the question of the donor's anticipated relationship with the donor-conceived child? What are donors' and recipients' moral duties and rights with respect to information and which of these should be enforced by law and regulation, or by clinic policies and professional guidelines? Farsides argues that there needs to be a 'fair contract' between gamete providers and recipients, one which clearly indicates the options for future interactions with the donor-conceived child. As regards health information, 'serious' health risks should be eliminated by careful selection (or rejection) of donors. However, it may also be important to provide recipients with additional health-related information about matters falling below the 'seriousness' threshold: for example, a recipient might want to know whether the donor experiences a range of mild reactions to common allergens such as cat fur, tree pollen or certain foods because of the environment in which they live; or recipients may wish to consider using a donor with a minor impairment (say, being 50 per cent deaf in one ear) if that donor is deemed to have other desirable features, even if this means that there is some risk of the child inheriting the impairment. In such cases, Farsides suggests, it is important for recipients to be offered information, not just about the physical facts but also, perhaps in personal narrative form, about the 'meaning' of the condition for the individual donor. Finally, and relating back closely to some of the questions raised in Part III regarding conceptions of what makes a 'good donor' and donor motives, Farsides discusses the extent to which recipients should be provided with information about donor motives and about the 'type of person' the donor is.

Overall, this collection reveals the complexity of the bioethical, empirical and regulatory picture. It also highlights the amount of important work that still needs to be done in this field, including with regard to issues – such as information disclosure and surrogacy – that have already been the subject of significant research to date. The global and rapidly changing nature of donation practices is particularly evident and the challenges this presents should not be underestimated.

1 The development of governance and regulation of donor conception in the UK

Martin Richards

Introduction

In this chapter, I will trace the development of the governance and regulation of donor conception in the UK. The clinical practice of artificial insemination (AI)[1] has a long history in Britain and a rather longer one abroad. There were early clinical experiments with AI in France and Germany and other European countries around the turn of the nineteenth century (Rohleder, 1934; Swanson, 2012). However, it was not until the 1930s that the clinical practice of AI was established in Britain; this was largely artificial insemination with semen from the husband (AIH), but there were also a few cases where artificial insemination with semen from a donor (AID) was used. This development largely took place in the context of newly set up specialist infertility clinics which were established in several parts of the country in the context of a growing concern about the falling birth rate (Jackson et al., 1948; Lane-Roberts et al., 1939; White and Green-Armitage, 1962).[2] While clinics could do nothing about the problem of 'voluntary childlessness', they were able to address some problems of marital infertility.

My survey will begin with these early developments and continue through the arrival of in vitro fertilisation (IVF) in the 1980s and will include the coming of legal regulation through the Human Fertilisation and Embryology Act 1990. Before the establishment of legal regulation, governance was largely a matter of standards for clinical professional practice which in the early years were developed in the face of criticisms of the practice of AID from the churches, and some members of the public and fellow professionals.

[1] Until the 1980s, the abbreviations that were generally used were A.I.H. and A.I.D., and subsequently became AIH and AID (and much later DI). For simplicity in my text and in the quotations, I use AIH and AID throughout. And following the practice of our time, I will use the term 'donation' throughout whether or not the provision of semen involves a gift relationship.

[2] The broader international context of the development of clinical AIH and AID is discussed by Schellen (1957) and Bartholomew (1958).

Churches and professional practice

The first move in regulation of AI came from the Catholic Church. In 1897, the Papal Office responded to an enquiry about AI with a laconic, 'non licere'. Over the following couple of decades, the Catholic position was elaborated (Glover, 1948). In essence, the Catholic Church objected to any departure from conception through marital congress, save only a sanctioned form of 'assisted reproduction' for married couples which involved the post-coital transport of semen with a syringe from the vagina into or beyond the cervix.

The artificial insemination of a wife with semen obtained from her husband by means of an act of self-pollution or onanistic, or condomistic intercourse with her, is gravely sinful and has the morality and malice of whichever of the above sinful practices was employed.

The artificial insemination of a married woman with semen taken from anyone other than her husband involves a moral sin of legal injustice and a mortal sin of commutative injustice. Such a procedure has the morality and malice of adultery.

The artificial insemination of a single woman with semen taken from an unmarried man is a mortal sin of legal injustice and has the morality and malice of fornication. If the man be married, a mortal sin of commutative injustice is added so that the procedure will have the morality and malice of adultery.

The doctor who advises or performs any type of sinful artificial insemination is a formal cooperator in an evil action and becomes guilty of a sin which has the gravity and malice of whatever sins are committed in the course of the whole procedure. (Glover, 1948: 148–9)

There were edicts from Pope Pius XII in 1949 and 1956 effectively reiterating the condemnation of all collaborative reproduction.

In 1946, the Archbishop of Canterbury set up a Commission to advise on these matters (Wand, 1948). The Church was moved to consider AI by a growing public and professional debate which followed papers in the medical press (e.g. Barton, Walker and Wiesner, 1945) about AI practice in Britain and also reports from the United States where the practice had become much more established and widespread than in the UK (e.g. Forbes, 1945). The Commission was hardly more permissive but it did extend the Catholic permitted form of assisted reproduction to include AIH. As the Commission set up by the Archbishop of Canterbury found:

When 'assisted insemination' is inapplicable, or ineffective, other methods of AI with husband's semen may be employed. Even if, for the insemination of a wife with her husband's semen, there is no practical alternative to masturbation by the husband, his act, being directed to the procreative end of the marriage, may be justifiable.

AI with donated semen involves a breach of marriage. It violates the exclusive union set up between husband and wife. It defrauds the child begotten and deceives both his putative kinsmen and society at large. For both donor and recipient the sexual act loses its personal character and becomes a mere transaction. For the child there must always be the risk of disclosure, deliberate or unintended, of the circumstances of his conception. We then judge artificial insemination with donated semen to be wrong in principle and contrary to Christian standards.

In our view, the evils necessarily involved in AI (donor) are so grave that early consideration should be given to the framing of legislation to make the practice a criminal offence. (Wand, 1948: 58)

The Church's call for criminalisation of AID was not heeded by the Government of the day and the practices of AIH and AID continued to be offered to a slowly growing number of couples by a handful of clinicians. But negative attitudes, not least from the medical establishment made the practice rather more secretive and under the counter during the late 1940s and 1950s (see Feversham, 1960).

To illustrate the ideology of the period we may note the eugenic stance of the Commission. They considered the use of AID for eugenic ends – an issue much discussed at the time. It noted that some of 'those who were most expert in the science of eugenics', who had given evidence to the Commission, 'deprecated some of the exaggerated claims made for the use of AID for this purpose and the supposed benefits it could confer on human kind' (Wand, 1948: 32) and they concluded that 'it is doubtful, however, whether the most potent effects for society of the practice of AID will be in the field of eugenics' (Wand, 1948: 34).[3] But, aside from such proposals to use AID as a tool for the eugenic betterment of society, the clinical use of AID which the committee considered was carried in a eugenic context with couples seeking infertility treatment being screened for their child worthiness' and donors selected for their eugenic potential. This remained a feature of most practice until the 1960s.

It is unclear whether any single women used AID during this early period. It seems likely that a few did[4] and at least this was a possibility advocated by the League of Bachelor Mothers (Swanson, 2012). But the Wand Commission Report was unequivocal in its condemnation of the possibility.

Problems of the gravest possible character would inevitably arise in the case of insemination of unmarried women. The motive for requesting AID in those cases might be represented to be, and in many instances would really be, the comparatively innocent one of a desire for motherhood. It might on the other hand arise from a wish to deceive a man with whom the women had had intercourse into a belief that she was pregnant by him. If such a deceit resulted in his being induced

[3] See Richards (2008) for an account of the eugenic history of AID.

[4] And they, and single men, had been able – and did – adopt children from the beginning of regulated adoption under the Adoption of Children Act 1926.

to marry her, the child would be treated (falsely) as his, even, in some cases, when born before the marriage, i.e. under the Legitimacy Act (1926). (Wand, 1948: 41)

The significance of regarding AID as adultery for both an inseminated wife and a married donor was not simply that adultery was seen as an immoral marital offence (though not illegal in the UK) but that it was grounds for divorce, as can be traced to the much cited Canadian case of *Orford* v. *Orford* which was decided by the Supreme Court of Ontario in 1921. This was a case in which the wife was suing her husband for alimony on the grounds of cruelty. She had attempted to account for the existence of a child she had produced while living on the other side of the Atlantic to him by claiming it had been conceived by AID. The court found that the child was the product of an adulterous relationship with another man. But in a dictum the court commented that if the wife's testimony had been accepted, her using AID without her husband's consent would have also amounted to adultery.

The essence of the offence of adultery consists, not in the moral turpitude of the act of sexual intercourse, but in the voluntary surrender to another person of the reproductive powers or faculties of the guilty person, and any submission of those powers to the service or enjoyment of any person other than the husband of the wife comes within the definition of 'adultery'... the introduction into her body of semen by unusual means... in itself was 'sexual intercourse'. (*Orford* v. *Orford*)

In the later House of Lords case of *Russell* v. *Russell*, one of their Lordships said 'fecundation *ab extra* is, I doubt not, adultery'.

Such positions were not universally accepted. For example, Alan Guttmacher, a US obstetrician and a leading AI practitioner at John Hopkins University, said that, 'to the obstetrical mind it sounds like so much balderdash' (Guttmacher, 1946). He argued that adultery and AI were the absolute antithesis of one another, one being to enjoy carnal pleasure while the other is to beget offspring without the emotional and physical enjoyment of coitus. And he pointed out that if adultery is the surrender of the reproductive powers, women who have had hysterectomies would be incapable of adultery (Guttmacher, 1946).

Beyond the question of a child's legitimacy,[5] the Archbishop's Commission pointed to other legal issues raised by AID. They suggested that the registration of a child begotten by AID as the child of the

[5] There was general agreement that a child born to married parents through AID would be illegitimate. This was the status accorded to a 'bastard' child conceived outside marriage. An illegitimate child would suffer significant legal disadvantages, as well as social stigma. Over time most of these legal distinctions were removed and the legal status was effectively abolished by the 1970s (Bainham, 2005).

husband would be a criminal offence under section 4 of the Perjury Act 1911. And, among the problems that could ensue if unmarried women were inseminated, was the point that donors would be liable for the financial maintenance of their offspring. However, practitioners arranged their practice in ways that might avoid or mitigate some of these problems. For instance, often couples would be advised to continue sexual intercourse during treatment and practitioners might mix donor and husband's semen or semen from several donors so that there would be uncertainty about paternity. They usually advised their patients to register the birth as a child of the marriage. Some also matched the blood groups of donor and the recipient's partner so that the paternity tests of the day could not detect 'non-paternity'. While using eugenic criteria for selection of donors, some endeavoured to match donors to characteristics of the husband in the hope that the child would not stand out because of a lack of familial resemblance. A report from the United States suggested that some doctors got husbands to press the plunger of the syringe used for insemination so that they can confirm they had impregnated their wives. Some doctors in Britain announced that they restricted their practice to married couples to avoid the complication of inseminating single women. Insemination was treated as secret, avoiding any possible connection of donors with recipients to avoid emotional complications, to protect the welfare of children and to keep knowledge of the husband's sterility private. Parents were advised not to tell their children of their donor origin as this would indicate their illegitimate status, knowledge that might threaten their well-being.

In the 1940s, the Medical Defence Union produced guidance for doctors using AID some of which is included as an appendix to the Wand report. This included pro forma consent forms. Those for couples, include the statement that we 'assure you that the birth of a child will not defeat the claims of any person to any titles, estates, interests or funds'. And that for the donor, 'it has been explained to me that the use of semen supplied by me for this purpose might be held to be adultery and I have accordingly only consented to supply semen on the condition that my name be not disclosed'. The general advice of the Medical Defence Union covered avoidance of negligence through such actions as appropriate screening of the donor and selecting characteristics and the 'race' of the donor with regard to those of the husband. There was an expectation that practitioners would try to avoid the possibility of dissolution of marriage through careful selection of couples for treatment and arranging other matters so that there would be a good defence to any charge of adultery in such a situation. This guidance makes clear that the legitimacy of AID children was uncertain and so there might be difficulties about the inheritance of property and so forth by offspring. This could raise a possibility that a doctor, together with the husband and wife and donor, might be sued for conspiracy to defeat the claims of those who would inherit in default of the husband and wife having legal issue – hence the statement included in the couple's consent form. This defensive legal advice may be contrasted with transatlantic advice from Professor Guttmacher.

> I believe that if a doctor is honest and uses his God-given common sense no serious problem exists in a heterologous insemination.
>
> Some months ago I summarised my own practice in the following credo:
>
> *Rule one*: The donor must remain completely anonymous to the recipient and the husband and the recipient and the husband must remain equally anonymous to the donor.
>
> *Rule two*: Before accepting artificial insemination, know the couple: their intellectual capacity and emotional stability, and if possible the likelihood of a permanent marriage. Only a small percentage of patients applying qualify for so radical a social procedure. When a doctor consents to do an artificial insemination from an unrelated donor, it is really the couple's insignia of good character. Artificial insemination must always be completely individualised. It should never be an assembly-line kind of medical treatment.
>
> *Rule three*: Never urge the procedure; if either husband or wife is lukewarm, drop it completely.
>
> *Rule four*: Forget signed papers. If the patients are carefully selected, contracts and agreements are unnecessary, and simply act as a permanent reminder of something which should be forgotten as quickly and completely as possible. In the ideal case, by the time the patient reaches term, the woman, the husband and the doctor have to think twice to remember that the pregnancy is physically not the husband's for psychically it has become his.
>
> *Rule five*: Accord paternity to the husband both in the hospital record and the birth certificate. Here a white-lie is a kindly, humane act.
>
> *Rule six*: Make the fees low, keep artificial insemination out of the mercenary column. View it as a personal medical service, the contribution of an aesculapiad to the happiness of some wretched, worthy, sterile couple. (Guttmacher, 1943: 589–90)

Guttmacher's position was explicitly followed by at least some UK practitioners. Lane-Roberts et al.'s (1939) account of the technique of AI concludes with a brief description of 'medico-legal aspects'. This cites Guttmacher's views and concludes that, 'it is psychically wiser to leave the procedure, untrammelled by legal formalities and unhappy reminiscent documents' (Lane-Roberts et al., 1939: 345–6).

By the mid-1950s, there was a slow rise in the numbers of those seeking AID in Britain, possibly driven, in part, by a decline in the number of babies available for adoption. Further, among some Protestant theo logians there was a growing tendency to distance their moral natural law arguments from those of the Catholics and to offer some qualified support for the use of AID by infertile couples and, perhaps even for treatment of single women (e.g. Fletcher, 1954).

Lawyers and professional practice

In 1958, in a case at the Court of Sessions in Edinburgh[6] it was held that AID without the husband's consent did not amount to adultery according to the laws of Scotland. In a subsequent debate in the House of Lords (26 February 1958), Lord Merriman said that this view would likely also prevail in an English court. While this may have settled the legal issue of adultery and donor insemination, a wider public and press discussion about AID was initiated.

In a debate in the House of Lords it was stated there was considerable public anxiety about the procedure and the Lord Chancellor announced the setting up of a Departmental Committee to consider the legal consequences of AI and whether any change in the law was necessary or desirable (Feversham, 1960). This Committee, chaired by the Tory peer, the Third Earl of Feversham, produced a long and detailed report. But its conclusions were very modest – that AID should be 'discouraged', but not declared criminal, nor be regulated by law. And there should be no amendment of laws relating to legitimacy of AID children or registration of their births. The only legal changes recommended were essentially technical matters of law related to divorce. These included making the use by a wife of AID without consent of her husband grounds for divorce, though a husband donating sperm without consent from his wife would not be grounds for divorce. Further, the birth of an AID child to a couple should be a bar to proceedings by either spouse for nullity of marriage on the grounds of impotence.

The Report stops short of calling for criminalisation of AID because:

> To attempt to prohibit by law a practice which is very difficult to detect, which is so far of very small extent[7] and not demonstrably harmful to the community

[6] *MacLennan* v. *MacLennan* (1958). We may also note that it is quite possible that the first use of AID in an infertility clinic in the UK also took place in Scotland in 1934 with Albert Sharman, of the Royal Samaritan Hospital for Women, the pioneer obstetrician practitioner involved (see Lane-Roberts et al., 1939).

[7] The Committee thought numbers were rising but remained at a level of somewhat over one hundred children conceived annually in the UK with some twenty doctors regularly engaged in providing AID but this made up a very small part of their infertility practice. This may well be an underestimate and some doctors may have wished to hide their

as a whole, which, if prohibited, might get into worse hands or offer scope for blackmail and which some people do not regard as morally wrong would, we think, be liable to encourage a general disrespect for the criminal law. (Feversham, 1960: 72)

The Report rejects AID for single women[8]:

The importance and possible difficulties of AID are such that it should never be undertaken if there is not in the home a husband who is prepared to exercise the responsibilities of fatherhood from the beginning. It is manifestly unfair to the child to impose on him the additional handicap of having no-one to look to as his father . . . the usual argument put forward in favour of AID is that a woman is married to a man who is physically incapable of giving her a child in the normal way, and this, ex hypothesi, cannot apply to an unmarried woman. (Feversham, 1960: 34)

Though the Committee did note that an adoption order can be made in favour of a single woman, it points out that 'the adopted child is already in the world, and it may occasionally be found that there is an unmarried woman – sometimes his own mother – who is, in all the circumstances, the most suitable person to give him a good home' (Feversham, 1960: 34).

For married women, the Committee concluded that AID may not constitute adultery because sexual intercourse is not involved:

The wife does receive the seed of a person other than her husband and this goes against what has hitherto been regarded as the essential nature of marriage. This may well cause emotional difficulties in her relationship with her husband. [And that while] it is claimed that AID is justified by the happiness it brings to an otherwise childless couple . . . it may be that a couple who are prepared to seek the solution of their problem are unsuited to become parents . . . the attempt to enable one of the spouses to beget a child when the other is sterile implies an excessive concentration on procreation which is not the principle object of marriage. (Feversham, 1960: 42)

professional practice in an era when there was wide disapproval from the Church and medical establishment.

8 Later in the Report the Committee discuss and reject the possibility of making it a criminal offence to undertake AID for a single woman. One of their arguments for rejecting this is that they had no evidence that AID with single women had ever taken place in the UK. I, too, have found no direct evidence of a single woman receiving AID in the UK before 1960. However, given that this matter had been widely discussed since the 1930s (at which time significant numbers of single women were adopting) and we know some single women had sought insemination, it would be surprising if none were able to arrange AID in, or outside, the clinic. It is very likely that clinicians would not wish it to be known that they had inseminated single women. Post-war attitudes to women rearing children on their own hardened, at least judging by adoption practice. It may well be that it would have been more difficult to find a clinician willing to inseminate unmarried women in the 1950s than it had been in the 1930s. But of course the DIY route was always open to women – single or married.

The Committee also set out a number of difficulties for children of AID conception and suggested it would not be in their interests to encourage AID and so it 'refrain[ed] from making any recommendation about the legal status of children conceived in this way [and] accordingly . . . recommend[ed] that there should be no amendment of the laws relating to legitimacy or regulation of birth' (Feversham, 1960: 57).

The Report discusses what some had seen as one of the gravest dangers of AID – the meeting and unwitting incestuous marriage of donor half-siblings.[9] It draws on evidence from Glass (1960) and Hajnal (1960):

> If 2000 live children per year were to be born in Great Britain as a result of the successful use of AID and if each donor were responsible for 5 children, an unwitting incestuous marriage is unlikely to occur more than once in about fifty to a hundred years. Thus, even if there was a twenty-fold increase in the use of AID . . . the possibility that two children having the same father would marry would be remote . . . The number of incestuous marriages occurring as a result of AID would be much smaller than those resulting from fornication and adultery. (Feversham, 1960: 12)

The Committee learnt of a donor who had fathered seventeen children, but were told that most practitioners set a limit at ten and few reached the limit. So on the basis of the demographer's modelling there was little cause for concern. However, it was noted that the situation might change if it became possible to preserve sperm and 'semen' banks were to be set up. But practitioners showed little interest in such possible developments as they felt it would mean that they could no longer be responsible for ensuring that donors were suited to couples.

But there was a crack in this establishment façade of disapproval. There is a Memorandum of Dissent included in the Report signed by Committee members Peggy Jay (the redoubtable Hampstead Labour Party grandee) and John Ross. While they agreed that AID should not be encouraged, they thought that 'given a stable marriage, AID may properly be employed in small numbers of cases provided that both applicants and donors are carefully and expertly selected'. They are also critical of a number of the conclusions in the Report. For instance, they argue that the statement that donation dissociates, 'responsibility for physical procreation from responsibility for the upbringing of the child thus created', places 'undue emphasis on the biological aspect of fatherhood' (Feversham, 1960: 83). They found it difficult to understand what is meant

[9] Marriage within the prohibited degrees of relationship of the wife and husband was (and is) a criminal offence.

by the statement that AID 'violates the principle of monogamy'. They concluded with their own two recommendations:

i. the definition of legitimacy should be extended to include a child born as a result of AID to which the husband of the mother has consented; and
ii. for the purposes of registration of the birth of such a child, the husband should be deemed to be the father of the child.

The Feversham Report had no discernible effect on clinical AID practice, though, ironically perhaps, its Memorandum of Dissent would prove influential and its two recommendations were later accepted by the 1973 British Medical Association Panel which considered AID.

The report was widely criticised for the negative attitude to AID it displayed. And for its approach in placing AID in the legal category of 'liberties', which, while not prohibited by law, will receive no kind of support or encouragement from the law. G.W. Bartholomew (a barrister and eugenicist who had written widely on AID) made such criticisms and concluded a lengthy and detailed analysis of the Report which he called 'a sterile solution':

> The Committee's analysis of the situation can only be regarded as superficial and totally inadequate. However one thing that emerges from the inadequacy is that a further enquiry will have to be held at which the evidence submitted will have to be more representative, and the factual ground provided will have to be more comprehensive. The Report of the Feversham Committee has added nothing but further confusion to the issue of artificial insemination. (Bartholomew, 1960: 225)

Beyond Feversham: practice standards and medical ethics

In the period from Feversham (1960) to the next Government Report, Warnock's (1984) Committee of Inquiry into Human Fertilisation and Embryology, there were a string of symposia and study groups that re-examined the question of AID. For the most part these were groups of clinicians and scientists, but invariably including legal and ethics contributions. Perhaps most significant of these was a British Medical Association Panel (Peel, 1973). This accepted AID as appropriate medical practice[10] and set out a position for its governance and practice in the National Health Service. It endorsed the recommendations of the Feversham Memorandum of Dissent and noted that these conclusions

[10] And I should note that in 1968 the Minister of Health had decided that both AIH and AID for medical problems could be offered by the NHS.

(and, by implication not those of the Report itself) 'also reflect the present trend in judicial thinking' (Peel, 1973: 3).

Before proceeding further with my discussion, I need a brief sideways step to describe something of the medical ethics of the period, and, in particular, the role of one man, Gordon Dunstan (1917–2004). Professor the Reverend Canon G.R. Dunstan was a Church of England priest and a leading moral theologian of the period who was committed to multidisciplinary discussions of issues related to the practice of medicine. He held that the concept of natural law was a necessary tool in analysing moral consequences of developments in medicine. Clinicians often treated him as the established voice of medical ethics (four of the medical royal colleges made him an honorary fellow) and he took part in all the discussions I describe here. Importantly, as he himself said, he changed his views of AID over the post-Feversham period. He provided written and oral evidence for Feversham on behalf of the Church of England. In essence, that evidence reiterated the position of the Archbishop's Commission. In 1973, he argued that the circumstances of inadequate law and a generally secretive and scientifically unassessed practice erected a barrier to the moral assessment of AID itself.

> At present, discussion of the personal and professional morality of the practice, like the discussion of its scientific validity, is inhibited because the practice has developed in ways unforeseen and unprovided for by law, with the result that existing legal categories have had to be bent, and even actively misused, in order to accommodate its consequences . . .
>
> It is a matter for serious concern that a new medical practice, grounded upon scientific research and so upon a high value put upon truth, should in fact result in, and to some extent require, deceit and uncertainty. The secrecy involved in AID obliges the practitioner, the husband and wife and the donor to conspire together to deceive the child and society as to the child's true parentage, his genetic identity. Truth is violated, credibility is undermined and this is a serious ethical matter. (Dunstan, 1973: 47f.)

By 1976, while the law had not changed, he saw a significant advance as he could cite an example of AID practice which was building in all the requirements of a scientific assessment. Now he argued that a couple, with a stable marriage would be without sin in using AID. Here he assumes that a couple will have rejected adoption because this is either unacceptable given 'a woman's intense desire to bear her own child' (Dunstan, 1976: 183–9), or unavailable. And that they may decide that 'the nexus between husband and wife excludes no more than physical congress' (Dunstan, 1976: 183–9) and that 'the seed of a third party is a mere fertilising agent whose part and product in conception imports nothing alien into their marriage relationship' (Dunstan, 1976: 183–9).

In such a situation, he suggests if they hold this view in conscience, properly advised and strictly formed, 'the orthodox Christian moral tradition holds them to be without sin in following it' (Dunstan, 1976: 183–9). But he adds, 'in a more strictly disciplined church, like that of Rome, they may still have to face the consequences of doing what has been clearly forbidden by the highest teaching authority since 1897' (Dunstan, 1976: 183–9).

As far as the law is concerned, he argued that the concept of bastardy (illegitimacy) should be abolished and the law revised, but until that is done he questioned whether it was just to conceive a child to be born into such disadvantage. Further, 'to register a birth as of the husband is an injustice to society as well as the child and erodes a common interest in truth. In particular, the falsehood threatens a vital interest in medical science, particularly in genetics. So for the practice to continue there is a clear moral case for removing this circumstantial legal handicap' (Dunstan, 1976: 183–9). He suggests 'the real issue is one of truth, and man's right to know their true identity. Only a register of genetic identity,[11] maintained alongside of the register of social identity will serve' (Dunstan, 1976: 183–9). He argued that in a changed legal context, secrecy could be avoided and a child told the truth. As far as the donor is concerned, following Titmuss's *Gift Relationship* (1971), he thought donors should not be paid because the 'introduction of payment can appeal to motives which may lead to the suppression or falsification of relevant medical history and so to the contamination of the gift' (Dunstan, 1976: 183–9).

So by 1976, Dunstan began to reconcile much of AID practice with his natural law principles – at least assuming changes in the legal status of donor offspring. And, indeed, in almost all discussions in this period there was wide agreement that legal changes of some kind are required to remove the stigma and legal disadvantages of illegitimacy from AID children and to permit the registration of their birth as children of the marriage. However, no moves were instigated to make such legal changes.

The three major discussion reports we have from the 1970s, the British Medical Association Panel on AI (Peel, 1973), the Ciba Foundation Symposium, The Law and Ethics of AID and Embryo Transfer (Wolstenholme and Fitzsimons, 1973) and the AI Study Group of the Royal College of Obstetricians and Gynaecologists (Brudenell et al., 1976) allow us

[11] This may be the first use of a concept of genetic identity in discussions about AID and perhaps it is worth noting that other philosophers rejected its use. Williams (1973), for example, in the same discussion, accepts a notion of bodily identity but does not align this with any idea of genetic origins. The notion remains controversial; for example, see Wilson (1997) and Richards (2014).

to see the 'pinch points' for AID: those critical aspects of practice which were then seen to be regulated through the responsibilities and professional ethics of clinicians. As noted earlier, the Medical Defence Union warned practitioners of the need to protect themselves against charges of negligence, or conspiracy in cases involving inheritance. Thus, in these reports there is much discussion of the necessary standards of practice in relation to such matters as the selection of patients for the procedure, the selection of donors and the need for counselling for parents.

Practitioners' duties in the selection of patients were seen to be wide-ranging: married couples only, and no lesbian couples, nor single women (for the sake of the children), and they were required to satisfy themselves of the stability of the marriage and the eugenic 'child worthiness' of the potential parents. So assessments are required of their general health (including 'the genetical equipment' of the mother-to-be), emotional stability and so forth. And counselling was needed to ensure that parents fully understood the procedures, and were warned about the emotional problems that might lie ahead. Careful selection of donors was required for their eugenic qualities – healthy, well endowed and a 'clean' family history. The use of medical students as donors was encouraged because it was thought to ensure high intelligence and a good 'background'.[12] Matching of blood groups and racial background was expected but it was recognised that close matching of physical features with the husband was not possible given the unpredictability of inheritance – beyond avoiding striking features that might aid identification. The donor should remain anonymous and on no account should his identity be revealed to the recipients.

Then there was the tricky matter of advising patients about the registration of the birth of AID children. To register a birth with the husband as father was a felony, while to state 'father unknown' potentially revealed the AID. Dr Margaret Jackson, a leading pioneer of AID, described her practice in typically forthright terms. 'I put two alternatives to the patients. I tell them that they can either put their own names on the form – because they are legally married to their wife – if they wish to do so, or they can leave it blank and then adopt the child later. They all choose the first alternative' (Brudenell et al., 1976: 176). She was also willing to advise parents to tell their children of their donor origins in certain specific situations, for example, where an inherited condition ran in the family and offspring might consider themselves to be at risk if they were the natural children of the father. She described a case of a family who

[12] We might note that at the time medicine was a largely male and a hereditary profession.

had a child who was blind because of an inherited condition. They subsequently had two further children through AID. She advised the parents to explain the situation to them and to tell them of their donor origins. They did so at 'an appropriate age' and she reported that 'the family has weathered the decision'. This example apart, practitioners strongly held that children should not be told of their donor origins because this would burden them with the knowledge of their illegitimate status. However, were the issue of the children's status to be fixed through legal changes, some thought, like Dunstan, that it was better for offspring to know of their donor origins – not least to protect them against inadvertent discovery and to avoid secrecy. But knowledge of the donor's identity was seen as being too emotionally troubling for both parents and for their children. Donors' names should be kept privy to the practitioner, records were often anonymised or names coded. When AID became possible on the NHS in 1968, a number of practitioners continued to restrict their AID practice to their private patients on the grounds that information about AID would not be sufficiently confidential in NHS records systems. So medical records of AID practice was a very fraught issue. Some argued for the need for evidence-based practice which would require follow-up studies of families and offspring. But many practitioners thought that the confidentiality of records was paramount and so no systematic follow-up should, or could, be carried out.

With wider adoption of the use of frozen sperm in the 1970s, questions were raised about its safety. In the absence of any direct evidence, the best that could be said was that the very wide use of AID with frozen sperm for livestock had not revealed any dangers for offspring.

The 1973 Ciba Symposium included a paper by Bob Edwards and Patrick Steptoe on embryo transfer. Of course, this predated the birth of the first IVF baby in July 1978. But the research was well advanced and Edwards (1973) had published a paper about the moral, ethical and legal issues related to IVF. Beyond the possibility of medical risks for the child and the potential use of 'host' [surrogate] mothers for the convenience of an embryo donor mother, he saw no major ethical problems. 'We believe that our studies conform with the Hippocratic Oath in that they are for the benefit of patients and not for their hurt or for any wrong – indeed we believe they hold out the prospect of widespread benefit' (Edwards and Steptoe, 1973: 17). Of course, with IVF would come the possibility of egg and embryo donation. Participants at this Ciba workshop accepted that while the woman carrying a pregnancy would be the legal mother, it would be helpful to get a legal ruling that this would remain the case when egg or embryo donation are involved. But interestingly, while issues about 'genetic' parentage were raised in relation to the use of donor sperm, and the need (as a few saw it) for children born following donor sperm conception to be made aware of the manner of their conception, no such issues were raised in connection with egg donation. Here, while the woman giving birth would be the legal mother, no one at this meeting saw any reason for the offspring to be told that a donor egg had been used in their conception. It would seem at least for participants in this workshop, eggs were not seen to have the same social, hereditary or genetic significance as sperm.

From Warnock to legislation

The news of the birth of Louise Brown in 1978, the first IVF baby, caused a very mixed global reaction: a triumph for 'high tech' medicine giving babies to infertile women, or a dangerous step too far into a perilous new world of scientific baby-making, spawning a whole new breed of 'test-tube babies'.[13] In July 1982, the Government set up an inquiry into 'recent and potential developments in medicine and science related to human fertilisation and embryology' to be chaired by the philosopher, Mary Warnock. In its work the Committee chose not only to engage with matters of practice but also with the underlying moral questions, focussing on the alleviation of infertility. With the recognition of the need for clear limits to bolster public confidence, it proposed a legal system of regulation of techniques of assisted and collaborative reproduction. Thus, the Committee held that the professional standards that had so far influenced the practice of AID were insufficient, and proposed curbing professional autonomy by putting in their place guidelines underwritten by legal enforcement. To do this would involve the establishment of a new statutory licensing authority to regulate the infertility services which practitioners might then provide under licence. The new body would hold centrally the medical records of practice, including donation, so that these would be outside NHS and General Practice record-keeping systems. Additionally, it might undertake follow-up research on the children and families of assisted reproduction, as well as regulating all embryo research. Unlike all previous committees of inquiry concerned with these matters, the Warnock recommendations were largely accepted by government and they led to legislation.

In terms of donor sperm and egg practice, what Warnock recommended was, broadly speaking, what would have been regarded as the

[13] The press in Britain and elsewhere described Louise Brown as a test-tube baby. However, the term had been long used in the United States and elsewhere to describe AID children and to signify the scientific manner of their conception (Squier, 1994).

standard clinical practice of the day, except that there would be systematic record-keeping with a national register of donors and recipient couples held by the regulatory body, and a process available to donor offspring whereby they could, when adult, access some minimal non-identifying information about their donor. The post-eugenic Committee, not wishing to encourage parents to seek donors with specific characteristics in the hope of producing a particular type of child, thought information about potential donors should be restricted to some basic facts 'such as his ethic group and his genetic heath' (Warnock, 1984: 24). It was this information that would be recorded and then then made available on request to offspring in adulthood. Egg and sperm donation were to be treated in exactly the same way in the arrangements, so that the social and hereditary determinative power of eggs was elevated to the same social status as sperm. As far as the organisation of services were concerned, recommendations were made about each health authority (i.e. the National Health Service) establishing appropriate specialist infertility services which should be available to those in need and not necessarily restricted to married couples. Warnock did not consider the possibility of infertility treatment being made available outside the NHS.

While the Report states that 'as a general rule it is better for children to be born into a two-parent family, with both father and mother' (Warnock, 1984: 11),[14] it says that 'hard and fast rules are not applicable' (Warnock, 1984: 12) and eligibility for treatment should be a matter for the judgement of practitioners. Thus, treatment for single women or same sex couples would not necessarily be ruled out.

While gamete donation was to be anonymous, children should not be deceived about the manner of their conception. The Report discusses sperm, eggs and embryo donation and overall, the same regulatory system was suggested for each. However, it was recognised that there were some different practical and legal considerations for egg donation. That, for instance, it might be difficult to maintain the anonymity of the egg donor who it was thought might well be a friend or relative of the mother; and that complications may also arise because eggs could not (at that time) be stored. 'In such cases particularly careful counselling for all concerned would be necessary and thought should be given as to how and at what stage the child should be told about its parentage [i.e. their donor conception, not the identity of the donor]' (Warnock, 1984: 37).

For all donor conception the Report recommended that parental rights and duties of gamete providers should be transferred to the recipients. But, of course, the then legal, and social, positions for sperm donors

[14] All quotations in this section are from Warnock (1984).

and egg donors were quite different. As I have described, sperm-donor offspring were regarded as illegitimate, as sperm providers were both progenitors and potentially pater. But not so egg donors, as it is the woman who gives birth who becomes the social and legal mother. Warnock regarded the egg donor as the 'genetic mother' thereby introducing uncertainty into the situation. Accordingly, the Report calls for legislation to establish that, when a child is conceived with a donor egg, the woman who gives birth be regarded in law as the mother and that egg donors should have no rights or obligations in respect of the child.[15]

As far as birth registration is concerned, it recommended that the law be changed to permit the husband (or male partner) to be registered as the father. In this case, as with egg donation, it is suggested that it should be made possible for parents to add, if they so wish, the words 'by donation' after the child's name on the birth certificate.

With respect to egg and embryo donation, it is of course the case that both of these procedures also involve IVF. Moreover, IVF was the procedure that caused all the furore after the birth of Louise Brown. But as far as Warnock was concerned, IVF was an acceptable means of treating infertility which had passed 'the research stage' and could be regarded as an established treatment. However, it was a treatment which some opposed on fundamentalist natural law grounds as being a deviation from sexual intercourse with its inseparable unitive and procreative aspects. But an issue which had even more purchase with some critics was that it usually produces more embryos than are likely to be used, so that some of those created which have the potential for human life will not survive. Some believed it was morally unacceptable to allow viable embryos to die. Thus, there were those who rejected the use of egg donation (as well, of course, as any use of IVF, or indeed embryos, reproductively, or for research). Warnock used utilitarian arguments to set aside such objections; IVF was an effective treatment for some cases of infertility, and infertility research involving embryos was justifiable.

The Government held a consultation on the Warnock Report which predictably revealed 'a diversity of strongly held views', especially about research involving human embryos. However, perhaps surprisingly, they acted rather quickly in a couple of areas where they believed there was widespread agreement. Thus, they prohibited commercial surrogacy agencies (Surrogacy Arrangements Act 1985) and took advantage

[15] It may be noted that this position is maintained for both traditional and gestational surrogacy where the surrogate mother, that is, the woman giving birth, is the legal mother.

of a Family Law Reform Bill to include a section which met that enduring call to remove donor conception from its legal limbo (Family Law Reform Act 1987). This effectively made the husband and wife parents of their donor children and removed all rights and duties of parenthood from gamete and embryo donors, and allowed the child's birth to be registered accordingly. There would be no obligation for parents to tell the registrar that a child was born following gamete or embryo donation and there was no provision to allow parents to add 'by donation' after a child's name on the birth certificate. But in all other matters related to the Report matters proceeded more slowly. Further consultation was followed with a White Paper, 'Human Fertilisation and Embryology: A Framework for Legislation' (Department of Health and Social Security, 1987) and following discussion of that, a Bill was laid before Parliament. Finally, the Human Fertilisation and Embryology Act came to pass in 1990.

Postscript

Of course, the Human Fertilisation and Embryology Act is not quite the end of the story of regulation. The Act was subsequently amended in 2004 to require the donor's identity be made available to all donor-conceived offspring when adult. There were further amendments of the Act in 2008 (HFE Act 1990, as amended 2008). Changes included the removal of the duty for clinicians in offering treatment to consider a child's need for a father and substituting a more general assessment of the ability of would-be parent(s) to offer 'supportive parenting'.

Historiography may tell us how we have reached the present position and may offer some kind of explanation of why, and how, the relationships between the various parties involved in reproductive donation have changed. However, it is also important to recognise that while the Warnock Report effectively established the regulatory system we have today, the context in which that system now operates has shifted in important ways. For instance, new technologies have been introduced which may have far reaching consequences. ICSI (intra-cytoplasmic sperm injection) provides a good example here. In this procedure, which was first used in Britain in 1992, a single sperm (and this can be an immature sperm removed surgically from the testes) is injected into an egg to effect IVF. Thus, a range of male infertility problems are circumvented and so cases where AID would have been required can now be treated with IVF and ICSI using the partner's sperm. So the use of AID began a dramatic decline. In 1992, there were some 25,000 donor insemination clinic treatments in the UK. By 2007, this had fallen to about 5,000 but by then there were over 15,000 ICSI treatments (HFEA, 2006). So, AID has become predominately a procedure for those who do not have an appropriate reproductive partner (single women and lesbian couples) rather than a remedy for male infertility.

At the time of Warnock, egg donation was a very recent development and there was little experience of its use. Under the Act the practices of egg donation were largely modelled on the established practice of what by then was called donor insemination. However, as research soon established, there were marked gender differences in representations of gamete donation and attitudes of the women and men who donate their gametes (Haines, 2002; Konrad, 1998; Price, 1995). While women often saw their donation as a sisterly gift to another woman, men generally regarded their donation as the provision of a bodily substance in return for a modest payment. At the time of the Act, sperm donors were generally paid (cash, plus reasonable expenses), while women who donated eggs only got expenses or were offered benefits in kind (in the private sector) such as free sterilisation or IVF treatment. (Later there was a change to system of reimbursement of expenses for all donors, and payment in kind for some egg donors.) And while recruitment of known sperm donors was discouraged, this was common with egg donation, with couples frequently making their own arrangements with sisters, other relatives or friends. Most egg donors questioned by researchers wanted to know the outcome of their donation – something not permitted under the regulations – and almost all of the known egg donors preferred that children were not told of the circumstances of their conception (Price, 1995). This, together with subsequent work (see Freeman, 2014) undermines the Warnock approach of modelling regulation of egg donation on that established for sperm donation. Most recently, the HFEA (2011) has again revised the system of reimbursement of expenses for donors by introducing a system of flat rate payment which can be supplemented by reimbursement of additional expenses.

An assumption of the Warnock Report was that infertility services would be offered by the National Health Service (NHS) and, indeed, the Report made recommendations about the development of such services. However, today only rather limited assisted reproductive services are available in the NHS and most of those seeking treatment turn to the private sector. Indeed, rather than thinking of patients, today we perhaps should be considering customers and consumers. The assisted reproductive service industry has all the trappings of a modern marketplace, including pop-up ads online to lead you to fertility clinics and an annual infertility trade fair where providers from home and abroad display their wares. And, significantly, this has become an international market with increasing numbers of UK residents choosing to seek treatments in clinics abroad – and thus receive treatment under a different regulatory regime than that which exists in the UK. For some at least, a reason for travel is that they are able to obtain a service not available, or permitted in Britain. For example, some may travel elsewhere in order to ensure that the gamete donation they use is anonymous. The net result of seeking cross-border services is that a significant, and apparently increasing number of UK residents, are using reproductive donation and other assisted reproductive services outside the UK-regulated system. In the case of insemination which, of course, does not need the services of a clinic, there have always been do-it-yourself solutions to problems of infertility, or the absence of an appropriate reproductive partner. And today it may be semen, not women, that travel across borders as it is now possible to order sperm online for delivery to your home. Developments in techniques for cryopreservation of eggs (Stoop, Coho and Silber, 2014) have stimulated an international market in eggs. In Chapter 2, Pennings discusses the example of prenatal genetic diagnosis where cross-border travel of tissue and genetic information may complicate issues of regulation. And we must recognise that a significant number of UK residents now receive fertility treatment outside the UK-regulated system.

Acknowledgements

I thank colleagues in the Centre for Family Research for discussion of some of the issues considered in the chapter and I am grateful to Jill Brown for secretarial assistance. Thanks for support to Oh My Darling, Ivan Drever, Blue Flint, Sister Rosetta Tharpe, Ray Charles, Bill Monroe, the Country Gentlemen, Woody Guthrie, K.D. Lang, Joan Baez, Bob Dylan and the Carter Family.

REFERENCES

Bainham, A. (2005). *Children. The Modern Law*, 3rd edn. Bristol: Family Law.

Bartholomew, G.W. (1958). 'The development and use of artificial insemination'. *Eugenics Review*, 49, 187–95.

Bartholomew, G.W. (1960). 'The report of the Feversham Committee – a sterile solution'. *University of Malaya Law Review*, 2, 201–25.

Barton, M., Walker, K. and Wiesner, B.P. (1945). 'Artificial insemination'. *British Medical Journal*, i, 40–43.

Brudenell, M., McLaren, A., Short, R. and Symonds, M. (eds.) (1976). *Artificial Insemination. Proceedings of the Fourth Study Group of the Royal College of Obstetricians and Gynaecologists*. London: Royal College of Obstetricians and Gynaecologists.

Department of Health and Social Security (1987). *Human Fertilisation and Embryology: A Framework for Legislation.* Cmd 259. London: HMSO.

Dunstan, G.R. (1973). 'Moral and social issues arising from A.I.D', in G.E.W. Wolstenholme and D.W. Fitzsimons (eds.), *Law and Ethics of A.I.D. and Embryo Transfer.* Ciba Foundation Symposium, 17, (New Series). Amsterdam: Associated Scientific Publishers.

Dunstan, G.R. (1976). 'Ethical issues relating to AID', in M. Brudenell, H. McLaren, R. Short and M. Symonds (eds.), *Artificial Insemination: Proceedings of the Fourth Study Group.* London: Royal College of Obstetricians and Gynaecologists.

Edwards, R.E. (1973). 'Fertilisation of human eggs in vitro: morals, ethics and the law'. *Quarterly Review of Biology,* 51, 367–91.

Edwards, R.G. and Steptoe, P.C. (1973). 'Biological aspects of embryo transfer', in G.E.W. Wolstenholme and Fitzsimons, D.W. (eds.), *Law and Ethics of A.I.D. and Embryo Transfer.* Ciba Foundation Symposium, 17, (New Series) Amsterdam: Associated Scientific Publishers.

Feversham (1960). Home Office and Scottish Home Department. *Report of the Departmental Committee on Human Artificial Insemination.* Cmnd 1105. London: HMSO.

Fletcher, J. (1954). *Morals and Medicine.* Princeton, NJ: Princeton University Press.

Forbes, R. (1945). 'The medico-legal aspects of artificial insemination'. *Criminology Review,* 12, 138–93.

Freeman, T. (2014). 'Introduction', in T. Freeman, F. Ebtehaj, S. Graham and M. Richards (eds.), *Relatedness in Assisted Reproduction: Families, Origins and Identities.* Cambridge University Press.

Glass, D.V. (1960). 'Human infertility and artificial insemination: the demographic background'. *Journal. Royal Statistical Society, Series A,* 123, 174–81.

Glover, W.K. (1948). *Artificial Insemination among Human Beings: Medical, Legal and Moral Aspects.* The Catholic University of American Studies in Sacred Theology. (Second Series), No. 15.

Guttmacher, A. (1943). 'The role of artificial insemination in the treatment of human sterility'. *Bulletin of the New York Academy of Medicine,* 19, 573–91.

Guttmacher, A. (1946). 'The legitimacy of artificial insemination'. *Human Fertility,* 11, 16–21.

Haines, E. (2002). 'Issues of gender in gamete donation'. *Social Science and Medicine,* 36, 85–93.

Hajnal, J. (1960). Artificial insemination and the frequency of incestuous marriage. *Journal of Royal Statistical Society. Series A,* 123, 182–94.

Human Fertilisation and Embryology Authority (HFEA) (2006). Unpublished statistics. London: HFEA.

Human Fertilisation and Embryology Authority (HFEA) (2011). *Donation Review. Compensation of Donors and Benefits in Kind.* London: HFEA.

Jackson, M.H., Malleson, J., Stallworthy, J. and Walker, K. (1948). *Problems of Fertility in General Practice.* London: Hamish Hamilton Medical Books.

Konrad, M. (1998). 'Ova donation and symbols of substance. Some variations on the themes of sex, gender and the partible body'. *Journal of the Royal Anthropological Institute.* (N.S.), 4, 643–67.

Lane-Roberts, C., Sharman, A., Walker, K. and Wiesner, B.P. (1939). *Sterility and Impaired Fertility. Pathogenesis, Diagnosis and Treatment.* London: Hamish Hamilton Medical Books.

Peel, J. (1973). 'Annual Report of Council. Appendix V: Report of Panel on Human Artificial Insemination'. *British Medical Journal*, Supplement, 3–5.

Price, F. (1995). 'The donor, the recipient and the child – human egg donation in licenced UK clinics'. *Journal of Child and Family Law Quarterly*, 7, 145–51.

Richards, M. (2008). 'Artificial insemination and eugenics: celibate motherhood, eutelegenesis and germinal choice'. *Studies in the History and Philosophy of Biology and Biomedical Sciences*, 39, 211–21.

Richards, M. (2014). 'A British history of collaborative reproduction and the rise of the genetic connection', in T. Freeman, S. Graham, F. Ebetahaj and M. Richards (eds.), *Relatedness in Assisted Reproduction: Families, Origins and Identities*. Cambridge University Press.

Rohleder, H. (1934). *Test Tube Babies: A History of the Artificial Impregnation of Human Beings.* New York: The Panurge Press.

Schellen, A.M.C.M. (1957). *Artificial Insemination in the Human.* Amsterdam: Elsevier Publishing Co.

Squier, S.M. (1994). *Babies in Bottles: Twentieth-Century Visions of Reproductive Technology.* New Brunswick, NJ: Rutgers University Press.

Stoop, D., Cobo, A. and Silber, S. (2014). 'Fertility preservation for age-related fertility decline'. *Lancet*, 384, 1311–9.

Swanson, K.W. (2012). 'Adultery by doctor: artificial insemination 1890–1945'. *Chicago-Kent Law Review*, 87, 561–633.

Titmuss, R.M. (1971). *The Gift Relationship.* London: Allen and Unwin.

Wand, J.W.C. (1948). *Artificial Human Insemination: The Report of a Commission Appointed by His Grace the Archbishop of Canterbury.* London: S.P.C.K.

Warnock, M. (1984). *Report of the Committee of Inquiry into Human Fertilisation and Embryology.* Cmnd 9314. London: HMSO.

White, M.M. and Green-Armitage, V.B. (1962). *The Management of Impaired Fertility.* London: Oxford University Press.

Williams, B. (1973). 'Contribution to discussion: moral, social and ethical issues', in G.E.W. Wolstenholme and D.W. Fitzsimons (eds.), *Law and Ethics of A.I.D. and Embryo Transfer.* Ciba Foundation Symposium, 17, (New Series). Amsterdam: Associated Scientific Publishers.

Wilson, S. (1997). 'Identity, genealogy and the social family: the case of donor insemination'. *International Journal of Law, Policy and the Family*, 11, 270–97.

Wolstenholme, G.E.W. and Fitzsimons, D.W. (eds.) (1973). *Law and Ethics of A.I.D. and Embryo Transfer.* Ciba Foundation Symposium, 17, (New Series). Amsterdam: Associated Scientific Publishers.

CASES

MacLennan v. *MacLennan* [1958]S.C.105.
Orford v. *Orford* [1921]58. D.L.R. 251.
Russell v. *Russell* [1924]AC 721.

LEGISLATION

The Adoption of Children Act 1926.
The Legitimacy Act 1926.
The Perjury Act 1911.
Family Law Reform Act 1987.
Human Fertilisation and Embryology Act 1990.
Human Fertilisation and Embryology Act 1990, as amended 2008.
Surrogacy Arrangements Act 1985.

Part I

International, cross-border and global issues

2 International regulation and cross-country comparisons

Guido Pennings, Robert Klitzman and Fernando Zegers-Hochschild

In the last two decades, most countries have adopted legislation regarding medically assisted reproduction. Yet, in some regions, such as South America as we show in this chapter, this process has only just started. However, statute law is only one form of regulation and in this chapter, we consider three different types of regulation: legislation both national and international, court decisions and professional guidelines. But it is difficult to see why certain matters are regulated by certain types of regulation. In our discussion, we will illustrate the broad lines of the evolution of the regulation in three continents: Europe, North America and South America.

The regulation of reproductive donation in Europe

It is well-known that Europe is characterised by diversity when it comes to regulation on assisted reproductive technologies (ARTs). There are no two countries with the same legislation (see Glennon, Chapter 3). This is true for different aspects of the treatment process: gamete donation, donor anonymity, age limits for treatment, access criteria for ARTs, reimbursement systems for costs, etc. This diversity provides the necessary conditions for cross-border reproductive care (Pennings, 2004). Many people believe that these cross-border movements are morally wrong and should be limited as much as possible. This judgment is made on the misleading assumption that movement across borders is done exclusively for the evasion of law. However, there are many different reasons why people look for treatment outside their own country. Those who oppose the transnational movement of patients seeking treatment have called for harmonisation of European legislation to limit this movement; however, this will not stop the movements. At most, harmonisation will stop the movements of patients between European Union (EU) member states. Moreover, those seeking harmonisation do not explain how this will be brought about. At present, most countries seem to be convinced of the superiority of their own legislation and insist that the other countries should adopt their laws. Such attitudes will not lead to harmonisation.

Ethical issues are usually considered to be the prerogative of the EU member states. Since legislation on medically assisted reproduction is largely based on ethical, religious and cultural beliefs, each European country has certain approaches that differ from other countries. Germany's views on pre-implantation genetic diagnosis is clearly influenced by that country's history of eugenics. The prohibition of gamete donation in Italy can be explained by the influence of the Catholic Church in their society. Most European institutions do not typically focus attention on these matters. Nevertheless, under the cover of economic integration, many documents of the European Council and Parliament cover ethical topics (Mahalatchimy, 2010; Pennings, 2004). There are two separate drivers at the European level that have an impact on the practice of ARTs: European directives and judgments in the European Court of Human Rights.

European directives

The first directive which has had a major impact on the daily practice of ARTs in the clinics and laboratories is the Tissues and Cells Directive.[1] This is a mainly technical directive that imposes numerous rules regarding freezing, storing, etc. of human tissue. This directive has been integrated into national legislation (at least most of it, in most EU countries) and its implementation is increasingly controlled by independent inspection. Part of the problem with the directive is that it ignores the specificity of gametes. Take serological screening as an example: according to the Directive 2006/17/EC 'biological screening must be carried out at the time of donation' of sperm and eggs in the case of partner donation. Although this stipulation seems fairly clear, there exists a whole spectrum of national interpretations (Wingfield and Cottell, 2010). Some countries like Ireland tested prior to each in vitro fertilisation (IVF) cycle while other countries, like Finland, tested every twelve to twenty-four months. The ironic part of this screening rule is that it applies to partners who are sexually active and who are actively trying to conceive. One may reasonably predict that if there is a risk of transmission of infection, it is unlikely to be during the IVF cycle. In the meantime, a new European rule regarding testing is in the making that recommends testing once per year (European Centre for Disease Prevention and Control, 2012).

[1] Directive 2004/23/EC.

Although the Directive was established to ensure uniform high safety and quality standards across Europe, it also contains a number of ethical principles. The most important principles are voluntary and unpaid donation, anonymity of both donor and recipient, altruism of the donor and solidarity between donor and recipient. The danger of commercialisation is of special concern to the European Parliament, and this has been expressed in several resolutions (European Parliament, 2012). Following a scandal in Romania where donors' rights were violated, one resolution specifically addressed the trade in eggs (European Parliament, 2005). It had been found that in some Romanian clinics, donors had not given informed consent, had received insufficient information about medical risks and had not received follow-up care when complications occurred (Magureanu, 2005).

The perennial problem is the distinction between compensation and payment for donation. In a strict interpretation, one could argue that compensation should be restricted to proven expenses. However, one could also argue for compensation for incidental effects of the procedure such as pain, missed opportunities, time and so on. The European resolutions and directives do allow compensation which is strictly limited to covering expenses and inconvenience related to the donation. But it is up to the member states to decide what this means. As could be expected, a very large variation in compensation schemes is applied (Pennings et al., 2014). This is especially true for egg donation (ED). In France, only proven expenses can be reimbursed for egg donors. Other countries offer a fixed amount: €250 in Finland, €627 in Portugal, €870 in the United Kingdom and €900 in Spain. In other countries, each clinic decides independently what amount is offered and there are huge differences between the clinics. Moreover, some countries, like the United Kingdom and Poland, recruit a large percentage of their donors from populations of people who are IVF patients, while others do not have the egg sharing schemes. Nevertheless, with a few exceptions, in most countries the majority of the egg donors still indicate that they mainly donate to help others (Pennings et al., 2014).

The second important directive is the Patient Mobility Directive (European Parliament and Council, 2009). Before the directive, patients who went abroad for treatment had to receive prior authorisation from their health insurer to be reimbursed.[2] This condition was largely abolished by this Directive. The Directive aimed at facilitating access to safe and high-quality cross-border health care and promoting cooperation on health

[2] This does not apply in the UK, where limited treatment is available with the National Health Service (NHS) and those who travel abroad are not reimbursed by the NHS.

care between member states. Patients will be allowed to receive health care in another member state and be reimbursed up to the level of costs that would have been assumed by the member state of affiliation. In other words, patient mobility is promoted by imposing the portability of health insurance.

Although the directive will facilitate cross-border movements for some groups of people, it will not make a difference for others. From the start, the member states have wanted to keep a certain degree of control, both on health care expenditures and on the type of treatment they would be obliged to pay for abroad. It was specified that they would not have to reimburse ethically controversial medical services such as euthanasia, DNA-testing or IVF when these services are not allowed or not reimbursed at home (European Parliament and Council, 2009). The authority to decide which treatments are unethical firmly remains with the member states. In the future, countries will have to decide when the conditions of a treatment abroad differ sufficiently from the system at home not to be accepted or reimbursed. This can be illustrated by the problems of United Kingdom courts when British couples go abroad and enter into commercial surrogacy arrangements which are not permitted in the UK (Cohen, 2013; see Gamble, Chapter 7). Similar decisions may be taken by other countries. Should one, for instance, reimburse a couple living in a country that ends donor anonymity when they had treatment with donor gametes in a country which retains donor anonymity? Although the impact of the Patient Mobility Directive is still unclear, it seems that it will lead to an (limited) ending of national prohibitions for some instances of cross-border reproductive care.

Judgments by the European Court of Human Rights

The main task of the European Court of Human Rights is to determine whether the human rights of European citizens, as set out in the European Convention on Human Rights, have been respected. This process has two steps: in the first step, the Court has to decide whether the right invoked applies to the specific case that is brought before the Court, and if it does, the Court has to decide whether the violation of the right is acceptable or not. The decision on the acceptability is made by applying the proportionality principle: is the violation necessary to reach a justified goal?

An important recent judgment by the European Court of Human Rights was issued in the case of *S.H. and others* v. *Austria*[3] (see also

[3] *S.H. and others* v. *Austria* [2011] ECHR.

Glennon, Chapter 3). In this case, two infertile couples challenged prohibitions in the Austrian law. The Artificial Procreation Act 1992 prohibits ED entirely and sperm donation in the context of IVF. The couples argued that these prohibitions violated their right to respect for private and family life (Article 8)[4] and that the inconsistency in allowing only some techniques of assisted reproduction was a form of unjustified discrimination (Article 14).[5] The Grand Chamber of the European Court of Human Rights ruled against the complainants on the basis of the margin of appreciation. The margin of appreciation has been described as having 'two functions':[6]

> First, it establishes an 'interpretative obligation' to respect the varying cultural traditions of the contracting states . . . Secondly, the margin . . . functions as a standard of review that enables the ECtHR to take a 'hands off' approach to certain issues where national authorities are better placed to make an assessment of proportionality.

In this specific case, the Court had to decide what the 'right to respect for private and family life' means in terms of access to ARTs. The next question was then whether the interpretation given by Austria fell within the margin of appreciation. In areas of contested morality (including ARTs), the Court allows for a relatively wide margin.[7] Very liberal legislation in countries such as the UK and Belgium as well as very restrictive legislation such as in Italy and Malta may fall within the margin. In conclusion, the Austrian prohibitions were upheld. If the Court had ruled otherwise, all member states would have been obliged to allow gamete donation. Those in favour of gamete donation obviously regret the Court's decision but one may wonder whether it would be right if ethical issues were decided at the European level and by an organ that is not democratically elected. There is a strong tension between the right of the member states to decide private matters and the wish to impose a universal reading of the principles in the human rights convention. At the same time, people should not have to turn to the European institutions to solve conflicts related to the interpretation of human rights. Every country should ask itself whether a new law violates a human right. Moreover, even though

4 European Convention on Human Rights, Article 8.

5 European Convention on Human Rights, Article 14.

6 See Wadham et al., *Blackstone's Guide to the Human Rights Act 1998*, 6th edn (Oxford: Oxford University Press, 2011), para 2.78, citing Clayton and Tomlinson, *The Law of Human Rights*, 2nd edn (Oxford: Oxford University Press, 2009), 315.

7 See, for example, *A, B & C* v. *Ireland*, App No 25579/05, (2011) 53 EHRR 13 (upholding the restrictive nature of Irish abortion law) and *Evans* v. *United Kingdom* (2007), App No 6339/05, (2008) 46 EHRR 34 (upholding the consent provisions of the United Kingdom's Human Fertilisation and Embryology Act (HFE) Act 1990).

the Court has been accused of being too culturally relativist, reasonable people may disagree on certain points and interpretations and pluralism and diversity of opinions are not necessarily bad things. In fact, the situation in Italy is an excellent illustration; the Constitutional Court has turned back almost every part of the law on assisted reproduction. After it rejected the embryo transfer policy and the prohibition on preimplantation genetic diagnosis, the Court recently struck down the ban on gamete donation (Benagiano et al., 2014; Corte Costituzionale della Repubblica Italiana, 2014; Gianaroli et al., 2014).

Regulation concerning reproductive donation in the United States

In the United States, several sets of federal and state regulations, as well as guidelines from professional organisations, shape the practice of reproductive donation. Overall, practices in the United States differ in key ways from those in many other countries. In the United States, the ART industry has successfully opposed many kinds of regulations that exist in other countries. Professional self-regulation and widely variable state-by-state regulations prevail. Many individuals who would not otherwise have been able to have children, have now been able to do so; but possibilities arise for exploitation and commodification. Key questions and concerns thus arise and need to be considered, as these practices continue to evolve.

The US Constitution dictates that certain realms are under federal jurisdiction, while others are covered by individual states. Thus, states tend to regulate many aspects of medical practice, especially insurance and family law.[8] Federal regulations concerning physicians' ART practices are limited, and state laws vary widely.

Nevertheless, several sets of federal guidelines concern quality control practices of ART clinics, seeking to maintain general standards of quality of ART clinics and laboratories. Specifically, Food and Drug Administration (FDA) regulations oversee the inspection of laboratories and facilities, including screening of eggs and sperm for infectious disease (Food and Drug Administration, 2005). The Centers for Medicare and Medicaid Services (CMS) through the Clinical Laboratory Improvement Act (CLIA) establishes basic quality standards for labs concerning accuracy and reliability for test results (Centers for Medicare and Medicaid Services, 2014). The Centers for Disease Control (CDC) has arranged for the collection of data, through the Society for Assisted Reproductive

[8] Constitution of the United States.

Technology (SART) – an affiliate of the American Society for Reproductive Medicine (ASRM). Through SART, the CDC maintains a publicly accessible database that lists information from clinics. In 2011, the most recent year for which information is available, the database contained information on practice patterns from 451 clinics, including numbers of cases of IVF and of fresh and frozen eggs and donor eggs cycles, average numbers of embryos transferred, and percentages that resulted in implantation or pregnancy and live births (Centers for Disease Control and Prevention, 2013).

Various federal and state laws also regulate insurance coverage, affecting which prospective parents can receive reproductive donations, and of what kinds. The fifty United States range widely in whether they have specific laws concerning insurance coverage for infertility; and, if so, for whom, under what conditions and how much. Though fourteen states mandate that certain kinds of health insurance plans cover certain infertility procedures (Arons, 2007), these laws differ considerably in whether patients must be married and must be heterosexual couples, whether the ages of patients is limited, whether patients on Medicaid are included, how infertility is defined (e.g. for how long couples need to have tried to conceive on their own or beforehand), how much coverage is provided (based on costs or types or numbers of procedures), whether patients must use only their own (rather than donated) gametes, and whether all institutions (including religiously affiliated ones) must comply.

But, unlike many of the other countries mentioned in this chapter, federal guidelines do not address physician decisions concerning whether, when and how eggs may be used, or how much compensation for these is offered. The ASRM has guidelines that address a series of important and controversial areas, including eggs, sperm, embryo donation and gestational surrogacy. The relevant regulations and guidelines concerning each of these domains are described below, along with various state laws that at times address these domains.

Egg donation

One of the areas in which practice in the United States differs perhaps most markedly from that in many other countries concerns reimbursement for ED. The United States is one of the few countries that permit payment for eggs, leading to a robust industry. ASRM has issued guidelines concerning aspects of this practice, but the possibility of compensation raises many complex questions, and controversies continue. The Ethics Committee of the ASRM (2007) states that:

(1) Financial compensation of women donating eggs for infertility therapy or for research is justified on ethical grounds.
(2) Compensation should not vary according to the planned use of the eggs retrieved, the number or outcome of prior donation cycles, or the donor's ethnic or other personal characteristics.
(3) Total payments to donors in excess of $5,000 require justification and sums above $10,000 are not appropriate.

Yet data suggest that these ASRM guidelines are not always followed (Keehn et al., 2012). Specifically, in an examination of 102 websites of egg donor agencies and IVF clinics, many failed to comply with ASRM's guidelines that prohibit varying payment based on a donor's traits (34 per cent). Of sites mentioning traits, the most commonly paid for trait was prior donation success (64 per cent) (Keehn et al., 2012). ASRM has also recommended the use of donors aged over twenty-one, yet 41 per cent of these websites sought younger donors (Keehn et al., 2012). The American Medical Association (AMA) has issued guidelines concerning health websites, requiring, for instance, that these sites present risks alongside compensation (American Medical Association, 2001). But 56 per cent of the websites in this study failed to do so (Keehn et al., 2012). Trait-based payment was more associated with agencies than clinics, with location in the western United States (v. elsewhere), with not being endorsed by ASRM or SART, and with mention of ASRM's compensation guidelines.

Debates emerge concerning not only how much donors should be compensated, but who should decide. Recently, a couple, unable to obtain a donor that they wanted because of these limited amounts of compensation, has sued the ASRM for price-fixing. The outcome of this case remains unclear, with many observers concerned that courts may reject ASRM limits (Krawiec, 2014).

ASRM (2010) has also issued guidelines concerning the upper age limits of potential egg or embryo recipients, stating that providers should discourage or deny treatment to all women over fifty-five, and to women over fifty who have medical problems that may increase risks. Yet, again, the ASRM does not monitor or enforce these guidelines.

In 2009, the case of Nadya Suleman, dubbed 'Octomom' in the media, brought wide attention to this problem, when she gave birth to octuplets after undergoing IVF (Garrison, Yoshino and Ho, 2009; Harris, 2010; Hennessy-Fiske, 2010; Lin, 2011; Yoshino, 2009). She was thirty-three years old, living on welfare food stamps and already had six children, three of whom were disabled and received federal Supplemental Security Income. Her California physician, Dr. Michael Kamrava had implanted twelve embryos in her womb, of which eight had been successful and gone to term, and were born nine weeks prematurely. ASRM guidelines

(Practice Committee of American Society for Reproductive Medicine, and Practice Committee of Society for Assisted Reproductive Technology, 2013a; Practice Committee of the Society for Assisted Reproductive Technology, and Practice Committee of the American Society for Reproductive Medicine, 2006) state that providers should not use more than two embryos, and ideally only one, for a patient of Suleman's age. Hence Dr. Kamrava's actions violated these guidelines. Dr. Kamrava was kicked out of the ASRM and his license was later revoked (Harris, 2010; Lin, 2011). Following this case, the California State Legislature considered increasing state regulations, but ultimately did not do so (Rao, 2011).

Sperm donation

Sperm donation has been the topic of less scrutiny, overall. However, anonymous sperm donation remains the standard, even though other countries, notably the UK have banned such anonymity. ASRM also recommends that a man should not donate for more than twenty-five births for a population region of 800,000 people (Practice Committee of American Society for Reproductive Medicine, and Practice Committee of Society for Assisted Reproductive Technology, 2013b). However, compliance with this guideline is not monitored or enforced.

Embryo donation

A few states have also enacted legislation concerning the disposal of unused frozen embryos. Florida mandates that prospective parents and the physician have a written agreement concerning the disposition of embryos and gametes, if the couples divorce or one of them dies. Louisiana sees an embryo as possessing the same legal rights as a child, barring destruction of embryos (Arons, 2007).

In addition, controversies have recently erupted concerning companies that create embryos from egg and sperm donations and then own and sell these embryos (Zarembo, 2012). While some of these embryos are created 'on demand' (i.e. when an individual or a couple request an embryo that will, they hope, have blonde hair and blue eyes), the company may then create extra such embryos at the same time that it can freeze and sell in the future. In part, the lack of a unified national policy, and certainly the lack of a prohibitive one, have enabled such a practice to develop. This practice raises, however, a series of ethical questions, in part because an embryo may arguably have higher moral status than either one of its constituent parts (i.e. sperm or egg), each of which are necessary but not sufficient to create a human being.

Traditional and gestational surrogacy

Debates continue within the United States regarding compensation for gestational surrogacy. The market for compensated gestational surrogates has grown rapidly, and state laws vary widely in whether they permit, prohibit or limit it, and enforce whatever prohibitions they may have (Cohen and Adashi, 2013). As of 2011, traditional surrogacy (when a woman agrees to be impregnated by a man and carry the foetus) is permitted (since it is not explicitly prohibited) in sixteen states, permitted by statute without much detail in five; permitted by statute with restrictions in two; permitted only if uncompensated in four; permitted but with unenforceable contracts in nine; practiced though contracts are prohibited in two; not practiced because contracts are prohibited in four and unpredictable in nine (Hinson and McBrien, 2011). In addition, gestational surrogacy laws (where a woman offers a 'host uterus' to carry a baby conceived with gametes from the receiving couple but not her own eggs) vary widely as well: gestational surrogacy is permitted by statute with regulatory structures in three states; permitted (since it is not explicitly prohibited) in twenty-two; permitted by statute without much detail in seven; permitted by statute with restrictions in six; permitted with unenforceable contracts in one; supported but with no statute in six; practiced, though contracts are prohibited, in five and not practiced since contracts are prohibited in Washington, D.C. (Hinson, 2013). States may vary in other ways as well – for example, how much compensation can be provided (e.g. whether it can exceed coverage of basic expenses); whether the surrogate can change her mind after birth and if so, for how long afterwards; whether court approval and state residency are necessary; whether at least one of the intended parents must provide gametes and whether the surrogate's eggs can be used (Arons, 2007).

The fact that ASRM guidelines, but not government laws have addressed many aspects of ARTs has several implications. Providers have been able to engage in certain practices that they would not be able to perform in many other countries. Hence, we could view this situation as maximising provider and patient autonomy. Moreover, the fact that an ASRM committee is the entity issuing guidelines – instead of a much larger federal government bureaucracy – has allowed for relatively rapid release of reports concerning emerging questions about these ever-evolving technologies and practices. Yet as mentioned above, clinics and providers who violate ASRM guidelines may have their membership revoked, or face 'name and shame' tactics; but these strategies may still allow the physician to practice. Hence, the effectiveness of these actions is often limited. Furthermore, certain providers, particularly egg donor agencies, exist as third-party businesses outside of professional medicine, and hence are not subject to professional codes of medical conduct, and thus appear even less affected by ASRM self-regulating. SART asks agencies voluntarily to agree to ASRM's guidelines in exchange for listing on ASRM's website as a professional endorsement (ASRM, 2010). But not all participating agencies fully comply (Luk and Petrozza, 2008). Important questions arise as to whether more oversight is needed.

Regulation concerning reproductive donation in South America

Background

ARTs have been practiced in Latin America since the early eighties, and the first baby was born in 1984. Since 1990, most institutions providing treatment in Latin America joined the Latin American Registry of ARTs (REDLARA). This registry gathered summary data, and since 2010, individualised data from 148 institutions in twelve countries in the region. The information available includes individualised data from the start of a cycle until birth or miscarriage. This registry has made it possible to look at regional trends as well as markers of access to treatment, safety and efficacy of different treatment alternatives.

The vast majority of countries in Latin America have not officially recognised infertility as a disease, therefore, this condition remains ignored as a public health issue. Also, due to the intervention of conservative groups, ART, although not prohibited, is not officially registered as a treatment procedure. Therefore, infertile couples cannot count on public or private health insurances to cover infertility treatments. These conservative groups, very much in accordance with the Catholic Magisterium, argue that ARTs constitute a threat to human life, embodied in the embryo. The vast majority of ART procedures are carried out in private institutions, generating inequality in access and leaving many infertile couples without possible medical treatment. So far, Argentina and Uruguay are the only countries in Latin America with laws regulating access to ARTs. Both laws refer to the WHO definition of infertility as a disease, and establish that access should be granted to women or couples with no discrimination in terms of their sexual preferences. Furthermore, after the ruling of the Inter-American Court of Human Rights, Costa Rica has been forced to pass a law making ARTs available to all citizens[9] (Zegers-Hochschild, Dickens and Dughman-Manzur, 2013a).

[9] *Artavia Murillo et al. ('In Vitro Fertilization')* v. *Costa Rica* [2012] I/A Court H.R. 12361.

Although the Court does not refer to specific situations such as single women and gay couples, the intention is to avoid discrimination on the grounds of financial incapacity. The law is not yet approved in Costa Rica, and there are strong disagreements centred on whether embryo freezing and gamete donation should be included in the law.

In the absence of national regulatory bodies, many important decisions are left uncontrolled: the number of embryos to be transferred, the age limits for undergoing ED, anonymity of donors, economic compensation and access to treatment for same sex couples and single women. There are regional guidelines provided by REDLARA as well as national guidelines provided by scientific societies, but none of these are enforceable except in Argentina and Uruguay, which now have laws regulating access to ARTs and to a certain extent, how ARTs should be performed.

Gamete donation

Although sperm donation has been practiced in Latin America for almost half a century, there has been no attempt to register these procedures, either nationally or regionally; for this reason, little is known about the welfare of offspring born after the use of donor semen. However, ED, which is part of ART procedures, has been reported and registered by REDLARA. The first fifty-eight cases were published in 1991 when ED represented 1.9 per cent of initiated ART cycles. Ten years later, 1,780 cases were reported, corresponding to 9.6 per cent of all procedures. The latest ARTs report, corresponding to procedures performed in 2011, included 6,258 ED cycles, representing 15.2 per cent of all initiated ART cycles. Thus, in twenty years, the proportion of ED cases increased from 1.9 to 15.2 per cent of all ART procedures.

This rise in the use of ED can result from the delay in the initiation of childbearing in Latin America. Between 2000 and 2010, the proportion of women equal or above forty years old requesting ARTs increased from 14.8 to 23 per cent (Zegers-Hochschild et al., 2011). Another reason is a shift from fully altruistic egg donors or infertile women who donate spare eggs (egg sharing) while performing an IVF procedure in exchange for a small contribution to cover the total cost of their IVF procedure; to healthy and fertile women, who are hormonally stimulated and their eggs recovered with the sole purpose of donating them (exclusive donation). These women are economically reimbursed and as a consequence the number of potential donors has increased, and as expected, the efficiency of the procedure has also improved. Today, the delivery rate per embryo transfer is 37.1 per cent (Zegers-Hochschild et al., 2013b).

In the data reported by REDLARA (Zegers-Hochschild et al., 2013b), 60 per cent of ED procedures are performed with exclusive donors, while the remaining 40 per cent are performed as part of an egg sharing arrangement. Although these two forms of reproductive donation pose similar bioethical and psychosocial challenges, egg sharing adds even more controversial issues because a limited number of eggs need to be distributed between the donor and the recipient, and this requires further regulation. No such regulation exists, but most institutions recognise that the egg sharers have the first choice, in cases where few eggs are harvested. The Federal Council of Medicine in Brazil clearly establishes that in cases of egg sharing, where the number of gametes is lower than expected, the donor of the gametes has priority to decide whether to donate (Conselho Federal de Medicina, Resolution N° 2.013/2013). It does not indicate however, what happens with the agreement that donors and recipients had reached prior to the egg collection.

Regulations

As noted earlier, Argentina and Uruguay have recently passed laws establishing universal access to ARTs, and in some ways, regulating how it should be practised. On the other hand, Costa Rica, again as noted earlier, was obliged by the Inter-American Court of Human Rights[10] to restore the legality of IVF, lost since 2000, and to make it available as part of their social security program. No other country in the region has passed laws regulating ARTs, but in general, possible laws that have been discussed in their parliaments have been very restrictive.

In the absence of legislative bodies regulating gamete and embryo donation, most institutions follow guidelines which are issued at three levels: (a) by each institution without an external regulatory body, (b) by ethics committees from national reproductive medicine professional societies and (c) by a national board of medicine such as the Federal Council of Medicine in Brazil, which is an independent body that regulates clinical and research activities in medicine for the whole country.

Most regulatory statements, irrespective as to whether they are produced by a professional body or national organisations, contain similar elements and deal with them in a similar way. These elements include:

(a) Anonymity between the donor and recipient is recommended. It is also recommended to avoid donation between individuals who are blood relatives. Although in some countries, organisations of infertile women have made important efforts to have the identity of gamete donors made available for donor offspring, this has been resisted and is not done. In Argentina, this issue has been discussed in the House of Deputies, but no changes have been achieved so far. On the other

[10] *Artavia Murillo et al. ('In Vitro Fertilization')* v. *Costa Rica* [2012] I/A Court H.R. 12361.

hand, Article 12[11] of the law recently approved in Uruguay establishes that donors and recipients must remain anonymous; however, Articles 10[12] and 21[13] establish the right of every person born to know how he or she was conceived, and in cases of gamete donation, it establishes the right of offspring to know the identity of the person who acted as donor. Although this is recognised as a right, the information must be granted in court. Whether this will restrict the number of potential donors is still unknown. In the rest of Latin American countries, guidelines produced by professional bodies or by the federal council as in the case of Brazil, are mostly in favour of retaining anonymity between donors and recipients.

(b) In general, gamete donation is supposed to be altruistic but donors can be compensated for travel costs, absence of work, etc. It must be recognised, however, that the majority of the donors are in need of financial support. Financial compensation for some women will amount to more than a month's salary for others. The concept of compensation is very much dependent on the social and economic position of the donor. The word 'altruistic' is incorporated in Article 12 of law 19.167 of The Republic of Uruguay, as well as in Article 4 of resolution CFM No 2.013/2013 of the Federal Council of Medicine, which regulates the practice of ART in Brazil. Furthermore, all professional bodies demand an altruistic approach to gamete donation. The question remains why it should be altruistic and whether altruism is incompatible with any financial compensation. There is no necessary contradiction between altruism and financial compensation; the wish to help others may still exist when financial compensation is offered (Pennings et al., 2014).

(c) In general, every regulatory body, whether national or institutional, comments on the need to limit the number of children conceived by

[11] 'Article 12 (gamete donation) states (authors' own translation from Spanish): Gamete donation will be performed anonymously and altruistically. The confidentiality of the identity of donors must be guaranteed, irrespective of what is established in Article 22 of the present law. Donation is authorised after due consent by the donor and can be revoked if the donor would need her gametes for personal use. The maximum number of gametes donated by each donor will be established by a special regulation.

[12] Article 10 (superior interest of the child) states (authors' own translation from Spanish): Children born with Assisted Reproductive Technology will have the right to know the procedure performed in their conception.

[13] Article 21 (authors' own translation of the key parts of this article from Spanish): Artículo 21 (identity of donors). The identity of the donor will be disclosed after a judicial order if newborns or their descendent specifically request the competent judge, what is established in Articles 22, 23 and 24 of the present law. This information will in no way imply the identity of the donor will be made public, nor will it produce a judicial effect concerning filiation.

each donor. For example, the Federal Council in Brazil establishes a maximum of two children per donor in a population of one million inhabitants. In this respect there are at least two problems. First, nobody really knows what the ideal number is according to a certain population density that will avoid or limit the chances of inbreeding. Many regulatory bodies establish two to four offspring per donor, but the scientific evidence is lacking. Second, even in those countries that arbitrarily establish a maximum number, there is no national donor registration. Therefore, a donor can make donations in different clinics without any control. In countries with laws regulating ART such as Argentina and Uruguay, the decision on the maximum number of offspring from each donor is left to the relevant professional body to decide (see Wright, Chapter 9 for further discussion of this issue).

(d) Some of the regulatory bodies in the region specify that in cases of egg sharing, the donor has priority over the recipient, but no procedure is established in cases where the number of eggs does not allow sharing, or how to distribute good quality eggs. A third matter has to do with the disclosure of the outcome experienced by each couple. Frequently, if a woman does not become pregnant and has shared eggs, she asks whether the recipient became pregnant with her eggs. This information can have great value for the donor because the quality of her eggs is assured by a pregnancy, irrespective of whether this took place for the donor or the recipient. The question of whether the results are to be disclosed to donors and recipients needs to be addressed prior to egg sharing.

(e) Generally, regulations for embryo donation are often very similar to gamete donation with the exception that in embryo donation, it can be argued that the person born is also entitled to the right to be told that he or she might have a genetic sibling. This information is difficult to share among families with grown-up children when a sibling embryo is to be donated. However, in some cases, embryo donors may not wish to know whether their donated embryo has become a person.

Other remarks on sharing information about the method of conception

Studies on disclosure to donor children highlight the need for parents to receive support from health care professionals. Guidelines are required about what may be best for the children (see Blake, Ilioi and Golombok, Chapter 13) and eventually when and how to share information with children and other family members. In Argentina, Silvia Jadur and

Constanza Duhalde have published a series of children's books[14] designed for families formed by ARTs, to help parents talk with their children about their mode of conception.

In general, very little is known about disclosure of the method of conception to donor children in Latin America. It is believed that the vast majority of persons born from ED are not aware that their mother is not their progenitor. But we do not even know what proportion of those conceived through reproductive donation are aware of their method of conception. In Argentina, CEGYR (Centro de Ginecología y Reproducción), one of the first institutions providing ART treatments in that country, conducted an anonymous online survey of mothers with children of at least three years old conceived with donated eggs. The survey revealed that only 9 per cent of egg recipients had in fact begun to tell their children how they were conceived. A much higher proportion (69 per cent) answered that they would disclose this information in the future, once the child was older, but it is uncertain whether this will ever happen.

Between 2,700 and 2,800 babies are born every year from ED in Latin America and although the perinatal data are accurately registered, there is almost no information on the psychosocial welfare of these children and their families (Zegers-Hochschild et al., 2014). Before any attempt is made to study the effect of ARTs and reproductive donation in the family and their children, we first need to learn whether parents disclose these important issues with their children and other family members. Only then, will we be able to conduct studies to assess the wellbeing of people born from ARTs and third party gametes.

General conclusions

Although regulation is very different between the continents, there are some similarities. In all three continents, tensions exist between the nation state level and supranational level. In Europe, this is expressed in the increasing interference of the European Parliament in domains that according to the European constitution fall outside its remit. In the United States, there is the battle between the federal state and the individual states. The existing patchworks of regulations in the three continents show that national values and sensitivities continue to play a role and that, at least for the moment, states resist the increasing pressure for harmonisation.

A second common element is the influence of the courts. More and more, courts are directing the laws. In Europe, the European Court

[14] An archive listing many of Jadur and Duhalde's books is available at http://www.booksfordonoroffspring.blogspot.co.uk/2012_11_01_archive.html.

of Human Rights is increasingly seen as the arbiter in disagreements between citizens and their government. In South America, the decision by the Inter-American Court of Human Rights limited the authority of Costa Rica to decide what should be allowed on its territory. It seems that today, with an increasingly empowered global network of human rights organisations defending reproductive rights, the original widely accepted subsidiarity principle is crumbling.

Finally, almost everywhere there exists a mix of different types of regulations: supranational rules, national laws, professional guidelines and local clinic rules. This mix of regulations frequently results in incoherent, contradictory and complex systems of regulation.

How these regulations will evolve over time is unclear – especially as these technologies continue to advance, and as state governments range widely in their approaches towards these domains. In comparing the histories of regulations among these three continents, no clear 'one size fits all' pattern emerges. Decisions regarding the scope and content of guidelines and self-regulation often get made through complex political, social, cultural and historical processes, including recent national scandals. The issues reflect rapidly advancing technology, sensitive topics and diverse beliefs about politics, morality and religion, the proper extent of government in private family and reproductive matters and traditional types of reproduction and families. Achieving consensus on these matters involves multiple stakeholders, including local, national and international political and professional organisations. The differences between these continents highlight the extent to which ART continues to raise controversial and competing ethical concerns that can manifest themselves in a wide variety of ways in our increasingly globalised world.

Acknowledgements

We would like to thank Jennifer Teitcher, B.A., and Patricia Contino, M.F.A., for their assistance with this chapter.

REFERENCES

American Medical Association (2001). 'Code of medical ethics'. Available at www.ama-assn.org/ama/pub/physician-resources/medical-ethics/code-medical-ethics.page.

American Society for Reproductive Medicine (ASRM) (2010). 'Oversight of assisted reproductive technology'. Available at www.asrm.org/uploadedFiles/Content/About_Us/Media_and_Public_Affairs/OversiteOfART%20(2).pdf.

Arons, J. (2007). 'Future choices: assisted reproductive technologies and the law'. Center for American Progress. Available at www.americanprogress.org/wp-content/uploads/issues/2007/12/pdf/arons_art.pdf.

Benagiano, G., Filippi, V., Sgargi, S. and Gianaroli, L. (2014). 'Italian Constitutional Court removes the prohibition on gamete donation in Italy'. *Reproductive BioMedicine Online*, 29, 662–4.
Centers for Disease Control and Prevention (2013). '2011 Assisted Reproductive Technology: Fertility Clinic Success Rates Report'. Available at www.cdc.gov/art/ART2011/PDFs/ART_2011_Clinic_Report-Full.pdf.
Centers for Medicare and Medicaid Services (2014). Available at www.cms.gov/.
Cohen, I.G. (ed.) (2013). *The Globalization of Health Care: Legal and Ethical Issues*. New York: Oxford University Press.
Cohen, I.G. and Adashi, E.Y. (2013). 'Made-to-order embryos for sale – a brave new world?' *New England Journal of Medicine*, 368, 2517–9.
Ethics Committee of the American Society for Reproductive Medicine (ASRM) (2007). 'Financial compensation of oocyte donors'. *Fertility and Sterility*, 88, 305–9.
European Centre for Disease Prevention and Control (ECDC) (2012). *Risk Assessment on Change of Testing Requirements for Partner Donation of Reproductive Cells*. Stockholm: ECDC.
European Parliament (2005). 'Planned egg cell trade'. European Parliament resolution on the trade in human egg cells. P6 TA (2005)0074.
European Parliament (2012). 'Voluntary and unpaid donation of tissues and cells'. European Parliament resolution of 11 September 2012 on voluntary and unpaid donation of tissues and cells (2011/2193(INI)). P7 TA(2012)0320.
European Parliament and Council (2009). 'Report on the proposal for a directive of the European Parliament and of the Council on the application of patients' rights in cross-border healthcare' (COM(2008)0414 – C6–0257/2008 – 2008/0142(COD)). Committee on the Environment, Public Health and Food Safety.
Food and Drug Administration (2001; updated 2005). 7341.002 – Inspection of Human Cells, Tissues, and Cellular and Tissue-Based Products (HCT/Ps) (Covers HCT/Ps recovered after 5/25/2005). Available at www.fda.gov/BiologicsBloodVaccines/GuidanceComplianceRegulatoryInformation/ComplianceActivities/Enforcement/CompliancePrograms/ucm095207.htm. Accessed 20 July 2015.
Garrison, J., Yoshino, K. and Ho, C. (2009). 'Octuplets' birth spawns outrage from public'. *The Los Angeles Times*, 7 February 2009. Available at www.articles.latimes.com/2009/feb/07/local/me-octuplets7.
Gianaroli, L., Crivello, A.M., Stanghellini, I., Ferraretti, A.P. et al. (2014). 'Reiterative changes in the Italian legislation on IVF: the effect on PGD patients' reproductive decisions'. *Reproductive BioMedicine Online*, 28, 125–32.
Harris, D. (2010). 'Octomom doc Kamrava: "it was done the right way"'. *ABC News*, 13 July 2010. Available at www.abcnews.go.com/Nightline/doctor-kamrava-octomom-nadya-suleman/print?id=11145533.
Hennessy-Fiske, M. (2010). 'Expert says fertility doctor implanted far too many embryos in Nadya Suleman'. *The Los Angeles Times*, 19 October 2010. Available at www.articles.latimes.com/2010/oct/19/local/la-meoctuplets-doctor-20101019.

Hinson, D.S. (2013). 'State by state surrogacy law: actual practices'. Available at www.creativefamilyconnections.com/state-map-surrogacy-law-practices.

Hinson, D.S. and McBrien, M. (2011). 'Surrogacy across America: both the law and the practice'. *Family Advocate*, 34, 32–6.

Keehn, J.E., Holwell, E., Abdul-Karim R., Chin, L.J. et al. (2012). 'Recruiting egg donors online: an analysis of IVF clinic and agency websites' adherence to ASRM guidelines'. *Fertility and Sterility*, 98, 995–1000.

Krawiec, K.D. (2014). 'Egg donor price fixing and Kamakahi v. American Society for Reproductive Medicine'. *American Medical Association Journal of Ethics*, 16, 57–62.

Lin, II R.-G. (2011). 'Michael Kamrava's medical license revoked'. *The Los Angeles Times*, 1 June 2011. Available at www.documents.latimes.com/michael-kamrava-disciplinary-decision/.

Luk, J. and Petrozza, J.C. (2008). 'Evaluation of compliance and range of fees among American Society for Reproductive Medicine listed egg donor and surrogacy agencies'. *Journal of Reproductive Medicine*, 53, 847–52.

Magureanu, G. (2005). 'Egg donation and conflict within the Romanian legal framework'. Paper presented at the CORE European seminar: Human egg trading and the exploitation of women. Brussels: European Parliament, 30 June 2005. Available at www.handsoffourovaries.com/pdfs/appendixg.pdf.

Mahalatchimy, A. (2010). 'Bioethics and European Union: the advanced therapy medicinal products' case'. *Opinio Juris in Comparatione*, 2, 1–22.

Pennings, G. (2004). 'Legal harmonization and reproductive tourism in Europe'. *Human Reproduction*, 19, 2689–94.

Pennings, G., de Mouzon, J., Shenfield, F., Ferraretti, A-P. et al. (2014). 'Socio-demographic and fertility-related characteristics and motivations of oocyte donors in eleven European countries'. *Human Reproduction*, 29, 1076–89.

Practice Committee of the Society for Assisted Reproductive Technology, and Practice Committee of the American Society for Reproductive Medicine (2006). 'Guidelines on number of embryos transferred'. *Fertility and Sterility*, 86, S51–S52.

Practice Committee of American Society for Reproductive Medicine, and Practice Committee of Society for Assisted Reproductive Technology (2013a). 'Criteria for number of embryos to transfer: a committee opinion'. *Fertility and Sterility*, 99, 44.

Practice Committee of American Society for Reproductive Medicine, and Practice Committee of Society for Assisted Reproductive Technology (2013b). 'Recommendations for gamete and embryo donation: a committee opinion'. *Fertility and Sterility*, 99, 47–62.

Rao, R. (2011). 'How (not) to regulate ARTs: lessons from octomom'. *Albany Law Journal of Science and Technology*, 21, 313–21.

Wadham, J., Mountfield, H., Prochaska, E. and Brown, C. (2011). *Blackstone's Guide to the Human Rights Act 1998*, 6th edn (Oxford: Oxford University Press), para 2.78, citing Clayton and Tomlinson, *The Law of Human Rights*, 2nd edn. (Oxford: Oxford University Press, 2009), 315.

Wingfield, M. and Cottell, E. (2010). 'Viral screening of couples undergoing partner donation in assisted reproduction with regard to EU Directives 2004/23/EC, 2006/17/EC and 2006/86/EC: what is the evidence for repeated screening?' *Human Reproduction*, 25, 3058–65.

Yoshino, K. (2009). 'House where octuplets' mother lives is in danger of foreclosure'. *The Los Angeles Times*, 19 February 2009. Available at www.articles.latimes.com/2009/feb/19/local/me-octuplets19.

Zarembo, A. (2012). 'An ethics debate over embryos on the cheap'. *The Los Angeles Times*, 12 November 2012. Available at www.articles.latimes.com/2012/nov/19/local/la-me-embryo-20121120.

Zegers-Hochschild, F., Dickens, B.M. and Dughman-Manzur, S. (2013a). 'Human rights to in vitro fertilization'. *International Journal of Gynecology and Obstetrics*, 123, 86–9.

Zegers-Hochschild, F., Schwarze, J.E., Crosby, J. and Do Carmo Borges de Souza, M. (2011). 'Twenty years of assisted reproductive technology (ART) in Latin America'. *JBRA Assisted Reproduction*, 15, 19–30.

Zegers-Hochschild, F., Schwarze, J.E., Crosby, J., Musri, C. and Do Carmo Borges de Souza, M. (2013b). 'Assisted reproductive technologies (ART) in Latin America: the Latin American Registry, 2011'. *JBRA Assisted Reproduction*, 17, 216–21.

Zegers-Hochschild, F., Schwarze, J.E., Crosby, J.A., Carolina Musri, C. and do Carmo Borges de Souza, M. (2014). 'Assisted Reproductive Technology in Latin America: the Latin American Registry, 2012'. *Reproductive BioMedicine Online*, 30, 43–51.

CASES

ITALY

Corte Costituzionale della Repubblica Italiana, 2014. Sentenza 162/2014 [Ruling 162/2014].

EU

S.H. and others v. *Austria* [2011]ECHR.
A, B & C v. *Ireland*, App No 25579/05, (2011) 53 EHRR 13.
Evans v. *United Kingdom* (2007) App No 6339/05, (2008) 46 EHRR 34.

COSTA RICA

Artavia Murillo et al. *('In Vitro Fertilization')* v. *Costa Rica* [2012]I/A Court H.R. 12361.

LEGISLATION AND DIRECTIVES

BRAZIL

Conselho Federal Dd Medicina (Federal Council of Medicine).
Resolution CFM No 2.013/2013. Article 4, Doacao de Gametas ou Embrioes (Gametes and embryo donation).

URUGUAY

Técnicas de Reproducción Humana Asistida. Ley N. 19.167.

AUSTRIAN LEGISLATION

Artificial Procreation Act 1992.

EU LEGISLATION

European Convention on Human Rights.

EU DIRECTIVES

Directive 2004/23/EC of the European Parliament and of the Council of 31 March 2004 on setting standards of quality and safety for the donation, procurement, testing, processing, preservation, storage and distribution of human tissues and cells.

Directive 2011/24/EU of the European Parliament and of the Council of 9 March 2011 on the application of patients' rights in cross-border healthcare.

Directive 2006/17/ EC and Patient Mobility Directive.

US LEGISLATION

Constitution of the United States.

3 Legal regulation of family creation through gamete donation

Access, identity and parentage

Theresa Glennon

Gamete donation has revolutionised family creation – and challenges deep-seated notions of reproduction, identity and kinship. Legal responses vary widely across states and continue to evolve. This chapter provides a brief review and analysis of developments in the legal regulation of gamete donation in the United States, United Kingdom, Canada and Europe with regard to three major issues: access to reproduction, challenges to donor anonymity and disputes regarding parentage.

Controversy will only intensify as use of gamete donation continues to grow. Claims for access to assisted reproduction as a human right have increased. Older adults, gay and lesbian couples and single individuals assert claims for access to reproduction – and where those claims are not met, they travel to more receptive countries. The expense of family creation through third-party involvement has drawn advocacy for increased public funding. Donor-conceived children have raised their own human rights claims, asserting that they are entitled to know the identity of all those involved in their conception. Finally, the legal status of families formed through gamete donation continues to be contested. These disputes may arise when parents choose to create their families outside medical channels or same-sex couples face barriers to legal parentage. Some have also challenged embedded views that children have, at most, two parents and raised questions over the role of parental agreements and functional parenthood.

This review addresses three broad issues raised by gamete donation. First, it explores how different states regulate access to services, with particular attention to restrictions by age, sexual orientation, relationship status and problems of access related to family income. Second, it examines laws surrounding access to donor identity. Third, it examines some of the legal controversies arising from known-donor sperm donation and parentage in same-sex and other non-traditional families. This analysis is limited to Europe, the UK, Canada and the United States. In each area, states have adopted varied legal approaches that reflect different normative commitments. However, because social understandings and legal approaches continue to evolve, this chapter is best understood as framing these central issues and providing a snapshot of legal approaches to them at this particular point in time.

Overview of gamete donation

This chapter uses the term 'assisted reproduction' (AR) to refer to medical interventions to aid conception, including use of donated eggs and sperm and in vitro fertilisation (IVF). Sperm donation has a long history and is performed quite safely in a clinical setting, where extensive regulation in most countries ensures the screening of prospective donors for medical conditions or genetic concerns and the clinical testing of donated sperm safety. Egg donation, a more arduous procedure for both donor and recipient, is more controversial and subject to greater variations in regulation. Egg extraction, fertilisation and embryo transfer are all performed in clinical settings (Glennon, 2010). Donating eggs, unlike donating sperm, carries health risks for the donor, although knowledge about the magnitude of those risks remains limited (Boutelle, 2014).

Because IVF with egg and/or sperm donation must be conducted in a clinical setting, states may more easily regulate issues of access, donor identity and parentage in this context. Sperm donation, however, may take place outside the clinical setting, which can provide access to those otherwise excluded by regulation or lack of financial resources. However, informal donation may not have the benefit of the same safety precautions, and complicated issues regarding donor identity and parentage may arise (Glennon, 2012).

Individuals and couples use AR and gamete donation for various reasons, and access to reproductive donation may be dependent on those reasons. Some individuals, for medical reasons, cannot produce eggs or sperm of adequate quality to support conception and pregnancy, which some refer to as 'functional infertility' (Daar, 2008: 23–24). Functional infertility has begun to lose its historical stigma and gain acceptance as a medical condition worthy of treatment, although this acceptance is often limited to those who are married and of typical reproductive age. Others may need AR and gamete donation due to 'structural infertility' that arises from 'the social structure with which they self-identify' (Daar, 2008: 24). Thus, single women and lesbian couples require donor sperm, while for single men and gay couples, egg donation is a necessary part of the surrogacy process.[1] Those who experience structural infertility

[1] It is also possible to use a traditional surrogate (whose own egg is fertilised); however, gay couples often use both an egg donor and a gestational surrogate.

face significant barriers in many countries to AR and gamete donation, although the trend is clearly towards increasing access (Daar, 2008).

Justifications and methods for legal regulation of gamete donation

The legal regulation of AR generally, and gamete donation more specifically, has been described as 'legal mosaicism' (Pennings, 2008), and this is certainly true with regard to access, donor identity and parentage issues. Where access to AR and gamete donation is forbidden, human health and safety is a frequently cited concern, particularly for restrictions based on age. Concerns such as those invoked by the UK – dignity and well-being of patients and donors, welfare of children and the special status of embryos – motivate a wide range of regulatory approaches to all three issues (HFEA, 2014a). Notions of morality, often based on dominant religious beliefs, animate other regulation. For example, the Catholic Church's view that IVF is 'morally illicit' has had a profound effect on assisted reproductive technologies (ARTs) legislation in some countries and may lead to greater restrictions on access (Ory, 2013). Those who prioritise reproductive liberty and are sceptical about societal consensus on concepts such as morality, dignity and children's welfare, as well as governments' ability to protect these interests through regulation in such a rapidly changing area, urge countries to minimise restrictions (Robertson, 1995). In some places, lack of regulation may reflect a state's inability to resolve these conflicting claims.

The debate over whether to require the provision of access to donor identity to donor-conceived children has generally focused on human rights arguments. Human rights advocates for donor-conceived children have argued for mandatory retention and provision of donor identity, while those opposed have argued that such schemes restrict the human right of intended parents to form a family without excessive state intervention (Clark, 2012). This debate does, however, also raise concerns regarding human health, as advocates for donor identity have argued that information related to genetic heritage may be important for medical treatment and other health-related concerns (Sabatello, 2014).

Debates over parentage itself often focus on whether the state controls parentage status or whether the parties themselves have the freedom to enter into effective written or oral agreements regarding parentage (Glennon, 2012). These debates arise most often where informal methods of reproductive donation have been used, where donors were not informed that medically assisted donation would deprive them of their parental rights, or where same-sex couples have used donation to create parent–child relationships that one member of the relationship later rejects (Glennon, 2012).

Regulatory restraint may be premised on classical liberal ideals that the state should intrude as little as possible into the realm of individual autonomy and neo-liberal tenets that primarily view AR as market-based services in which individual actors are best able to make their own decisions. Liberal and neoliberal notions of autonomy, however, often exclude from their view whether individuals have the means to effectuate their desire to reproduce. These financial limitations can greatly restrict individuals' reproductive autonomy (Herring, 2006; Lui and Adashi, 2013). Lui and Adashi (2013) also exclude from view the ways 'in which structural inequality and social circumstances constrain choice' (Mutcherson, 2013: 193).

In most European countries and the UK, legal regulation at the national level is extensive and largely governs all AR practices of clinics, including gamete donation. Canada's Assisted Human Reproduction Act governed many facets of AR until many of its provisions were struck down by the Supreme Court of Canada as an invasion of provincial jurisdiction (In Reference re Assisted Human Reproduction Act, 2010). While a few provinces such as Quebec have issued regulations regarding AR, many have not yet done so. In the United States, national regulation is spare. Even at the state level, legal regulation is minimal – leaving clinicians to obtain guidance from professional associations and state courts to adjudicate disputes with little legislative guidance. Thus, much of what is known about legal regulation regarding access to gamete donation, donor identity and defining parent–child relationships in the United States has developed through case law rather than legislation.

Access to reproduction through gamete donation

Countries generally fall into one of three categories regarding restrictions on access to gamete donation: some, like the UK and United States, are permissive; others impose some restrictions but still provide significant access; while a third group either completely bans or greatly restricts gamete donation. Almost all European countries, Canada, the UK and the United States allow sperm and egg donation (Ory, 2013). While many countries permit the use of donor embryos, Denmark and Sweden prohibit such donations to ensure that children have a genetic link to at least one parent. France largely prohibits embryo donation except under judicial supervision (Berg Brigham, Cadier and Chevreul, 2013). Austria, Germany, Norway and Switzerland permit semen donation but prohibit egg donation, and Austria also forbids the use of donor sperm for IVF

(Ory, 2013).[2] Turkey prohibits the use of gamete donation completely (Berg Brigham, Cadier and Chevreul, 2013). In 2004, Italy passed a law prohibiting all use of donor eggs and sperm. This aspect of the Italian law was found to be unconstitutional by the Constitutional Court of Italy in April 2014 (Day, 2014).

The diversity of approaches to gamete donation reflects different religious and moral traditions and beliefs regarding the state's role in enforcing ethical values. For example, Italy's restrictions on AR, including the complete ban on gamete or embryo donation, were widely considered to be based on the Roman Catholic Church's opposition to all forms of AR (Fineschi, Neri and Turillazzi, 2005; Zanini, 2011). And in fact the Vatican publicly protested the decision by the Constitutional Court of Italy that found the ban on donor gametes unconstitutional (Day, 2014). Similarly, Turkey's restrictive approach, based on religious values, not only prohibits gamete donation but imposes civil and criminal penalties on all involved if patients travel to other countries to obtain donor gametes. Turkey supports fertility treatments only where treatment aids the creation of a traditional nuclear family – 'a married mother and father with their genetically related offspring'. This approach upholds Sunni Muslim religious tenets on AR, which view a child as legitimate only if it is genetically related to both of its married parents (Gürtin, 2011). In contrast, the UK's generally permissive rules on gamete donation reflect a secular regulatory process that has been open to adaptation based on evolving ideas of equality (Appleby, Jennings and Statham, 2012). The United States, with almost no regulation, reflects the belief that the state's role in ethical decisions related to gamete donation is minimal.

The European Court of Human Rights (ECtHR) has been reluctant to second-guess these value-laden choices. Austria's Artificial Procreation Act permits the *in vivo* use of donor sperm where a husband or male partner is infertile, but prohibits the use of donor sperm for IVF and completely prohibits egg donation. The Act otherwise permits the use of IVF. This law was challenged on the basis that these restrictions violated the 'right to respect for private and family life' under Article 8 of the European Convention on Human Rights. The ECtHR Grand Chamber held that this law did not violate Article 8 and that the government should be given a wide margin of appreciation as the law (1) balanced the interests of those facing fertility problems with the protection of economically disadvantaged women; (2) prevented risks that IVF may be used for non-therapeutic purposes, such as 'selection' of children;

[2] *SH* v. *Austria*, 2011.

(3) avoided disputes between genetic and birth mothers and, more generally, (4) addressed 'questions of a social and ethical nature on which there was not yet a consensus in the society and which had to take into account human dignity, the well-being of children thus conceived and the prevention of negative repercussions or potential misuse'.[3] Developments since this decision include the ECHR's decision in *Costa and Pavan* v. *Italy*, which rejected Italy's ban on pre-implantation genetic diagnosis for a couple who carried the gene for cystic fibrosis, and the decision by the Italian Constitutional Court requiring provision of access to donor gametes (Day, 2014).[4] These decisions may indicate that the trend recognised by the ECtHR in *S.H.* v. *Austria* towards greater use of donor gametes will result eventually in a revised view by the ECtHR towards requiring access to donor gametes.

Even the most legally restrictive approaches face limits. Those with sufficient resources 'exit' restrictive regimes by travelling to other jurisdictions. For example, during the ban on donor gametes, many Italians travelled to other countries to obtain gamete or embryo donations. This led to feelings of abandonment, anger and disappointment with their national institutions for, in their view, requiring them to travel to obtain services they needed in order to reproduce (Zanini, 2011).

States have also found it difficult to deny parentage claims on behalf of children born through actions taken in other countries to escape local regulation or prohibitions. Thus, English judges have expressed frustration that they are forced to recognise the children resulting from overseas surrogacy arrangements that violate English law limiting payment for surrogacy services because otherwise the children born through those illegal arrangements would be parentless and stateless.[5] France, which refuses to recognise the effects of illegal surrogacy arrangements, was recently rebuked by the ECtHR for rejecting requests by children for legal recognition of the parent–child relationships created through overseas surrogacy arrangements. These arrangements had been made in the United States to circumvent France's prohibition on surrogacy. The ECtHR found that France was entitled to a wide margin of appreciation in relation to its surrogacy laws, 'in view of the difficult ethical issues involved and the lack of consensus on these matters in Europe'. Yet it determined that the children's right to respect for their private life under Article 8 of the European Convention on Human Rights had been violated because failure to recognise this parent–child relationship undermined 'the children's identity within French society'. In particular, their

[3] *S.H.* v. *Austria*, 2011, ¶113. [4] *Costa and Pavan* v. *Italy*, 2013.
[5] Re: X and Y, 2008.

status as French nationals was unclear despite their biological father's French citizenship, the children's inheritance rights would be limited, and France had refused to recognise their legal relationship with their biological father.[6] Thus, European countries face limits to their ability to reject the outcomes of reproductive decisions and actions taken by their citizens in other countries on their return home.

Age

Age restrictions on gamete donation or IVF are often justified by concern for the physical health of older birth mothers and their children as well as the ability of older parents to care for children through their childhood. Advanced maternal and paternal age has been linked to increased risks during pregnancy, including higher rates of miscarriage and preeclampsia, and of disorders in children, including impaired neurocognitive outcomes, schizophrenia and epilepsy (Dain, Auslander and Dirnfeld, 2011). Some researchers argue limitations on patient autonomy are justified by the medical profession's charge to do no harm (Schutte et al., 2008). Other researchers argue that with careful screening of older prospective mothers, IVF with donor oocytes is safe (Grossman, Korth and Sauer, 2012). An Italian court demonstrated concern over older parents' ability to meet their one-year-old child's needs when it terminated parental rights of the child's mother, age fifty-seven, and father, age seventy, finding that they had been neglectful and were too old to be fit parents (Gulino et al., 2013). This ruling was upheld by a four-judge appellate court panel in 2012 (Cook, 2012).

States diverge over limiting access to AR based on maternal age. Countries including Austria, Finland, Germany, Portugal, Spain, the UK and United States have no restrictions based on maternal age. Others impose a fixed age cut-off for women, after which access to IVF, and therefore egg donation, is no longer available. These include Denmark and the Netherlands (forty-five years old) and Greece (fifty years old) (Berg Brigham, Cadier and Chevreul, 2013). In Belgium, egg extraction must be performed by age forty-five, and embryo transfer by age forty-seven (Pennings, 2007). A third group of countries, including France, Italy, Russia and Sweden, take a capacity-based approach and restrict access to ART based on the 'child bearing age' of the mother (Berg Brigham, Cadier and Chevreul, 2013; Svitnev, 2010).

Most European countries also impose age restrictions on public financing for assisted reproductive services. Austria and Germany impose a

[6] *Mennesson* v. *France* and *Labasson* v. *France*, 2014.

strict maternal age limit of forty years old and paternal age limit of fifty. Other countries with fixed age cut-offs include Denmark (up to forty), the Netherlands and Spain (forty years old), Belgium and France (forty-three years old) and Greece (fifty years old). Swedish law does not specify an age limit for funding, but regional authorities have placed restrictions starting at age thirty-eight up to age forty-three (Berg Brigham, Cadier and Chevreul, 2013; Ory, 2013; Pennings, 2007; White & Case, 2009). The UK's National Health Service generally follows professional guidelines to limit funding up to age 42 (NHS Choices, 2013). Italy and Spain take an evaluative approach and disallow public financing of IVF after a woman has exceeded 'child bearing' age. Quebec leaves decisions regarding the physical and psychosocial capacity of the woman for childbearing to the clinical judgment of the physician (Quebec AR Program, Eligibility). Finland and Portugal do not restrict on the basis of age even if public financing is necessary to the individual's treatment (Berg Brigham, Cadier and Chevreul, 2013; Pennings, 2007; White & Case, 2009).

In the United States, public financing for most AR services is not available, and only fifteen states require insurance companies to provide coverage for fertility services. Some of those states, such as Connecticut and New York, permit insurance companies to extend coverage only up to a certain age, ranging from forty to forty-six. Other states, such as Maryland and Hawaii, exclude age-related infertility from the list of covered conditions (Liu and Adashi, 2013; Resolve, 2014).

The varied approaches demonstrate little agreement over how to determine when age-related health risks for mothers and children and concerns over older parents' ability to properly rear their children should restrict patient autonomy.

Sexual orientation and sexual identity

Parenthood, widely regarded as a vital part of human existence, is no less important for lesbian, gay, transgendered, intersex, or other individuals who do not fit sexual norms (Bauermeister, 2014). States have taken three different approaches to AR for gay and lesbian couples. Countries that adhere to traditional family norms for parenting, including even some states that permit same-sex marriage, either ban sperm or egg donation for all individuals, or exclude same-sex couples from access to these treatments. For example, the French Bioethics Law of 2004 restricts the use of IVF to situations where a 'man and woman making up the couple' face medical infertility or risks of transmitting serious genetic disorders (Berg Brigham, Cadier and Chevreul, 2013). In Portugal, only opposite sex couples may obtain AR services after a diagnosis of infertility and/or genetic, infectious, or analogous disease (Machado and Brandão, 2013).

A second group of countries protects access to AR services by gay and lesbian couples through non-discrimination laws. For example, the UK protects gay and lesbian individuals from discrimination in receipt of AR services, and gay couples in legally recognised relationships may obtain Parental Orders to obtain legal parentage of children born to a surrogate (Norton, Huson and Culley, 2013). Denmark started providing lesbian couples access to insemination in 2005 (Adrian, 2010), and it has since passed extensive protection from discrimination for its gay and lesbian citizens (European Network). Only a small number of US states prohibit sexual-orientation discrimination, and in one such state, California, a court ruled that a clinic may not refuse treatment based on the physicians' religious beliefs.[7] The Ethics Committee of the American Society for Reproductive Medicine (ASRM) urges equal treatment on the basis of sexual orientation and marital status (Ethics Committee of the ASRM, 2006), but clinic practices vary. State laws that require insurance coverage for fertility treatment often exclude gay and lesbian couples. They allow insurance companies to either cover only married persons or to limit treatment to cases of 'medical necessity' or infertility (Resolve, 2014).

A third group of countries, which includes most of the United States, remains silent on the rights of gay and lesbian couples to access gamete donation and other fertility treatments. This silence invests clinics with the power to determine access themselves.

Gay men who wish to donate sperm may face additional hurdles. Both Canada and the United States bar gay men from donating sperm anonymously. Both countries provide a limited way to avoid this ban for known donors: the United States has a 'directed donor' category while in Canada gay men may apply for a 'special access program' (Kelly, 2013; United States Food and Drug Administration, 2007). In contrast, in the UK, gay men are protected from discrimination on the basis of sexual orientation and cannot be excluded as sperm donors simply because they are sexually active (HFEA, 2014a: 11.19).

Marital or relationship status

Single individuals also confront difficulty gaining access to AR services. Many physicians are wary of serving single individuals (Gurmankin, Caplan and Braverman, 2005; Záchia et al., 2011). Some countries refuse to assist reproduction by single individuals because it violates traditional

7 *North Coast Women's Medical Group, Inc.* v. *San Diego County Superior Court*, 189 P. 2d 959 (California, 2008).

family norms, while others protect single individuals from discrimination in treatment. Yet others have taken no stance on this issue and leave it to clinicians to decide whether to treat single individuals.

European countries including Austria, Croatia, the Czech Republic, Slovenia, France, Italy, Norway, Slovenia, Sweden, Switzerland and Turkey reject AR by single individuals. Some European countries limit access to AR to married couples, or, like Italy, to married or cohabiting opposite sex couples (Fineschi, Neri and Turillazzi, 2005). The trend is towards more inclusion, however. Denmark recently changed its law to allow single women access to gamete donation and fertility treatment, joining other countries such as Belgium, Bulgaria, Finland, Greece, Hungary, Latvia, Russia and Spain (Ory, 2013). Russian clinics that had refused treatment to single women have changed their practices since two courts established their right to treatment, but clinics continue to refuse treatment to single men through surrogacy despite equal treatment provisions of the Russian constitution (Svitnev, 2010).

In Canada the Assisted Human Reproduction Act protects individuals who want to use AR from discrimination on the basis of marital status. Quebec, the only province to provide full insurance coverage for AR, includes single women in its program (Quebec AR Program, Eligibility). The UK generally provides access to AR without regard to marital or relationship status. The Equality Act, 2010, protects against discrimination based on marriage or cohabitation, but it does not prohibit discrimination based on one's status as single (Equality Act, 2010). In 2008, the UK Parliament eliminated the requirement that clinics consider the future child's need for a father, a statutory provision that had led some clinics to reject single parents as patients, substituting instead a requirement to consider a child's need for 'supportive parenting' (Human Fertilisation and Embryology (HFE) Act, 1990, as amended (2008): §13(5)). However, the surrogacy provisions of the Act still require that the petitioners for a parental order be either a married or cohabiting couple (HFE Act, 1990, as amended (2008): §54(2)). Thus, single parents may not use surrogacy for their family planning. The United States is silent on this issue. Few states protect single and unmarried individuals from marital status discrimination, and clinics may deny services on that basis (Storrow, 2012). State-mandated insurance coverage related to egg or sperm donation may also be limited to married persons (Resolve, 2014).

Financial access to gamete donation

Gamete donation can be quite expensive; prices and availability of insurance for fertility treatments varies. US law treats fertility treatment and gamete donation as a commercial market; in stark contrast, European countries view fertility treatment as an aspect of their public commitment to health care and base gamete donation on altruism rather than profit (Spar and Harrington, 2009). While many European countries provide funding for AR, most Canadian provinces and the United States do not provide any assistance for these services, and private insurance for AR is very limited. These variations have a mixed impact on access, as many European countries face a shortage of gamete donations but actually demonstrate a higher rate of access to AR services generally. However, in many of the countries studied, it is common for patients to cross borders to obtain needed services either because of limited gamete supplies or expense.

US sperm banks and egg donation agencies face no legal restrictions on fees. However, the Ethics Committee of the ASRM found that monetary compensation is consistent with altruistic motive. Compensation should 'reflect the time, inconvenience, and physical and emotional demands associated with the oocyte donation process' (Ethics Committee of ASRM, 2007: 308). Payments for one cycle of egg extraction generally should be limited to $5,000 and under no circumstances should exceed $10,000. It notes that while sperm donors received on average $60 to $75 for a vial of sperm, the greater time, risk and physical discomfort involved in egg donation justifies the considerably higher compensation. Payment should not vary based on donor characteristics or egg number or quality. The opinion approves of egg sharing programs that reduce expenses for patients who are willing to donate excess eggs to other patients as long as the donor's interests are protected (Ethics Committee of ASRM, 2007).

Despite the Committee's guidance, varying fees based on personal characteristics are common in the United States. Fees charged may vary depending on the characteristics of the donors or their willingness to open their identity or be in contact with donor-conceived families (Acker, 2013; Keehn et al., 2012). Sperm banks and egg donor agencies often include additional fees for more donor information and other related services. Egg donor agencies set fees for their services and then leave it to individual egg donors and recipients to negotiate donation fees (Almeling, 2007). The extensive fees for both sperm and egg donation price many prospective parents out of the gamete donation market (Acker, 2013).

Altruism, not the market-based approach of the United States, is the guiding principle for gamete donation for Canada, the UK and Europe. Canada permits donor compensation only for actual expenses (Downie and Baylis, 2013). Members of the European Union are obliged to ensure that donations of tissues, including gametes, are 'voluntary and unpaid' and that compensation is limited to 'making good the expenses and inconveniences related to the donation' (European Tissues and Cells Directive, 2004/23/EC). Countries must balance these restrictions with their desire to increase donation. Thus, the UK increased donor compensation in 2011, raising fixed payments to sperm donors to £35 for each donation by a sperm donor and £750 for egg donors for each cycle of donation (HFEA, 2014b). Similarly, Spain sets compensation for egg donation at approximately €900 per cycle and has not experienced any unmet demands (García-Ruiz and Guerra-Diaz, 2012). In Germany, men are paid €100 for a usable donation (Lutticke, 2013). In Denmark, which has a very robust supply of sperm donors, a study of sperm donor attitudes found that the most frequently stated rationale for sperm donation was altruism, but only 14 per cent of donors stated that they would have agreed to donate without financial compensation, which averages €33 per vial (Bay et al., 2014).

In the United States and elsewhere, the costs associated with gamete donation are often covered by patients themselves. Only Massachusetts requires insurance companies to cover sperm, egg, or inseminated egg procurement (Massachusetts General Laws). The Affordable Care Act, which broadened access to health insurance in the United States beginning in January 2014, does not treat AR as an 'essential health benefit', so the law is unlikely to improve access to these services (Liu and Adashi, 2013). Although Canada has a national health service, individual provinces determine whether to cover AR. Only Quebec covers gamete donation under its health plan (Leader, 2013).

Many European countries, including the UK, at least partially cover some expenses related to AR, although the specifics vary dramatically. The UK may cover the entire cost through its National Health Service but this treatment is limited and most of those seeking ARTs need to turn to the private sector (Jenkins and Fleming, 2005). Countries may, like Denmark, limit coverage to a first child, while others, such as Portugal, Hungary and France, restrict the number of IVF cycles that may be used. Sweden and Finland cover 60 per cent of the costs and Norway covers up to a certain amount of the expenses, while other countries, such as the Czech Republic, cover some services and not others (Gissler et al., 2004; Ory, 2013).

The high costs associated with many forms of AR and gamete donation have a significant impact on their use. In the United States, where public or insurance funding for such services is very limited, only half of women with infertility seek treatment. Europe and the UK have much higher rates of usage because their health care systems often cover at least some types of treatment (Daar, 2008).

Donor identity

The ideal family form has long been based on a genetic and social connection between both parents and their offspring, and families created by gamete donation have felt stigmatised due to the lack of genetic connection to one or both parents (van den Akker, 2006). Until recently, most gamete donation through clinics was anonymous, and parents decided whether to tell their children about their conception.[8] However, the trend is towards increasing access to donor information based on concern for the human rights of donor-conceived offspring. This shifts control of donor information from parents to governments, who have begun to develop registries to maintain information and to provide identifying information about their donor once a donor-conceived individual reaches eighteen. Open donor identity is now official policy in some countries, including the UK, Austria, the Netherlands, Norway, Iceland, Sweden and Switzerland (Klotz, 2013; Ory, 2013; Ravelingien and Pennings, 2013). Denmark permits donors to choose whether to donate anonymously or not, and one study showed that 70 per cent of donors remained anonymous (Bay et al., 2014).

The UK's detailed regulations regarding donor identity provide prospective parents with non-identifying information about donors, including the number, sex and year of birth of other offspring with the same donor (HFEA, 2014a: Guidance 20.1). Donors may receive non-identifying information about the number, sex and date of birth of their donor-conceived children (HFE Act, 1990, as amended (2008): ss31ZD). Upon reaching sixteen, individuals may contact the national donor registry to determine whether they were conceived with donor gametes (HFE Act, 1990, as amended (2008): ss31ZA). If conceived with a donation made after April 2005, they receive information about the donor's ethnic group, marital status and details of donor screening tests and medical history; once they reach the age of eighteen they can also receive identifying information about the donor (HFE Act, 1990, as amended (2008): 31ZA). With mutual consent, they may also receive identifying information about donor-conceived genetic siblings (HFE Act, 1990, as amended (2008): ss31ZE). At age sixteen, children conceived with donations made after April 2005 may discover if they are genetically related through gamete donation to an intended spouse or intimate partner (HFE Act, 1990, as amended (2008): ss31ZB). Donors prior to April 2005 may elect to remove their anonymity (HFEA, 2015).

[8] However, it is still the case that most heterosexual couples using donor gametes do not tell their children of their donor conception (see Blake, Ilioi and Golombok, Chapter 13).

The HFE Act requires donors to be contacted to let them know that identifying information has been requested (HFE Act, 1990, as amended (2008): ss31ZC). It also requires an offer of counselling to donor-conceived offspring (HFE Act, 1990, as amended (2008): 31ZA). Some researchers have argued that these open identity requirements have led to shortages in donor gametes (Bernstein, 2010).

Germany, which permits sperm but not egg donation, has no clear policy on donor identity. Anonymity was the dominant practice until 2013, when a young woman, Sarah P., obtained a judgment from the regional appeals court in Hamm that she was entitled to the name of her donor-father (Klotz, 2013). Until this issue is decided at a higher judicial level, the current situation provides clinicians discretion about anonymity. Their refusal to preserve donor records may thwart successful plaintiffs such as Sarah P., where the defendant physician asserts that donor records cannot be located (Lutticke, 2013).

Other countries, such as Austria, the Czech Republic, Greece, Hungary and Latvia, permit offspring to request non-identifying information at a certain age. Some, like France, restrict even non-identifiable information to circumstances where a special commission has approved its release, while Spain permits identifying information to be disclosed where there is a serious illness (Ory, 2013).

Canada does not require donors to reveal their identity, although open-identity donors have become a favoured option among Canadians using sperm donation. Olivia Pratten, a donor-conceived individual, challenged her lack of access to identifying donor information as a violation of the Canadian Charter of Rights and Freedoms. The British Columbia Court of Appeals found that there was 'no positive right to know one's past'.[9] That ruling was allowed to stand by the Supreme Court of Canada.

In the United States, for the most part, donor identity is treated as a market commodity rather than a human right (Waldman, 2006). Gamete donation is most often anonymous, but prospective parents may pay a premium for record maintenance and access to identifying information (Cahn, 2009). However, Washington State recently became the first to legislate on this important topic. It requires gamete donors to provide identifying information and a medical history at the time of donation. Donor-conceived individuals may obtain this information at eighteen unless the donor had signed an affidavit of non-disclosure. In that case, only non-identifying medical history is revealed (Washington (State) Statutes: s26.26.750). This statute shifts the presumption to open

[9] *Pratten* v. *British Columbia*, 2012, ¶7.

identity, which may signal that Europe's human rights concerns about access to donor identity are beginning to gain traction in the United States.

European and North American countries may look to the experiences and research coming from Victoria, Australia, which has a broad donor identity law, as they consider whether to enact or further broaden open identity statutes. Victoria first established a mandatory registry of donors and donees in 1988. Donor-conceived children born from donations made between 1988 and 1998 have the right to request donor identity information from the Voluntary Register, but they receive the information only with the donor's consent and likewise, donors may receive information only with the consent of the donor-conceived individual. Since 1998 donors have been required to consent at the outset to allow donor-conceived individuals to obtain identifying information at eighteen. In both time periods, parents may request identifying donor information before their children turn eighteen, but they will receive that information only with the donor's consent (Hammarberg et al., 2014).

In addition, Victorian law now requires that when donor-conceived individuals apply for birth certificates, they must be provided an addendum to their birth certificate that states that more information is available about their birth (Births, Deaths and Marriages Registration Act, 1996: s17B). This prospective requirement went into effect in 2010. This means that all individuals born after 2010, once they reach the age of eighteen, who happen to request their birth certificate, could stumble upon the information that they were donor-conceived even if their parents have not chosen to reveal that information. This goes beyond the UK approach, which requires adults to specifically request information regarding whether they were conceived through donor gametes. They are most likely to do this only if their parents have revealed to them that donor gametes were used in their conception.

The Victorian Law Reform Committee proposed to go even further and make all donor identities available to donor-conceived individuals, even if they were conceived prior to 1998. However, in part based on research demonstrating that the majority of surveyed pre-1998 donors did not want this information provided without their consent, Victoria has not adopted retrospective release of donor identity (Hammarberg et al., 2014). It has, however, established a counseling service that must be offered to all donor-conceived individuals who seek information, and the Victoria Assisted Reproductive Treatment Authority conducts public education to encourage donors and donor-conceived individuals to take advantage of the Voluntary Register (Hammarberg et al., 2014; Wise and Kovacs, 2014).

Legal regulation of family relationships

Gamete donation raises new challenges to legal family forms. In countries that permit gamete donation, the consent of two married persons to gamete donation is generally adequate to ensure both legal parentage. Married gay and lesbian couples often benefit from this legal clarity as well.

There is less guidance as family forms created through gamete donation diverge from the traditional institution of marriage. Is a known sperm donor to an unmarried lesbian couple a father or donor? Does a man who provides sperm to a single woman have parental rights and responsibilities? When, if ever, can more than two people have parental rights in relation to any given child? Courts must balance often conflicting claims of procreative liberty and may do so in situations where the parties disagree about the terms of their pre-conception agreements.

In the United States, state courts have struggled to interpret state laws intended to cover only sperm donation to married couples. Single women who use anonymous donor sperm have been protected from paternity claims by donors, but claims by known donors have varied outcomes. While a California court denied parental status to a sperm donor who did not live with the recipient,[10] a New Jersey court imposed paternity on an informal donor under similar circumstances.[11] Courts have differed on whether strict adherence to statutory requirements for physician-assisted insemination is essential to avoid donor parentage.[12] The UK has a similar unresolved ambiguity. For those seeking to become parents outside legally recognised relationships, the HFE Act focuses on consent as the basis for assigning parental status and limits its reach to those obtaining treatment in licensed clinics (HFE Act, 1990, as amended (2008): ss36–37, 43–44). Thus, single individuals or couples who make informal arrangements with a sperm donor are not assured that the sperm donor will be barred from asserting parentage claims, nor can the sperm donor rest easy that he will not be liable for child support (Truescott and Williams, 2007).[13]

In part, these controversies concern the ability of states rather than parents to control legal parentage. While some US state courts have accepted the right of individuals to make their own decisions about parentage through pre-conception agreements, others have rejected this liberty claim and reassert the state's role in defining parental rights and responsibilities.[14] In Kansas, a sperm donor unknowingly lost his parental

[10] *Steven S.* v. *Deborah D.*, 2005. [11] *E.E.* v. *O.M.G.R.*, 2011.
[12] *McIntyre* v. *Crouch*, 1989; *C.O.* v. *W.S.*, 1994. [13] *Re: B (Parentage)*, 1996.
[14] *In re Sullivan*, 2005; *Ferguson* v. *McKiernan*, 2007; *E.E.* v. *O.M.G.R.*, 2011.

rights by failing to follow the statutory requirement for a written agreement preserving paternity.[15] The UK regulations, in contrast, inform donors that they are waiving their parental rights through notice of consent to the legal effects of the donation as long as they use regulated treatment (Human Fertilisation and Embryology Act, 1990). As in the United States, parentage in Canada is regulated at the provincial level. British Columbia bars a donor from raising a claim of parentage absent a pre-conception agreement assigning parental status to the donor. Absent this agreement, the child's birth mother and a person with whom the birth mother is in a marriage or marriage-like relationship are the only legal parents (British Columbia Family Law Act: ss27–30).

US states have also looked to the post-birth conduct of the parties to determine whether a sperm donor or non-biologically related partner has acted as a parent with the consent of the other parent. Some US state courts have followed this 'functional' approach to defining parentage rather than relying on a formalistic reading of state law.[16] This approach has been adopted by at least one Canadian court. In Alberta, Canada, two members of a couple agreed that the man was not the father of a child born to the woman via an anonymous sperm donor. The couple, however, continued to live together with the child. The court rejected their request for a declaration that the man was not a father, finding that any future court will have to consider the parties' actions with regard to the child to determine whether the man has exhibited a settled intention to be a father. Their agreement could not trump the child's interest in a developed and functional parent–child relationship.[17] One US state court has found that the failure to provide unmarried male sperm donors who have cohabited with the mother and child a way to establish their paternity would violate their US constitutional right to due process.[18]

In disputes between members of a lesbian relationship at the time the relationship dissolves, some birth mothers have tried to deny the other's parentage, even of partners who donated eggs and are genetically related to the children. These disputes highlight the very shaky legal ground on which many gay and lesbian couples had to tread in the United States in states prior to the recognition of marriage rights to shore up parent–child relationships, and that unmarried gay and lesbian couples may continue to confront. When faced with such a dispute, the California Supreme Court creatively interpreted its statute to treat the partner who donated the egg and helped raise the children as a legal parent.[19] In Florida, however, the Supreme Court agreed with the lesbian

[15] *In re: K.M.H.*, 2007. [16] *Mintz* v. *Zoernig*, 2008; *Breit* v. *Mason*, 2011.
[17] *Doe* v. *Alberta*, 2007. [18] *L.F.* v. *Breit*, 2013. [19] *K.M.* v. *E.G.*, 2005.

birth mother that the assisted conception statute limiting joint parentage rights to a heterosexual 'commissioning couple' deprived her former partner, who was also the genetic mother, of parental rights. However, the Court also struck down the statute for violating the genetic mother's due process rights under the United States and Florida constitutions.[20]

Similarly, an Alberta court found that gay partners should have the same right as heterosexual partners to rely on their relationship status to confirm parentage under the Canadian Charter of Rights and Freedoms.[21] British Columbia explicitly permits both members of a gay couple to obtain parentage through surrogacy.[22] In the UK, only the birth mother is identified as the 'mother' (HFE Act, 1990, as amended (2008): s33). The husband or same-sex legal partner (through civil partnership or marriage) of a woman who conceives through sperm donation is the father or female parent unless it is shown that he or she did not consent to the procedure, whether the procedure is conducted within or outside the United Kingdom (HFE Act, 1990, as amended (2008): s35, s42). The UK also permits two men to obtain Parental Orders to become parents through surrogacy.

Those whose families go beyond these more 'traditional' family forms to include more than two parents, or parenting across different households, may face even greater barriers to legal recognition (Kelly, 2013). To date, in Canada, only British Columbia and the Ontario Court of Appeal have expressly recognised families with more than two parents, while an Alberta court has rejected that idea (Kelly, 2013).

Conclusion

States face significant challenges to respond to the rapidly changing landscape of gamete donation. As this analysis makes clear, these challenges have led to a wide variety of responses, and this variety highlights the sharply conflicting values at stake in gamete donation. The freedom to procreate and form family relationships as one may desire conflicts with state control over reproduction and family formation. In general, states have moved in the direction of increasing access to AR and protection for their citizens from discrimination in receipt of those services. This trend, though, is uneven, and has been resisted by countries that seek to maintain the traditional family form, often to reflect religious values. Parents' rights to determine their children's access to donor identity have been limited by countries that find these rights in conflict with the human

[20] *D.M.T.* v. *T.M.H.*, 2013. [21] *H. (D.W.)* v. *R. (D.J.)*, 2011.
[22] British Columbia Family Law Act: ss27–30.

rights of donor-conceived children, though perhaps at the cost of greater access to donation, while other countries have resisted adopting this new 'right'. Finally, new family forms created through gamete donation, particularly those formed without clear legal guidance, will continue to prompt legal disputes and the need for states to further evaluate the legal bases of parent–child relationships.

REFERENCES

Acker, J. (2013). 'The case for an unregulated private sperm donation market'. *University of California Los Angeles Women's Law Journal*, 20, 1–38.

Adrian, S.W. (2010). 'Sperm stories: policies and practices of sperm banking in Denmark and Sweden'. *European Journal on Women's Studies*, 17, 393–411.

Almeling, R. (2007). 'Selling genes, selling gender: egg agencies, sperm banks and the medical market in genetic material'. *American Sociological Review*, 72, 319–40.

Appleby, J., Jennings, S. and Statham, H. (2012). 'Reproductive donation and justice for gay and lesbian couples', in M. Richards, G. Pennings and J.B. Appleby (eds.), *Reproductive Donation: Practice, Policy and Bioethics*. Cambridge University Press.

Bauermeister, J.A. (2014). 'How statewide LGB policies go from "under our skin" to "in our hearts": fatherhood aspirations and psychological well-being among emerging adult sexual minority men'. *Journal of Youth and Adolescence*, 43, 1295–305.

Bay, B., Larsen, P.B., Kesmodel, U.S. and Ingerslev, H.J. (2014). 'Danish sperm donors across three decades: motivations and attitudes'. *Fertility and Sterility*, 101, 252–57.

Berg Brigham, K., Cadier, B. and Chevreul, K. (2013). 'The diversity of regulation and public financing of IVF in Europe and its impact on utilization'. *Human Reproduction*, 28, 666–75.

Bernstein, G. (2010). 'Regulating reproductive technologies: timing, uncertainty and donor anonymity'. *Boston University Law Review*, 90, 1189–219.

Boutelle, A.L. (2014). 'Donor motivations, associated risks and ethical considerations of oocyte donation'. *Nursing for Women's Health*, 18, 112–21.

Cahn, N.R. (2009). *Test Tube Families: Why the Fertility Market Needs Legal Regulation*. New York University Press.

Clark, B. (2012). 'A balancing act? The rights of donor-conceived children to know their biological origins'. *Georgia Journal of International and Comparative Law*, 40, 619–61.

Cook, M. (2012). 'Legal adventures 1: Italian IVF baby removed from elderly "narcissistic" parents'. *Bioedge*. Available at www.bioedge.org/index.php/bioethics/bioethics_article/10298.

Daar, J.F. (2008). 'Accessing reproductive technologies: invisible barriers, indelible harms'. *Berkeley Journal Gender Law and Justice*, 23, 18–82.

Dain, L., Auslander, R. and Dirnfeld, M. (2011). 'The effect of paternal age on AR outcome'. *Fertility and Sterility*, 95, 1–8.

Day, M. (2014). 'Italy drops ban on infertile couples using donated eggs or sperm'. *The British Medical Journal*, 348, g2722.

Downie, J. and Baylis, F. (2013). 'Transnational trade in human eggs: law, policy, and (in)action in Canada'. *Journal of Law, Medicine and Ethics*, 41, 224–39.

Ethics Committee of the American Society for Reproductive Medicine (ASRM) (2006). 'Access to fertility treatment by gays, lesbians, and unmarried persons'. *Fertility and Sterility*, 86, 1333–35.

Ethics Committee of the American Society for Reproductive Medicine (ASRM) (2007). 'Financial compensation of oocyte donors'. *Fertility and Sterility*, 88, 305–09.

European Network of Legal Experts in the Non-Discrimination Field, Country Reports (European Network). Available at www.non-discrimination.net/law/national-legislation/country-reports-measures-combat-discrimination. Accessed 3 March 2014.

Fineschi, V., Neri, M. and Turillazzi, E. (2005). 'The new Italian law on AR'. *Journal of Medical Ethics*, 31, 536–39.

García-Ruiz, Y. and Guerra-Diaz, D. (2012). 'Gamete and embryo donation: a legal view from Spain', in M. Richards, G. Pennings and J.B. Appleby (eds.), *Reproductive Donation: Practice, Policy and Bioethics*. Cambridge University Press.

Gissler, M., Klemetti, R., Sevón, T. and Hemminki, E. (2004). 'Monitoring of IVF birth outcomes in Finland: a data quality study'. *BMC Medical Informatics and Decision Making* 4, 3. Available at www.biomedcentral.com/1472-6947/4/3.

Glennon, T. (2010). 'Choosing one: resolving the epidemic of multiples in AR'. *Villanova Law Review*, 55, 147–204.

Glennon, T. (2012). 'UK and US perspectives on the regulation of gamete donation', in Richards, M., Pennings, G. and Appleby J.B. (eds.), *Reproductive Donation: Practice, Policy and Bioethics*. Cambridge University Press.

Grossman, L., Korth, D.H. and Sauer, M.V. (2012). 'Managing AR in women over the age of 50 years: a clinical update'. *Expert Review Obstetrics and Gynecology*, 7, 525–33.

Gulino, M., Pacchiarotti, A., Montanari Vergallo, G. and Frati, P. (2013). 'Is age the limit for human AR techniques? "Yes", says an Italian judge'. *Journal of Medical Ethics*, 39, 250–52.

Gurmankin, A.D., Caplan, A.L. and Braverman, A.M. (2005). 'Screening practices and beliefs of assisted reproductive technology programs'. *Fertility and Sterility*, 83, 61–67.

Gürtin, Z.B. (2011). 'Banning reproductive travel: Turkey's ART legislation and third-party assisted reproduction'. *Reproductive Biomedicine Online*, 23, 555–64.

Hammarberg, K., Johnson, L., Bourne, K., Fisher, J. et al. (2014). 'Proposed legislative change mandating retrospective release of identifying information: consultation with donors and Government response'. *Human Reproduction* 29, 286–92.

Herring, J. (2006). *Medical Law and Ethics*. Oxford University Press.

Human Fertilisation and Embryology Authority (HFEA) (2014a). *Code of Practice*, 8th edn. London: HFEA.

Human Fertilisation and Embryology Authority (HFEA) (2014b). 'Potential donors information and advice'. Available at www.hfea.gov.uk/egg-donation-and-egg-sharing.html. Accessed 27 October 2014.

Human Fertilisation and Embryology Authority (HFEA) (2015). 'Re-register as an identifiable donor'. Available at www.hfea.gov.uk/1973.html. Accessed 6 March 2015.

Jenkins, J. and Fleming, R. (2005). 'Key facts on infertility, IVF and NHS provision'. *British Fertility Society Factsheet*. Available at www.britishfertilitysociety.org.uk/public/factsheets/docs/BFS-keyfacts.pdf.

Keehn, J., Holwell, E., Abdul-Karim, R., Chin, L.J. et al. (2012). 'Recruiting egg donors online: an analysis of IVF clinic and agency websites' adherence to ASRM guidelines'. *Fertility and Sterility*, 98, 995–1000.

Kelly, F. (2013). 'One of these families is not like the others: the legal response to non-normative queer parenting in Canada'. *Alberta Law Review*, 5, 1–21.

Klotz, M. (2013). 'Genetic knowledge and family identity: managing gamete donation in Britain and Germany'. *Sociology*, 47, 939–56.

Leader, A. (2013). 'What are we waiting for?' *Journal of Obstetrics and Gynaecology Canada*, 35, 499–500.

Liu, J.J. and Adashi, E.Y. (2013). 'Selective justice: state mandates for assisted reproductive technology and reproductive justice'. *American Journal of Clinical and Experimental Obstetrics and Gynecology*, 1, 53–61.

Lutticke, M. (2013). 'No anonymity for sperm donors, court rules'. *Deutsche Welle*, February 7, 2013.

Machado, T.C. and Brandão, A.M. (2013). 'Regulating lesbian motherhood: gender, sexuality and medically assisted reproduction in Portugal', *Laws*, 2, 469–82.

McCandless, J. and Sheldon, S. (2010). 'The Human Fertilisation and Embryology Act (2008) and the tenacity of the sexual family form'. *The Modern Law Review*, 73, 175–207.

Molinelli, A., Bonsignore, A., Daretta, V. and Anserini, P. (2012). 'Results and unsolved problems following the amendment to the Italian Law on AR brought about by the Constitutional Court'. *European Journal of Obstetrics and Gynecology and Reproductive Biology*, 163, 1–4.

Mutcherson, K. (2013). 'Transformative reproduction'. *Journal of Gender, Race and Justice*, 16, 187–234.

NHS Choices (2013). 'Can I get IVF treatment on the NHS?' Retrieved from: www.nhs.uk/chq/Pages/889.aspx?CategoryID=54.

Norton, W., Huson, N. and Culley, L. (2013). 'Gay men seeking surrogacy to achieve parenthood'. *Reproductive BioMedicine Online*, 27, 271–79.

Ory, S.J. (ed.) (2013). *IFFS (International Federation of Fertility Societies) Surveillance 2013*. Available at www.c.ymcdn.com/sites/www.iffs-reproduction.org/resource/resmgr/iffs_surveillance_09–19–13.pdf.

Pennings, G. (2007). Decision-making authority of patients and fertility specialists in Belgian law'. *Reproductive BioMedicine Online*, 15, 19–23.

Pennings, G. (2008). 'International evolution of legislation and guidelines in medical AR'. *Reproductive Biomedicine Online*, 18, S15–8.

Ravelingien, A. and Pennings, G. (2013). 'The right to know your genetic parents: from open-identity gamete donation to routine paternity testing'. *The American Journal of Bioethics*, 13, 33–41.

Robertson, J. (1995). 'Liberalism and the limits of procreative liberty: a response to my critics'. *Washington and Lee Law Review*, 52, 233–67.

Sabatello, M. (2014). 'Disclosure of gamete donation in the United States'. *Indiana Health Law Review*, 11, 29–81.

Schutte, J., Schuitemaker, N., Steegers, E. and Roosmalen, J. (2008). 'Maternal death after oocyte donation at high maternal age: case report'. *Reproductive Health*, 5, 1–4.

Spar, D. and Harrington, A. (2009). 'Building a better baby business'. *Minnesota Journal of Law, Science and Technology*, 10, 41–69.

Storrow, R.F. (2012). 'Marital status and sexual orientation discrimination in infertility care'. *Law Journal for Social Justice*, 3, 99–120.

Svitnev, K. (2010). 'Legal regulation of AR treatment in Russia'. *Reproductive BioMedicine Online*, 20, 892–94.

Truescott, C. and Williams, R. (2007). 'Lesbian mother hits back in row over donor's support payments'. *The Observer*, 4 December, retrieved from The Observer website: observer.guardian.co.uk.

van den Akker, O. (2006). 'A review of family donor constructs: current research and future directions'. *Human Reproduction Update*, 12, 91–101.

Waldman, E. (2006). 'What do we tell the children?' *Capital University Law Review*, 35, 517–61.

White & Case, LLP. (2009). 'European laws governing in vitro fertilization'. Memo to the Center for Reproductive Rights. Available at www.federa.org.pl/dokumenty_pdf/invitro/jbf_European_laws_governing_in_vitro_fertilization%5B2%5D.pdf.

Wise, S. and Kovacs, G. (2014). 'Secrecy, family relationships and the welfare of children born with the assistance of donor sperm: developments in research, law and practice', in A. Hayes and D. Higgins (eds.), *Families, Policy and the Law: Selected Essays on Contemporary Issues for Australia*. Commonwealth of Australia. Available at www.aifs.gov.au/institute/pubs/fpl/fpl.pdf.

Záchia, S., Knauth, D., Goldim, J.R., Chachamovich, J.R. et al. (2011). 'Assisted reproduction: what factors interfere in the professional's decisions? Are single women an issue?' *BMC Women's Health*, 11, 21–31.

Zanini, G. (2011). 'Abandoned by the State, betrayed by the Church: Italian experiences of cross-border reproductive care'. *Reproductive BioMedicine Online*, 23, 565–72.

LEGAL REFERENCES (BY COUNTRY OR REGION)

VICTORIA, AUSTRALIA

Legislation

Births, Deaths and Marriages Registration Act 1996, §17B (Vic)(as amended by the *Assisted Reproductive Treatment* Act, 2008).

CANADA

Cases

Doe v. *Alberta* (2007). ABCA 50.
H. (D.W.) v. *R. (D.J.)*, 2011 CarswellAlta 2178, 2011 ABQB 791.
In Reference re Assisted Human Reproduction Act [2010]3 SCR 457.
Pratten v. *British Columbia* [2012]BCCA 480.

Legislation

Assisted Human Reproduction Act, S.C. 2004, ch.2 (Canada) (AHRA).

EUROPE

Cases

Costa and Pavan v. *Italy*, Application Number 54270/10, European Court of Human Rights Second Section (2013).
Mennesson v. *France*, Application Number 65192/11 and Labassee v. France, Application Number 65941/11, European Court of Human Rights, Fifth Section (2014).
S.H. v. *Austria*, Application No. 57813/00, European Court of Human Rights Grand Chamber (2011).

Legislation and regulation

Directive on Setting Standards of Quality and Safety for the Donation, Procurement, Testing, Processing, Preservation, Storage and Distribution of Human Tissues and Cells (Directive 2004/23/EC).

UNITED KINGDOM

Cases

Re: X and Y (*Foreign Surrogacy*) [2008]EWHC 3030 (Fam).

Legislation and regulation

Equality Act 2010.
Human Fertilisation and Embryology Act 1990.
Human Fertilisation and Embryology (HFE) Act 1990, as amended (2008).

UNITED STATES

Cases

Breit v. *Mason*, 718 S.E. 2d 482 (Virginia App., 2011).
C.O. v. *W.S.*, 639 N.E.2d 523 (Ct. Common Pleas, Ohio, 1994).
D.M.T. v. *T.M.H.*, 129 So.3d 320 (Florida, 2013).
E.E. v. *O.M.G.R.*, 20 A.3d 1171 (New Jersey Superior Ct., 2011).
Ferguson v. *McKiernan*, 940 A.2d 1236 (Pennsylvania, 2007).
In re: K.M.H., 169 P.23d 1025 (Kansas, 2007).
In re Sullivan, 157 S.W.3d 911 (Texas App. – Houston [14th Dist.], 2005).
L.F. v. *Breit*, 736 S.E. 2d 711 (Virginia, 2013).

McIntyre v. *Crouch*, 780 P. 2d 239 (Oregon App. 1989).
Mintz v. *Zoernig*, 198 P. 3d 861 (New Mexico, 2008).
North Coast Women's Medical Group, Inc. v. *San Diego County Superior Court*, 189 P. 2d 959 (California, 2008).
Steven S. v. *Deborah D.*, 25 Cal. Rptr. 3d 482 (California Ct. App. 2d. Dist. 2005).

Legislation

Fertility Clinic Success Rate and Certification Act of 1992, Public L. No. 102–493, 106 Stat. 3146 [FCSRCA] (US).
Massachusetts General Laws Annotated, Ch. 175, Section 47H, ch. 176A, Section 8K, ch.176B, Section 4J, ch 176G, Section 4, and 211 CMR 37.00.
United States Food and Drug Administration (2007). 'Guidance for Industry Eligibility Determination for Donors of Human Cells, Tissues, and Cellular and Tissue-Based Products (HCT/Ps)'.
Washington (State) Statutes, s26.26.750.

Organisation websites

Quebec AR Program, Eligibility. Available at www.sante.gouv.qc.ca/en/programmes-et-mesures-daide/programme-quebecois-de-procreation-assistee/admissibilite/. Accessed 15 July 2014.
Resolve (2014). 'Insurance Coverage in Your State'. Available at www.resolve.org/family-building-options/insurance_coverage/state-coverage.html. Accessed 15 July 2014.

4 Reproductive donation in the context of environmental and global justice

Anja J. Karnein and Mattias Iser

Faced with the ever accelerating phenomenon of climate change – and environmental pollution more generally – we know that many of our actions will, by emitting CO_2, have harmful consequences, not only for those living in the present but also for those who will exist in the future.[1] There is thus a strong moral and political imperative to prevent this harm both by reducing emissions and by offsetting them as far as possible (see Broome, 2012, especially Chapters 4 and 5). Merely compensating future persons for the harm we impose on them would be highly problematic (see Shiffrin, 1999).

In this vein, it has been suggested that we, that is, those living today, need to seriously rethink our approach to reproduction because by bringing new children into the world we create more 'harmers'. John Broome states it poignantly: 'The more people there are, the more carbon they raise' (Broome, 2012: 169). Philip Cafaro puts the same point more positively claiming that 'less people is the environmental gift that keeps on giving. *Those people are not there*, and need not show any foresight or discipline in order to make their contributions to decreased resource use. They and their non-existent non-descendants just do the right environmental thing – nothing – and the Earth's existing inhabitants benefit' (Cafaro, 2012: 47–48, original emphasis). On a collective level we thus seem to face the political imperative to effectively control population, which, in turn, elicits the question on the individual level of how many children it is permissible for each person to have.

However, even if one agreed with this, it does not seem to matter at first sight how the number of children permitted by such an approach

[1] For this chapter, we just presuppose that it is possible to wrong future persons by acting in a way that will be more harmful with regard to the very position that they will occupy in a future society than if one would not have so acted. Thus, we believe that one can circumvent the non-identity problem. For an account along these lines, see Kumar (2003) and Karnein (2012a, Chapter 6).

came into being, that is, by 'traditional' sexual intercourse, by reproductive donation or by any other form of assisted reproductive technologies (ARTs). Thus, one may wonder what any of this has to do with reproductive donation. For while there may be an abundance of reasons for and against allowing or even promoting reproductive donation, as witnessed by the contributions to this volume, environmental impact does not seem to be one of them, since this will broadly be the same regardless of the method of procreation used.

Reproductive donation begins to look more problematic from an environmental perspective once we take into account that children created via ARTs will, for the most part, be born in western industrialised countries. This means that those children will typically be more likely to emit high volumes of CO_2 than those born in developing countries. Thus, the above quote by Broome is, in all its poignancy, too undifferentiated. The increase in carbon emissions is not merely a function of the number of persons inhabiting the world but of the product of their number and per capita emissions, with the latter, again, resulting from the combination of affluence and technological efficiency.[2] It is, after all, not the existence of additional persons we are concerned about but the harmfulness of their behaviour – via emitting – towards future people (and perhaps even towards the environment as such).

Yet, there is still an argument missing as to why the probability of more harmful behaviour by future persons in western industrialised countries should have any direct bearing on the issue of ARTs (including reproductive donation). If, say, every inhabitant of western industrialised countries would be permitted to create a certain number of children (but not more): why would it matter how the existence of such children came about?

There are two reasons for analysing the relationship between reproductive donation on the one hand and environmental and global justice on the other in more detail. First, what gives this issue specific salience globally is the potential hypocrisy involved in trying to decrease birth rates in developing countries while at the same time engaging in extra and often costly efforts to create more children in the West. This is valid especially for medically assisting persons who otherwise could not become parents by, for instance, providing them with access to donated eggs or sperms. This requires resources and money that could be spent elsewhere. Thus, there seems – at least at first sight – to be a mismatch between the demands placed on developing countries and those imposed on 'ourselves'. This is a particularly pressing concern once one realises

2 For the original formulation of the IPAT equation (Impact = Population × Affluence × Technology), see Ehrlich and Holden (1972: 20), also Heyward (2012: 706).

that the western industrialised countries are mainly to blame for climate change and the resulting need to decrease population in the first place.

Second, if one therefore believes that the western industrialised countries should bear the main burden with regard to decreasing birth rates, there is an argument to be made for either banning or at least not supporting reproductive donation. This argument turns on the different means that can be used in order to influence the reproductive choices of parents. Whereas fertile couples would have to be prevented, perhaps forcefully, from having (more) children, it seems comparatively unproblematic not to promote reproductive donation. Not helping people to have children is more like withholding a service than violating individuals' reproductive autonomy. Thus, this argument goes, if we cannot solve the problem of climate change by 'merely' overcoming excessively affluent lifestyles or by devising more efficient technologies, then we ultimately have to decrease population. If this is the case, we should use the phasing out of ARTs before we force couples who are not in need of ARTs to abstain from reproducing.

In this chapter we discuss these two issues in order, arguing, first, that the discourse on overpopulation is often misleading because it exhibits an inherent tendency to mistakenly focus on population size instead of emissions. Once one realises that it is the inhabitants of western industrialised countries who are 'overemitting', policy recommendations follow that do not exclusively or even primarily target population.

Second, to the extent that all countries have to reduce their birth rates we argue that it would constitute a specific kind of injustice to phase out ARTs or reproductive donation. Rather, other means to lower fertility levels have to be found. Here we argue in favour of specific taxation measures.

Population control in the context of global justice

There is no denying the seriousness of the concern about overpopulation. Overpopulation, in tandem with economic output (IPCC, 2014: 18), threatens the sustained availability of finite resources such as the absorptive capacity of the atmosphere. The number scholars are responding to with some anxiety is 9.2 billion, the probable world population in 2050.

In response to this number, some have suggested limiting birth rates by endorsing radically anti-natalist policies in high fertility countries (Cafaro, 2012). Hereby they are reviving the classic discourse on population that is characterised by highly questionable proposals, such as reducing population by withholding aid from the poor. Already in 1798, in his *An Essay on the Principle of Human Population*, Thomas Malthus famously argued that population growth was something to be feared. He was concerned that while the production of food could only grow arithmetically (2, 4, 6, 8 . . .), population grows geometrically (2, 4, 6, 16 . . .) so that, sooner rather than later, there would be too many people to be fed on this planet (Malthus, 1798: Chapter 2). While his originally proposed remedy lay in denying aid to the poor (since he thought that giving aid would only lead them to have more children), he later (in the 1803 edition of his essay) changed his stance to proposing moral restraint in reproducing on everyone. What Malthus had not foreseen was industrialisation and with it, the exponential growth of food production. He had also been wrong in thinking that greater wealth correlates with having more children. As economies began to grow and people became richer (and more educated), fertility levels started stabilising, and eventually dropping to where western industrialised countries are now.

There was another surge in population right after World War II when improved medicine led to lower child mortality, a factor that had thus far counteracted very high fertility rates in developing countries. At that point a wave of neo-Malthusians began reviving arguments against aid to the global poor in order to discourage them from reproducing. Garrett Hardin, for instance, reasoned that

> [i]f poor countries received no food from the outside, the rate of their population growth would be periodically checked by crop failures and famines. But if they can always draw on a world food bank in time of need, their population can continue to grow unchecked, and so will their 'need' for aid. In the short run, a world food bank may diminish that need, but in the long run it actually increases the need without limit. (Hardin, 1974: 10)

Paul Ehrlich had expressed the same sentiment even more radically in his book *The Population Bomb* from 1968:

> A cancer is an uncontrolled multiplication of cells; the population explosion is an uncontrolled multiplying of people. Treating only the symptoms of cancer may make the victim more comfortable at first, but eventually he dies – often horribly. A similar fate awaits a world with a population explosion if only the symptoms are treated. We must shift our efforts from treatment of the symptoms to the cutting out the cancer. (Ehrlich, 1968: 152)

Hardin as well as Ehrlich were heavily criticised both for the perceived inaccuracy of their predictions as well as for their morally dubious proposals to counteract the threats of overpopulation by letting 'superfluous' people die in order to cure the 'patient humanity'. For a long time then, even talking about population was seen as a potentially explosive topic that was better to be avoided.

Recently there have been a few renewed attempts to address the problem, this time, however, in more uncontroversial terms. These proposals depart from the earlier writings in two ways. First, they are all sensible enough to stress the need to reduce overconsumption (or per capita emissions), a task mostly burdening the western industrialised countries. Second, they mostly focus on measures not intended to prevent a certain part of the population from reproducing but to decrease birth rates by improving individual (reproductive) freedom. This change in outlook can mostly be ascribed to the insight that a discourse that is primarily focused on population is ideological in nature, that is (a) empirically as well as (b) normatively inappropriate.

(a) Any attempt to reduce population that primarily seeks to influence the reproductive choices of individuals within societies that have fertility rates above replacement level – be it coercive or non-coercive – faces the challenge that, in the world we live in, the overwhelming majority of such individuals are located in very poor areas in the developing world. But because the per capita emissions in these countries are relatively low, reducing the number of these populations seems to be an insufficient remedy. Cafaro, a contemporary proponent of the potentially permissible use of force to control population (Cafaro, 2012: 50), implicitly admits this by further arguing that immigration from developing countries to western industrialised nations, especially to the United States, should be brought to a halt in order to counteract resource depletion (Cafaro and Staples, 2009; see also Cafaro, 2012: 49).[3] He thus assumes – and rightly so – that the same person will have more negative impact on the environment living in the United States than if she spent her life in Mexico or Kenya. While not endorsing Cafaro's proposals regarding immigration, we take his view to suggest that if any number needs to be restricted it is that of the globally privileged.[4]

(b) But focusing on controlling population primarily in high fertility countries is not only an ineffective tool to fight global climate change, it is also normatively problematic. After all, the reasons for high fertility levels in those areas are partly cultural but largely economic. Children are frequently the only old-age insurance available. Having many may be

[3] Counter to what Cafaro is suggesting, immigration is not a problem but a promising solution to the problems faced by the economies of western industrialised societies (see in more detail below).

[4] If one regarded the issue of sperm donation from other, mostly developing countries (as discussed in some chapters of this volume) as another kind of 'indirect immigration' this very reasoning would imply that such donation might not be legitimate either. See also footnote 7.

a matter of survival. It is here that considerations of global justice come into play. Arguably, it is members of the western industrialised countries who are in some measure to blame for allowing global poverty on this scale to persist, by, for instance, supporting global economic structures that systematically place poor countries at a disadvantage while benefiting the already rich and powerful (Pogge, 2008; Young, 2011; on the role of local factors, see Rawls, 1999: 108). It thus seems that it is the task of the western industrialised countries to render it unnecessary for people in the developing world to have so many children. Thus, even if (growing numbers of) inhabitants of developing countries cannot but harm future persons in order to secure a decent living standard for themselves or even just their subsistence,[5] they may be excused to some extent.

This does not imply that there is no responsibility on the side of developing countries. Even if it is unfair and hypocritical of western industrialised countries to demand a decrease in children per person in the developing countries, the inhabitants of the developing world might still have duties towards future people. Thus, depending on how demanding a reduction of children is contemplated and how much this would prevent the inhabitants of developing countries from leading a decent life, we might think that their states wrong future persons if they do not reduce their population. This might be valid even if the western industrialised countries are mostly to blame for this state of affairs.[6]

Additionally, developing states not reducing their population might pose a further problem. If development brought us closer to achieving greater global justice, the children born in these states might end up contributing about as much as children in western industrialised countries. We should still aim for such an equalisation of opportunities for a flourishing life. But this goes to show that if we want to improve global and environmental justice at the same time, we indeed have to worry about the number of people populating the planet because everyone who is born should have the right to demand the resources (and necessary emissions) they need in order to lead a decent life. That means that we have to think about compensatory steps in the dimensions of population as well as affluence and technology.

For this reason it is disconcerting to look at another discourse, which is perhaps even more familiar from daily news sources to those of us living in western industrialised countries: fertility levels are at an all-time low

[5] On the difference between subsistence and luxury emissions, see Shue (1993).

[6] For an account that clearly distinguishes between fairness between duty holders and duties towards third parties, see Karnein (2014).

and this has worrying economic implications. Some predict, for instance, that the ratio between potential workers and retired persons will be 2:1 by 2050 (down from 5:1 in 1985). This places heavy strains on pension and social insurance systems, threatening to render the fulfilment of any form of intergenerational contract impossible (whereby those currently productive finance those who have retired). It also threatens to set in motion a vicious cycle leading to even fewer births, since working adults will have to pay for so many more retired persons that they are likely to find it harder to afford having children to begin with.

Because western industrialised countries are facing serious economic problems due to low fertility rates, some have proposed to promote limited pro-natal attitudes in low fertility countries (up to the replacement level of 2.1 children per couple). However, this neat sounding proposal, again, is diametrically opposed to what seems to be most appropriate right now, namely strongly pushing for anti-natalist policies. Trying to square this circle might mean embracing low fertility rates in western industrialised countries and opting – contra Cafaro – for more immigration (including, perhaps, international egg and sperm import[7]).

However, the argument about reducing population in developing countries might, after all, be one about feasibility. It would go like this: Surely we have to substantially reduce our emissions per capita as well as reduce population in order to limit the total emission of CO_2. The task of reducing per capita emissions clearly falls to the western industrialised countries (which should then transfer these technological innovations to the developing countries, perhaps even for free). But when it comes to population, we should look to those quarters of the world where we have the best prospects of reducing overpopulation very easily and especially by using non-coercive measures.

Admittedly, some have argued that unless very repressive means are used, there is no real way to influence the reproductive choices of individuals. Part of the reason for China's oftentimes draconian measures to control its population (forced abortions and sterilisations, for instance) was that these policies militated against deep-seated cultural reproductive

[7] Obviously, there are differences here. Whereas in the case of immigration already existing persons enter another state, in the case of sperm donation only an 'ingredient' is imported to create the child within the western industrialised country satisfying a deeply held desire for children entertained by citizens of this state. Due to this difference, such import creates new problems of justice on its own because one might believe that the inhabitants of developing countries are – due to their underprivileged status – used or even exploited. Here it would be interesting to compare such cases with problems of justice involved in (a) international adoption as well as (b) domestic reproductive donation by underprivileged people. We can obviously not pursue these intriguing questions in the narrow confines of this chapter.

norms (Huang, 1982: 775). But as the evidence from other countries has shown, there are more benign ways of influencing the number of children individuals choose to have. Among them are reducing poverty, educating women and influencing the social culture within which such choices are made. In Brazil, for instance, it seems to have been largely the increased ability to view telenovelas which portrayed the one-child family as an ideal that reduced birth rates (La Ferrara, Chong and Duryea, 2008). Such measures are a promising route indeed (Sen, 1994) but they do not suffice to show that it is only the developing countries which should decrease their birth rates (as the suggestion of a division of labour would have us believe). As long as the western industrialised countries have not succeeded in seriously reducing their per capita emissions they have to consider limiting population as well.

Population policy and reproductive donation

If we assume that the burden to decrease birth rates should not only fall on the developing countries, we face the challenge of how to lower western fertility rates below its already modest level. Let us assume that there is a duty of justice for every individual not to further contribute to harmful climate change (Broome, 2012: 54–64, 73–96), and that this also extends to the moral duty not to bring even more harmful emitters into the world, that is, by either refraining from procreating or by offsetting all emissions hereby added. Which means are permissible in a government's attempt to control population politically? Consider the following non-exhaustive list of policy options:

(1) legal prohibition of reproduction beyond a specific number of children, as in the case of China's one-child policy, backed by either
   (a) extremely coercive measures such as forced abortions or sterilisations or
   (b) other coercive measures such as punishment (ranging from imprisonment to fines);
(2) financial incentives, by either
   (a) withholding support for children and child services or
   (b) introducing taxation for children;
(3) promoting positive attitudes towards having small families, consisting of maximally one child;[8]

[8] The negative side-effect of such a promotion of positive attitudes towards small or no families might – if it proves to be very successful – be the stigmatisation of all those who have more than one child, a stigmatisation that would necessarily be a consequence of embracing option (1) and possibly of option (2), depending on how the financial incentives are justified. We will return to the latter issue below.

(4) changing the background structure (by, for instance, improving social security and education systems for women) to enable individuals to choose autonomously to have fewer children.[9]

Some authors, for example, Elizabeth Cripps (forthcoming) and Clare Heyward (2012), argue that the only kind of population control that could ever plausibly be defended, are non-coercive measures like (3) and (4). We have already established that especially option (4) is unproblematic because it increases individual autonomy and does not curtail it. Option (3) might meet with more scepticism depending on whether one believes that there is something objectively valuable about bringing children into the world. If one holds such a view one might believe that option (3) is akin to manipulation or instilling false beliefs even if it does not do so coercively. However, as long as people come to hold these views autonomously because they have been properly enabled by policies such as (4), this is hopefully not too worrisome a path to follow from a liberal perspective.

Option (2) looms large within the ethics of reproduction because many authors regard having children as a personal matter of 'expensive taste,' the costs of which have to be internalised by the parents alone and must not be externalised (some may say, not even partly) to the state and all other citizens. However, usually it is accepted that societies depend on children in order to reproduce or – as we have seen with regard to the demographic discourse in western industrialised countries – in order to maintain their social security and pension systems as well as the workings of the economy. With the introduction of the harmful effects of emissions, however, these benefits seem to be counteracted, if not even outweighed, by harms so that some might be justified in complaining about the harmful reproductive behaviour of others. Now, two things are important to note: first, within the context of western industrialised countries it is unlikely that the benefits of population increase for the particular society would be outweighed by the harms endured by that society due to the population increase. But even if that were the case, second, viewing child bearing as just another case of consumption (Young, 2001) disregards that it makes a difference whether one person excessively consumes or whether she creates another person, to whom we owe respect, so that in the end two people consume the same amount (but do not do so excessively as individuals). Thus, Heyward is correct in alerting us to the danger that any coercive population policy (option 1) – and we might

[9] This policy is often recommended with regard to developing countries, as shown above, but may also be important for at least some parts of the population in western industrialised countries who suffer from relative deprivation.

add, cultural pressures that may come as a side-effect of options (1)–(3), see footnote 8 above – may signal to the new person that she is not welcome but rather seen as a burden or as a harmful entity (Heyward, 2012: 716–7).[10] We will return to this issue at the end of the paper.

For now we want to argue that attempts at targeting specific potential parents are much more problematic and that compared to such proposals even option (1) might look comparatively promising because it at least holds on to the idea of equal access to procreative rights. One such proposal that we want to criticise seeks to dissuade those from reproducing who cannot do so without the help of ARTs. It holds that there is a reason not only to regulate assisted reproduction, but also to systematically discourage the practice altogether. This may be true especially for reproductive donation because this form of assistance potentially increases the individual/child ratio by enabling singles to have children (if each person had one child then we would automatically be at replacement levels of reproduction – so one might claim that with couples, at least, two are sharing one child).

In this vein, Heyward has argued that once the time has come at which we inevitably need to address population, one of the places to inquire about would be ARTs:

> There are other attitudes toward procreation that might be reconsidered. One would be the strong preference to bring up children who are biologically related to oneself. While it would be rather unsympathetic to those who undergo the emotional and physical trauma of IVF to argue that support for assisted reproduction should be phased out, it is at least worth considering whether it should be presented as the first port of call for infertile couples. Adoption, including of older children, could be more widely promoted and presented as a positive choice. Remaining childless could perhaps be shorn of some of its stigma. (Heyward, 2012: 724)

While Heyward seems to argue against phasing out ARTs, she recommends a change in parents' attitudes: they should not be encouraged to go out of their way to try to insure having a biologically related child. However, her reluctance to come down disfavourably on ARTs might not be shared by everyone and thus it seems plausible to consider how this thought may be picked up in three different ways.

First, following Heyward one might want to suggest that the importance of having a biologically related child should be reconsidered, either only by those needing ARTs or by everyone, that is, both by those

[10] Yet, whether this effect will take place may depend on the kind of sanction applied (it should try to avoid targeting the child or her welfare) and on whether changing the attitude of people might involve inclining people to condemn 'surplus' children.

who need reproductive assistance as well as by those who do not (a). Second, one could think that, *pace* Heyward, one should 'phase out' assisted reproduction (b). Finally, one may argue (and would thereby only very loosely be depending on Heyward's claim) that the public money that is currently spent on high-tech ART solutions would be better spent on alleviating poverty or combating climate change (c).

(a) The most 'benign' proposal, that is, that of weakening the grip of biological ties on our social imagination is unproblematic as it seems to open up new horizons rather than close them off. The increasing willingness to adopt a child can be welcomed from several perspectives, including that of already existing children who wish to be adopted. Such a proposal would only be problematic if it did not address everyone but was meant to primarily target parents who are in need of ARTs – and this is indeed one possible reading of Heyward's proposal. Such parents might come to perceive their desire to have a biologically related child as unjustified whereas potential parents needing no medical assistance would not have to question their choice to reproduce 'naturally'.

A more general uncoupling of social (as well as legal) parenthood and biological relatedness may turn out to have serious (and perhaps surprising) implications for the practice of reproductive donation. There might, for instance, be an increased need for reproductive assistance and gamete donation. Instead of wanting their own genetically related child, couples might seek to 'optimise' the genetic heritage of their children by opting for donated sperm or egg cells rather than using their own. This may aggravate ethical concerns that are already an issue today because, at least in the United States, which is a market driven system, not just any potential gamete donor is encouraged to donate, but only those who fulfil certain 'quality' standards, such as being above a certain minimal height, heterosexual, not older than 40 and having a college degree (see Glennon, Chapter 3; Wright, Chapter 9).[11] It therefore may end up being only a very limited elite group of women and men whose services came to be in high demand. Thus, some worry that allowing individuals to choose the gamete donor of his or her child expresses the wrong kind of (instrumentalising) attitude towards gamete providers and the children conceived this way (Warnock, 1984). Others have, in principle at least, defended the practice of choosing one's donor

[11] See, for instance, the policies of leading sperm banks such as California Cryobank (www.spermbank.com/how-it-works/sperm-donor-requirements, retrieved 24 November 2014) or The Sperm Bank of California (www.thespermbankofca.org/content/how-qualify-sperm-donor, retrieved 24 November 2014). In the latter case, it is not specified whether or not the donor can be homosexual.

on the grounds that 'respect for the autonomy of the recipients and the reduction of the anxiety caused by the uncertainty constitute the main reasons for allowing the choice of the donor' (Pennings, 2000: 514).

So once genetic kinship is no longer of the great importance it is today, there might be an interesting ethical controversy to look forward to. However, at this point such worries (about genetic connections losing their significance) still seem somewhat far-fetched. And there are other argumentative routes someone may choose to pursue in light of Heyward's suggestion.

(b) Although Heyward does not explicitly embrace it, she is at least insinuating that 'phasing out' ARTs might be a more benign method of population control than state coercion. However, it is not clear that this is more benign if we consider where the real harm in prohibiting reproduction lies, that is, using option (1b). If this prohibition is not effected by violating a person's bodily integrity (forced abortion and sterilisation), then the harm of limiting reproduction lies in not allowing individuals to raise a second or third child (assuming that having one child would have to be permitted under all circumstances). But, of course, worse harm would occur if people were systematically barred from using ARTs since they presumably are prevented from being able to raise even one child.

Rejecting ARTs in such a fundamental manner becomes even more implausible if we consider how similar some forms of assisted reproduction are to what is commonly perceived as non-assisted reproduction. Sperm donation, for instance, may require as little as the use of a turkey baster to successfully 'assist' in producing a pregnancy.[12] Non-medically assisted reproduction may on occasion need much more elaborate tools to lead to a pregnancy. But if the line between what we conventionally call assisted and non-assisted reproduction is more fuzzy than commonly assumed, then either a number of common practices of non-assisted reproduction would have to be 'phased out' along with reproductive donation (at least of sperm donation) or we ought to rethink this suggestion again.

Perhaps someone following in Heyward's footsteps would respond by saying that she is referring only to high-tech kinds of reproductive assistance (excluding such low-tech methods as using a turkey baster, for instance). But why would this make a difference given that the parents could pay for it themselves? Unless someone were to refer to dubious assumptions of 'natural ways' to create children this is a non-starter.

[12] We are grateful to Lisa Tessman for pointing this out to us.

After all, individuals invest a great deal to make their procreative wishes come true and to let their children flourish afterwards. Nobody worries about any of these private efforts and expenses.

(c) The following idea may be more promising: The state must not coercively prevent people from using ARTs, option (1b), but it does not have to promote them either because there is a morally relevant difference between preventing individuals from doing what they would naturally just do (such as procreate in a low-tech fashion) and not enabling individuals to have children by providing them with high-tech assistance. The state could thus embrace option (2a) still leaving intact the negative right to bear children in whichever way one pleases as long as one pays for the necessary efforts oneself. In fact, someone may object to public resources being allocated to assisted reproduction (thereby leading to the birth of further individuals in an already overcrowded world) instead of allocating these resources to fighting poverty or climate change. However, this is a short-sighted concern, focusing on a single issue (assisted reproduction) rather than keeping in mind the whole picture.

We spend many resources on the provision of positive rights (such as social rights) and do not restrict state spending on the protection of negative rights – as libertarians propose who emphasise law enforcement as the main task of a minimal state (paradigmatically Nozick, 1974: Part 1). But why should we conceptualise a right to have children as a positive right rather than as a negative one? Such an account has to be grounded in the value of having a child and thus founding a family. If one views the experience of accompanying a child towards her or his independence as specifically valuable (see in more detail Karnein, 2012b: 56) one has to enable every member in society to participate in this specific form of intersubjective recognition (on the latter see Iser, 2013: Section 2.4, and Iser, forthcoming: Section 3.3.1). A merely negative right of non-interference would not protect equal access to this important sphere of experience, just as a merely negative right to education would not be able to insure any (let alone equal) access to education.[13]

It is therefore promising to posit a legal right to state support in bringing at least one child to life. After all, given the high costs of pregnancies quite generally, it would seem strange, especially in light of a concern about overpopulation, to publicly support a couple, let us call it AA, in receiving their fourth child (via taxes) but refusing to help an infertile

[13] Admittedly, a right to education may be seen as providing access to a precondition of autonomy whereas the right to have children rather protects the (autonomous) pursuit of a valuable end. We still believe that the similarities are sufficient to draw this analogy.

couple, let us call it BB, to receive their first child via ARTs or reproductive donation. If we assume that the costs for one child born to BB via ARTs are not higher than the costs for the three additional children of AA, there seems to be no reason to favour AA over BB but there is a reason of equal access to favour BB over AA. Favouring three children over the birth of only one might have made sense when governments were contemplating how to achieve higher birth rates without spending too much, but it certainly does not hold once the focus turns to the right of parents to have their own child, and especially not in the context of a threat of overpopulation. Opponents of the view proposed here might hold that *any* public support for bearing children should be phased out. However, this would not only constitute a radical break with current practice but would render having children a privilege of the wealthy.

There are certainly reasons to doubt that parents can only partake in the special experience of child rearing if they care for their own biologically related offspring. The spread of patchwork families has rendered the romantic idea of parents' love manifesting itself (only) in the product of the sexual union of a heterosexual couple rather anachronistic (Honneth, 2014: 169). Adoption and its accompanying idea of social parenthood thus offer a powerful alternative. However, as long as our social culture promotes the idea that biological relatedness is a source of specific value, society should guarantee all their members the opportunity to partake in this promulgated value. Thus, the default position seems to be at least to promote the desire of all citizens to have one biologically related child if that is their wish.

In light of this brief digression on the value of having one's own child, it seems obvious that there are far more expensive goods of much lesser value we might turn to for re-allocating resources, such as public funding of sports or space exploration. So there seems to be no reason for singling out the creation of children by means of assisted reproduction from other ways people 'have' children. Both groups should have the same reproductive standards applied to them: if there is a one-child policy, for instance, this should apply to those reproducing without assistance to the same extent it applies to those who need it.

Where does this leave us? Promoting ARTs as well as reproductive donation as a means to ensure the equal access of all persons to having at least one child, that is, distributive justice, is perfectly compatible with state measures to decrease the population overall in a fair way. We have only been trying to show that 'phasing out' ARTs (be it by prohibition or eliminating state funding) should not, counter to what arguments along the lines suggested by Heyward may suggest, be a preferred method for implementing such a policy. Rather, if population is to be controlled at all, it should be limited across the board. Thus, we are back to a more general discussion of the list of policy options sketched above.

There is, in any case, a fundamental problem with restricting the number of children by law as option (1a) and (1b) would suggest. At this moment, western industrialised countries do not even need such a law given the already low birth rates. Thus, the question arises whether any law restricting the number of children to below the average birth rate would not pay too high a price in terms of liberty. Because, as we have argued, such a policy would have to apply across the board, only three possibilities seem feasible. The first is a blanket prohibition to procreate. This would, if applied universally, lead to the extinction of the human race so it does not seem to be a desirable option. The second is to grant the right to have two or three children. This would restrict the right to procreate but would not lead to any significant decrease of birth rates within the western industrialised countries. The third option is to introduce a one child policy. This might significantly decrease population.

Whether such a restrictive policy will ever be necessary is hard to tell. We have argued that it would leave intact the equal chance to partake in an experience of intersubjective recognition many cherish. What it would prohibit is twofold, namely (a) the child's experience of having biologically related siblings (which might very well be counteracted by having social siblings) as well as (b) the realisation of any conception of a good life that includes having two or more (biologically related) children. Although this may not amount to an impossible burden for a political justification to meet (especially given the threat of catastrophic climate change), it must be acknowledged that a restriction of such a kind comes at very great costs to individual freedom.

That such a one-child policy is highly problematic can also be seen if one examines what such a policy might plausibly mean for reproductive donation. Two readings are possible. First, strictly interpreted, one might take a one-child policy to imply that each individual is entitled to contribute to the creation of exactly one child. This would mean that singles could make use of donated gametes but only from individuals who have not contributed (and will themselves then no longer be entitled to contribute) to the creation of another child. This may or may not be a good solution for individuals whose only chance of parenting a child would be through gamete donation, given that they would have to be prevented – perhaps by force – from being able to raise their own biologically related child (since another person/couple would be presumably doing that).

This problematic result is avoided by the second, looser interpretation. According to this reading, a one-child policy may have fewer consequences for reproductive donation: while having a child – the one each individual is entitled to – may become more precious and so each person may be more selective about her choice of partner or gamete donor, as long as there was only one child per couple, the regulation of reproductive donation itself may not have to change very much. Individual women could still donate several of their eggs (the one they are entitled to plus one for each woman who cannot herself produce an egg) and men could father a number of children (again, the one they are entitled to as social parents themselves plus one for each other man who does not want to or cannot father his own children).

Depending on the community within which this one-child policy was applied, a smaller birth cohort may, of course, raise concerns about incest to a greater extent than it does today or would occur in societies with a more permissive population policy. It might therefore provide reasons for limiting the number of offspring an individual may contribute to in addition to the limit posed by being able to donate only for those who cannot contribute their gametes themselves.[14]

The greater problem might be the following: If these donors decided to have a relationship with all their biological children – as some suggest they permissibly may or even, as Velleman (2008) insists, should have – the one-child policy would *not* apply to them. Donors would potentially be able to have a relationship with more than one biologically related child. This may raise issues of fairness since 'naturally' reproducing people could only ever have a relationship with the one child they are biologically related to. For an account that emphasises equal access this may not be a convincing route to take.

Thus, both readings present their own problems. Whereas according to the first, restrictive reading, donors could only provide sperms or eggs for one biologically related child hereby forfeiting the right to raise their own biologically related child (later), the second, looser interpretation, circumvents this problem, but only at the price of not really being a one-child policy for donors anymore. These problems might provide us with a further reason to eschew option (1), that is, legal prohibitions by the state, in general.

The most promising route left open to anyone who wants to manage population thus seems to be either disincentivising children by withholding state support or by taxation that applies to all children equally, be they created with or without medical assistance, that is, options (2a) or (2b).[15] Withholding state support as well as introducing new forms

[14] For a much fuller discussion of these issues, see Chapter 9 by Katharine Wright.

[15] We are grateful to Stephen Wilkinson for urging us to elaborate on this point.

of taxation merely changes the incentive structure of people without prohibiting any particular choices. Admittedly, taxation is coercive in the sense of punishing those who try to evade such taxes. However, withholding state support may be thought of as especially unfair as it primarily affects poorer parents and is therefore also ineffective as it does not sufficiently target the rich. Thus, some form of taxation may look more promising as it applies to everyone and may be progressive, so that wealthier persons pay more than poorer persons.

When it comes to population policies one might initially be tempted to tax parents for every new child (perhaps even taxing them more for any additional child beyond the desired number).[16] The rationale for such a 'head tax' might be twofold: first, creating a negative incentive and second, to use the money to either offset the added emissions or – where this is not possible – to at least enable future persons to adapt to the adverse effects every new person causes. However, a head tax is obviously not specific enough in order to address either the problem of offsetting or that of adaption. It also raises the question of whether it is unfair towards poorer parents.

Thus, it makes much more sense to directly tax all activities or items of consumption in proportion to their carbon emissions or environmental pollution. As mentioned at the very beginning of this chapter, it is not the number of people one ought to be concerned about but the pollution and future harm they cause. Thus, instead of coming up with a tax for every new child, we believe that it would be more plausible to generally tax goods in such a way as to either offset the produced emissions or to cover the environmental costs (including harm to future persons) caused by them. Population growth would hereby be influenced only indirectly as a side-effect.

The introduction of such taxes will probably render having more children increasingly expensive. And this might, again, allow richer people to afford a greater number of children. However, given the rising costs for child care this is already the case. Moreover, this effect can, first, be somewhat counteracted through general redistributive measures, and, second, by enabling parents to lower the costs for every additional child by engaging in less environmentally harmful activities with them.

[16] Cafaro even proposes fining parents for 'having more than two children' (2012: 51). However, fines carry the additional condemnatory meaning of having done something wrong whereas taxes do not. This is actually a further argument in favour of taxation because it prevents people from regarding the creation of new humans as something blameworthy.

What is more, the implausibility of the head tax proposal can readily be seen when looking at the ever expanding life expectation of persons.[17] The longer people live the more they supposedly emit and destroy the environment (although it might be less likely that very old people will engage in highly polluting activities such as frequent intercontinental travel). This obviously neither speaks in favour of letting them die prematurely by, for instance, not providing them with intensive care anymore, nor of taxing anybody who was about to prolong the lives of their nearest (hereby creating an incentive not to do so). Taxing (years of) human lives in themselves is a normatively much more problematic proposal than taxing activities that create harmful emissions.

Of course, giving birth and prolonging life are dissimilar in several aspects. One significant difference is that prohibiting persons to procreate does not kill them. Their right to reproduce may be violated or infringed but not their right to life and no 'merely potential child' has a right to be born (see in more detail Karnein, 2012a: 20–26). In contrast, creating incentives to let people die by not providing them with the care they need clearly constitutes a wrong against persons. Thus, in the case of prolonging lives the only sensible option seems to be to tax activities and goods with regard to their emissions in order to create an incentive to reduce these emissions either via adapting a less affluent lifestyle or by further improving technological efficiency. And this also seems to speak in favour of applying such a taxation scheme to all polluting activities.

However, the main incentives such a tax provides are to decrease emissions by either consuming less or by increasing efficiency. The advantage that this tax only indirectly affects reproductive choices may turn into a disadvantage once the need to decrease population becomes inescapable. In such a case – which hopefully will be avoided – recourse to either a head tax for children or even coercive measures of type (1b), applied equally to everyone, might become universally acceptable after all.

Conclusion

We have argued that, if (environmental and global) justice has anything to say about regulating population, the main burden of what has to be done has to be shouldered by individuals living within western industrialised countries. This is first and foremost a task of reducing affluence as well as improving technological efficiency, but may involve reducing birth

[17] We are, again, indebted to Stephen Wilkinson for alerting us to the potential analogy between giving birth and prolonging lives.

rates as well, even though fertility levels are low here already. This is because western industrialised countries are mainly to blame both for (a) perpetuating global poverty which is a chief cause for high fertility levels in some countries and (b) for depleting vital resources, such as the absorptive capacity of the atmosphere, and thus for the limited ability of the earth to support a growing population.

We then explored what decreasing already low fertility levels might mean for western industrialised countries. We argued against an implicit suggestion made by Heyward, namely that 'phasing out' ARTs may constitute a promising option. Rather, we claimed that the right to reproduction should be read as a positive right granting everyone access to the possibility of at least socially parenting one biologically related child. The burden of reducing overpopulation has to be distributed equally and cannot be shouldered by those in need of ARTs and reproductive donation alone.

Finally, we discussed the merits of either legally prohibiting reproduction beyond certain numbers across the board – and what that would mean for reproductive donation – or introducing a taxation scheme. We argued in favour of the latter and distinguished between a head tax for every new child and taxing emissions directly. Again, we held that we should not be misled by the discourse on overpopulation and forget that it is emissions that count. Thus, we proposed to directly tax emissions instead of children. Otherwise we risk falling prey to the danger of hypostasising the number of existing people when what matters is really their impact on the environment – a danger that has always been inherent in the discourse on population.

REFERENCES

Broome, J. (2012). *Climate Matters. Ethics in a Warming World.* New York: W.W. Horton.

Cafaro, P. (2012). 'Climate ethics and population policy'. *WIREs Climate Change*, 3, 45–61.

Cafaro, P. and Staples, W. (2009). 'The environmental argument for reducing immigration into the United States'. *Environmental Ethics*, 31, 3–28.

Cripps, E. (forthcoming). 'Acknowledging the Elephant: Population, Justice and Urgency'. Paper manuscript on file with the authors.

Ehrlich, P. (1968). *The Population Bomb.* New York: A Sierra Club/Ballantine Book.

Ehrlich, P. and Holden, J. (1972). 'A Bulletin dialogue on the closing circle: critique of "One Dimensional Ecology"'. *Bulletin of the Atomic Scientists*, 28, 16–27.

Grant, J., Hoorans, S., Sivadasan, S., van het Loo, M. et al. (2004). *Low Fertility and Population. Ageing Causes, Consequences, and Policy Options*. Leiden: RAND Europe.

Hardin, G. (1974). 'Lifeboat ethics: the case against helping the poor'. *Psychology Today*, 800–12, reprinted in: W. Aiken and H. LaFollette (eds.) (1996). *World Hunger and Morality*, 2nd edn. Englewood Cliffs, N.J.: Prentice Hall, 5–15.

Heyward, C. (2012). 'A growing problem? Dealing with population increases in climate justice'. *Ethical Perspectives*, 19, 703–32.

Honneth, A. (2014). *Freedom's Right. The Social Foundations of Democratic Life*. New York: Columbia University Press.

Huang, L.J. (1982). 'Planned fertility of one-couple/one-child-policy in the People's Republic of China'. *The Journal of Marriage and Family*, 44, 775–84.

IPCC (2014). 'Technical Summary'. *Climate Change 2014: Mitigation of Climate Change*. Working Group III. Fifth Assessment Report. Available at www.report.mitigation2014.org/drafts/final-draft-postplenary/ipcc_wg3_ar5_final-draft_postplenary_technical-summary.pdf.

Iser, M. (2013). 'Recognition', in E.N. Zalta (ed.), *Stanford Encyclopedia of Philosophy*. Available at www.plato.stanford.edu/entries/recognition/.

Iser, M. (forthcoming). *Indignation and Progress. Foundations of a Critical Theory of Society*. New York: Oxford University Press.

Karnein, A. (2012a). *A Theory of Unborn Life. From Abortion to Genetic Manipulation*. New York: Oxford University Press.

Karnein, A. (2012b). 'Parenthood – whose right is it anyway?', in M. Richards, G. Pennings and J.B. Appleby (eds.), *Reproductive Donation: Practice, Policy and Bioethics*. Cambridge University Press, 51–69.

Karnein, A. (2014). 'Putting fairness in its place: Why there is a duty to take up the slack'. *The Journal of Philosophy*, 111, 593–607.

Kumar, R. (2003). 'Who can be wronged?' *Philosophy & Public Affairs*, 31, 99–118.

La Ferrara, E., Chong, A. and Duryea, S. (2008). 'Soap operas and fertility: evidence from Brazil'. *BREAD Working Paper*, 172. Available at www.iadb.org/res/files/WP-633updated.pdf.

Malthus, T.R. (1798). *An Essay on the Principle of Population*, G. Gilbert (ed.) (2004). Oxford University Press.

Nozick, R. (1974). *Anarchy, State, and Utopia*. New York: Basic Books.

Pennings, G. (2000). 'The right to choose your donor: a step towards commercialization or a step towards empowering the patient?' *Human Reproduction*, 15, 503–14.

Pogge, T. (2008). *World Poverty and Human Rights. Cosmopolitan Responsibilities and Reforms*, 2nd edn. Cambridge: Polity Press.

Rawls, J. (1999). *The Law of Peoples*. Cambridge, MA: Harvard University Press.

Sen, A. (1994). 'Population: delusion and reality'. *The New York Review of Books*, September 22, 62–71.

Shiffrin, S. (1999). 'Wrongful life, procreative responsibility and the significance of harm'. *Legal Theory*, 5, 117–48.

Shue, H. (1993). 'Subsistence emissions and luxury emissions'. *Law and Policy*, 15, 39–60.

Velleman, D. (2008). 'Persons in prospect'. *Philosophy and Public Affairs*, 36, 221–88.

Warnock, M. (1984). *A Question of Life. The Warnock Report on Human Fertilisation and Embryology*. Oxford: Blackwell.

Young, I.M. (2011). *Responsibility for Justice*. New York: Oxford University Press.

Young, T. (2001). 'Overconsumption and procreation: are they morally equivalent?' *Journal of Applied Philosophy*, 18, 183–92.

5 Normative and regulatory issues in cross-border reproductive health care

Guido Pennings

Introduction

In the literature, most discussions about cross-border reproductive care (CBRC) are focused on ethical and legal issues, and amongst these especially legislation and commercialisation. The trend towards cross-border care is supported by individualisation (the individual as separate and independent from the community in which he or she lives) and consumerism (the idea that a person should be able to purchase the goods and services he or she desires). However, other aspects are overshadowed when the focus is on the travelling patient. This chapter will shed light on some of these other issues.

New developments

We continue to lack basic information about CBRC and its extent. In the future we will probably be able to obtain more information through national statistics on health care expenditure. However, since many travellers pay privately the picture will still be incomplete. Currently, most of what we know comes from qualitative studies of travellers. Such studies help us to get a better idea of the experiences of patients, the process of decision making and the factors involved (Bergmann, 2011; Hudson and Culley, 2011; Rozée Gomez and De la Rochebrochard, 2013). The general conclusion from all these studies is that there is no single 'cross-border patient'. The more information we have, the more we find that it is difficult to make general statements about cross-border reproductive care. Many relevant factors can be distinguished: the type of patient, the country of origin and of destination, the type of treatment and so on (Hudson et al., 2011).

The internet plays an ever-greater role in cross-border care. It also makes things uncontrollable. For example, Belgian women go onto the websites of international sperm banks and order sperm for self-insemination, thus avoiding all the local restrictions imposed on donor selection (Pennings, 2011). The commercialisation of CBRC is nowhere more visible than on the internet. New players such as brokers, travel agents and tourism firms enter the field and guide patients through the maze (Inhorn and Patrizio, 2012; Speier, 2011). The travelling patient increasingly becomes a consumer to whom services are marketed.

With more regulation of quality and safety, the costs for in vitro fertilisation (IVF) clinics have grown considerably. The European Tissues and Cells Directive has also led to higher costs for clinics (more paper work, certified personnel, higher investment cost in laboratories and so forth) (UK Association of Clinical Embryologists, 2005). As a consequence, scaling-up is an economic necessity for many clinics to survive. Performing more cycles, treating more patients and analysing more samples is frequently the only way forward. Cooperation with other clinics, whether local or abroad, can help clinics to reach critical thresholds. Clinics in Belgium, the Netherlands and Germany have made deals with each other to perform parts of an IVF cycle in order to increase their efficiency.

Little is known about institutional connections between clinics and the referral of patients. Equally sparse is information on connections between clinics and health insurers. Health insurance companies obviously have strong financial reasons to make deals with clinics to offer infertility treatment at lower cost. They can then oblige their clients to go to those clinics. Such institutional agreements and contracts may provide a more stable basis for movements than the flows that are the result of an accumulation of individual patient decisions. Nevertheless, studies on collaborations between clinics across borders for general medical services show that such collaborations only survive when all parties involved consider it to be in their own interests (Glinos and Wismar, 2013). Although clinics claim that these arrangements are made to serve the patients, the patients' needs are rarely the crucial driver of collaborations. There is no reason to believe that this would be any different in the context of medically assisted reproduction rather than general medical services.

Judging patient flows

Interestingly, collaboration between clinics is regarded with suspicion for some assisted reproduction treatment (ART) applications and as normal and beneficial for others. When people are referred abroad for egg donation, many considered this to be inappropriate. In the context of prenatal genetic diagnosis (PGD), however, 'transport PGD' is widely recommended as a means to improve reliable diagnosis for specific diseases in European reference centres, to lower the burden for patients and to lower the price for patients and clinics. Many fertility centres send their samples (polar bodies, blastomeres or trophectoderm biopsies) to other clinic laboratories that may be located abroad (Couture et al., 2014). In the only European study on the topic, about one third of the samples for PGD came from abroad (Corveleyn et al., 2008). Given the high cost of PGD, high numbers of cycles have to be carried out to make it economic (Wells and Fragouli, 2013). Thus commercial survival and profit underlies the development of transport PGD. Harton et al. recommended that IVF and PGD centres make a formal agreement to deal with the different aspects involved in the collaboration (Harton et al., 2011). The recommendations that this group make could as well be applied to collaboration for other types of infertility treatments.

Attitudes towards CBRC may depend on specific elements of the situation. CBRC is not restricted to patients moving across borders (Pennings and Gürtin, 2012). Although less visible, transport of material may be more common than travelling patients. The Danish sperm bank Cryos, for instance, exports 85 per cent of its 15,000–20,000 sperm donations to more than 400 clinics in sixty countries (Anonymous, 2009). Again, the general view of this type of CBRC is negative. However, CBRC is not necessarily bad because it involves patients crossing borders, and good because embryos or gametes are travelling. The ethical evaluation is highly context-dependent. Moreover, it seems that this context is constructed in a biased or preselected way. Take the example of transport PGD again. In this case, parts of embryos are travelling, apparently without objections. Numerous things may contribute to a positive image of PGD and thus of transport PGD. People think of families with disabled children and the suffering of a child with a disease. PGD is a way to avoid all this and is thus seen to be good. Moreover, these diseases, contrary to infertility, are perceived as serious diseases by everyone. However, also for PGD, questions arise about the evasion of the law and dodging moral standards on embryo selection. Most countries have regulation for PGD; they allow it with minimal limitations, impose strict restrictions on the diseases for which diagnosis and selection may be performed or forbid it entirely. It would be fairly easy for patients (and clinics) to bypass the restrictions in their country by shipping the embryos for diagnosis to countries such as Belgium, where very few limitations are imposed on PGD use. Rapp (2011) described two US sex selection clinics that established satellite clinics in other countries where the US personnel collected biopsied cells, flew these to the United States for sexing and then phoned the clinic abroad to tell them which embryo to replace.

It could be argued that in all these cases the selective transfer is a legal violation since this transfer takes place in the home country of the patient. But the movement of tissue and information is hard to control.

In almost all cases, additional information is made available about the embryo that may confuse the issue: information on other genetic diseases or predispositions, embryo quality based on morphological criteria and so on. Suppose there is information on a few hundred diseases. Two situations should be considered: (1) the penetrance of a disease is lower (but not zero) in one sex (unequal sex ratio) and (2) the expression of the gene is lower in one sex. How much should the incidence of a certain illness decrease before sexing is acceptable (Pennings, 2002)? The point here is that almost every decision on sex selection can be turned into a 'medical decision'. So it would be very hard to prove that the doctor has violated the law on social sex selection. Moreover, the clinician may condemn sex selection in general, but may still find it hard not to give in to the patients' request in these specific circumstances. There may, for instance, be several embryos approximately similar in all aspects apart from their sex. The physician will be informed about the sex because of the sex-linked differences in penetrance and expression of many diseases is an integral part of the information provided by the laboratory.[1] What is he supposed to do: roll the dice? This argument would be considerably stronger when we talk about 'minor' diseases. When the doctor has information on the presence of a disease that is not on the list of eliminable diseases, he should ignore it when selecting embryos. When the patients know that this information was available to the doctor and they get a child with the disease, can you imagine the fix he is in?

Some may argue that the doctor should not impart all test results that he received from testing abroad. This opens a general discussion as to who owns or has decisional authority over the data. This is a difficult balance as there are circumstances where we believe that patients should receive the genetic information on the embryo and simultaneously circumstances where genetic information should be withheld because of a right to privacy of the future person. Still, by withholding test results, one treats patients as suspects who will take the wrong decision on the basis of these results while there may be many reasons why people may want to be informed (Dondorp et al., 2013).

In the future, it will be even more difficult to keep control of information when next-generation sequencing becomes the standard method for

[1] These dilemmas are created by a technical change and commercial decision by the laboratory. In principle, the laboratory could supply only requested information to a clinician. However, testing is carried out using standard chips which cover a wide range of diseases. It is more efficient and cheaper to use such standard chips – rather than a test for a specific condition that a clinician might request. And labs return all the information derived from the chip, leaving it to the clinician to decide which information to use.

testing. All PGD use will become suspicious since patients in countries which allow PGD only for lethal early-onset diseases will then receive information on less serious diseases with lower penetrance. Up till now, this point has been largely ignored. It makes one wonder how public opinion will change when cases are made public in the media about patients going abroad to perform PGD for a 'trivial' disease, or sex selection. Interestingly, the geneticists have, thus far, managed to separate the tricky matter of social sex selection from the tricky matter of selecting for diseases.

The responsibility of the physicians

When a person commits a crime, his liability will depend on his contribution (causality, *actus reus*) and on his intention (*mens rea*). A similar structure applies to an accomplice. A person becomes an accomplice when he gets involved in a wrongful act, or when he helps another person to commit a crime. The discussion in common law is about whether intention is necessary and/or sufficient to make someone an accomplice or whether causation is sufficient (Moore, 2007). When causation is considered sufficient, an important question is the degree of contribution to that causation by an individual.

The physician is responsible for the health (well-being) of his patient. One problem with CBRC is to determine who is the treating doctor. Is it the doctor who received the original request or the foreign doctor who provides the actual treatment? Do they share the responsibility? In fact, apart from the distance and the communication issues, this problem is not different from doctors in the same country or clinic collaborating in the treatment of a patient.

Fertility treatment can be split up in several steps (diagnosis, hormonal stimulation, cycle monitoring, oocyte pick-up, fertilisation and embryo transfer or embryo freezing). Each part of the treatment can be done by different persons in different places. French lesbian couples who go to Belgium often received part of their treatment at home (Van Hoof, Pennings and De Sutter, 2015). Also in the European context, the majority of the cross-border patients (59 per cent) received some form of help from their local doctor. The doctor prescribed drugs (17 per cent), monitored the cycle (17 per cent) or did both (26 per cent) (Shenfield et al., 2010). In some cases, the geographic spread may be enormous and the contribution of the different actors may involve much more than mere support. The Sims clinic in Ireland has a program whereby frozen sperm is sent from Ireland to Ukraine where it has a partnership with a fertility clinic (Walsh et al., 2010). This clinic provides the donor oocytes and carries out the fertilisation. The frozen embryos are then returned to Ireland to be transferred to the would-be parents (www.sims.ie).

The ultimate goal of the overall treatment is the birth of a healthy child. The doctor collaborates in the parental project of the patients who are considered as the principals. As long as the parental project is ethically and legally acceptable, there is no problem. Obviously, a person cannot be condemned for complicity when there is no crime or wrongful act. However, when the parental project of the parents contains elements that render it unacceptable, either from a legal or an ethical point of view, things become problematic. Let us look at some examples. A couple goes to a clinic for surrogacy. This clinic is located in a country where surrogacy is forbidden by law. The couple proposes that the clinic does the hormonal stimulation, pick-up and fertilisation and then ships the embryos to the United States to be replaced in a surrogate. All the arrangements in the United States have been made by the couple without any intervention of the clinic. Nevertheless, the clinic knows about the intentions of the couple. If there is any wrong involved, it does not lie in the treatment itself (hormonal stimulation, fertilisation and so forth) but in the treatment as part of a project that is legally prohibited.

Take another example, a couple wants to have a daughter and they are prepared to have IVF and embryo sex selection to reach this goal. In most European countries, sex selection for social reasons is forbidden. If the couple is fertile, this would be the end; no clinic should start treatment. However, suppose the couple lies to the doctor and he concludes that this is a case of unexplained infertility. In that case, and of course when they really have an infertility problem, they could have IVF without mentioning their intention to select on the sex of the embryos. When the embryos have been created, they put in their request for sexing. Up to that point, the clinic was part of what they thought to be a normal parental project: it cannot be held responsible for the steps before the patients change the project unilaterally. But what about the next steps? When the couple asks the clinic for their embryos to be shipped to another country, the clinic cannot refuse. First, the clinic has no decision-making authority over the embryos. Second, the patients are just asking the clinic to send the embryos abroad. Given the points made above, the clinic would only be justified in refusing to ship when there is a sufficiently direct link between the action they perform (shipping) and the wrongful act (the selection of embryos leading to the birth of a child with the desired sex). In my opinion, this link is not close enough. First, it is not certain that the patients will have the sexing done when they arrive in the United States. They may find out that the biopsy lowers the chance of implantation, or that the costs are higher than they thought and so forth. Second, it may be that after the biopsy there are no (good quality) embryos of the desired sex and they may decide to have the others replaced. Moreover, the centre does not have the intention to enable the couple to choose the sex of their child and intention is a condition for complicity (Kadish, 1987). Nevertheless, it is possible to determine whether a clinic is intentionally helping a patient. In a famous case in Belgium, a doctor was sending sperm to the United States for selection after which he inseminated his patients with the selected sperm. This case was the reason why the Belgian law, that originally only forbid selection of embryos for sex determination, was amended to include also selection of gametes. In such a scenario, it would be impossible for the doctor to argue that he was not intentionally helping patients to choose the sex of their future child. Notice in this regard that knowledge of something cannot be equated with intention: it is not because the clinic knows that the parents are planning to have the embryos sexed, that releasing the embryos to the parents automatically means that the clinic shares this intention. It also becomes clear that the ethical and legal responsibilities are merging together through the common elements of causality and intention.

The determination of complicity is linked to the question of extraterritoriality. Downie and Baylis (2013) discuss what is referred to as the 'qualified territorial application' to determine whether the Canadian law would apply beyond Canada's border. In order for this application to apply, two conditions have to be fulfilled: first, there is a 'real and substantial link' between Canada and the offence, and second, prosecution would not offend against international comity. The question of complicity is connected to the first condition. Although there is room for discussion in many situations, some cases would clearly qualify. A Canadian woman who orders eggs from a US clinic and pays with her credit card would undoubtedly be violating the Canadian law which prohibits payment for eggs. However, other cases are less clear. Would ovarian stimulation of a Canadian woman who then travels to another country to sell her eggs be sufficient to trigger the application of the law (Downie and Baylis, 2013)?

Referral and complicity

An interesting test case of complicity is that of referral. In Belgian law (and in the laws of many other countries), the right to conscientious objection of doctors that applies to abortion and euthanasia is extended to include medically assisted reproduction treatment (Belgian Parliament, 2007). Belgian ART centres are allowed to refuse treatment by just sending a letter to the patient stating that they have a conscientious objection. No further explanation or reason is required. Still, the centre has a legal obligation to provide the patient with the address of another centre if the patient asks for this (Belgian Parliament, 2007: Art. 5, 1°). This is a very open obligation and the centre may fulfil its duty by referring the patient to a website where all clinics are listed. One may even wonder whether this should be called a referral. This legal clause raises some intriguing questions: does a clinic have a conscience and, if so, what is the relationship with the conscience of the persons working in the clinic?

Two ethical questions can be raised about the referral: can it be seen as a form of helping a person to perform a wrongful act, and if yes, is the involvement sufficient to call it complicity? In general, the referral is presented as a compromise position between on the one hand the right of the doctor not to have to do things that he considers to be morally wrong and the right of the patient to receive treatment (McLeod, 2008). The ethical and legal duty to refer is justified by the duty to protect the well-being of the patient. A broad philosophical discussion can be found on this point in the literature. Interestingly, it is rarely mentioned whether the duty to refer also implies that a doctor should refer or should be allowed to refer a patient to a clinic abroad in case the patient demands a treatment not permitted at home. It seems unlikely that the legal duty would include referral for an unlawful action. However, there might still be a moral duty based on the rights of the patient. According to Heng, doctors should not refer patients abroad out of respect for their local community and the medical profession. They have a moral obligation to uphold the spirit and essence of the local legislation (Heng, 2006). In some countries, laws exist that make referral for certain treatments punishable. Doctors in Turkey can be put in prison for helping patients to have third-party reproductive assistance (donor gametes and surrogacy) which is forbidden in Turkey (Gürtin, 2011). Until recently, German doctors feared prosecution for referring patients for pre-implantation genetic diagnosis abroad (Corveleyn et al., 2008). Evidence from a qualitative study of French lesbians who went to Belgium for donor insemination shows that not a single lesbian couple had been referred by either their general practitioner or their gynaecologist (Van Hoof, Pennings and De Sutter, 2015).

Several elements will determine the degree of responsibility or liability: specificity, necessity and causality. For instance, how specific is the referral? Is the patient referred to Spain or to a clinic in Spain? If the doctor refers to a specific clinic, he should be fairly certain that this clinic follows good practice standards, especially because this is probably the message the patient will receive when she is referred to a specific clinic, even when this is not explicitly stated. The ESHRE Task Force on CBRC also mentioned this point in their good practice guide to CBRC (Shenfield et al., 2011). Still, if something undesirable happens to the patient (for instance, she comes back with triplets), the main responsibility would still lie with the treating doctor (who replaced several embryos) and not with the referring doctor.

One important specification needs to be added regarding referral. When patients are referred to a clinic with which the doctor has a contractual and/or financial connection, the responsibility of the doctor remains almost intact. Such contracts generally include fee-splitting, a practice that is almost universally condemned because it creates a conflict of interest: the doctor to whom the patient is referred is not chosen on the basis of the patient's best interests but on the size of the fee for the referring doctor. The doctor violates his professional ethics when such motives guide his referrals (Dickens and Cook, 2006). Although doctors are obliged to reveal possible conflicts of interest, it needs no argument to see that transparency will be hard to obtain.

Information provision and complicity

In 2012, Dr. Grall, Director General of Health in France, wrote a letter to all heads of fertility clinics in France stating that doctors who provided information on foreign clinics and organisations that practiced gamete donation in a way that deviates from the French law could go to prison for five years and be fined €75,000. Dr. Grall specifically mentioned Spain as a popular destination for egg donation (Grall, 2012).

In a later letter of 30 April 2013, Dr. Grall maintained his position by stressing which elements were important in the French law: a heterosexual couple, alive, at the age of procreation, anonymity of donor and recipient, altruistic motivation and finally screening of donors (Grall, 2013). The problem with Spain apparently was the payment of donors. However, according to the Spanish centres donors are not paid in Spain. The €900 that Spanish donors receive is compensation for travelling, loss of time, inconveniences and so on. In Europe, a large variety of reimbursement systems is used. According to a large European study on egg donors in eleven European countries, France is the only country that strictly reimburses proven expenses (Pennings et al., 2014). As a consequence, even though French doctors would in theory be allowed to provide information regarding clinics abroad or send patients to these, there is not one country that actually fulfils the condition of having the same rules.

The French government clearly believes that doctors who provide information (for instance in the form of a leaflet) about foreign clinics in a different jurisdiction, or who refer patients to clinics in other countries, are helping patients to evade the law. This is a very wide restriction that goes much further than a prohibition on referral. Interestingly, one may question whether this decision by the French authorities violates Article 10 of the European Convention on Human Rights. The right to freedom of expression includes the right to 'impart information and ideas without interference by public authority and regardless of frontiers'. This initiative is remarkable because it is well-known that the clinics in France are unable to recruit enough donors to cover the demand (as the Director General himself admits). According to a report by the General Inspection of Social Affairs, between 1,800 and 3,600 French women leave France for oocyte donation per year and this number is increasing steadily (Aballea, Burstin and Guedj, 2011). Ironically, the French social security system partially reimburses patients who go abroad for egg donation. The same report indicates that 649 demands for reimbursement of treatment outside France were received, of which 76.6 per cent were from Spain, 13.5 per cent from Belgium, 3.5 per cent from Greece and 3.4 per cent from Czech Republic (Aballea, Burstin and Guedj, 2011). In a recent case, a French Court decided that the social security system should reimburse an IVF treatment with oocyte donation performed in Barcelona by a French citizen (Court d'appel de Rennes, case nr. 91/10 of 3 March 2010) (Lucas-Baloup, 2013). Reimbursement seems to be a much stronger form of participation in the wrongdoing than information provision mainly because without it, the treatment might not have taken place. Without the physician's information, there is still a relatively high chance that the patient will find his or her own way to a clinic abroad.

A duty to inform

In the section above, we have looked at information provision from a particular angle, that is, as contributing to law evasion. Information about treatment abroad can however also be evaluated from the point of view of the autonomy of the patient. The Ethics Committee of the American Society for Reproductive Medicine takes this position. The Committee starts from the principle that respect for patient autonomy implies that the patient is provided with the information necessary to understand his or her diagnosis and treatment options. So when the patient asks for options abroad, the physician should tell him or her what he knows. He is not obliged, however, to do research to find out more or to offer the possibility of fertility travel as a treatment option (Ethics Committee of the ASRM, 2013).

These subtle phrasings demonstrate a very cautious position. The absence of a duty to investigate (regarding, for instance, the risks and benefits of treatment abroad) avoids a possible accusation of negligence: a doctor cannot be accused of negligence when he sends a patient abroad without checking the circumstances of treatment there. Is it part of his responsibility to verify that things are done according to good clinical practice in the country of referral? Four elements need to be proved to establish negligence: the defendant owed the patient a duty of care; the defendant was in breach of that duty; the breach of duty caused the damage and the damage was not too remote. Every element is debatable for the issue of cross-border referral. For instance, no one doubts that there is a duty on the part of the physician to promote the health of the patient but what does this duty imply in this specific context? The doctor cannot be expected to scrutinise different countries and inform the patients about the treatment options in other countries. This would be an unreasonable request in the first place but even more so since he is no longer the treating physician (Ethics Committee of the ASRM, 2013).

The duty to inform could be transferred from individual doctors to, or shared by, institutions and patient organisations. For instance, the Human Fertilisation and Embryology Authority (HFEA) lists some issues that patients planning to seek treatment abroad should consider, also based on the principle of respect for autonomy (HFEA, 2009). Full knowledge of the risks and benefits empowers the patients. Although their list only mentions negative aspects and risks, it is still a much more open position than the French one. Patient organisations such as the Infertility Consumer Support for Infertility (2008) have adopted a similar stance. The main problem with this approach is that it will in practice be impossible for people to do what is recommended in the list. This highlights a typical conflict between trying to protect patients from taking the wrong decisions and respecting patients' autonomy. The higher one estimates the risks of treatment abroad, the more one tends to favour a paternalistic stance. However, the premise that treatment abroad is more dangerous than treatment at home has not been substantiated for well-regulated countries. Without this premise, there is little justification for paternalism left.

Finally, when the patient has decided to go abroad (independently and not from information or referral by the local doctor), the doctor should still provide all information that may be relevant for her treatment abroad (particular risks, test results and so forth). The data acquired during the doctor-patient relationship belong to the patient and not to the doctor.

As a consequence, a copy of the medical file should be available to the patient whenever she requests it.

Regulation and extraterritoriality

Why regulate when people can evade the laws? To answer this question, we have to determine the purpose of legislation and regulation. In a democracy, political parties are elected to realise their programme. This programme includes views on the organisation of politics, economics and society. Laws on medically assisted reproduction more than other laws express views on the family, sexuality, morality and religion. Legislation (or at least part thereof) is meant to indicate what people can, must or should not do in the country. However, law makers should also respect the autonomy and private lives of people. The purpose of legislation cannot be to control all behaviour of citizens regardless of where it is performed. Allowing people to travel is in that sense a minimal form of tolerance for the views of the minority (Pennings, 2004).

It is important to clarify one frequent misunderstanding from the outset: people who go abroad to obtain treatment that is forbidden in their home country do not commit a crime or break the law, unless the law is extraterritorial. Almost all legislation only applies to the territory of the country. Only in very specific cases such as treason and espionage do countries introduce extraterritorial laws (Chehtman, 2010). Regarding the protection against bodily harm and integrity, three examples of extraterritoriality can be found: abortion, child sexual abuse and female genital cutting (Van Hoof and Pennings, 2011). Generally speaking, exterritorial legislation is only justified when the act in question is unambiguously morally wrong. Obviously, this will be a matter of debate but the idea is that whenever there are reasonable arguments in favour of a certain application (even if the overwhelming majority of the people believe these to be wrong), no extraterritoriality should be introduced. Apart from reproductive cloning (at least at the moment), no application of medically assisted reproduction qualifies. Acts such as sex selection are not obviously wrong. (Is the child harmed or wronged by the selection? Are the consequences of this selection harmful to society?) Some people (such as the present author) have argued that reasonable arguments can be advanced to allow at least a limited form of sex selection (Pennings, 1996). In short: legislation should fit the moral views of the majority to a certain extent, but the majority should have the intellectual honesty to recognise that it may be wrong and it should demonstrate a certain restraint when legislating.

Restrictions in the country of destination

Most discussions on cross-border movements are focused on the home country of the patients. However, it takes two to tango: also the country of destination carries moral responsibility for the treatment.

Foreign patients should receive the same quality of treatment as local patients (Shenfield et al., 2011). The application of this principle would avoid a large number of problems. There are for instance some indications that more embryos are replaced in foreign patients (Pennings et al., 2009). The explanation probably lies in a number of objective differences in the population group such as a higher percentage of previous failed cycles and higher mean age. But there surely is also increased pressure exerted by the patients themselves. Given the time, money and effort they have invested in their treatment abroad, they want to maximise their chances of success by demanding replacement of more embryos. Although a relaxation of some rules is understandable, the extra effort of foreign patients cannot justify high risk-taking for both the welfare of mother and child.

When patients travel to avoid restrictive legislation at home, it is difficult to see why a country would want to uphold the restrictions applied in another country (i.e. the country from which the patients have come) (Mutcherson, 2012). When French lesbians go to Belgium for donor insemination, the Belgian clinics will welcome them since this patient group is fully accepted (both ethically and legally) in Belgium.

Why would a destination country limit the inflow of foreign patients? The most likely reason would be that the number of foreign patients negatively affects the situation for the local patients. Three possibilities come to mind: increased shortage of donors, longer waiting times for treatment and higher fees. There is little evidence for any of these possible effects. No information is available regarding increased prices or longer waiting time for ART (independent of the shortage of donor gametes) in European countries. There are some indications that countries may take action against an increased shortage of donor gametes. Belgium receives minimally 750 women per year for donor insemination (each receiving a mean number of four inseminations), the majority being lesbian couples from France (Pennings et al., 2009). Apparently for a few months (we are writing this in February 2014), there has been a waiting list for sperm donation. The shortage seems to have been contained by the import of Danish sperm. Almost all Belgian clinics import sperm from Denmark (Thijssen et al., 2014). Without this import, they would not be able to recruit a sufficient number of donors to cover the internal demand, let alone the extra demand by the foreign patients. At the same time, many Belgian clinics have adopted a protectionist position regarding donor eggs. A number of these clinics only treat foreign candidate recipients of donor eggs when they bring their own donor (Pennings et al., 2009). This condition is not imposed on local patients although it is also recommended for them if they want to have treatment without a long waiting time. A similar debate has been conducted in relation to organ donation. In the Istanbul Declaration on organ transplantation and transplant tourism the following statement is included: 'Travel for transplantation becomes transplant tourism if it involves organ trafficking and/or transplant commercialism or if the resources (organs, professionals and transplant centres) devoted to providing transplants to patients from outside a country undermine the country's ability to provide transplant services for its own population.' (Participants in the International Summit, 2008). The country's ability to provide for its own population is a basic duty of social security systems based on solidarity. As a consequence, measures can be adopted (residency requirements or maximal percentages of transplantations for foreign nationals) to avoid these negative effects.

As far as higher prices are concerned, there is to my knowledge only one study that points to this effect and this, strangely enough, from India. The focus in India on the western reproductive patient makes it increasingly difficult for middle-class Indian couples to access high-quality fertility care. Moreover, the prices have gone up due to the influx of richer western patients, thus forcing the Indians to travel themselves (Inhorn, 2012).

A second reason why countries could restrict access to certain categories of people would be the welfare of the children resulting from the treatment. In the field of medically assisted reproduction, the most famous example is surrogacy (see Jadva, Chapter 6 and Gamble, Chapter 7). A large number of countries (such as Germany, Italy, Spain and France) forbid surrogacy or have no regulation on surrogacy (such as Belgium and Denmark) (Trimmings and Beaumont, 2013). As a consequence, the commissioning parents who used surrogacy services abroad frequently have enormous difficulties in bringing their child into the country. In most cases, and frequently after months of legal battle, the judge will allow the child to enter and will assign legal parenthood to protect the best interests of the child (Gamble, Chapter 7).

Art. 34 § 19 of the Assisted Reproductive Technologies Draft Bill in India states the following:

> A foreigner or foreign couple not resident in India, or a non-resident Indian individual or couple, seeking surrogacy in India shall appoint a local guardian

who will be legally responsible for taking care of the surrogate during and after the pregnancy as per clause 34.2, till the child/children are delivered to the foreigner or foreign couple or the local guardian. Further, the party seeking the surrogacy must ensure and establish to the assisted reproductive technology clinic through proper documentation (a letter from either the embassy of the Country in India or from the foreign ministry of the Country, clearly and unambiguously stating that (a) the country permits surrogacy and (b) the child born through surrogacy in India, will be permitted entry in the Country as a biological child of the commissioning couple/individual) that the party would be able to take the child/children born through surrogacy, including where the embryo was a consequence of donation of an oocyte or sperm, outside of India to the country of the party's origin or residence as the case may be (Ministry of Health and Family Welfare, Government of India, 2010).

This is an interesting development that can be explained in different ways. The most charitable is that the Indian government is concerned about the welfare of the children. It is obviously far from ideal when the family involuntarily has to stay in another country for a long period and when the future of the child is uncertain. However, other explanations are possible. These legal fights damage the reputation of India and, equally importantly, it gives the industry a bad name. Although this bill has not been the subject of a vote in Parliament yet, the Indian government already introduced a medical visa in which these conditions are included (Foreign and Commonwealth Office, 2013). In fact, the conditions included in the medical visa are even stricter than those foreseen in the Draft Bill since single women and gay couples are also excluded. The impact on the industry will have to be determined by empirical studies.

There are other situations where the welfare of the child is jeopardised. Suppose that a lesbian couple lives in a country where homosexuality is not accepted and homosexuals are discriminated against. The clinic that treats them should take into account the possible effects on the child as a consequence of the lack of recognition of the family. One consequence could be that, although they presented themselves and were evaluated as a couple for treatment, the two women will not be able to live as a family in their home country. This is not necessarily the case. French lesbian couples do not feel discriminated against in their daily life by their social environment and they do not expect any difficulties for their child later (Van Hoof, Pennings and De Sutter, 2015). Again, the position of France is rather inconsistent because lesbian and gay couples cannot obtain infertility treatment but they can marry and adopt children. So since the new law, the social mother is able to adopt the child and become the legal parent. Still, the legal situation remains confusing (Gamble, Chapter 7). In May 2014, a few months after the law, the court in Versailles refused to allow the adoption by the social mother, arguing that the couple had defrauded the French law by having treatment in Belgium. The court stated that it was 'banning the adoption of an illegally conceived child' (Willsher, 2014). This decision will most likely not be maintained since the European Court of Human Rights in June 2014 condemned France for refusing to grant legal recognition in France to parent–child relationships that had been legally established in the United States between children born as a result of surrogacy treatment and the couples who had had the treatment (European Court of Human Rights, 2014). The situation of the lesbian couples who go abroad for donor insemination is very similar. Although such cases of differing circumstances between countries may be rare, the question is whether the clinic in the destination country should exclude foreign candidate patients on this basis. It seems unlikely that the clinic is better able to judge the threat to the welfare of the child than the would-be parents.

Positive measures

When the reasons why patients cross borders are known, one indirectly also knows what can be done to prevent this. Most measures that countries consider to stop CBRC are negative or prohibitive measures such as forbidding patients to go or introducing extraterritorial laws. Most of these measures are ineffective for the simple reason that the rules cannot be imposed. The effect of a prohibition on information provision will be very limited when patients can easily access this information on the internet. It is almost impossible to prevent people from going because the authorities rarely know why people go abroad. The only instance where control is possible to a certain extent is surrogacy because the parents have to bring a child into the country that they did not have when they left. The most important point is however that such measures focus on the symptoms and do not tackle the underlying causes of the movements. The empirical studies indicate that the two main reasons for going abroad are restrictive legislation and the lack of donor gametes, and more specifically donor eggs (Shenfield et al., 2010). While relaxation in legislation may be an option, it is difficult to explain this to the public. It is not likely that a country will adopt a more flexible law on ART when it finds out that many citizens are leaving the country. This question is part of an unresolved discussion on the effects of cross-border movements. I have argued that it may soften politicians because they see that the law will have little effect. However, others have argued that the existence of an escape route may actually encourage politicians to adopt stricter regulation than they otherwise might (Storrow, 2010). The latter interpretation is indirectly confirmed by the comments in the judgment of the European

Court of Human Rights in the case of *S.H. and others* v. *Austria*. The Grand Chamber stated, as part of its defence of the acceptability of the Austrian law, that patients always had the possibility to go abroad:

> In this connection the Court also observes that there is no prohibition under Austrian law on going abroad to seek treatment of infertility that uses artificial procreation techniques not allowed in Austria and that in the event of a successful treatment the Civil Code contains clear rules on paternity and maternity that respect the wishes of the parents (European Court of Human Rights, Grand chamber, 2011).

The dissenting judges of the Grand Chamber rightly pointed out that first, this does not answer the real question of interference of the Austrian law with the right to respect for private and family life under Article 8 of the European Convention on Human Rights (ECHR) and second, this point undermines a number of the arguments advanced by Austria to maintain their law (concerning the resistance to atypical families and the child's best interests).

Improving the availability of donor gametes in each country would have a double positive effect: it would enable local patients to have treatment within a reasonable time period and it would curb the outflow of patients. At the moment, governments are not eager to start large scale promotion campaigns for gamete donation. In fact, very little is done in the European member states. The United Kingdom seems to be the exception with the National Gamete Donation Trust. In theory, the Agence de la Biomédicine has a similar role in France but their campaigns are very low profile and, judging by the national numbers of donors, not very efficient (Le Lannou, 2013). These efforts are a fraction of what is being done to promote donation of organs and blood. The ethical sensitivity of gamete donation is the most likely explanation for this discrepancy. Still, if all countries became self-sustaining for donor gametes, the number of cross-border movements would strongly diminish. An additional advantage would be that countries would also control the circumstances in which donors are recruited and how they are treated. When a country has enough altruistic donors, it does not have to worry about its citizens using paid donors abroad.

Conclusion

Many ethical questions remain regarding specific aspects of cross-border reproductive travelling. The collaborative nature of the phenomenon emphasises the ethical concepts of complicity and responsibility. It is important that the analysis of these problems goes hand in hand with empirical studies on what people do and what kind of arrangements constructions they make. In addition, this patient–doctor interaction takes place in a social and legal context that is constantly changing. Changes in legislation (see India and France) may have immediate repercussions that are worth studying if only to find out how these elements interact with each other. This contextual approach will avoid unjustified generalisations and will bring forward important distinctions that might be lost in a top-down approach. A consequence of the contextual approach is that the ethical evaluation should also be adapted to this level.

REFERENCES

Aballea, P., Burstin, A. and Guedj, J. (2011). *Etat des lieux et perspectives du don d'ovocytes en France*. Rapport tôme I. IGAS: Inspection Généraledes Affairs Sociales.

Anonymous (2009). 'Business booms at world's biggest sperm bank'. Available at www.google.com/hostednews/afp/article/ALeqM5hBNU1WQrNjm PogMWhQc1XYQly65Q?hl=en Last. Accessed 3 March 2014.

Bergmann, S. (2011). 'Reproductive agency and projects: Germans searching for egg donation in Spain and the Czech Republic'. *Reproductive BioMedicine Online*, 23, 600–8.

Chehtman, A. (2010). 'The extraterritorial scope of the right to punish'. *Law and Philosophy*, 29, 127–57.

Corveleyn, A., Zika, E., Morris, M., Dequeker, E. et al. (2008). *Preimplantation Genetic Diagnosis in Europe*. Luxembourg: Office for Official Publications of the European Communities.

Couture, V., Drouin, R., Tan, S.-L., Moutquin, J-M. et al. (2014). 'Cross-border reprogenetic services: a narrative overview and thematic analysis of the literature'. *Clinical Genetics*, doi: 10.1111/cge.12418.

Dickens, B.M. and Cook, R.J. (2006). 'Conflict of interests: legal and ethical aspects'. *International Journal of Gynecology and Obstetrics*, 92, 192–7.

Dondorp, W., De Wert, G., Pennings, G., Shenfield, F. et al. (2013). 'ESHRE Task Force on Ethics and Law 20: Sex selection for non-medical reasons'. *Human Reproduction*, 28, 1448–54.

Downie, J. and Baylis, F. (2013). 'Transnational trade in human eggs: law, policy, and (in)action in Canada'. *Journal of Law, Medicine and Ethics*, 41, 224–39.

Ethics Committee of the American Society for Reproductive Medicine (ASRM) (2013). 'Cross-border reproductive care: a committee opinion'. *Fertility and Sterility*, 100, 645–50.

European Court of Human Rights (2014). Totally prohibiting the establishment of a relationship between a father and his biological children born following surrogacy arrangements abroad was in breach of the Convention. Press release issued by the Registrar of the Court, 26.06.2014. Available at www.hudoc.echr.coe.int/sites/eng-press/pages/search.aspx?i=003–4804617–5854908.

Foreign and Commonwealth Office (2013). 'Surrogacy overseas'. Available at www.gov.uk/government/uploads/system/uploads/attachment_data/file/288902/Surrogacy_overseas__updated_February_2014_.pdf.

Glinos, I.A. and Wismar, M. (2013). 'Hospital collaboration in border regions: observations and conclusions', in I.A. Glinos and M. Wismar (eds.), *Hospitals and Borders: 7 Case-Studies on Cross-border Collaboration and Health System Interactions*, 11–31. Observatory Studies Series 31. World Health Organization: Geneva. Available at www.euro.who.int/__data/assets/pdf_file/0019/233515/e96935.pdf.

Grall, J.-Y. (2012). 'Lettre du 21 Décembre 2012.' Ministére des Affairs Sociales et de la Santé'. French Government.

Grall, J.-Y. (2013). 'Lettre du 30 Avril 2013. Ministére des Affairs Sociales et de la Santé'. French Government.

Gürtin, Z.B. (2011). 'Banning reproductive travel: Turkey's ART legislation and third-party assisted reproduction'. *Reproductive BioMedicine Online*, 23, 555–64.

Harton, G., Braude, P., Lashwood, A., Schmutzler, A. et al. (2011). 'ESHRE PGD consortium best practice guidelines for organization of a PGD centre for PGD/preimplantation genetic screening'. *Human Reproduction*, 26, 14–24.

Heng, B.C. (2006). '"Reproductive tourism": should locally registered fertility doctors be held accountable for channelling patients to foreign medical establishments?' *Human Reproduction*, 21, 840–2.

Hudson, N. and Culley, L. (2011). 'Assisted reproductive travel: UK patient trajectories'. *Reproductive BioMedicine Online*, 23, 573–81.

Hudson, N., Culley, L., Blyth, E., Norton, W. et al. (2011). 'Cross-border reproductive care: a review of the literature'. *Reproductive BioMedicine Online*, 22, 673–85.

Human Fertilisation and Embryology Authority (HFEA) (2009). 'Considering fertility treatment abroad: issues and risks'. Available at www.hfea.gov.uk/fertility-clinics-treatment-abroad.html.

Infertility Consumer Support for Infertility (2008). 'Travelling abroad for assisted reproductive technology (ART) treatment'. Available at www.icsi.ws.

Inhorn, M.C. (2012). 'Reproductive exile in global Dubai: South Asian stories'. *Cultural Politics*, 8, 283–306.

Inhorn, M.C. and Patrizio, P. (2012). 'The global landscape of cross-border reproductive care: twenty key findings for the new millenium'. *Current Opinion in Obstetrics and Gynecology*, 24, 158–63.

Kadish, S. (1987). 'A theory of complicity', in R. Gavison (ed.), *Issues in Contemporary Legal Philosophy: The Influence of H.L.A. Hart*. Oxford University Press.

Le Lannou, D. (2013). 'Quelle stratégie pour améliorer le recrutement des donneurs de gamétes?' *Gynécologie Obstétrique et Fertilité*, 41, 711–14.

Lucas-Baloup, I. (2013). 'GPA et AMP: soupçons / condamnations (les circulaires incohérentes)'. *Gynéco Online*, February 2013. Available at www.gyneco-online.com

McLeod, C. (2008). 'Referral in the wake of conscientious objection to abortion'. *Hypatia*, 23, 30–47.

Moore, M.S. (2007). 'Causing, aiding, and superfluity of accomplice liability'. *University of Pennsylvania Law Review*, 156, 395–452.
Mutcherson, K.M. (2012). 'Welcome to the Wild West: protecting access to cross border fertility care in the United States'. *Cornell Journal of Law and Public Policy*, 22, 349–93.
Participants in the International Summit (2008). 'The Declaration of Istanbul on organ trafficking and transplant tourism'. *Kidney International*, 74, 854–9.
Pennings, G. (1996). 'Ethics of sex selection for family balancing – Family balancing as a morally acceptable application of sex selection'. *Human Reproduction*, 11, 2339–43.
Pennings, G. (2002). Personal desires of patients and social obligations of geneticists: applying preimplantation genetic diagnosis for non-medical sex selection. *Prenatal Diagnosis*, 22, 1123–9.
Pennings, G. (2004). 'Legal harmonization and reproductive tourism in Europe'. *Human Reproduction*, 19, 2689–94.
Pennings, G. (2011). 'Sperma op maat: een patiëntenrecht'. *Tijdschrift voor Geneeskunde*, 67, 1154–9.
Pennings, G., Autin, C., Decleer, W., Delbaere, A. et al. (2009). 'Cross-border reproductive care in Belgium'. *Human Reproduction*, 24, 3108–18.
Pennings G., de Mouzon J., Shenfield F., Ferraretti A.P. et al. (2014). 'Sociodemographic and fertility related characteristics and motivations of oocyte donors in eleven European countries'. *Human Reproduction*, 29, 1076–89.
Pennings, G. and Gürtin, Z. (2012). 'The legal and ethical regulation of transnational donation', in M. Richards, G. Pennings and J. Appleby (eds.), *Reproductive Donation: Policy, Practice, and Bioethics*. Cambridge University Press.
Rapp, R. (2011). 'Reproductive entanglements: body, state, and culture in the dys/regulation of childbearing'. *Social Research*, 78, 693–718.
Rozée Gomez, V. and De La Rochebrochard, E. (2013). 'Cross-border reproductive care among French patients: experiences in Greece, Spain and Belgium'. *Human Reproduction*, 28, 3103–10.
Shenfield, F., de Mouzon, J., Pennings, G., Ferraretti, A.P. et al. (2010). 'Cross border reproductive care in six European countries'. *Human Reproduction*, 25, 1361–8.
Shenfield, F., Pennings, G., De Mouzon, J., Ferraretti, A.P. et al. (2011). 'ESHRE's good practice guide for cross-border reproductive care for centers and practitioners'. *Human Reproduction*, 26, 1625–7.
Speier, A.R. (2011). 'Brokers, consumers and the internet: how North American consumers navigate their infertility journeys'. *Reproductive BioMedicine Online*, 23, 592–9.
Storrow, R.F. (2010). 'The pluralism problem in cross-border reproductive care'. *Human Reproduction*, 25, 2939–43.
Thijssen, A., Dhont, N., Vandormael, E., Cox, A. et al. (2014). 'Artificial insemination with donor sperm (AID): heterogeneity in sperm banking facilities on a single country (Belgium).' *Facts, Views and Vision in ObGyn*, 6, 57–67.
Trimmings, K. and Beaumont, P.R. (eds.) (2013). *International Surrogacy Arrangements: Legal Regulation at the International level*. Oxford: Hart Publishing.

UK Association of Clinical Embryologists (2005). 'Response to the 'EU Draft technical requirements for the coding, processing, preservation, storage and distribution of human tissues and cells'. Available at www.ec.europa.eu/health/archive/ph_threats/human_substance/oc_tech_cell/docs/ev_20050624_co10_en.pdf. Accessed 2 March 2014.

Van Hoof, W., Pennings, G. and De Sutter, P. (2015). 'Cross-border reproductive care for law evasion: a qualitative study into the experiences and moral perspectives of French women who go to Belgium for treatment with donor sperm'. *Social Science and Medicine*, 124, 391–7, doi:10.1016/j.socscimed.2014.09.018.

Van Hoof, W. and Pennings, G. (2011). 'Extraterritoriality for cross-border reproductive care: should states act against citizens travelling abroad for illegal infertility treatment?' *Reproductive BioMedicine Online*, 23, 546–54.

Walsh, A.P.H., Shkrobot, L.V., Omar, A.B., Walsh, D.J. et al. (2010). 'EU screening applied to anonymous oocyte donors from Ukraine: logistics, results and reproductive outcomes from an Irish IVF programme'. *Human Reproduction*, 25, i154.

Wells, D. and Fragouli, E. (2013). 'Preimplantation genetic diagnosis', in K. Coward and D. Wells (eds.), *Textbook of Clinical Embryology*. Cambridge University Press.

Willsher, K. (2014). French court blocks gay woman from adopting partner's child born by IVF. The Guardian, 2 May 2014.

LEGISLATION

Belgian Parliament (2007). 'Law on medically assisted reproduction and the destination of supernumerary embryos and gametes', 17 June 2007. *Belgisch Staatsblad*, 177, 38575–86.

European Convention on Human Rights, Council of Europe. Available at www.echr.coe.int/Documents/Convention_ENG.pdf.

Ministry of Health and Family Welfare, Government of India (2010). 'The Assisted Reproductive Technologies (Regulation) Bill – 2010'.

LEGAL CASES

European Court of Human Rights, Grand chamber. (2011). *Case of S.H. and others* v. *Austria*. Strasbourg, 3 November 2011.

6 Surrogacy

Issues, concerns and complexities

Vasanti Jadva

Introduction

One of the difficulties in evaluating the impact of surrogacy for the individuals involved is the great variability in the way in which surrogacy is accepted, legalised and practised in different countries.[1] These factors are likely to have an impact on the psychosocial experiences of intended parents, surrogates and the resultant child. Furthermore, the increase in the number of surrogacy arrangements taking place across national borders and jurisdictions means that the impact of surrogacy for those concerned needs to be discussed and evaluated at a global level (see Pennings, Klitzman and Zegers-Hochschild, Chapter 2 and Gamble, Chapter 7). In this chapter, I will discuss the available findings from research carried out with intending parents, surrogates and children born using surrogacy and highlight the shortcomings in our understanding of the impact of surrogacy on those directly involved.

In practice, there are two different ways in which a surrogate may achieve pregnancy, these are distinguished by whether the gestating surrogate's own egg is fertilised (traditional surrogacy, also referred to as straight or genetic surrogacy), or not (gestational surrogacy or host surrogacy). In traditional surrogacy, the surrogate is inseminated (naturally or artificially) with the sperm of the intending father so the child is genetically related to him and to the surrogate who carries the pregnancy. While in gestational surrogacy, the intending couple may use their own gametes, or those of a donor, for in vitro fertilisation (IVF), and the resulting embryo is then transferred to the surrogate, who is (usually) genetically unrelated to the child she carries. Choices related to the use of donor gametes will be influenced by medical reasons, as well as whether the intended couple are a heterosexual couple, same-sex couple or a single man or woman. Furthermore, the chosen surrogate may be someone previously known to the intended couple, that is, a friend or family

[1] Trimmings and Beaumont (2013) provides accounts of surrogacy arrangements in twenty-five countries.

member, or someone who was previously unknown found through a surrogacy organisation, agency or clinic. Sometimes, the surrogate remains anonymous during and after the pregnancy, this may be referred to as a 'closed' surrogacy arrangement (Ragoné, 1994). Thus, there are many diverse ways in which surrogacy can be practised and each of these raises different questions for the people involved. Terminology can be a contentious issue, and can ascribe different meaning for different people (Jadva and Imrie, 2014). Here the person who commissions a pregnancy will be called the 'intended' or 'intending parent(s)'. The woman who gestates the pregnancy for the intending parents will be the 'surrogate' and children born as a result of a surrogacy will be called 'surrogacy children'.

The extent to which the use of donor gametes may have an impact on the psychological development of children has been studied within families of heterosexual and lesbian couples and single women. Overall, children born using donor gametes do not suffer psychological problems as a result of their donor conception (Golombok et al., 2013). Most heterosexual couples using donor gametes do not tell their child of their donor origins, whereas single women and lesbian couples are more likely to say that donor gametes were used (Appleby, Blake and Freeman, 2010). Children who are aware of their donor conception vary in their feelings about this (see Blake, Ilioi and Golombok, Chapter 13). This may be influenced by their age, and the age at which they found out about their conception (Blake et al., 2013; Jadva et al., 2009; Scheib, Riordan and Rubin, 2005). The amount of information a child has about their donor may also have an effect on their feelings about being donor-conceived. Scheib, Riordan and Rubin (2005) found that children born using identity release sperm donation (where the name of the donor can be revealed to the child at the age of eighteen years) reported being comfortable about their origins but almost all indicated that they would request the identity of their donor.

Surrogates and the gestational connection

In cases of surrogacy, children may or may not have a genetic connection with their parents; however, they all lack a gestational connection with their mother. How important is this gestational connection for parents and children? The term 'prenatal attachment' has erroneously been used to describe the mother's relationship with her unborn child. In the psychological literature, the term 'attachment' is used to refer to the reciprocal relationship that develops between the child and the mother (or other attachment figures) whereas the mother's relationship with the child is referred to as 'bonding'. Thus the prenatal relationship between the mother and her unborn child should be described and conceptualised as an emotional bond.

Researchers have examined and discussed whether surrogates develop a bond with the unborn child that they gestate. Studies of surrogates from different countries have documented that the surrogate is able to distance herself from the foetus, such that she is aware from the outset, and through the pregnancy, that the child she carries is not her own (Hibino and Shimazono, 2013; Ragone, 1994; Teman, 2010). Whilst this detachment from the foetus may make the process of handing over the child easier, it has been suggested that this could lead to the surrogate putting her own health or the unborn child's health at risk by engaging in harmful behaviours such as smoking or drinking (Agnafors, 2014; British Medical Association, 1996) although no studies have found that surrogates do engage in such behaviour. Whereas gestational surrogates in the UK and Thailand have reported that their lack of a genetic connection to the child can help them distance themselves from the child (Hibino and Shimazono, 2013; Jadva and Imrie, 2014), in contrast Indian gestational surrogates have been found to talk of their connection to the child through blood and breast milk (Pande, 2009). Pande carried out a detailed ethnographic study of Indian surrogates and reported that surrogates believed that the foetus is nourished by the surrogate's blood and that this blood contributes to the child's identity (Pande, 2009). Although not yet fully understood, recent scientific evidence suggests that maternal-foetal cellular exchange and epigenetic factors may form a biological connection between the foetus and surrogate (Loike and Fischbach, 2013). Fischbach and Loike (2014) argue that intending parents and the surrogate need to be aware of this biological connection and of any health risks that may be associated with it.

Surrogates from diverse cultures may conceptualise their 'connection' to the child differently from women who are pregnant with children they intend to raise, perhaps in ways that may optimise their ability to hand over the child to the intending parents. Even in traditional surrogacy where the surrogate uses her own egg, she sees a surrogacy child as different to a child in her own family (Jadva and Imrie, 2014). The main factor here appears to be the *intention* for the pregnancy to be a surrogacy pregnancy (Berend, 2012). While earlier research found that surrogates tend to act either as traditional or gestational surrogates, recent studies have found that some women have carried out both types of surrogacy arrangements (Jadva and Imrie, 2013). These surrogates do not appear to have greater or fewer difficulties in handing over the child according to the type of surrogacy that they have undergone (Jadva and Imrie, 2014).

Much of the research on surrogates has examined their motivations and characteristics (Ciccarelli and Beckman, 2005). Many women give altruistic reasons for being a surrogate (Blyth, 1994; Jadva et al., 2003; Ragone, 1994; van den Akker, 2007). Even in countries where commercial surrogacy is allowed, financial incentives are often mentioned in combination with motivations such as wanting to help a childless couple and enjoyment of pregnancy (Hibino and Shimazono, 2013; Ragone, 1994). The main motivation for Indian surrogates has been reported to be financial gain though some also acknowledge that they are doing something noble (Karandikar et al., 2014). Some studies explored whether surrogates have particular characteristics that enable them to act as surrogates. Braverman and Corson (1992) examined psychopathology and personality characteristics in eleven gestational surrogates, sixteen intending mothers and sixteen intending fathers as they embarked on a surrogacy programme at a clinic in the United States. They found that surrogates had lower self-esteem and lower self-confidence when compared to intending mothers and displayed narcissistic needs that were fulfilled by their role as surrogates (Braverman and Corson, 1992). A later study of forty-three women who were planning on being surrogates (Pizitz, McCullaugh and Rabin, 2013) found that, in comparison to population norms, surrogate candidates were more assertive and more resilient to stress whilst also showing lower levels of anxiety and higher feelings of contentment and self-worth. According to the authors, these attributes enabled these women to manage their surrogate role which requires them to be emotionally strong to deal with the surrogacy arrangement. In terms of psychological health after the birth of the child, some UK surrogates report minor difficulties in the weeks following the birth which dissipated over time (Jadva et al., 2003) and the majority of surrogates do not experience psychological problems six months to one year following the birth (Jadva et al., 2003; van den Akker, 2007). In the longer term, our own research has found that surrogates do not have psychological problems ten years following the birth of the child (Imrie and Jadva, 2014; Jadva, Imrie and Golombok, 2015). Notably, studies assessing the psychological well-being of surrogates have largely been carried out in the United States and UK. As yet, little is known about the impact on the psychological health of surrogates in other countries.

Surrogacy families

In terms of the outcomes for surrogacy families, the UK Longitudinal Study of Assisted Reproduction Families has been following up parents with a child born using surrogacy in comparison with children born through egg donation, sperm donation and natural conception (Golombok et al., 2013). Families were first seen when the child was aged one year (Golombok et al., 2004) and subsequent data were collected when the child was age, two (Golombok et al., 2006a), three (Golombok et al., 2006b), seven and ten years (Golombok et al., 2013). The study examined aspects of parenting associated with warmth, sensitive responding and disciplinary control. These dimensions of parenting have been found to be associated with positive and negative outcomes for children. Observational assessments were also used to assess mother–child and father–child interactions. In the latter two phases, the children were also interviewed about their family relationships, and those who were aware of their surrogacy origins were asked what they understood about their conception and how they felt about it. The children's teachers were asked to complete questionnaires in order to obtain an independent assessment of the children. This research has found few differences in parents' psychological wellbeing, the quality of parent–child relationships and child outcomes during the pre-school years between surrogacy families and a comparison group of families where parents had not had any medical assistance in conceiving their child, suggesting that families in which a mother lacks a gestational connection to the child are similar to those where she does not. At the age seven assessment, children born using surrogacy showed higher adjustment problems (as measured by the Strengths and Difficulties Questionnaire), in comparison to children born using gamete donation, although, and importantly, all children were found to score within the normal range showing that they were not experiencing any psychological problems. Furthermore, this difference disappeared by the time the children were aged ten years. No differences were found in the quality of parenting between surrogacy, gamete donation and natural conception families (Golombok et al., 2013). It is important to note that the surrogacy children in the longitudinal study were all aware of the circumstances of their birth and all intended parents had used domestic surrogacy and become legal parents of the child. The extent to which these factors contribute to child outcomes is unclear.

The majority of research examining surrogacy families has focused on families headed by heterosexual couples. Much less is known about families headed by gay couples who use surrogacy to have a child. Bergman et al. (2010) interviewed forty gay men (from forty couples) who had a child using surrogacy. The men were recruited through a single surrogacy agency based in California, United States. They found that these men tended to be highly affluent, experienced a similar transition to parenthood as other parents and felt very proud and positive about becoming parents. A separate study of fifteen gay couples who were seeking surrogacy at a clinic in Connecticut, United States, found that gay men choosing surrogacy were in a committed relationship and had carefully considered becoming fathers with the vast majority reporting that their families were supportive of their decision to use assisted reproduction (Greenfield and Seli, 2011). Whilst these studies shed some light on the motivations and characteristics of gay men using surrogacy, it is essential that more is understood about the processes within these families including what impact it has on the children. As yet, no study has assessed family functioning and child outcomes for gay men who have used surrogacy to have a child. A study of parenting and child development in gay father families created by surrogacy is currently being conducted at the Centre for Family Research.

There is also a dearth of research on single men using surrogacy. Although the prevalence of such arrangements is unknown, the media have reported cases in the United States and UK. In the UK, a single man cannot obtain legal parentage of a child born using surrogacy via a parental order. However, he can obtain parentage in other ways and surrogates have been found to be carrying out traditional surrogacy for single men (Imrie and Jadva, 2014). For example, a surrogate involved in the study by Imrie and Jadva reported that her name remained on the child's birth certificate. She felt the relationship with the single intended father and his child was different when compared to other couples that she had also helped as a surrogate, specifically, she felt that the single intended father sought more contact from her. Much more research is needed to increase understanding of single men becoming parents using surrogacy.

Although not widely practiced, some fertile heterosexual couples and single women may use surrogacy through choice because they do not want to undergo the pregnancy themselves (sometimes referred to as social surrogacy). Reasons for this appear to include the impact a pregnancy would have on the woman's career or her body as reported by an article in Elle magazine in 2014 (www.elle.com/life-love/society-career/birth-rights). It is not known how prevalent social surrogacy is. A doctor in San Diego, quoted in the article by Elle, stated that social surrogacy made up less than 5 per cent of his 2,500 cases. Social surrogacy raises questions over who should and should not have access to surrogacy. Society's attitudes to this type of surrogacy may be more negative as the reasons for using surrogacy shift from an *inability* to carry a baby to *choosing* not to carry a baby.

The children of surrogacy

Surrogacy in the UK and the United States share some similarities in that the surrogate and intended parents are often in contact with each other and can sometimes develop close relationships that last beyond the arrival of the baby (Braverman, Casey and Jadva, 2012). This relationship, typically maintained between the surrogate and the intending mother (MacCallum et al., 2003), can continue as the child grows up and comes to understand their birth using surrogacy (Jadva et al., 2012). Children who are aware of their surrogacy origin, report positive feelings about their birth and towards their surrogate saying, for example, 'I think she is kind and she's lovely and funny' (Jadva et al., 2012). Although surrogacy children may be comfortable discussing surrogacy within their family it is possible that they may find explaining their birth to their friends and peers more challenging. For example, one ten-year-old child said:

> . . . some people at school sometimes bring it up, and they ask me [if] I'm adopted and I'm like [bored voice] "No, I'm surrogate, don't let me explain it, it takes forever" because I just can't tell anybody, well I can, but I just can't put it in the right words and they just don't understand me, and looking at me like I'm some weird person [laughs] so I try not to tell. (Child born through surrogacy from Golombok et al. (unpublished data))

It is possible that the positive feelings about surrogacy that have been observed amongst ten-year-old children may change as children grow older and gain a more sophisticated understanding about their birth. Furthermore, as children enter the period of adolescence, where identity development gains more relevance, they could form a more critical view of their surrogacy birth (Jadva et al., 2012).

For intending couples and surrogates who remain in contact with each other, the type of contact they maintain, and the closeness of the relationship formed, can vary from an exchange of letters or cards once or twice a year to frequent phone calls and family gatherings (Jadva et al., 2012; Jadva and Imrie, 2014). These get-togethers can involve the intending parents' family and the surrogate's family, such that the children from the respective families also grow up knowing each other (Jadva and Imrie, 2014). A study of thirty-six children of surrogate mothers aged between twelve and twenty-five years found that children of surrogates generally felt proud of their mother's role as a surrogate. Just under half were in contact with the surrogacy child with 40 per cent referring to the surrogacy child as a sibling or half-sibling (Jadva and Imrie, 2014). Surrogates who were no longer in contact with the intended parents reported being happy with this decision, provided that this had been decided from the outset. In contrast, some surrogates whose contact was stopped by the intending parents, despite an initial agreement to keep in touch, have been found to report feelings of disappointment (Ciccarelli and Beckman, 2005; Imrie and Jadva, 2014). It is not known whether or not contact with the surrogate is important for the child's social and emotional development and whether the type of surrogacy, that is, traditional or gestational, mediates this relationship.

Going abroad and remuneration

The UK has seen a rise in the number of surrogacy arrangements taking place abroad, which may partly be attributed to the recent change in law enabling gay couples to obtain legal parentage of the child via a Parental Order (see Gamble, Chapter 7). It is thought that increasing numbers may be going to India or the United States for surrogacy although it is difficult to know the exact number (Crawshaw, Blyth and van den Akker, 2012). When parents go abroad they may not know who their surrogate or egg donor is. The process of going abroad may put an additional psychological strain on intended parents. On the other hand, it is possible that dealing with a clinic or a surrogacy agency, rather than the surrogate directly (as is usually the case in the UK), may lessen anxiety during the pregnancy. It is also not known how children will feel about having a surrogate and possibly an egg donor who is from a different country, culture and ethnicity to their parents, and what, if any, information they would want about such surrogates (Braverman, Casey and Jadva, 2012).

There are a number of reasons why intending parents may look to go abroad for surrogacy. A survey carried out by Surrogacy Australia (Everingham, 2014) found that the most common reason for Australian intending parents going abroad for surrogacy was because they were concerned about the risk of the surrogate keeping the baby if the surrogacy was undertaken in Australia. Just under half of the 217 Australians surveyed thought that asking a surrogate to carry 'for love', that is, for altruistic reasons, seemed an unfair exchange. Other reasons included finding no-one suitable to act as a surrogate, and that surrogacy in Australia was a lengthy and complicated process. At the time the survey was carried out, most Australians were going to India for overseas surrogacy with an estimated 200 births in 2012 attributed to Indian surrogacy. It is possible that British intending parents would have similar reasons for going abroad for surrogacy to those in Australia, as the legislation regarding payment is similar. The Brazier report expressed great unease about commercial surrogacy and recommended that only reasonable expenses should be received by the surrogate (Brazier, Campbell and Golombok,

1998, see Wells-Greco, 2013, for arrangements in the UK). Concerns included how the child would feel about significant sums of money changing hands and whether commercialisation would lead to exploitation of surrogates. Currently we do not know how payment to surrogates may impact on the surrogate and on the child's feelings about their surrogacy birth.

In a study of thirty-four British surrogates, most were happy with the current law allowing only reasonable expense as they felt that it prevented women from receiving large sums of money whilst also providing some flexibility in the amount received (Jadva and Imrie, 2013). However, the surrogates in this study had been critical of other aspects of legislation including the need to have their name on the birth certificate. Several surrogates felt it unfair that the intended parents who provided their gametes could not be named on the birth certificate and had to acquire legal parentage of their own biological child through a legal process. For example, as one surrogate said:

> If it is host surrogacy and the egg is the mother's and the sperm is the dad's then I see no reason at all why I have to be on the birth certificate, at all, I just find that just stupid, that's just bizarre. Um, and then the whole adoption thing, I just think, is just ridiculous as well, you know, again it's probably different if it was straight surrogacy, but from my point of view, from host [gestational] surrogacy, both [intended parents] should have been on the birth certificate from the very beginning and they shouldn't have had to adopt their own child. (Surrogate mother from Jadva and Imrie (unpublished data))

From the intended parents' perspective it is possible that having a surrogate who is motivated by money may appear less of a threat. In terms of the amount of money received by the surrogate, there appear to be minimal differences. For example, in the UK the surrogate may receive £15,000 and in the United States typical amounts are between $20,000 and $30,000 (Gamble and Prosser, 2013). Thus it appears that the difference between the UK and the United States may sometimes hinge on terminology – 'altruistic versus compensated' – rather than the amount a surrogate receives. Of course, not all UK surrogacy arrangements involve large sums of money and most surrogates have been reported to be motivated by a desire to help others, rather than for financial reasons (Imrie and Jadva, 2014; Jadva et al., 2003). In cases where the amount received by the surrogate is perceived to be high, then intended parents and surrogates may be put in a very difficult position jeopardising their chances of obtaining a Parental Order. This scenario is perhaps more common for intending parents who go abroad to access commercial surrogacy, although as yet, no intended parent has been denied a Parental Order because of the amount the surrogate has received. As Gamble (Chapter 7) points out, it is not illegal for surrogates to be paid, though in practice intended parents and surrogates may feel that it is. In the UK, it is thought that not all parents seek a Parental Order when they return home (Crawshaw, Blyth and van den Akker, 2012) as some countries allow the intended parents to be named on the birth certificate, although according to British law these parents would not be considered legal parents (Blackburn-Starza, 2013). Studies are needed to assess the impact for the couple of using surrogacy abroad and of raising the child once they return home. It is not known, for example, how intended parents who choose not to obtain a Parental Order, and so would not be legal parents of the child, would be affected in their role as a parent. Does the uncertainty over their legal parentage make them feel less secure in their parental role? Do they keep the surrogacy birth secret from their family and friends given that they had not formally disclosed it to the authorities, and if so, what impact does this have on family relationships and on the child? Also, how may the surrogacy child feel about their surrogate or donor being from another country or of a different race or culture? For those families who choose to stay in contact with their surrogate, how do families maintain a relationship across different countries and cultures and does contact taper off over time in the same way as it has been found to do for British parents who had carried out domestic surrogacy arrangements?

Changes in legislation or surrogacy practice can have immediate consequences for those concerned. For example, in July 2012 the Government of India, Ministry of Home Affairs, instructed that all oversees intending parents seeking surrogacy in India would require a medical visa instead of a tourist visa. Such medical visas are issued following a letter from the Indian clinic involved (see Gamble, Chapter 7). Furthermore, to access surrogacy, medical visas would only be issued to couples who have been married for at least two years. Given that India does not recognise gay marriages, this meant that gay couples and single men were no longer able to access surrogacy in India. This sudden change in the eligibility criteria meant that intended parents found themselves in a situation where they were unsure whether they would be able to take their baby home. It was later made clear that the guidelines would not apply to those who were in the middle of treatment; however, it did affect couples who had embryos in storage in India who, as a result of these new rules, would not be able to have them transferred into a surrogate. India's restrictions led to many couples travelling to alternative destinations such as Thailand, Malaysia, Kenya and Ukraine, which at the time had no such limitations in access to surrogacy.

Surrogacy in a context in which the surrogate is paid and where there is no perceived shortage of surrogates can also lead to intending parents requesting that more than one surrogate undergoes embryo transfer in order to increase the chances of a pregnancy. If two surrogates become pregnant this results in a unique type of 'twins' or 'twiblings' (a term coined by the media), where the intending parents raise two children of a similar age, but where the children do not share their gestational mother. In some instances the two surrogates may each carry twin pregnancies resulting in a rare situation of two sets of twins, that is, four children, as reported by the BBC in 2013 (see www.bbc.co.uk/news/uk-24670212). Although the Indian clinic involved in this case was surprised and concerned when they discovered both surrogates were carrying twins, the couple were reported to be overjoyed. Couples can view multiple births as a means of creating an 'instant family' (Baor and Blickstein, 2005). However, multiple births carry health risks for the gestating woman, such as high blood pressure, pre-eclampsia, anaemia and gestational diabetes, and also for the babies, including preterm delivery, low birth weight and perinatal mortality and disability (Olivennes et al., 2005). In addition to the medical risks, parents may be unprepared for the additional physical, emotional and financial burden of caring for twins or triplets and mothers of twins born through assisted reproduction have been found to experience greater parenting stress and depression in comparison to mothers of singletons (Freeman et al., 2007; Olivennes et al., 2005).

Conclusions

Whilst studies have found that, on the whole, surrogacy does not lead to psychological problems for either surrogacy families or surrogates involved in domestic surrogacy arrangements in the UK and United States, many questions remain unanswered. Although some children born using surrogacy in the UK appear comfortable with the circumstances of their birth, their views as they grow up and gain a clearer understanding of what and who was involved may change. It is of paramount importance that their perspective is evaluated and ultimately taken into account in the practice and regulation of surrogacy. In addition, the question of how contact with the surrogate and her family may affect the surrogacy family needs to be better understood. For example, is it desirable for children to have contact with the surrogate as they grow up? For those who have no contact or do not know their surrogate, is it in their best interests to have access to identifying information about their surrogate when they reach adulthood? The impact of surrogacy for surrogates also needs to be better understood in the context of the country in which they reside. The increase in the number of people going abroad for surrogacy means that surrogacy must be evaluated globally. This raises many complications. Legislation and practice differ between countries and perceptions of surrogacy differ between different cultures and the various communities within them. As the practice of surrogacy evolves, so does the need for more empirical research in order to fully evaluate this form of assisted reproduction for surrogates, the intending parents and the resultant child.

REFERENCES

Agnafors, M. (2014). 'The harm argument against surrogacy revisited. Two versions not to forget'. *Medicine, Health Care and Philosophy*, 17, 357–63.

Appleby, J.B., Blake, L. and Freeman, T. (2010). 'Is disclosure in the best interests of children conceived by donation?', in M. Richards, G. Pennings and J.B. Appleby (eds.), *Reproductive Donation: Practices, Policies and Bioethics*. Cambridge University Press.

Baor, L. and Blickstein I. (2005). 'En route to an "instant family": psychosocial considerations'. *Obstetrics and Gynecology Clinics of North America*, 32, 127–39.

Berend, Z. (2012). 'The romance of surrogacy'. *Sociological Forum*, 27, 913–36.

Bergman, K., Rubio, R.J., Green, R.J. and Padron, E. (2010). 'Gay men who become fathers via surrogacy: the transition to parenthood'. *Journal of GLBT Family Studies*, 6, 111–41.

Blackburn-Starza, A. (2013). 'International surrogacy arrangements need parental orders'. *BioNews*, 707. 3 June 2013.

Blake, L., Casey, P., Jadva, V. and Golombok, S. (2013). '"I was quite amazed": donor conception and parent–child relationships from the child's perspective'. *Children and Society*, doi: 10.1111/chso.12014.

Blyth, E. (1994). '"I wanted to be interesting. I wanted to be able to say 'I've done something interesting with my life"': interviews with surrogate mothers in Britain'. *Journal of Reproductive and Infant Psychology*, 12, 189–98.

Braverman, A.M. and Corson S.L. (1992). 'Characteristics of participants in a gestational carrier program'. *Journal of Assisted Reproduction and Genetics*, 9, 353–57.

Braverman, A., Casey, P. and Jadva, V. (2012). 'Reproduction through surrogacy: the UK and USA experience', in M. Richards, G. Pennings and J.B. Appleby (eds.), *Reproductive Donation: Practices, Policies and Bioethics*. Cambridge University Press.

Brazier M., Campbell A. and Golombok S. (1998). *Surrogacy: Review for Health Ministers of Current Arrangements for Payments and Regulation*. Report of the Review Team. Cmnd: 4068. Department of Health, London: HMSO.

British Medical Association (1996). *Changing Conceptions of Motherhood. The Practice of Surrogacy in Britain*. London: British Medical Association.

Ciccarelli, J.C. and Beckman, L.J. (2005). 'Navigating rough waters: an overview of psychological aspects of surrogacy'. *Journal of Social Issues*, 61, 21–43.

Crawshaw, M., Blyth, E. and van den Akker, O. (2012). 'The changing profile of surrogacy in the UK – implications for national and international policy and practice'. *Journal of Social Welfare and Family Law*, 34, 267–77.

Everingham, S. (2014). 'Use of surrogacy by Australians: implications for policy and law reform', in A. Hayes and D. Higgins (eds.), *Families, Policy and The Law: Selected Essays on Contemporary Issues for Australia*. Melbourne: Australian Institute of Family Studies.

Fischbach, R.L. and Loike, J.D. (2014). 'Maternal-fetal cell transfer in surrogacy: ties that bind'. *American Journal of Bioethics*, 14, 35–6.

Freeman, T., Golombok, S., Olivennes, F., Ramogida, C. and Rust J. (2007). 'Psychological assessment of mothers and their assisted reproduction triplets at age 3 years'. *Reproductive BioMedicine Online*, 15, 13–17.

Gamble, N. and Prosser, H. (2013) 'The "Brilliant Beginnings" of surrogacy reform in the UK'. *Bionews*. 27 August 2013.

Golombok, S., Murray, C., Jadva, V., MacCallum, F. and Lycett, E. (2004). 'Families created through surrogacy arrangements: parent–child relationships in the first year of life'. *Developmental Psychology*, 40, 400–11.

Golombok, S., Murray, C., Jadva, V., Lycett, E., MacCallum, F. and Rust, J. (2006a). 'Non-genetic and non-gestational parenthood: consequences for parent–child relationships and the psychological well-being of mothers, fathers and children at age 3'. *Human Reproduction*, 21, 1918–24.

Golombok, S., MacCallum, F., Murray, C., Lycett, E. and Jadva, V. (2006b). 'Surrogacy families: parental functioning, parent–child relationships and children's psychological development at age 2'. *Journal of Child Psychology and Psychiatry*, 47, 213–22.

Golombok, S., Blake, L., Casey, P., Roman, G. and Jadva, V. (2013). 'Children born through reproductive donation: a longitudinal study of psychological adjustment'. *Journal of Child Psychology and Psychiatry*, 54, 653–60.

Greenfield, D.A. and Seli, E. (2011). 'Gay men choosing parenthood through assisted reproduction: medical and psychosocial considerations'. *Fertility and Sterility*, 95, 225–29.

Hibino, Y. and Shimazono, Y. (2013). 'Becoming a surrogate online: "message board" surrogacy in Thailand'. *Asian Bioethics Review*, 5, 56–72.

Imrie, S. and Jadva, V. (2013). 'Surrogacy law: a call for change?' *Bionews*. 5 August 2013.

Imrie, S. and Jadva, V. (2014). 'The long-term experiences of surrogates: relationships and contact with surrogacy families in genetic and gestational surrogacy arrangements'. *Reproductive BioMedicine Online*, 29, 424–35.

Jadva, V., Freeman, T., Kramer, W. and Golombok, S. (2009). 'The experiences of adolescents and adults conceived by sperm donation: comparisons by age of disclosure and family type'. *Human Reproduction*, 24, 1909–19.

Jadva, V., Blake, L., Casey, P. and Golombok, S. (2012). 'Surrogacy families 10 years on: relationship with the surrogate, decisions over disclosure and children's understanding of their surrogacy origins'. *Human Reproduction*, 27, 3008–14.

Jadva, V. and Imrie, S. (2014). 'Children of surrogate mothers: psychological well-being, family relationships and experiences of surrogacy'. *Human Reproduction*, 29, 90–6.

Jadva, V., Imrie, S. and Golombok, S. (2015). 'Surrogate mothers 10 years on: a longitudinal study of psychological wellbeing and relationships with the parents and child'. *Human Reproduction*, 30, 373–9.

Jadva, V., Murray, C., Lycett, E., MacCallum, F. and Golombok, S. (2003). 'Surrogacy: the experiences of surrogate mothers'. *Human Reproduction*, 18, 2196–204.

Karandikar, S., Gezinski, L.B., Carter, J.R. and Kaloga, M. (2014). 'Economic necessity or noble Cause? A qualitative study exploring motivations for gestational surrogacy in Gujarat, India'. *Journal of Women and Social Work*, 29, 224–36.

Loike J.D. and Fischbach, R.L. (2013). New ethical horizons in gestational surrogacy. *In Vitro, IVF-Worldwide, Reproductive Medicine, Genetics & Stem Cell Biology*. doi:10.4172/jfiv.1000109.

MacCallum, F., Lycett, E., Murray, C., Jadva, V. and Golombok, S. (2003). 'Surrogacy: the experience of commissioning couples'. *Human Reproduction*, 18, 1334–42.

Olivennes, F., Golombok, S., Ramogida, C., Rust, J. and Follow-Up Team. (2005). 'Behavioral and cognitive development as well as family functioning of twins conceived by assisted reproduction: findings from a large population study'. *Fertility and Sterility*, 84, 725–33.

Pande, A. (2009). '"It may be her eggs but it's my blood": surrogates and everyday forms of kinship in India'. *Qualitative Sociology*, 32, 379–97.

Pizitz, T.D., McCullaugh, J. and Rabin, A. (2013). 'Do women who choose to become surrogate mothers have different psychological profiles compared to a normative female sample?' *Women Birth*. 26, e15–20. doi: 10.1016/j.wombi.2012.06.003. Epub 2012 Jul 21.

Ragoné, H. (1994). *Surrogate Motherhood: Conception in the Heart*. Oxford: Westview Press.

Scheib, J.E., Riordan, M. and Rubin, S. (2005). 'Adolescents with open-identity sperm donors: reports from 12–17 year olds'. *Human Reproduction*, 20, 239–52.

Teman, E. (2010). *Birthing a Mother*. Berkeley, CA: University of California Press.

Trimmings, K. and Beaumont, P. (eds.) (2013). *International Surrogacy Arrangements*. Oxford: Hart Publishing.

van den Akker, O. (2007). 'Psychosocial aspects of surrogate motherhood'. *Human Reproduction Update*, 13, 53–62.

Wells-Greco, M. (2013). 'United Kingdom', in Trimmings, K. and Beaumont, P. (eds.), *International Surrogacy Arrangements*. Oxford: Hart Publishing.

7 A better legal framework for United Kingdom surrogacy?

Natalie Gamble

Introduction

Surrogacy has never been illegal in the United Kingdom, but UK law has historically focused on discouraging rather than supporting it. In the 1980s it was hoped that, with restrictive law, surrogacy would 'wither on the vine' (Brazier, Campbell and Golombok, 1998: para 2.23). In fact, it has not – far from it: surrogacy has blossomed as a practice both in the UK and internationally.

The UK is not alone in grappling with the growth of surrogacy. In a modern world of globalised travel and information, increasing numbers of parents living in countries with restrictive surrogacy laws (including many European countries, Australia and China) are crossing borders to build their families through surrogacy. Although the focus of this chapter is the UK, the issues discussed echo similar themes in many other countries.

It is clear that the number of UK parents conceiving through surrogacy has risen dramatically over the past five years. Without a proper legal framework, UK data are piecemeal. However, there are now three non-profit-making surrogacy agencies in the UK (COTS, Surrogacy UK and Brilliant Beginnings) and more UK parents are accessing surrogacy services overseas. Statistics from the General Register Office show that the number of post-birth parental orders registered rose from fifty-one in 2007 to 213 in 2012. At the same time press reports (which I have heard confirmed by UK government officials as realistic) suggest that the number of children born through surrogacy in India to UK parents may be as high as 1,000 per year (Bhatia, 2012). This makes it clear first that the numbers are rising quickly and second that growing numbers of parents are not taking the proper steps to secure parentage. In this context, reform of UK law is necessary and overdue.

But the case for UK legal reform is a positive as well as a pragmatic one. With thirty years of experience, we know that surrogacy can be a positive and enriching experience with a good outcome for all involved (see Jadva, Chapter 6). Permissive changes have recently been made to UK surrogacy law (including allowing same-sex parents to apply for parental orders[1] and extending maternity leave rights[2]) which, although peripheral to the overall framework, indicate our growing acceptance of surrogacy as a practice to be supported by the law.

A more wholesale review must be the next step, looking at surrogacy policy with a clean sheet of paper and a fresh mind. The era of hoping that surrogacy will go away is clearly over; and there is no reason why it should. If there are complex issues to resolve, they can be tackled better within a proper legal framework than by keeping surrogacy on the margins of the law.

Law and policy: surrogacy services

The Surrogacy Arrangements Act 1985 was the UK's first piece of legislation dealing with UK surrogacy. It was rushed through Parliament in reaction to press coverage of the 'baby Cotton' case,[3] and aimed to halt the growth of surrogacy in the UK. It was (and is) restrictive rather than regulatory in approach.

The 1985 Act prohibits advertising in connection with surrogacy, creating criminal offences for those who place advertisements, and those who publish them, if they are based in the UK. The offences cover adverts by prospective parents (that they are looking for a surrogate), advertisements by surrogates (that they are willing to carry a pregnancy) and advertisements by third parties (that they facilitate surrogacy arrangements).[4]

The intent was to stop surrogacy in its tracks by limiting the means by which connections could be made between prospective parents and surrogates who did not already know each other. However, in practice, the advertising offences in the 1985 Act have never been enforced. Just a few clicks on Google will uncover UK prospective parents and surrogates connecting with each other on busy online surrogacy forums and social networking pages. Advertisements by commercial surrogacy providers (mainly from outside the UK) are also regularly published in UK magazines and featured at UK exhibitions. There has never been a prosecution.

The development of UK surrogacy agencies

The 1985 Act also restricts the arrangement of surrogacy by third parties. Originally, the Act made it an offence for third parties to keep lists of

1 Human Fertilisation and Embryology Act 1990, as amended (2008), § 54; in force from 6 April 2010.
2 Children and Families Act 2013 and associated regulations.
3 *Re C (A Minor)* (1985) FLR 846.
4 Surrogacy Arrangements Act 1985, § 3.

potential intended parents and surrogates, to introduce people with a view to their making a surrogacy agreement, and to negotiate the terms of a surrogacy agreement, for 'any payment'.[5] Again, the intent was to limit the ability of surrogates and intended parents to find each other, by preventing third parties from arranging surrogacy on an organised basis.

In practice, Childlessness Overcome Through Surrogacy (COTS) was founded in the UK by Kim Cotton in 1988 to provide a matching service for surrogacy. More recently Surrogacy UK (SUK) has run social events which facilitate prospective parents and surrogates mixing to make connections. Both COTS and SUK charge a membership fee to intended parents and are run largely by volunteers.

COTS and SUK originally operated, at best, on the fringes of the law. When the Human Fertilisation and Embryology Act 1990 was reviewed in 2008, the opportunity was taken to encompass them within it. As from 6 October 2009, the 1985 Act was amended to include an exemption which allowed non profit-making organisations to keep lists of prospective surrogates and intended parents, to introduce them to each other and to advertise their services supporting surrogacy (although there remain restrictions regarding the fees charged and negotiation of individual arrangements).

As with the advertising offences, there has never been a prosecution under the 'brokering' offences in the 1985 Act, either before or after the 2009 changes. However, in 2013 another agency, the British Surrogacy Centre of California (an Essex-based agency run by a high profile gay couple with children through US surrogacy), was referred to the authorities for criminal investigation by Mrs Justice Theis who heard a parental order application in the High Court Family Division involving parents who had used their services.[6]

There have also been issues associated with the quality of service offered by UK surrogacy agencies. In 2007, Mr Justice McFarlane dealt with a case in which COTS had matched a UK surrogate with a Turkish couple who were then unable to obtain a parental order because they were not domiciled in a part of the UK, resulting in a complex legal situation which required nine months of litigation to resolve. He said:

> The court's understanding is that surrogacy agencies such as COTS are not covered by any statutory or regulatory umbrella and are therefore not required to perform to any recognised standard of competence. I am sufficiently concerned by the information uncovered . . . to question whether some form of inspection or authorisation should be required in order to improve the quality of advice

[5] Ibid., § 2. [6] *J* v. *G* (2013) EWHC 1432 (Fam), ¶ 6.

that is given to individuals who seek to achieve the birth of a child through surrogacy. Given the importance of the issues involved when the life of a child is created in this manner, it questionable whether the role of facilitating surrogacy arrangements should be left to groups of well-meaning amateurs. To this end, a copy of this judgment is being sent to the Minister of State for Children, Young People and Families for her consideration.[7]

In September 2013, the team at law firm Natalie Gamble Associates set up Brilliant Beginnings as a third non profit-making UK surrogacy agency in order to support parents and surrogates preferring a more structured surrogacy service. Brilliant Beginnings complies with the current framework under the 1985 Act, but is run by full-time professional staff with an approach more akin to a US agency. Matching of parents and (gestational) surrogates takes place after in-depth discussions and a screening process, and the process is then actively managed for all parties throughout the fertility treatment, pregnancy and birth, including the arrangement of medical treatment and legal advice and counselling at appropriate stages. This aims to cater for those UK parents who prefer a more managed approach to surrogacy, but who have until now had to look outside the UK for this.

The availability of international surrogacy

One of the main motivations for establishing Brilliant Beginnings was the fact that the difficult landscape for surrogacy matching in the UK was driving UK parents abroad. Since the first UK case to ratify an international surrogacy arrangement in 2008,[8] our legal practice has advised more than 250 UK parents on actual or planned international surrogacy arrangements. India, the United States and Eastern Europe are the major destinations. (In 2013, India represented 38 per cent of our cases, the United States 25 per cent and the Ukraine 7 per cent, with the remainder spread across a range of destinations or with the destination not yet chosen.) We see daily that the key drivers for parents choosing overseas surrogacy services are the ease of matching with surrogate mothers (and egg donors), the professional services available and the perceived legal security.

However, the ballooning of cross-border surrogacy has created a host of new challenges for UK law (just as it has for other countries which prohibit or restrict commercial surrogacy). In permissive surrogacy destinations, the law typically treats the intended parents as the legal parents

[7] *Re G (Surrogacy: Foreign Domicile)* (2007) EWHC 2814 (Fam).
[8] *Re X and Y* (2008) EWHC 3030 (Fam).

from birth. However, UK law does not recognise the foreign birth certificate (instead treating the foreign surrogate and her husband as the legal parents), and there is a long, complex and often expensive process to get the right documentation to bring the child home and to secure parentage. As well as creating issues for parents, cross-border surrogacy raises concerns about potential exploitation of foreign surrogate mothers, lack of regulation of foreign surrogacy providers, fraud and child protection (e.g. fake overseas surrogacy agencies which disappear after taking large deposits from intended parents), as well as problems for children whose parentage is not properly resolved.

While the focus of this chapter is the regulation of surrogacy in the UK, such issues are of growing global concern. The Hague Conference on Private International Law has recently begun investigating whether a global treaty on cross-border surrogacy/parentage is desirable and, if so, whether it might be feasible. The Permanent Bureau's preliminary report to the Hague Convention Members dated 3 April 2014 stated:

> Whilst cross-border problems concerning legal parentage are already occurring in multiple different contexts including in non-surrogacy cases, the problems occurring for children in the context of international surrogacy arrangements (ISAs) are undoubtedly the most acute and urgent. This is due to (1) the number of ISA cases taking place today and the likely thousands of children implicated; (2) the fact that cross-border legal status issues arise in the overwhelming majority of these cases due to their factual specificities; and (3) the serious broader concerns, implicating the fundamental rights of children and women, which also arise in ISA cases. . . .
>
> The far more difficult questions remain in the realm of feasibility: that is, whether, bearing in mind the diverse approach of states to questions concerning legal parentage in internal and private international law, as well as the difficult questions of public policy raised in an area traditionally strongly connected with States' cultural and social milieu, common ground can be found to move forward towards a multilateral approach to the cross-border aspects of legal parentage. (Hague Conference on Private International Law, 2014: para. 41)

It is clear that the problems associated with the growth of international surrogacy arrangements are being widely felt, but that international measures are not likely to provide any short term solution, making it even more important that we take steps to reform UK surrogacy.

The need for regulation in the UK

The original hope underpinning UK surrogacy legislation was that the restrictions imposed would halt the development of surrogacy altogether. In fact, rather than limiting surrogacy, the law has created a landscape in which UK surrogacy services have been provided exclusively by unregulated organisations.

This has been perhaps most pertinently observed by Baroness Warnock, chair of the Committee of Inquiry on Human Fertilisation and Embryology,[9] who in 2008 expressed regret about her prejudice against surrogacy:

> I had great difficulty and failure of imagination. I just could not imagine acting as a surrogate mother myself. I've always adored being pregnant and having children and so I just couldn't conceive of giving them up . . . Now, I think, looking back on it, that . . . I was wrong . . . I think it would have been much better if we had had fully open regulation of surrogacy. Because I think even to this day, it's very often done, if at all, in a rather 'hole and corner' way. (Warnock, interview, 2008)

The continuing absence of regulation is indeed hard to understand given that UK surrogacy is thriving in the wider context of a heavily regulated UK fertility sector. Gamete donation, by contrast, takes place under Human Fertilisation and Embryology Authority (HFEA) licence and with careful control of the information and support which must be offered to parents and donors before they embark on treatment, a requirement to consider the welfare of the child, and measures to control how information is stored and accessed by the child. Although in surrogacy cases parents and surrogates are arguably entering into an even more complex arrangement, which they hope will lead to the conception and birth of a child, there is currently no framework to provide for any of these issues, nor any oversight of the quality of support or the accuracy of information provided.

Law and policy: individuals involved in a surrogacy arrangement

The law governing the position of individuals conceiving through reproductive donation is contained in the Human Fertilisation and Embryology Act 1990 (now updated by the Human Fertilisation and Embryology Act, 1990, as amended (2008)). However, the only mention of surrogacy in the original version of the 1990 Bill was the well-known rule that UK surrogacy agreements are 'unenforceable'.[10] Presuming that in a high proportion of arrangements, the birth mother would bond with the

[9] The Committee's 1984 report, which became known as the 'Warnock Report', provided the architecture for the Human Fertilisation and Embryology Act 1990 and the system of UK regulation of assisted reproduction.

[10] Surrogacy Arrangements Act 1985, § 1A.

baby; this rule was designed to protect the surrogate's rights if she did not wish to hand the child over having given birth.

Again, the theme was to discourage surrogacy, by sending a clear message that, while parents and surrogates could enter into surrogacy arrangements, they did so at their own risk, with no guarantees and no recourse to the law if things went wrong. In interview in 2008, it was put to Baroness Warnock that 'One legacy of your committee was a slight "turning up of the nose" at surrogacy that has influenced subsequent legislation in a way that says "we'd rather it didn't happen"'. Baroness Warnock replied: 'Absolutely, you've got it absolutely right, yes' (Warnock, 2008).

In practice, UK surrogacy arrangements have rarely gone wrong in the way envisaged, perhaps surprisingly so given the support the law gives to a surrogate to allow for a change of heart. The lack of enforceability of UK surrogacy arrangements has also not discouraged parents from pursuing surrogacy altogether, as was hoped, but has instead driven them abroad to jurisdictions which offer the comfort of a legally enforceable agreement.

For those who do pursue UK surrogacy arrangements, the current structure of the law creates an imbalance in the surrogacy relationship. It is to the detriment, not just of parents, but of surrogates too, and their husbands (and now civil partners and same-sex spouses as well), who are burdened with all the responsibilities of legal parenthood for a child they do not consider theirs. We are commonly asked by prospective surrogate mothers what would happen if the intended parents reneged on their promises. We have to tell them that the law currently provides that commissioning parents have no legal responsibility for the life they have created.

Legal parentage and parental orders

The 1990 Act (now updated by the 2008 Act) also dealt with UK legal parentage for children conceived through assisted reproduction. The primary focus of the 1990 Act's parentage rules was donation: clarifying that legal motherhood in egg donation cases went to the birth mother rather than the egg donor, and protecting the parentage of husbands conceiving through sperm donation.

The new rules on legal parenthood would, in surrogacy cases, make the surrogate the legal mother and her husband the legal father, irrespective of what the parties to a surrogacy arrangement intended, or whether either or both of the intended parents was the child's biological parent. There was no redress for parents through surrogacy in the original version of the Human Fertilisation and Embryology Bill (leaving adoption as the only possible remedy by which they could acquire legal parenthood). However, a retrospective mechanism for reassigning parentage (in the form of parental orders) was ultimately added to the Bill after Michael Jopling, MP, raised the case of a couple in his constituency who had twins through surrogacy and did not wish to adopt their own biological children. At the time, surrogacy was rare, and gestational surrogacy (in which an embryo is transferred to a surrogate who is therefore not the biological mother, a practice which is now commonplace) was apparently entirely unprecedented, with Michael Jopling commenting: 'I think I am right in saying that my constituents are the first example of such a thing happening in this country.'[11] Parental orders were therefore never a considered legal framework for surrogacy in the UK, but rather a fix, an afterthought. They were added to the Bill just five weeks before the final reading and there was virtually no Parliamentary debate on the detail. They have, however, remained the basis of UK surrogacy law for the past twenty-five years.

The rules set out in section 30 of the 1990 Act (now section 54 of the 2008 Act) demonstrate the hesitant attitude to surrogacy which so clearly prevailed in 1990, the legislation setting out various strict criteria which must be met for the court to be empowered to make a parental order transferring parentage. This whole approach is, of course, flawed. The law essentially seeks to shape the nature of UK surrogacy arrangements into an 'acceptable' model after the event, applying policy in hindsight rather than in advance. The obvious problems with this framework have been aptly demonstrated in practice, as shown below.

The surrogate mother must consent

For a parental order to be granted (by which the UK family court reassigns parentage permanently to the intended parents after the birth), the surrogate (and her husband if she is married) must 'have freely, and with full understanding of what is involved, agreed unconditionally to the making of the order'[12] and (in the case of the surrogate mother) the consent must be given not less than six weeks after the birth. The child's home must also be with the parents at the time of the application and the making of the order.

This, of course, is a further extension of the policy that surrogacy agreements are unenforceable. The logic was that the birth mother should

[11] HC Deb 2 April 1990, vol. 170, cols. 944–45.
[12] Human Fertilisation and Embryology Act (1990), as amended (2008), § 54(6).

have an absolute right to change her mind, and that the family court should not become involved in transferring parentage unless everyone agreed and the baby had already been handed over. This is not, however, how things have worked in practice.

As noted above, UK surrogacy arrangements have resulted in a failure to hand over the child much more rarely than was expected. Notwithstanding the protection given to surrogate mothers to change their minds, there are only three reported legal cases of surrogacy disputes of this kind in the United Kingdom,[13] as against the many parental orders now successfully granted. Of course there may be other cases which have not been taken to court, or not legally reported, but our experience of over 400 surrogacy cases over many years is that it is incredibly rare for a surrogate to refuse to hand a baby over at birth. Our experience is that surrogates go into arrangements with a very clear mindset that the baby they are carrying is not their own (see Jadva, Chapter 6), whether or not the surrogate is the biological mother.

In the three reported legal cases involving such disputes, the family court has not (in line with the apparent intention of the law) simply upheld the surrogate's position, but has instead considered what is in the child's best interests and made flexible use of the law to uphold this. In 2011,[14] the family court allowed a surrogate to retain care of a child she had given birth to, after weighing up where the child was most likely to thrive. In 2007[15] (applying the same test), care of an eighteen-month-old boy was transferred to an intended parent couple after they discovered that their surrogate had feigned a miscarriage. The Court of Appeal upheld the decision, saying that the order was in the child's best interests and (most surprisingly) that the order transferring residence was valid even though the surrogate was married and so neither intended parent was a legal parent. In 2015,[16] the High Court transferred care of a fifteen-month-old girl to her father and his same-sex partner, having found that the birth mother had deceived the intended parents in order to conceive a child she had no intention of relinquishing and then embarked on a homophobic campaign against the father and his partner.

This demonstrates that, in practice, the family courts have ignored Parliament's intention to safeguard the surrogate mother's right to change her mind, and instead taken a more flexible child-focused approach. However, the court's power to arbitrate such disputes is limited, since it has only been able to award residence in these cases and not to

[13] *Re N* (2007) EWCA Civ 1053 and *Re TT* (2011) EWHC 33 Fam and *H* v. *S* (Surrogacy Agreement) (2015) EWHC 36 Fam.

[14] *Re TT* (2011) EWHC 33 Fam.

[15] *Re N* (2007) EWCA Civ 1053.

[16] *H* v. *S* (Surrogacy Agreement) (2015) EWHC 36 Fam.

re-allocate legal parenthood. This meant that the boy in the 2007 case was allowed to live with his biological father and intended mother, but his legal parents remained the surrogate and her husband. Whether or not this was in the child's best interests, the court had no power to make a parental order.

The policy that a surrogate mother must consent to a parental order is therefore, in its practical application, not quite what it seems. In reality, the courts have applied a more flexible approach, undermining the apparently inalienable rights given to surrogates.

Relationship status of the parents

The legislation also tries to enforce policy in respect of what constitutes an acceptable family form. Under the 1990 Act, the applicants for a parental order could only be a heterosexual married couple. As from 6 April 2010, the 2008 Act extended the categories of applicants to include same-sex and unmarried couples.

However, the law still excludes single applicants. This issue was raised when the 2008 Act was discussed in Committee and the government expressly declined to adopt a tabled amendment which would have allowed applications by single parents (something which would have brought the law into line with that on both adoption and access to donor insemination treatment). Minister for Health Dawn Primarolo said:

> Surrogacy is such a sensitive issue, fraught with potential complications such as the surrogate mother being entitled to change her mind and decide to keep her baby, that the 1990 Act quite specifically limits parental orders to married couples where the gametes of at least one of them are used. That recognises the magnitude of a situation in which a person becomes pregnant with the express intention of handing the child over to someone else, and the responsibility that that places on the people who will receive the child. There is an argument, which the Government have acknowledged in the Bill, that such a responsibility is likely to be better handled by a couple than a single man or woman.[17]

For single mothers, the legal difficulty of establishing motherhood (given that the surrogate will always be the mother) deters women from pursuing surrogacy. It is very difficult to find a surrogate in the UK, and accessing surrogacy services overseas may create serious difficulties bringing the child home.

The position is easier for single fathers who, provided the surrogate is unmarried, can be recognised as a legal parent from birth. We have worked with many single fathers through surrogacy, mainly UK

[17] HL Deb 13 June 2008, cols. 244–249.

fathers who have arranged the conception of their own biological children through surrogacy overseas in the United States. Contrary to the policy expressed by the Minister in 2008, UK law does not prevent single fathers from conceiving through surrogacy, but simply denies them the legal solution which would give their children secure and resolved legal status in the UK. Most are therefore caring for children without parental responsibility and with the surrogate remaining the legal mother, a highly unsatisfactory position. The law's exclusion of single applicants for parental orders is potentially challengeable on human rights grounds.

The rule against single applicants also causes difficulties where a couple embarks on a surrogacy arrangement but is no longer a couple by the time the order is applied for. In a case in 2011, Mrs Justice Theis made a parental order in favour of a widow and her late husband after the applicant father died during the course of the court proceedings.[18] The judgment is a wonderful example of the court bending the rules to reach the right outcome for the child, but also makes clear that this was possible only because the intended father survived long enough to issue the application. We have dealt with a case where a widowed father was prevented from securing parentage because his wife had died during the pregnancy, and another where the application was issued just hours before an intended mother died. Since intended parents often go into surrogacy following a history of medical difficulties (often cancer) the likelihood of an intended parent dying between conception and birth is not remote, and where it happens the surviving parent can be denied parentage of their own child.

Separation is another serious cause of difficulty. In a recent case heard by Mrs Justice King,[19] a child born through surrogacy was left a permanent ward of the court (with the court powerless to transfer parentage to the mother who had cared for him since birth, or to extinguish the surrogate's responsibilities) because the parents separated without applying for a parental order.

The rule against single applicants for parental orders is causing real difficulties in practice. It is also difficult to understand the justification for maintaining the policy. What was the evidence basis of the Minister's assertion that only couples should be permitted to embark on surrogacy? Does any research show that surrogacy arrangements entered into by single parents are more likely to break down? It seems likely that the historic prejudice against women conceiving on their own (evident in the now-reformed 1990 Act's requirement for clinics to consider the child's

[18] *A* v. *P* (2011) EWHC 1738 (Fam). [19] *JP* v. *LP* (2014) EWHC 595.

'need for a father' before offering treatment) has simply been transplanted to a new prejudice against (largely) men conceiving on their own through surrogacy.

Other criteria

The inflexibility of some of the other requirements for obtaining a parental order is also problematic. One or both of the intended parents must be 'domiciled' in the UK, a policy designed to create a jurisdictional limitation for parents without sufficient UK connections (as seen in the case involving the Turkish couple). In practice, this causes difficulties for parents who need a parental order because they are living in the UK, but retain links with other countries and so are not eligible to obtain one.

The legislation also says that the application 'must' be made within six months of the birth. Although understandable that there should not be excessive delay in making an application which rewrites a child's birth certificate, it is hard to understand why the family court was given no discretion to extend the deadline in any circumstances. In a recent judgment involving parents of a child born through surrogacy in India who had not applied for a parental order in time and then experienced legal difficulties after a separation, the President of the Family Division Sir James Munby held that a parental order could in fact be made by the court out of time, notwithstanding the legislation. He said:

> Can Parliament really have intended that the gate should be barred forever if the application for a parental order is lodged even one day late? I cannot think so. I assume Parliament intended a sensible result. Given the subject matter, given the consequences for the commissioning parents, never mind those for the child, to construe the law as barring forever an application made just one day late is not, in my judgment, sensible. It is the very antithesis of sensible; it is almost nonsensical.[20]

This is perhaps the clearest expression yet of the court's frustration with the restrictive criteria.

The child must also be conceived through artificial insemination or IVF and at least one of the intended parents must be his or her biological parent. The child can therefore have been conceived through artificial insemination by private arrangement at home, or (more commonly now) as a result of fertility treatment at a clinic using the intended parents' sperm and/or eggs (but not both donated eggs and sperm). Policy in effect defines the limits of the reproductive context: conception must

[20] *Re X (A Child) (Surrogacy: Time Limit)* (2014) EWHC 3135 (Fam), ¶ 55.

be artificial and, if there is no gestational connection with the parents, there must be a genetic one. However, the requirement for a genetic connection is inconsistent with wider UK policy on reproduction, given that in UK donation cases there is no requirement for any genetic link in conferring parenthood.

Payments to surrogates

It is a popular misconception that it is illegal to pay a surrogate in the UK more than her reasonable expenses. In fact, neither parents nor surrogates commit any kind of offence under UK law no matter how much is paid. The issue is relevant only as part of a parental order application where, before transferring legal parentage, the court must be satisfied that no payments have been made other than for 'expenses reasonably incurred'[21] or must decide to authorise the payment.

What is difficult about the policy against payments in surrogacy cases is that the law, bizarrely, seeks to prevent payments after they have already been made. Parliament therefore undermined its own policy from the outset, by giving the court an explicit discretionary power to authorise payments retrospectively. While the intention was no doubt that this power should be exercised only rarely, its inclusion shows an awareness that policy against payments could not always be upheld in practice.

In its application, the law is both confusing and ineffective. First, there is no definition of what 'reasonable expenses' means. COTS has for many years advised parents to pay UK surrogates a lump sum (now £12,000 to £15,000) in addition to various out-of-pocket costs. This was noted in 1998 by the Brazier, Campbell and Golombok's Report which said:

> From the evidence that we have received during the course of the Review, it is clear that in many cases a component of the amount paid to the surrogate mother is a direct payment for services rendered rather than the reimbursement of actual expenses. We have received accounts from COTS and elsewhere suggesting that payments of £15,000 or more are being made by commissioning couples to surrogate mothers, with a number of payments being in the range of £10000–£15000. (Brazier, Campbell and Golombok, 1998: paras. 5.3–5.4)

This picture echoes our experience on the ground, where we see magistrates dealing with UK surrogacy cases in the Family Court routinely making parental orders in such cases, implicitly accepting such 'inconvenience' payments without reference to identified expenses as reasonable.

More recently, international surrogacy cases have pushed the boundaries further with the *fait accompli* of openly commercial payments. The

[21] Human Fertilisation and Embryology Act 2008, § 54(8).

first case of this kind in 2008 involved a British married couple who conceived twins with the help of a married Ukrainian surrogate.[22] The court had to decide how to deal with the compensatory payment of €27,000 made to the surrogate under Ukrainian law. Mr Justice Hedley exercised his discretion to authorise this payment, given the dire straits the children were otherwise in. Ukrainian law said that the commissioning couple were the legal parents, while UK law attributed parenthood to the Ukrainian surrogate and her husband; the result was a conflict of law which meant that the children were born 'marooned stateless and parentless' in the Ukraine. Mr Justice Hedley drew attention to the fact that welfare and public policy on payments were 'two competing and potentially irreconcilably conflicting concepts'. The children's welfare ultimately had to take priority, although he set out the considerations the court had to first make (including the scale of the payment and the applicants' good faith) before authorising a payment.

His approach has been echoed in every subsequent international surrogacy case, of which there have now been many. The court has set out various additional issues which need to be taken into account before payments can be authorised, including that there are no child protection issues, that payments do not 'overbear the will' of the surrogate, and more recently that payments to foreign agencies need authorisation as well as payments to surrogates.

However, the welfare of the child is the 'paramount consideration' and the court has made clear that a parental order would only be withheld if a case represented the 'clearest abuse of public policy'.[23] In practice, an order has never been refused, and it is difficult to conceive of any circumstances in which it would be, unless the court was so concerned about a child's welfare that it would in any event be contemplating proceedings to have the child removed (which mirrors the position for any parent and has no bearing on the issue of payments). Parental orders have now been granted following substantial payments (the highest yet reported figure being a payment of $56,750 plus significant expenses to a US surrogate mother,[24] although payments to Indian surrogates are often more significantly life-changing in value. Our practice has dealt with many international surrogacy cases, and it is clear on the ground that (while the court will apply the process rigorously, particularly with regard to confirming that the surrogate is appropriately involved) the amount of the payments is virtually immaterial. It is simply far too late by the time a child has been born for the court to do anything other than ratify the arrangement.

22 *Re X and Y* (*Foreign Surrogacy*) (2008) EWHC 3030 (Fam).

23 *Re L* (*A Child*) (2010) 3146 (Fam).

24 *J* v. *G* (2013) EWHC 1432 (Fam).

This makes UK policy against payments for surrogacy now entirely redundant in practice. However, more interestingly, the policy itself is questionable, with a clear argument that compensation for inconvenience should be permitted. Surrogacy typically takes at least a year and involves hard work and considerable inconvenience for surrogates and their families. The doctors, nurses, lawyers and everyone else involved in the surrogacy during this process can be paid, but the woman who makes the most significant contribution (and notably the only contribution which is uniquely female) is expected to do so without being compensated for her inconvenience at all.

In other jurisdictions, a surrogate's right to make autonomous choices in respect of her own body (including as to payments for inconvenience) is viewed as her right rather than an undermining of her will. The California Supreme Court, for example, has said:

> The argument that a woman cannot knowingly and intelligently agree to gestate and deliver a baby for intending parents carried overtones of the reasoning that for centuries prevented women from attaining equal economic rights and professional status under the law. To resurrect this view is both to foreclose a personal and economic choice on the part of the surrogate mother, and to deny intending parents what may be their only means of procreating a child of their own genetic stock.[25]

It is time for us to take a similarly enlightened approach, which respects a woman's ability to make an informed choice to carry a pregnancy for someone else and to be compensated for her inconvenience.

It is notable that in related areas there has already been a softening of UK policy, and that such move for surrogacy might not therefore be an enormous leap. For example, the HFEA's introduction of a flat rate payment of £750 per cycle for egg donation in place of the previous requirement to pay actual identified expenses implicitly permits an element of payment for inconvenience (albeit not described as such) (HFEA, 2011b: para. 4.3). Egg-sharing arrangements, in which women can receive a subsidy of their own fertility treatment if they donate their eggs, also in effect involve an element of reward or compensation (HFEA, 2011a).

A map for the future

We need better law for managing surrogacy for UK parents, surrogates and children. There is a strong pragmatic case for reform. The law already, in practice, allows payments for surrogacy and takes a flexible

[25] *Johnson* v. *Calvert* (1993) 5 Cal.4th 84: 97.

fact-specific approach if the surrogate changes her mind, so why not allow this with more honesty and transparency? Doing so would allow us to have greater control to ensure that surrogacy is managed ethically and responsibly.

It would also remove the major incentives which are currently driving parents overseas. With the security of meaningful surrogacy contracts, a shift towards a more structured and managed process with openness about permitted compensation, and (hopefully) a resulting rise in the numbers of UK women prepared to become surrogates, fewer UK parents would need to go overseas. Our experience is that the vast majority of parents choose international options with reluctance, and would prefer to stay in the UK. Of course, international surrogacy will never disappear, but the numbers of UK parents going abroad would almost certainly be reduced if there were a safe and viable alternative in the UK.

But there is also an argument of principle: that surrogacy law needs reviewing because, with thirty years of experience, it is time to re-visit our initial reluctance about supporting it as a practice. We now know that surrogacy arrangements do not regularly result in the surrogate keeping the baby; that women can make informed rational choices to carry a pregnancy for someone else and be expected to honour that commitment; that surrogacy offers hope and the birth of a much-wanted child and that children are cherished and thrive in non-traditional families created by choice. If, at the base of our law, we have the attitude that surrogacy (where properly managed) is a benefit, our focus will be on how best to support it rather than how to discourage it.

We should therefore be focusing on encouraging well-managed surrogacy, something which can cross a broad range of factual scenarios, but which always involves a positive and appropriate balance of power in the relationship between the surrogate, the parents and any intermediary.

The United States offers perhaps the best model: there are processes to ensure that everyone is well-informed and advised at the outset (including medical and psychological screening and legal advice for all parties), and the agency acts as a professional facilitator of the direct relationship. While the professional aspects are commercially run, this does not mean that the relationship is purely contractual, and it is much more typical for parents and surrogates to form warm bonds. I have heard the US surrogacy system described as giving rise to a personal relationship between the surrogate and the parents which exists amidst commercially run professional services supporting that relationship, and this description is, in my experience, extremely apt.

Elsewhere, the balance of power can be less well managed. In India, for example, there is very little, if any, direct relationship between the parents and the surrogate, making the primary relationship between the parents and the clinic (which recruits the surrogates, many of whom are poor and illiterate, and houses them together, usually away from their families, in order to manage them closely throughout the process). While surrogacy may be a welcome and life-changing opportunity for Indian women, the clinic's power within the dynamic is disproportionate. Without regulatory safeguards, this creates a clear risk that surrogates may not be properly informed of risk, and may not be fairly or ethically treated.

By contrast, the current UK framework is not one which promotes an equally balanced relationship, with the surrogate's position given disproportionate weight and a lack of support and structure which makes surrogacy essentially an informal adventure. Parents and surrogates are expected to muddle through themselves and then, only after a successful outcome, resolve the legal position. Although the imbalance rarely results in the surrogate seeking to keep the baby, we have seen considerable practical difficulties. This includes surrogates who, once pregnant, demand increasing sums of money from parents who feel they have no choice but to pay (BBC, 2014); parents who proceed with fertility treatment without discussing critical issues (such as views on termination) because they are frightened of undermining their chance at parenthood and arrangements which break down because parents and surrogates have inadequate support for resolving relatively simple issues. Although many arrangements proceed smoothly, there is often considerable anxiety and distress which could easily be avoided.

What should a UK legal framework for surrogacy look like?

We should abolish the existing law on surrogacy in the 1985 Act and under the Human Fertilisation and Embryology Act 1990 and Human Fertilisation and Embryology Act 1990, as amended (2008) and replace it with new surrogacy legislation.

Surrogacy services

Those providing third party surrogacy services should adhere to a Code of Practice which ensures that prospective parents and surrogates are given accurate information, appropriate screening and support at the outset to ensure that they are suitable and sufficiently prepared, support throughout the process and appropriate help with dealing with long-term issues including future communication with the child and any long-term contact. However, surrogacy arrangements should continue to be permitted outside this framework (to enable individuals to engage in family arrangements and overseas arrangements without the involvement of a UK agency).

It should also be remembered that surrogacy is a form of reproduction, and that suitability-vetting for parents should be based on that for parents conceiving through assisted reproduction, rather than for those adopting unrelated children. Where conception takes place at a UK licensed fertility clinic, measures can be put in place for information regarding genetic and gestational parenthood to be recorded, in line with the procedures for gamete donation and the HFEA's Register of Information.

Surrogacy agreements

Intended parents and surrogates should be encouraged to enter into surrogacy agreements to agree key issues at the outset. Such contracts can be validated in a number of possible ways, for example, by requiring the parties to have a prior assessment or consultation with a psychologist or social worker (as in South Africa), and/or prior independent legal advice (as in many US states). Such measures can be validated by a court process which ratifies the agreement during the pregnancy (i.e. a pre-birth order, as in many US states).

Where the parties remain in agreement, this court order should enable the intended parents to be recognised as the legal parents immediately their child is born, and named as such on their child's original birth certificate. The value of this legal change is not to make contracts enforceable if the surrogate changes her mind, but to enable a streamlining of the process and a protection of the child's identity immediately from birth where all goes smoothly (as it does in the vast majority of cases).

Agreements should be available to those entering into surrogacy arrangements in the UK without the involvement of an agency (e.g. family arrangements), so that such arrangements are not excluded from the system, and a range of surrogacy choices remains available.

Thought should also be given as to how the pre-birth UK court process can be used by parents in international cases so that they can be recognised as legal parents from birth. This will ensure that appropriate nationality status is conferred promptly and will avoid children being stranded overseas or left with unresolved legal parentage.

A more sophisticated mechanism where things go wrong

Surrogacy disputes (which concern children) should not be arbitrated as if they were commercial contracts, and so, if either the surrogate or the intended parents wishes to dispute the arrangements agreed in the contract, the matter must be arbitrated by the family, rather than the civil, court. In cases where a challenge is brought, the family court should resolve parenthood and care arrangements based on the framework which applies to all other UK children proceedings (the child's welfare being paramount and assessed with reference to the statutory 'welfare checklist').[26] The family court is experienced in weighing and assessing competing interests on a case-specific basis, and already applies this framework in practice in surrogacy disputes as we have seen.

The law could limit the basis on which challenges can be brought (providing, e.g. that there must have been a change in circumstances) or there could be no such limitations, which would allow for a change of heart more generally. There could also be a time limit for challenging a surrogacy contract, perhaps within six months unless there are exceptional circumstances, to prevent applications affecting parentage being made long after the birth of a child.

As we have seen, the family court already has flexibility to deal with disputed surrogacy situations, and the change proposed would implement a change of presumption rather than enforceable surrogacy. The benefits are twofold: first, the court would have greater powers to deal with parenthood as well as care arrangements where there is a dispute (which would mean that children would not be not left in the care of adults who were not legally their parents, as they are now); second, the presumption would favour what we now know to be the more likely scenario (i.e. that there is no dispute) so that in those cases there is an immediate and appropriate recognition of parenthood.

With a proper framework to support the relationship from the outset, it would be hoped that the incidence of disputed cases (already rare) would be further reduced. The burden on the court system would also be lightened as against the current requirement for a complex court application even in cases where there is no dispute.

Payments

Parents should be permitted, if desired, to compensate their surrogate for her inconvenience (as distinct from making payments to buy a child). While it may be tempting to fix a maximum amount, in practice it will be difficult to police payments in a process which involves so much independent interaction between the parties. Facilitating honesty and transparency captured in a clear written contract is a much better approach.

It is interesting that in the United States, where payments for surrogacy are regulated by no more than market forces, the compensation

[26] Children Act 1989, § 1.

paid to surrogate mothers is reasonably standard ($25,000–$30,000 plus expenses) and little more than the £15,000 commonly paid to UK surrogate mothers. We see on the ground that the profile of compensated US surrogates is often very comparable to UK surrogates, with altruism often a significant motivator.

One of the major concerns about allowing payments is exploitation; in other words, that 'unsuitable' women who would not otherwise consider being surrogates might be coerced, by the offer of payment, to do so against their better interests. Such a view fails to appreciate that the risk of exploitation is much more complex. The offer of payment does not necessarily preclude an informed choice; and nor does the absence of payment ensure it. A much more sophisticated approach is to require regulated intermediaries to ensure that surrogates and parents are given good quality information about the risks and offered counselling to reflect on the long term commitment involved before they proceed. Regulation can also enforce other parameters if desired, such as age restrictions, health requirements and perhaps a requirement that the surrogate has completed her family or at least already had a child successfully.

Purely altruistic arrangements, where the surrogate does not wish to receive any compensation for inconvenience above her actual expenses (or even at all), should also be permitted provided the surrogate has been properly informed and not taken advantage of.

Alternative family forms

The above procedures should be available to single parents as well as couples, and to parents conceiving with donated eggs and sperm, so there is no requirement for the intended parents to use their own gametes. This would be consistent with wider law for parents building families through fertility treatment and adoption.

Thought needs to be given to the jurisdictional limitations. If there are no status restrictions, the UK could easily become a surrogacy destination (particularly within Europe) and this may not be desired. However, it would be sensible for eligibility to be founded on the basis of habitual residence in the UK as well as UK domicile (as is the case for adoption) as this would limit those cases where parents living in the UK are barred from securing their parentage here.

Conclusions

UK law originally aimed to discourage surrogacy practice generally, but at the same time provided a mechanism by which parentage could be resolved after the event, thereby supporting individual surrogacy arrangements which took place. The flaws of this system have been aptly demonstrated by the way the law has been applied in practice, and a comprehensive review of UK law is needed, particularly in the light of the international context.

A legally supported framework for surrogacy arrangements in the UK would allow no more than is already happening in practice. However, it would do so with clarity and honesty, and it would create a healthier balance of power between UK surrogates and parents which would help minimise the risk of exploitation. Where everyone agrees, it would provide a simple and straightforward process for securing children's legal identity within their families promptly, and enable children born abroad to be brought home to the UK quickly and easily. It would also remove the incentives which are fertilising international surrogacy and afford support in the UK at the right time to minimise the risk of difficulties occurring. And where, rarely, there are difficulties it would provide a more honest and appropriate mechanism for arbitrating them.

Surrogacy has long been viewed, unfairly, as a thorny and contentious issue. In fact, it is one of the most positive forms of human collaboration where properly managed, and the framework needed for more appropriate law in the UK is now obvious and straightforward. It is time for us to grasp the nettle and finally design a proper legal framework for surrogacy in the UK.

REFERENCES

BBC (2014). 'Fake surrogate mother Louise Pollard jailed'. Available at www.bbc.co.uk/news/uk-england-devon-27868511.

Bhatia, S. (2012). *Revealed: How More and More Britons are Paying Indian Women to Become Surrogate Mothers*. Available at www.telegraph.co.uk/health/healthnews/9292343/Revealed-how-more-and-more-Britons-are-paying-Indian-women-to-become-surrogate-mothers.html.

Brazier, M., Campbell, A. and Golombok, S. (1998). *Surrogacy: Review for Health Ministers of Current Arrangements for Payments and Regulation. Report of the Review Team*. Cm 4068. London: Department of Health.

Committee of Inquiry into Human Fertilisation and Embryology (1984). *Report of the Committee of Inquiry into Human Fertilisation and Embryology* ('Warnock Report'). London: HMSO.

Hague Conference on Private International Law (2014). *The Desirability and Feasibility of Further Work on the Parentage/Surrogacy Project*. Available at www.hcch.net/upload/wop/gap2014pd03b_en.pdf.

Human Fertilisation and Embryology Authority (HFEA) (2011a [2009]). *Code of Practice*, 8th edn. London: HFEA. Available at www.hfea.gov.uk/496.html.

Human Fertilisation and Embryology Authority (HFEA) (2011b). *Donation Review: Compensation of Donors and Benefits in Kind*. London: HFEA.

Warnock, M., interview by Martin Johnson and Sarah Franklin, 11 June 2008, interview C1324, transcript, The History of Mammalian Developmental Biology Interviews, British Library, London.

CASES

UK

A v. *P* (2011) EWHC 1738 (Fam).
J v. *G* (2013) EWHC 1432 (Fam).
JP v. *LP* (2014) EWHC 595.
Re C (A Minor) (1985) FLR 846.
Re G (Surrogacy: Foreign Domicile) (2007) EWHC 2814 (Fam).
Re L (A Child) (2010) 3146 (Fam).
Re N (2007) EWCA Civ 1053.
Re TT (2011) EWHC 33 (Fam).
Re X (A Child) (Surrogacy: Time Limit) (2014) EWHC 3135 (Fam).
Re X and Y *(Foreign Surrogacy)* (2008) EWHC 3030 (Fam).
H v. *S (Surrogacy Agreement)* (2015) EWHC 36 (Fam).

UNITED STATES

Johnson v. *Calvert* (1993) 5 Cal.4th 84.

UK LEGISLATION

Children Act 1989.
Children and Families Act 2013.
Human Fertilisation and Embryology Act 1990.
Human Fertilisation and Embryology Act 2008.
Surrogacy Arrangements Act 1985.

HANSARD REPORTS

HC Deb 2 April 1990, vol. 170, cols. 944–945.
HL Deb 13 June 2008, cols. 244–249.

Part II

How many children per donor?

8 Sperm donors limited

Psychosocial aspects of genetic connections and the regulation of offspring numbers

Tabitha Freeman, Vasanti Jadva and Jenna Slutsky

Introduction

Sperm donation enables a single man's gametes to be used to conceive multiple children in multiple families. Regulatory and ethical debates about whether to limit the number of offspring or families to be created from one donor – and if so, what that limit should be – have a long history. Although the specified limits, and the arguments for these limits, have varied over time and place, these discussions contain implicit assumptions about the meaning and significance of the genetic connections created through donor conception. In particular, perceived risks associated with the genetic connection between donor-conceived individuals who share the same donor – referred to in this chapter as 'same donor offspring'[1] – underpin widely accepted arguments for limiting donor offspring numbers. For example, in the UK context, these arguments have shifted from concerns about unintentional consanguinity to the psychosocial impact of the discovery of large numbers of genetic half-siblings (for further discussion, see Wright, Chapter 9). Despite the significance bestowed upon the genetic link between same donor offspring, it is only very recently that empirical evidence has become available on how these connections are perceived by those involved. Furthermore, beneath the argumentation, the specification of the actual maximum number of donor offspring has been viewed by some as arbitrary and unfounded, leading to calls for a more evidence-based approach.

[1] As will be discussed further, terminology in this area is very problematic. Although our preferred term in this chapter is 'same donor offspring', there are a number of alternative terms for donor-conceived individuals who share the same gamete donor. In particular, terms which stress the kinship dimension such as 'donor sibling' have gained wide currency, particularly in the United States. Furthermore, similar kinship terms have slipped rather uncritically into regulatory discourse: for example, in the UK, the Human Fertilisation and Embryology Act (1990), as amended (2008) refers to 'donor-conceived genetic siblings', which even in its own terms is misleading as these are technically genetic half-siblings.

The aim of this chapter is to present empirical findings from psychosocial research with donor conception families that may be brought to bear when considering the regulation of donor offspring numbers. To this end, we outline new data from our exploratory study of 'donor sibling' groups in the United States. This study comprises the first in-depth interviews with mothers of young donor-conceived children about their experiences of seeking and finding families who share the same donor: nine mothers were interviewed, including seven who had conceived by sperm donation, one by egg donation and one by both sperm and egg donation.[2] By drawing on this qualitative material, our discussion sheds light upon the different ways in which connections between families who share the same donor may be perceived and managed in practice, assessing the implications of these descriptive narratives for ethical and regulatory discussions about donor offspring limits. In doing so, the chapter seeks to question both the limitations of psychosocial evidence in informing regulatory and ethical debates as well as the limitations of regulation in defining the quantity and quality of the complex relationships created through reproductive donation. In order to set this discussion in context, the chapter opens by identifying key assumptions underpinning ethical and policy arguments for limiting donor offspring numbers and the empirical questions raised.

Regulating offspring numbers: policy and practice

Historically, arguments for limiting offspring numbers have principally concerned the risk of unwitting incestuous relationships between donor-conceived individuals who share the same donor. Up until the 1960s, these concerns were generally framed in terms of the risk of unlawful marriages between genetic relations; for example, as Richards describes in his account of UK governance of donor conception in Chapter 1, the Feversham Report (1960)[3] discusses the need to control the potential for 'unwitting incestuous marriages' (p. 12). Concerns about the illegality of these relationships subsequently gave way to medicalised concerns about unwitting procreation between genetic relations, or what is variously described as 'inbreeding,' 'half-sibling mating' or 'consanguinity'.

[2] As with much policy and research literature on donor offspring numbers, our discussion is principally focused on sperm donation, although we shall flag up issues raised by other forms of reproductive donation, such as egg donation and surrogacy, where possible.

[3] The Feversham Report (1960) was commissioned by the government to consider the moral and legal implications of the practice of artificial insemination and whether any change in the law was necessary or desirable. Further discussion of both the content of the report and the Committee which produced it can be found in Richards (Chapter 1).

Such concerns were largely presented in a vocabulary of genetic risk concerning the transmission of autosomal recessive disorders and other negative genetic outcomes. Whilst there was – and remains – varying opinions about the scale of these health risks, the overall impression is that 'expert' and 'lay' perceptions of the consequences of consanguinity may be out of kilter: as concluded in the Warnock Report, 'the true medical and genetic consequences of inadvertent incest or marriage within the prohibited degrees are often over-stated' (Warnock Report, 1984: 4.13).[4] An underlying reason for this disparity is that discussions of marital and procreative relationships between half-siblings necessarily tap into deeper cultural taboos concerning sexual relations between close family members. The incest taboo is deemed to be one of the true cultural universals, manifest in the prohibition of sexual relations between siblings and between parents and children.[5] The extent to which cultural anxieties about intra-familial procreation reflect medical 'realities' about the risks involved thus remains open to question; it may be more the case that 'scientific' legitimations are called upon to justify a cultural taboo.[6]

Not only are the risks of the potential outcomes of incestuous relations perceived to be both grave and over-stated, but the probability of such accidental incest occurring is deemed to be very low and controllable by limiting donor offspring numbers. Indeed, looking at the Feversham Report (1960) and the Warnock Report (1984), there is a certain confidence that controlling offspring numbers would reduce the likelihood

4 Alongside the risk of consanguinity, associated medicalised concerns that sometimes feed into debates about donor offspring numbers relate to the perceived need to curb the risk of donors transmitting genetically inherited disorders to large numbers of people. Whilst there have been some high profile cases of sperm donors passing on serious genetic disorders (e.g. Ahmad, 2012), it has been suggested that these risks are perceived to be greater than the actuality, especially as the screening of donors in UK clinics at least is regarded as thorough and effective (for further discussion, see Nuffield Council on Bioethics, 2013). A related discussion concerns the extent to which gamete donation impacts on genetic variation amongst the general population, where again arguments for limiting donor offspring numbers to minimise the potentially negative impact of donor conception have been challenged (see Janssens, 2003). In all these discussions, similar tensions between 'expert' and 'lay' perceptions of risk arise. For example, despite the screening of donors, many parents of donor-conceived children express concern over the potential impact of their child's lack of medical history, as do donor-conceived people themselves (e.g. Ravitsky, 2012).

5 There are of course numerous historical, cultural and individual examples of the incest taboo being broken; however, the deep-seated nature of this taboo is not in question. Discussions of the origins and significance of the incest taboo can be found in both anthropological and psychoanalytic literature; see, for example, Freud (1986 [1905]).

6 It is interesting to observe that concerns about consanguinity resulting from sperm donation largely relate to half-sibling relationships: the greater cultural taboo of potential parent–child (i.e. father–daughter) incest is rarely mentioned although this is also theoretically possible, especially at a time when men commonly donated sperm at a young age.

of incestuous relations to a negligible level;[7] for example, in the latter, 'unwitting incest between children of the same donor' is described as a 'remote possibility' with the associated risks being 'largely reduced by limiting the number of children fathered by one donor' (4.26). The determination of the actual numerical limit is also viewed as lacking firm empirical grounding, despite various attempts over the years to calculate the possibility of unwitting incest based on population demographics and modelling (e.g. Curie-Cohen, 1980; Hajnal, 1960). For example, the Warnock Report concluded that 'there was no conclusive argument for any particular figure' whilst agreeing the need to stipulate a number, so in the absence of any compelling reason, selected the limit of ten children per donor.[8]

Concerns about the risk of unwitting marital, procreative and sexual relationships between same donor offspring were forwarded at a time when donors were anonymous and donor-conceived people generally remained unaware of the nature of their conception. Whilst anxieties about 'donor sibling' incest remain prevalent in the public mind when considering donor offspring numbers,[9] regulatory debates now also foreground the potential psychosocial impact of the discovery of large numbers of offspring and half-siblings (Human Fertilisation and Embryology Authority (HFEA), 2011). The concern has thus shifted from potentially negative genetic outcomes of same donor offspring *not knowing* who each other is and *unintentionally* forming procreative relationships to potentially negative psychosocial outcomes of same donor offspring *knowing*

[7] The Feversham Report (1960) reasons that: 'If 2000 live children per year were to be born in Great Britain as a result of the successful use of AID and if each donor were responsible for 5 children, an unwitting incestuous marriage is unlikely to occur more than once in about fifty to a hundred years. Thus, even if there was a twenty-fold increase in the use of AID . . . the possibility that two children having the same father would marry would be remote . . . The number of incestuous marriages occurring as a result of AID would be much smaller than those resulting from fornication and adultery' (p. 12).

[8] The current UK limit of ten families per donor follows this recommendation although modifying the specified unit from ten children to ten families. This was largely for pragmatic reasons concerning difficulties of regulating offspring limits in practice; for example, due to parents' common wish to have further children using the same donor. This sense of the arbitrary nature of donor limits is also reflected in the extent of international variation in regulation. Whilst a couple of countries (e.g. Canada and Sweden) have no limits, most countries have specified limits but the number varies from three offspring per donor (e.g. Hong Kong and Singapore) and one family per donor (e.g. Taiwan), up to twenty-five offspring per donor (e.g. United States and the Netherlands) and ten families (e.g. UK, New Zealand and Victoria, Australia). One interesting pattern is that countries where the limits are lowest have anonymous donors whilst countries with highest limits have identifiable donors (Janssens, Nap and Bancsi, 2011).

[9] This is evident, for example, in the right of adults in the UK from age sixteen to check with the Human Fertilisation and Embryology Authority if they are donor conceived and if so, if they share the same donor as a potential partner.

each other and *intentionally* forming kin relationships. In part, this shift reflects wider changes in the cultural and regulatory climate; in particular, the greater openness around donor conception and the importance placed on 'genetic identity' and an individual's right to knowledge of their 'genetic origins'. In the UK, for example, donor anonymity was replaced by identity-release donation in 2005. This was swiftly followed by the introduction of the right of donor-conceived individuals at age eighteen to access identifying information about any other donor-conceived offspring conceived with their donor's gametes, provided that these 'genetic siblings' consent to such disclosure (Human Fertilisation and Embryology Act, 1990; Human Fertilisation and Embryology Act, 1990, as amended (2008)).[10]

As with arguments about the health effects of sibling incest, those about the psychosocial impact of discovering large numbers of half-siblings mask normative assumptions about the nature and significance of potential relationships between those who share the same donor. Why should the discovery of a large number of offspring who share the same donor be viewed as problematic, and what constitutes a large number? In itself, the identification of the relationship between those who share the same donor as 'half-siblings' ascribes kinship significance to these 'genetic' connections in social terms. Thus, whilst open to interpretation, a 'large' number seems to refer loosely to anything beyond the 'normal' maximum of siblings one might expect in a family unit. The very concept of 'donor sibling' is relatively new and illustrates the social contingency of kin relationships. For example, the recent cultural and regulatory emphasis on the potential significance of these half-sibling relationships does not give equal weight to comparable genetic connections: although a gamete donor's own child shares an equivalent genetic connection to any offspring conceived using his or her gametes, this half-sibling relationship has been relatively invisible in policy debates in the UK and elsewhere compared to the relationship between half-siblings who are both

[10] A further proviso is that the disclosure must not lead to the release of the donor's identity unless the donor also consented or provided gametes at a time when the regulations require this information be provided. Clearly the implementation of a donor-conceived individual's right to information about what this Act terms as their 'donor-conceived genetic siblings' depends on their being aware of their donor conception. Indeed, the various arguments about the introduction of identity-release donation both reducing the risk of unwitting incest and increasing concerns about the impact of the discovery of large numbers of half-siblings are generally premised on the unsubstantiated assumption that having identifiable donors will lead to parental disclosure. Although the actual impact of the removal of donor anonymity on parental disclosure rates has not yet been established, the contemporary climate has arguably given rise to the creation of both greater opportunities and a greater desire to seek out one's 'donor siblings', regardless of whether one was conceived using an anonymous or an identifiable donor.

donor-conceived. The contingency of social interpretations of genetic relatedness is further illustrated by the greater cultural and psychological significance seemingly attributed to half-sibling relationships created by sperm donation as compared to those created by egg donation.[11] Understanding the significance (or not) of these half-sibling relationships – and the number of half-siblings one has – depends on relative cultural and psychological meanings attributed to genetic relatedness. Regulators and policy maker contribute to this meaning-making process and can influence how these relationships are perceived.

The empirical grounding for concerns about the psychosocial implications of same donor offspring meetings is also very limited, perhaps inevitably so given that the formation of such connections is a relatively recent phenomenon (Freeman, Appleby and Jadva, 2012). A proliferation of positive stories of contact between 'donor siblings' in both the media and research has been reflected in a largely welcoming regulatory attitude towards facilitating such connections. However, there is as yet little evidence concerning the longer-term outcomes or indeed, of people's experiences of meeting large numbers of same donor offspring. Policy discussions tend to work on the assumption that meeting a moderate number of same donor offspring may be beneficial but that meeting too many may be overwhelming, although the exact nature of these concerns and negative outcomes are rather loosely defined.

Finally, when considering arguments about offspring limits, there are always somewhat less tangible, gendered concerns about the need to curb a man's potentially 'unlimited' reproductive possibilities. By contrast, female forms of reproductive donation (i.e. egg donation and surrogacy) are perceived, to a certain extent at least, to have 'natural' limits; the notion of a serial female propagator conjures up very different images to a serial male one. Indeed, although the aversion to a donor having multiple offspring may be cast in medicalised terms of genetic risk (see footnote 4), as ever, this veils more deeply entrenched cultural concerns. The idea of a man 'fathering' multiple children via sperm donation calls upon negative archetypes of men wildly 'spreading their seed' as an egotistical reproduction of self or a symbol of potency and dominance. Such images allude to dangerous and uncontrolled aspects

[11] Reasons for the contrasting perceptions of sperm donor siblings and egg donor siblings are very complex and touch on both quantitative and qualitative differences between these two forms of reproductive donation; for example, in terms of the greater numbers of sperm donor offspring compared to egg donor offspring and the different gendered meanings attributed to the genetic connections between donor offspring and their donors in the case of egg donation and sperm donation (for further discussion, see Freeman, Bourne, Jadva and Smith, 2014).

of male sexuality as well as cultural anxieties around 'feckless fathers' procreating without any notion of paternal responsibility, particularly in economic terms (Freeman, 2003). Such negative stereotypes are frequently played out in media representations of sperm donors, where cases of single donors 'fathering' large numbers of children are spotlighted as distasteful examples of unchecked masculine egotism, falsely dressed up as altruism and masking dubious sexual motivations. Of course, this is not just media sensationalism; there are several examples of men who have 'fathered' high numbers of children through sperm donation, including cases where men have been found to have sexually exploited women.[12] Although disproportionate media attention may be given to such 'extreme' cases, concerns about the 'seedy side' of sperm donation have a long history, with 'normal' sperm donors sometimes being viewed suspiciously and even being referred to as 'perverts' or 'psychopaths' (Haimes, 1993).[13]

Our aim in this chapter is to pull together new empirical insights regarding psychosocial aspects of the genetic connections between same donor offspring that may be valuable for regulatory discussions around donor offspring numbers. As this overview of the regulatory and ethical arguments suggests, several assumptions are made about these psychosocial considerations that are open to empirical question. What is the risk that same donor offspring will unwittingly meet and establish relationships? Is this a calculable risk or an unwarranted fear that donor conception families experience? What motivates same donor families to seek contact with each other? Are there any risks in making these connections? If so, are these risks exacerbated by the number of offspring found? What is the psychosocial impact of meetings between same donor offspring? Are there any negative outcomes when same donor families meet? What are the longer-term outcomes of the developing relationships between same donor offspring? What terms are used to describe

[12] For example, at the time of writing, a UK professor reported as 'fathering' fifty-eight children as a private sperm donor has been convicted of two counts of sexual assault. At the same time, widespread media attention has been given to recent HFEA figures concerning donor offspring numbers; for example, the Daily Mail ran a headline that 'Britain's top 500 UK sperm donors have "fathered" more than 6,000 children between them – and some have twenty children each' (Hodgekiss, 20 August 2014).

[13] It is pertinent in this context to note that the reference to sperm donors as 'psychopaths' was taken from the Feversham Report, which said of sperm donation, 'it is an activity which might be expected to attract more than the usual proportion of psychopaths' (quoted in Haimes, 1993: 87). Considerations of sperm donors' motivations impact on regulation: for example, in the UK at least, the historical tendency has been to package 'altruism' as the only acceptable motivation for donation, as evidenced by a deep reticence to promote financial payment. Further discussion of the regulation of the 'good donor' is found in Graham et al., Chapter 10.

these relationships? An 'evidence-based' answer to these questions will depend on how connections between donor relations are perceived and negotiated in practice by the people and families involved. We now turn to our empirical data to explore these issues further.

Psychosocial aspects of limiting donor offspring numbers

The empirical findings reported in this chapter derive from an exploratory study conducted within the north-eastern United States. Semi-structured interviews were carried out with a sample of mothers who had conceived at least one child by gamete (i.e. sperm and/or egg) donation, recruited through assisted reproduction support organisations, including one specifically for 'solo mothers by choice' (i.e. women who conceive a child without a partner). Nine mothers, ranging in age from thirty-nine to fifty-eight years (mean age forty-seven years), were interviewed in total, of whom seven were solo mothers and two were in a heterosexual couple; all mothers identified as heterosexual except one solo mother who was bisexual. All mothers had carried one full-term pregnancy, of which four resulted in twins. The thirteen resulting children (six female, seven male) ranged in age from nine months to ten years (mean age three and a half years). Of these nine families, five were members of the Donor Sibling Registry (DSR), an online forum that enables families created by 'anonymous' donor conception to seek families who share the same donor as well as the donors themselves. Six families reported that they had connected to varying numbers of same donor offspring, one family had searched but found no relations and two had not yet attempted to locate same donor offspring. While same donor offspring were largely clustered in age, the group sizes varied significantly from one to at least twelve known same donor offspring. Same donor offspring tended to be geographically concentrated, although there were several exceptions with donor sibling groups distributed both across the United States and internationally.

Before considering the findings, it is worth commenting on the high proportion of solo mothers in this sample and the low ages of their offspring. Although as an exploratory, qualitative study with a small sample, no claim for representativeness is being made, the focus on solo mothers might still be viewed as limiting the wider value of these findings for discussions about donor offspring limits in other family types. However, not only do solo mothers now constitute a significant and increasing proportion of donor conception families, but research with solo mother families may be particularly informative because both parents and offspring in these families have been identified as having high levels of interest in 'donor relations' (Freeman et al., 2009; Jadva et al., 2010): since discussions about donor offspring limits focus on outcomes when donor-conceived individuals make contact with each other, it is instructive to explore the experience of groups who are most likely to seek contact. Further, although research ascertaining offspring's own perspectives is of vital importance,[14] it is also prescient to access parents' perspectives since, as the experience of the DSR suggests, it has been parents of young children who have been the driving force behind making these connections. Finally, whilst family structure should be viewed as significant contextual information for interpreting the following empirical data, as will become apparent, there is a great deal of individual variation in the meanings attributed to genetic connections between same donor offspring that is not reducible to the gender, sexuality or marital status of their parents.

What are parents' motivations for forming connections between same donor families?

In line with previous research (Freeman et al., 2009), a variety of reasons for wishing to establish contact with same donor families were raised in the interviews, including curiosity, the child being an only child and simply because it seemed easy and there was no reason not to. Mothers often described searching on behalf of their children in case they wished to seek these connections in the future. As one mother explained:

> I just realised there's nothing lost in contacting them at this point. If we all get along, it's great, you know we'll have the contact, if we don't then we can all back off, leave it to the kids when they become older and understand the concept more . . . I've made a lot of decisions that, you know, are conventional, unconventional that affected [daughter]'s life and I wanted her to have as many answers as she could . . . I think there's a lot of information and solidarity that can come from siblings, other kids in the same situation. (Solo mother by sperm donation)

This sense of community, solidarity and information that can be gleaned from making contact with these families was a key theme in the narratives, emerging in different ways. For example, mothers may have concerns about their child's future health and welcomed the opportunity to exchange medical information with other families who had used the

[14] It is particularly important to gain insight into the perspectives of adolescents and young adults who may be in the position to make decisions about whether or not to seek contact with same donor offspring. The authors are currently conducting such a study with donor-conceived adolescents in the United States and preliminary findings will be referred to where relevant.

same donor. Indeed, one of the most fascinating insights from this study is that parents are using these connections to counter their lack of knowledge about the donor, especially in medical terms: meeting other families and seeing the health and characteristics of same donor offspring can be reassuring. Parents may also seek same donor families to find more vials of their donor's sperm.[15] Thus whilst parents' and offspring's interest in same donor offspring is often perceived as being greater than their interest in the donor, our findings suggest that the two may be closely interlinked.

How are connections between same donor families being made?

Mothers' narratives of how connections between families were forged and the quality of the 'donor sibling' networks that developed were unique. Families reported a diverse and decentralised process of first locating, then initiating contact with same donor families. Parents may embark on a search for same donor offspring at various points in their child's development. One mother chose to seek same donor offspring *prior* to her child's birth, while another still demonstrates a reticence ten years after the birth of her children. Routes to initiating contact also vary and may be complex. Whilst three mothers reported locating families through the DSR, two mothers were met with disappointment when the DSR yielded no matches, only then to locate donor siblings through their sperm banks' private forums. In addition, one mother who located a same donor family through the DSR explained how one family served as a sort of 'connector' to no fewer than three other same donor families. The lack of a centralised US system for locating donor relations contributes to an unpredictable pattern of donor sibling networking as well as a lack of certainty about the true number of same donor offspring. It also demonstrates that parents and families will seek different ways of forming connections, despite the regulation within the particular jurisdiction. A particularly poignant example is that of seeking 'pre-conception' connections with families who have, or are intending to use, the same donor, enabling a degree of planning and choice about whom one's child's donor relations might be. The intentional use of the same donor may therefore act as a mechanism for creating new forms of kinship relationships and communities extending beyond the traditional isolated nuclear family model.

15 In the United States, it is possible for parents to buy additional vials of their donor's sperm to store in case they want to use it to have further children.

How common are unwitting meetings between same donor offspring?

In this small sample, there were two reported instances of unwitting or accidental meetings of mothers who conceived, or were pregnant, with the same sperm donor. In one case, the mothers had initially met each other through a solo mother support group, only finding out that they had conceived by the same donor after being re-introduced by another mutual donor sibling parent. Likewise, another mother was re-introduced by a donor sibling mother to a long known acquaintance before discovering that their children had the same donor. In our ongoing study with DSR members (see footnote 14), we have so far come across two more instances of such meetings within a sample of thirty families.

The unexpectedly high frequency of accidental meetings between same donor families encountered in our research raises questions about what has previously been viewed as the 'remote' possibility of same donor offspring unwittingly meeting and forming relationships. Our current sample was based in the United States, where the unregulated commercial donor conception market contributes to large numbers of offspring being conceived from one donor. Some donor sibling groups of over a hundred have been reported (Freeman et al., 2014), which, even if offset against the large population overall, is perhaps not insignificant. However, there are a number of other contributing factors that may impact on the likelihood of unwitting meetings including the similarity in age between same donor offspring, the localised concentration of donor conception families and the catchment areas of particular clinics and sperm banks. As such, it is possible that same donor offspring will meet at a later age and establish friendships without being aware of their 'genetic connection', for example, through attending the same school or college, and there are some anecdotal examples of this happening. Whether or not these meetings may also lead to unwitting intimate relationships remains unknown, although it seems the former confidence of its near impossibility may have been undermined. A trace of earlier anxieties around sibling incest also hangs over these discussions. For example, the controversial phenomenon of 'genetic sexual attraction' (i.e. the experience of sexual attraction between genetic relations) that has been reported in cases of adoption reunions involving birth parents and children or siblings who have grown up separately (Greenberg and Littlewood, 1995), could be perceived as a risk with donor sibling meetings and indeed, with meetings between donors and their donor-conceived offspring.[16]

[16] This is an extremely controversial area, open to anecdote and speculation. Although there is as yet little publicly available evidence regarding the extent of this form of

Although both donor conception parents and offspring are generally aware of the issue of consanguinity, their perception of the extent of this risk may vary. Within the current sample, the risk of consanguinity was mentioned, although commonly expressed with a relaxed stance. One mother remarked that although she has not yet pursued same donor offspring, she wonders how many siblings exist, acknowledging with a tone of acceptance that:

> I think [my children] are gonna have to have DNA testing when they go to have a child, because who knows? Because I know that the female donor donated a lot. And she's not that far away, I mean who knows . . . maybe they'd be attracted to someone that's from their make up. (Heterosexual couple mother by egg donation)

A solo mother's concerns about consanguinity were tinged with resentment towards heterosexual couples who 'are embarrassed to tell because the husband was infertile'. Thus she views consanguinity as a result of parents' failure to disclose rather than an inevitable consequence of gamete donation.

How is contact between same donor families being established?

Once initial contact has been made, families report even more diverse narratives of navigating these novel and complex relationships. As with previous research (Freeman et al., 2009), a consistent finding is of initial hesitancy as parents come to know and trust each other and gradually grant donor relations greater access to their family. After first emailing, contact often shifts to more intimate settings, such as phone calls or face-to-face meetings. Some parents report large gatherings bringing together groups of families who share the same donor. Only after testing the relational waters do repeated meetings and shared holidays sometimes follow.

Transitions in mothers' feelings about contact were a frequent theme, both in the relief from anxiety some mothers experienced on meeting and the sense that these meetings exceeded their expectations. Initial trepidation about embarking into what one mother described as 'unchartered territory', could be replaced by a sense of intimacy, warmth and connectedness. One solo mother explained, 'it is stressful to meet people that you have this connection with that you might have a life-long connection to and have no idea who they are or whether you're gonna

incestuous experience, there is some suggestion that a confusion of sexual boundaries may occur when 'donor relations' meet (Freeman et al., 2014).

like them', but now considers her child's same donor offspring to be 'in the family'. Another described how she 'didn't think we would have a connection that was like family members . . . it's definitely become more than I thought'.

There could, however, be discrepancies in parents' feelings about meetings within what are sometimes referred to as 'dibling' groups, with some mothers reporting how others had initially been very 'cautious', 'guarded' or 'hesitant'. For example, one mother described the first mother she contacted as 'very nice', but 'very concerned about privacy and so it made it very awkward feeling'; by contrast, she described another mother as 'very open . . . it's actually been very easy, very welcoming'. Furthermore, the evolution of these relationships was not necessarily linear. Dependent on numerous factors ranging from the practical (e.g. geographic distance) to the emotional (e.g. feeling connected or distant from other parents), mothers emphasised their sense of agency in managing such connections. They regulated the degree of intimacy according to their comfort level while simultaneously carefully cultivating these relationships should their young children grow to desire them in the future. Indeed, only one mother in this study made reference to an 'instantaneous' bond between her child and 'his half-brother'. More frequently, the connections between the same donor offspring were viewed as having the potential to become more meaningful should their children wish to pursue them.

What are the outcomes when same donor families meet?

Positive outcomes of meetings between same donor families have been fairly well documented (Freeman et al., 2009; Jadva et al., 2010) and are widely quoted in the literature on donor offspring limits as providing evidence for the benefits of enabling connections between 'donor siblings' and conversely, of the minimal risks of negative psychosocial outcomes (Janssens, Nap and Bancsi, 2011). However, the limitations of this empirical evidence and the caveats that need to be born in mind when interpreting these findings can sometimes become lost (Freeman, 2015). More in-depth studies shedding light on the complexities of the relationships between same donor families over time are required and indeed, in the current study, parents report various relationship complications.

In particular, as these relationships are primarily viewed as optional, parents and children appear to evaluate their donor relations in terms of their degree of alignment in personality and thought. Whilst similarities and complementarities can lead to the formation of close relationships, divergences potentially lead to conflict. For example, one mother reported disliking her daughter's donor sibling but maintained the relationship both in the hope that the child might mature and out of fondness for this child's mother. Also, within a network, same donor offspring might develop dyadic relationships of differing qualities, feeling a greater sense of loyalty and affiliation to some. The dynamics and complexities of these new relationships can lead to the sorts of complications commonly observed in more 'traditionally' conceptualised families and friendship groups (see also Wright, Chapter 9); indeed, as a same donor network grows closer, both positive and negative aspects of familial relationships emerge. Furthermore, these relationships are not static over the long term; for example, one mother described changes in their network following the recent separation of the 'connector' couple, a lesbian couple whose separation reverberated beyond their family unit into the same donor network.

What is the quality of the relationships between same donor families and does the number of offspring have any impact?

Mothers expressed different perspectives on the psychosocial impact of the number of same donor offspring found. Some highlighted the benefits of large groups in terms of giving greater choice about which families to connect with, whilst others expressed a preference for the intimacy of smaller groups. For example, a solo mother who had connected with one family describes:

> I'm both lucky and unlucky in that some of my friends where there's 20 families you can like some of them and not like some of them . . . I'm lucky because I don't have a choice in a way or unlucky 'cause this is who I have. But it also it makes it special, I mean it's hard to have this relationship with 10. (Solo mother by sperm donation)

As with any other interpersonal relationship, it appears that a multitude of factors contribute to shaping the quality of these relationships and indeed, whether or not a relationship evolves in the first place. As one mother describes:

> Just because you share genetics doesn't mean you're best of friends . . . You know some siblings bond and some don't. (Solo mother by sperm donation)

In the above quote, having a genetic connection is not deemed to be sufficient to lead to the creation of a social bond. By contrast, the following quote illustrates how the genetic link may be attributed a fundamental role when close kin relationships are formed:

I would have never believed that just having a shared gene would make people bond like that but they were completely bonded and they have been incredibly close ever since, totally sibling like.

The contingency of the meanings ascribed to the genetic connection between same donor offspring underpinned the high levels of perceived agency and choice exercised in establishing, maintaining and negotiating these relationships. Whilst choice potentially has negative connotations of transience or a lack of commitment, it is perhaps more fitting to see the connections between same donor offspring as a flexible, elastic form of kinship.[17] Indeed, the conscious choice to ascribe psychosocial significance to these genetic connections could form the basis of a positive sense of commitment and obligation between these mothers, echoing more traditional family relationships. As one mother articulates:

It is my choice to have a relationship. I could say it doesn't matter to me, we just bought the same pair of boots . . . I chose to give it significance . . . I think we're gonna be in each other's lives for you know for the long haul . . . I feel an obligation to her [mother of same donor offspring], I mean in the most – not in a negative way. I feel connected to her and I've chosen to make it important. (Solo mother by sperm donation)

A mutual sense of obligation, support and friendship could also develop amongst a larger group, leading to a sense of community that appeared to arise as much from the shared enterprise of having children as from having a shared donor:

We're kind of a convenience family. None of us picked the other ones to sort of be parents of relatives, but at the same time, our kids are related. But on the other hand, like if you have a family member that you really don't like, you can't necessarily avoid them. These guys, I mean, it's all voluntary so there's nobody in the group I dislike. Everybody that I talk to seems perfectly nice, we're all of course focused on our babies. Some of them are different from me. I don't know how close we'll be as the kids grow, but I mean we have something very important in common which was that all of us have very wanted children that we dote on. (Solo mother by sperm donation)

Whilst the 'voluntary' nature of these commitments could also lead to a degree of selectivity as well as a degree of ambiguity and uncertainty about their long-term future, in the main, their present benefits appeared to outweigh the potential harms.

Although these relationships echo both the strengths and tensions of other types of interpersonal relationships, mothers also articulated

[17] This interplay between choice and commitment is reminiscent of other accounts of assisted reproduction families and kin relationships, such as Donovan, Heaphy and Weeks (2001) and Carsten (2004).

some of the specific complexities of seeking to establish these new and hitherto 'undefined' forms of kinship connections. For example, parents might disagree on the appropriate nature of the relationship, as well as the preferred terminology for referring to each other, although frequently such disagreements were resolved. Whilst discussions over terminology give fascinating insight into the complexities of negotiating these relationships, it is not always possible to read off the emotional weight given to these connections from the terms used. Indeed, the crux of the problem was often perceived to be the lack of any adequate terminology, with some mothers preferring to use familiar terms like 'cousin', particularly in public contexts, because it demands no explanation, whilst others opted to develop their own hybrid terms like 'dibling' or 'brousin' for use amongst themselves. Furthermore, it is clear from these narratives that whilst some parents were open to using sibling terms like 'brother' or 'sister' for those with whom their children had bonded, for others, the use of such kinship terminology was wholly inappropriate:

> I wouldn't call her a sister and in fact doing so would make me feel actually really weird and uncomfortable. (Solo mother by sperm donation)

> The other families call them all brothers and sisters like 'oh here's your brother'... They're just not brother and sister. In my mind the relationship is what I would consider a cousin type of relationship... I've always really tried not to use words that are not true. And to me a sibling relationship, a real sibling relationship, has a social component, so I guess it doesn't feel true to me to say brother and sister... It just carries like some kind of expectation that I am not ready to fulfil. (Solo mother by sperm donation)

This distancing of same donor offspring from being a 'sibling' in any meaningful sense is a useful reminder that regulators should not be too swift to assume that these genetic connections will be experienced and perceived to be more important than social connections. Indeed, whilst genetically equivalent to a conventional half sibling relationship, the social meaning attributed to the connections between same donor offspring is very much open to interpretation by those involved.

Conclusions

The empirical data presented in this chapter highlight the problematic nature of regulating the number of offspring conceived from any one donor based on assumptions about the meaning of the potential relationships between donor offspring. Indeed, even with a small sample, it is evident that there is a great deal of individual variation in the significance that is – or is not – attributed to the genetic connections between same donor offspring and how these relationships are – or are not – played out. Whilst establishing these connections may bring unanticipated benefits for all involved, providing supportive communities between parents and potentially meaningful close relationships between donor offspring, there is no guarantee how these relationships will work out. Indeed, it is evident that a variety of factors come into play and it is therefore likely that people's notions of a desirable number of same donor offspring will also vary.

Whilst our discussions have shown that concerns about the psychosocial impact of having large numbers of 'donor siblings' are hard to quantify, there is clearly scope for further research. Within this sample, the number of same donor offspring found ranged from none to twelve; empirical data from parents and offspring who have discovered larger numbers would be informative, as would research tapping into the perceptions of donor offspring themselves. Indeed, there are indications from our ongoing study with donor-conceived adolescents that larger numbers of same donor offspring can sometimes be experienced as 'too many', perceived as overwhelming or a source of revulsion to some. Furthermore, there is evidence that if these groups connect with the donor, donors themselves may find high numbers of donor offspring unmanageable, leading to instances where donors have imposed a maximum number of offspring with whom they are willing to establish contact (Freeman et al., 2014). Not only does this suggest that images of donors thoughtlessly creating large numbers of offspring for dubious reasons are probably misplaced, it illustrates that when considering donor offspring limits, it is vital to consider donors' perspectives too. As we have suggested, issues that arise concerning the relationship between same donor offspring are closely interlinked with issues concerning the connection between offspring and the donor.

Whilst longstanding regulatory and ethical concerns about unwitting incest are also hard to quantify, as instances of accidental meetings between same donor offspring families come to light, it becomes harder to dismiss the possibility. The common assertion that such risks can, and have been, reduced with the introduction of identity-release donation rest on rather tenuous grounds. Even if a donor-conceived individual is aware of their donor conception – and to this day, that is far from always being the case – to expect or assume that they will disclose the nature of their conception to potential romantic partners seems unreasonable and insensitive.

As well as suggesting that the empirical evidence for or against raising donor offspring numbers is limited, our discussion also highlights the limits of regulation itself. In particular, the agency of individuals to seek and define connections is evident in these mothers' narratives, as are the potential unintended consequences of regulatory interventions. For example, access to same donor offspring gives parents and offspring a means of creating 'families of choice' (Weston, 1991), a flexible concept of kinship that may be taken a step further by developing such networks at a preconception stage. In addition, access to same donor offspring may provide a new source of pooling and exchanging information about the donor that may reduce or even negate the significance of seeking the donor's identity.

Even where carefully considered, regulation is further limited in practice by the wider economic and commercial environment of donor conception. Localised concerns about shortages of eggs and sperm and the increasingly global donor conception market place competing pressures on the management of donated gametes; at the same time, the growth in cross-border donation and internet connection websites for linking potential recipients and donors open up new avenues for seeking gametes. Indeed, in part due to the introduction of identity-release donation, there has been a growing demand for greater choice about donors from recipients; conversely, donors themselves may wish to exercise choice about who, and how many people, they help to conceive. Whilst in the UK, individual clinics are expected to monitor the usage of donated gametes to ensure that the individual limits are not exceeded, this may be hard to track in practice. Such constraints have given rise to both 'over-use' and 'under-use' of sperm.[18]

Within such a context, it is perhaps advisable to adopt a cautious approach to regulating donor offspring numbers. As this chapter has highlighted, understandings of what an appropriate number of offspring per donor should be rest on cultural and individual assumptions about the meaning of genetic connections. Therefore, rather than chasing conclusive evidence about whether or not to alter donor offspring limits, it is perhaps better to focus our attention on further understanding why some people wish to seek same donor offspring and what contributes to positive and negative outcomes when they do so. It is also important to recognise that regulation is itself part of this process, contributing to the complex cultural, social and personal framework in which people navigate the relationships that may be created through assisted reproduction. Therefore, any change regarding offspring number limits should be considered carefully in terms of the potential messages this may send out regarding the (in)significance of these connections.

[18] Whilst it is hard to get accurate estimates, most HFEA-registered sperm donors are used to create one or two families in the UK (HFEA, 2011). For further discussion, see Wright, Chapter 9.

REFERENCES

Ahmad, A. (2012). 'Danish sperm donation law tightened after donor passes on rare genetic disease'. *BioNews*, 675.

Beeson, D.R., Jennings, P.K. and Kramer, W. (2011). 'Offspring searching for their sperm donors: how family type shapes the process'. *Human Reproduction*, 26, 2415–24.

Blyth, E. and Frith, L. (2009). 'Donor-conceived people's access to genetic and biographical history: an analysis of provisions in different jurisdictions permitting disclosure of donor identity'. *International Journal of Law, Policy and the Family*, 23, 174–91.

Carsten, J. (2004). *After Kinship*. Cambridge University Press.

Curie-Cohen. M. (1980). 'The frequency of consanguineous matings due to multiple use of donors in artificial insemination'. *American Journal of Human Genetics*, 32, 589–600.

Donovan, C., Heaphy, B. and Weeks, J. (2001). *Same Sex Intimacies: Families of Choice and Other Life Experiments*. London: Routledge.

Feversham (1960). Home Office and Scottish Home Department. *Report of the Departmental Committee on Human Artificial Insemination*. Cmnd 1105. London: HMSO.

Freeman, T. (2003). 'Loving fathers or deadbeat dads? The crisis of fatherhood in popular culture', in Earle, S. and Letherby, G. (eds.), *Gender, Identity and Reproduction: Social Perspectives*. Basingstoke: Palgrave Macmillan. 33–49.

Freeman, T., Jadva, V., Kramer, W. and Golombok, S. (2009). 'Gamete donation: parents' experiences of searching for their child's donor siblings and donor'. *Human Reproduction*, 24, 505–16.

Freeman, T., Appleby, J.B. and Jadva, V. (2012). 'Identifiable donors and siblings: implications for the future', in M. Richards, G. Pennings and J.B. Appleby (eds.), *Reproductive Donation: Practice, Policy and Bioethics*. Cambridge University Press.

Freeman, T., Bourne, K., Jadva, V. and Smith, V. (2014). 'Making connections: contact between sperm donor relations', in Freeman, T., Graham, S., Ebtehaj, F. and Richards, M. (eds.), *Relatedness in Assisted Reproduction: Families, Origins and Identities*. Cambridge University Press.

Freeman, T. (2015). 'Gamete donation, information sharing and the best interests of the child: an overview of the psychosocial evidence'. *Monash Bioethics Review*, 33, 45–63.

Freud, S. (1986 [1905]). 'Three essays on the theory of sexuality', in Freud, A. (ed.), *Sigmund Freud: The Essentials of Psychoanalysis*. London: Penguin.

Greenberg, M. and Littlewood, R. (1995). 'Post-adoption incest and phenotypic matching: experience, personal meetings and biosocial implications'. *British Journal of Medical Psychology*, 68, 29–44.

Haimes, E. (1993). 'Issues of gender in gamete donation'. *Social Science and Medicine*, 36, 85–93.

Hajnal, J. (1960). 'Artificial insemination and the frequency of incestuous marriages'. *Journal of the Royal Statistical Society. Series A (General)*, 182–94.

Hertz, R. and Mattes, J. (2011). 'Donor-shared siblings or genetic strangers: new families, clans, and the internet'. *Journal of Family Issues*, 32, 1129–55.

Hodgekiss, A. (2014). 'Britain's top 500 UK sperm donors have "fathered" more than 6000 children between them – and some have TWENTY children each'. *Daily Mail*, 20th August.

Human Fertilisation and Embryology Authority (HFEA). (2011). 'Donation review – family limit', Human Fertilisation and Embryology Authority Paper, HFEA (13/07/2011) 604.

Jadva, V., Freeman, T., Kramer, W. and Golombok, S. (2010). 'Experiences of offspring searching for and contacting their donor siblings and donor'. *Reproductive BioMedicine Online*, 20, 523–32.

Jadva, V., Freeman, T., Kramer, W. and Golombok, S. (2011). 'Sperm and oocyte donors' experiences of anonymous donation and subsequent contact with their donor offspring'. *Human Reproduction*, 26, 638–45.

Janssens, P., Nap, A. and Bancsi, L. (2011). 'Reconsidering the number of offspring per gamete donor in the Dutch open-identity system'. *Human Fertility*, 14, 104–12.

Janssens, P. (2003). 'No reason for a reduction in the number of offspring per sperm donor because of possible transmission of autosomal dominant diseases'. *Human Reproduction*, 4, 669–71.

Nuffield Council on Bioethics (2013). *Donor Conception: Ethical Aspects of Information Sharing.* London: Nuffield Council on Bioethics.

Ravitsky, V. (2012). 'Conceived and deceived: the medical interests of donor-conceived individuals'. *The Hastings Center Report*, 42, 17–22.

Sawyer, N. and Macdonald, J. (2008). 'A review of mathematical models used to determine sperm donor limits for infertility treatment'. *Reproductive BioMedicine Online*, 14, 411–17.

Sawyer, N. (2009). 'Who's keeping count? The need for regulation is a relative matter'. *Fertility and Sterility*, 92, 1811–17.

Sawyer, N. (2010). 'Sperm donor limits that control for the 'relative' risk associated with the use of open-identity donors'. *Human Reproduction*, 5, 1089–96.

Scheib, J.E. and Ruby, A. (2008a). 'Contact among families who share the same sperm donor'. *Fertility and Sterility*, 90, 33–43.

Scheib, J. and Ruby, A. (2008b). 'Beyond consanguinity risk: developing donor birth limits that consider psychosocial risk factors'. *Fertility and Sterility*, 91, 12.

Warnock, M. (1984). Report of the Committee of Inquiry into Human Fertilisation and Embryology. Cmnd 9314. London: HMSO.

Weston, K. (1991). *Families We Choose: Lesbians, Gays, Kinship.* New York: Columbia University Press.

LEGISLATION

Human Fertilisation and Embryology Act 1990.

Human Fertilisation and Embryology Act 1990, as amended 2008.

9 Limiting offspring numbers

Can we justify regulation?

Katharine Wright[1]

Introduction

The question of what limit should be placed on the number of people who can be born as a result of sperm or egg donation from a single donor, or indeed whether there is any place for such a limit in regulation, is a contested one (Human Fertilisation and Embryology Authority (HFEA), 2011). Drawing on the empirical evidence presented earlier in this collection by Freeman, Jadva and Slutsky (Chapter 8), this chapter will explore the ethical issues at stake, in particular those relating to the perceived harms of higher or lower donor offspring limits, and the associated questions that arise as to the role of the state in intervening in what many see as a private domain. These issues will be considered from a variety of perspectives, including those of donor-conceived people themselves, of parents and prospective parents, of donors and of those tasked with the responsibility of regulating donor conception practices.

As I will go on to discuss later, the choice of terminology with respect to the genetic connections created when people are conceived as a result of donation is highly value-laden. In this chapter, I will use the expressions 'same donor offspring' or 'donor siblings' to refer to people living in different social families but genetically connected via the same donor, and I refer to 'limiting offspring numbers' as a shorthand for 'limiting the number of people who can be born as a result of sperm or egg donation from a single donor'. In doing so, I recognise that the terminology of 'offspring' is itself not uncontentious.[2]

[1] I am Assistant Director of the Nuffield Council on Biorethics and I draw on the Council's 2013 report on 'Donor conception: ethical aspects of information sharing'. However, I write here in a private capacity.

[2] 'Offspring' is thus used here to describe the biological progeny of a man or woman, both during childhood and adulthood, in the absence of any relationship of nurture and care. In general usage, however, 'offspring' may be used to refer to the children of anyone, without necessarily implying the absence of conventional parent/child relationship (essentially the gender neutral equivalent of 'son' or 'daughter'). The issue of whether a donor's *naturally* conceived children should 'count' when considering offspring limits is alluded to later in this chapter, and demonstrates the terminological challenges in this field.

Defining the issue

To start at the beginning: why might it be thought necessary or appropriate to limit offspring numbers? As Freeman, Jadva and Slutsky note in Chapter 8, the rationale offered to justify the need for regulatory limits has taken very different forms over time. In the early days of donor conception, when anonymous donation was the norm, the main anxiety expressed in connection with high, or no, limits on offspring numbers related to anxiety about the risk of inadvertent consanguineous sexual relationships between donor-conceived people. Such relationships might arise either because one (or both) parties to the relationship did not know that they were donor-conceived, or because even if they did know, they had no access to information about their donor. Thus this first concern might be characterised as the need for *avoidance* between people who share a donor, for fear of the consequences of inappropriate relationships. Clearly the lower the number of people 'sharing' the same donor, the easier it would be for each to avoid the others.

More recently, however, as social policy and regulation in a number of countries has shifted towards identity-release donation,[3] anxiety about limiting offspring numbers has taken a very different form: that of concern about the implications of managing relationships with large numbers of genetic half-siblings ('donor siblings' or 'same donor offspring') born as a result of donation from the same donor. Fears are expressed that it may become very burdensome to create and maintain these relationships if there are 'too many' of them. In some cases, anxieties are also expressed that too many half-siblings might limit or impair the prospect of any kind of meaningful relationship with the donor and his or her own family (see Freeman, Jadva and Slutsky, Chapter 8). Thus the nature of the problem appears to have been turned on its head. Instead of the need for *avoidance*, the difficulties associated with high or no limits on offspring numbers derive from the value placed on the *creation* of family-like relationships based on genetic connection, and the difficulties inherent in making those relationships meaningful if they come in large numbers.

Alongside either or both of these competing sets of concerns, a third anxiety may also commonly arise: that of discomfort with the idea of

[3] Particularly within Northern Europe (e.g. in Finland, the Netherlands, Sweden and the UK) and in Australia and New Zealand. The shift, however, is far from universal, and other European countries such as France and Belgium actively mandate anonymity. The United States provides a contrasting approach in that whether or not donors are anonymous or identity-release is entirely driven by consumer demand, and not seen as a matter for regulation (see Glennon, Chapter 3; Graham, Mohr and Bourne, Chapter 10; Nuffield Council on Bioethics, 2013: paragraphs 2.30–2).

the multiple donor as 'weird' or distasteful. A person who is willing, or indeed enthusiastic, to help create very high numbers of offspring is often regarded with some suspicion: their motivations are regarded as dubious, and their behaviour seen as feckless. Parental views reported in a recent Australian study illustrated this anxiety vividly: 'I get images of . . . what is the right word? You know, like wacko priest type prophet cult sort of numbers. You know, like that one bloke can create 100 children' (Millbank, 2014).

It is clear, even from this very brief sketch of the various reasons presented as justification for regulation to limit offspring numbers, that there is a great deal more to be said, both in terms of exploring just what is *actually* at stake in each case, and in terms of analysing the assumptions implicitly embedded in the expression of those concerns. For example, it is worth considering how we understand and value genetic connections that arise independently of any social relationship, and what we believe the proper role of regulation to be. Before we start to explore these questions in more detail, however, two important points need to be made.

First, while the rationales cited to justify limiting offspring numbers have evolved in a way that would have been quite unimaginable fifty years ago, it cannot be assumed that this 'shift' has now been completed: that the first set of concerns identified above has been entirely replaced by the second. While concerns about inadvertent consanguinity have their roots in anonymity and secrecy, and desires to form meaningful relationships with genetic half-siblings have developed out of greater openness and access to donor information, the picture is nevertheless much more complicated than that. To begin with, it is important to recognise that anonymous donation has not, itself, been consigned to the past. Donor conception services cross national boundaries, and despite the growing emphasis on identity-release donation, there are still many countries where anonymous donation is the norm (see Graham, Mohr and Bourne, Chapter 10). It is not very difficult for British families to travel to Spain for treatment, if they wish to do so. Moreover, where regulatory change has taken place to introduce identity-release donation, it still takes a generation for such change to take full effect. Even those conceived immediately after the UK's introduction of identity-release donation in 2005,[4] for example, have yet to reach their tenth birthdays. Perhaps most importantly, though, it is crucial to note that 'identity-release' donation and parental disclosure to children about their origins are far from the same thing.

[4] Through the *Human Fertilisation and Embryology Authority (Disclosure of Donor Information) Regulations 2004*, SI 2004/1511.

'Identity-release' donation means that donor-conceived people may, on reaching the age determined by their national law, obtain identifying information about their donor. However, they will not do so if they have never been told by their parents that they are donor-conceived – and the evidence suggests that there are significant numbers of parents who do not feel able to talk to their children about the way in which they were conceived (e.g. Readings et al., 2011; Sälevaara, Suikkari and Söderström-Anttila, 2013). So there may still be plenty of donor-conceived people whose donors are potentially identifiable, but who do not in fact know that they are donor-conceived. On the other hand, to complicate the picture further, most of the evidence available about connections being made and relationships formed between donor siblings derives from donor-conceived people who do *not* have regulatory access to identifying information about their donor, but who have joined matching services such as the Donor Sibling Registry (DRS) (see Freeman, Jadva and Slutsky, Chapter 8). Such connections can be made in the absence of identifiable donor information through the use of unique donor codes which enable donor-conceived people to 'match' themselves both with their donor (if he or she has registered on the same database), and with any donor siblings who have chosen to register. These donor codes are widely available in the United States, but are no longer made available in the UK because of concerns that they could be used to subvert the regulatory regime by potentially facilitating contact between donors and donor-conceived people during the latter's childhood (HFEA, 2009).

The second point to make relates to gender. While it is generally assumed that the question of offspring limits arises primarily in connection with *sperm* donation, this should not be taken for granted: the small-scale study presented in the earlier chapter by Freeman, Jadva and Slutsky, for example, included at least one egg donor (who 'donated a lot'). However, it is the case that almost all the empirical evidence available, such as that from the DSR, relates to sperm donation, and at points in what follows, questions of gender do arise.

Possible harms: consanguinity

The question of *harm*, and the ethical imperative to avoid, or at least minimise, harm as much as possible, is a common thread in all the reasons offered for limiting offspring numbers. In order to consider how best to minimise harm to all those concerned with donor conception practices, it is essential to obtain a clear idea of the nature of the potential harms identified. The correlation of 'harm' and consanguineous relationships is perceived so widely that the actual nature of that harm is rarely explored.

However, as Freeman, Jadva and Slutsky note in their earlier chapter, these concerns actually derive from two quite distinct sources. The first is *medical*: it appears to be very widely taken for granted that children born as a result of a consanguineous relationships are almost bound as a result to suffer from serious genetic disorder (Nuffield Council on Bioethics, 2013). However, such an assumption may greatly overstate the *specific* risk in any particular case.

A pattern of reproduction within close families, such as regular cousin marriage, is certainly likely to lead to greater prevalence of otherwise rare genetic disorders: the *Born in Bradford* study, for example, found that cousin marriage led on average to an increase from 3 to 6 per cent of children born with congenital medical conditions such as heart or lung problems (Sheridan et al., 2013). In short, the more the parents share common genes, the greater the risk that a genetic mutation associated with a particular condition will be found in their child. Cousins on average share 12.5 per cent of their genes (although this will be higher in populations where cousin marriage is repeated throughout the generations), while same donor offspring share 25 per cent of their genes. The empirical risk of a child developing a recessive genetic condition has been put at 8–10 per cent if the child's parents are half siblings, although it would of course be higher if one of the parents was known to be a carrier of a particular condition (Saggar and Bittles, 2008). This is not an insignificant level of risk – but it seems unlikely that an equivalent degree of risk would *automatically* prevent couples outside the context of donor conception choosing to have children together. So, it may well be the case that these widely expressed medical concerns are actually a proxy, cloaked in respectable 'scientific' language, for another anxiety: the universal *taboo* on sexual relationships between siblings (see Freeman, Jadva and Slutsky, Chapter 8).

Such an analysis prompts a further question about what it is we understand by 'harm'. Medical or physical harms may be the easiest forms of harm to recognise and seek to guard against – but they are not the only kind of harms that 'matter'. Social or psychological harm as a result of breaching cultural taboos may be just as damaging to the individuals concerned. The fact that a particular practice is either forbidden or promoted in a particular culture does not, of course, render it immune from challenge, whether at the level of the individual or society. The current worldwide campaign against the practice of female genital mutilation, with its known terrible physical and psychological harms, provides an example of how deeply embedded practices and beliefs *can* be challenged. Given the widespread acceptance of a taboo on sibling sexual relationships, however, such a challenge seems unlikely – and it is certainly not the intention of this chapter to argue in favour of one. The point at stake here is that, whatever the medical consequences for any resulting children, inadvertent consanguineous relationships undoubtedly pose a threat of social and psychological harm to those entering into them.

The next question, then, in this exploration of possible harms is to identify the likelihood of this particular harm eventuating. No 'hard' figures relating to consanguineous relationships exist, and Freeman, Jadva and Slutsky (Chapter 8) allude to the imperfections of the existing statistical models used to estimate how likely initial chance meetings between donor siblings might be. Thus, they note, while the 1960 Feversham report estimated a risk of an 'incestuous marriage' arising once every fifty or hundred years in the UK, estimations based simply on the annual number of donor-conceived people born do not take account either of the increasingly globalised nature of sperm exports, nor of social factors that may lead to localised concentrations of donor-conceived families.[5] Nevertheless, the HFEA was satisfied in 2011 that the actual risks were low and 'that the risk would probably remain low unless the limit was increased greatly' (HFEA, 2011, paragraph 8.6). The Nuffield Council on Bioethics reached similar conclusions (Nuffield Council on Bioethics, 2013).

Does that mean, then, that the concerns generated by the risk of consanguineous relationships can thus be safely ignored? The quick answer must be 'no'. The argument was made very powerfully in evidence to the recent Nuffield Council Working Party on sharing donor information that, however statistically low the risks, there is a genuine *fear* among donor-conceived people and their families about the possibility of their inadvertently entering into a relationship with a donor sibling. That fear itself is a source of harm. And even though the perceived risk (however low in practice) may be reduced further by increased openness in families and knowledge about donors, it may still be unrealistic to imagine that donor-conceived young people will make careful enquiries before entering into a new relationship. Indeed, the number of people applying to the UK Human Fertilisation and Embryology Authority for this information (to which they have been entitled since regulation began in 1991) is very small.[6] So it seems likely that the question of the risk of consanguineous relationships may represent a latent anxiety – not necessarily acute, but nonetheless real – for many donor-conceived people. The scale of that

[5] See also HFEA (2011) for a helpful overview of the various statistical modelling methods used, and the associated limitations.

[6] Human Fertilisation and Embryology Authority (HFEA) (2014). Personal communication.

anxiety may be directly affected by knowledge of the existence of controls over the numbers of donor siblings who may be 'out there'.

The discussion above sought to identify more precisely the *nature* of the harm that might arise from a consanguineous relationship. The fact that we have identified such a harm (albeit in rather different terms from those generally expressed) does not, of course, of itself demonstrate a rationale for the state, or other regulator, to intervene. There are multiple interests involved in donor-conception: those of donor-conceived people, certainly, but also those of the parents of donor-conceived people, 'potential parents' seeking treatment and donors. The Nuffield Council report argued strongly that any analysis of the interests at stake in donor conception must take account of all such interests, and that there could be no justification for *automatic* prioritisation of the interests of one party, although a case might be made to privilege one over the other in any particular set of circumstances. So, having analysed the nature of the harm presented by the risk of consanguineous relationships, and the extent to which those harms may be increased by higher (or no) limits on the numbers of children born from one donor, we need to set that against any competing harms or benefits. We return to this point after discussing other potential harms.

Harms: managing multiple relationships

The question of how many 'donor siblings' along with their families is acceptable (or beneficial, or problematic) is one that has attracted considerable recent attention, and the views of a number of US families on this volume in Freeman, Jadva and Slutsky's chapter (see Chapter 8) cast a fascinating light both on the *actual* relationships being developed between donor-conceived families, and on the *prospect* of such relationships. (It is noteworthy that a number of families interviewed in Freeman's study sought early contact with families 'just in case' their children, when older, might want to take advantage of this.) Companion data from Australia, focusing directly on the views and experiences of 18 families created through sperm donation with respect to limits on same donor offspring, has also recently been published (Millbank, 2014). It is useful to be able to draw on the empirical evidence reported from Australia alongside that from the United States, because of the very different regulatory regimes: most of the parents taking part in the Australian study had created their families under a regime of identity release donation, while anonymous donation remains the norm in the United States. However, the fact that families from both countries had drawn on donor/sibling linking services (the DSR and private sperm bank registers) to make sibling connections via their unique donor number illustrates how the actual *identity* of the donor is not necessarily part of the equation. It also highlights how the children born from donors' own relationships tend to be excluded from the discussion of 'donor sibling' relationships, although the degree of genetic relationship between donor-conceived people and the offspring of their donor is clearly just the same as that between donor siblings.

The empirical accounts set out by Freeman, Jadva and Slutsky (see Chapter 8) and Millbank provide a vivid illustration of the way families[7] approach the question of making contact with other families formed with the help of the same donor, and what it is they value (or think their children will value) in these contacts. All the conversations reported in the studies, in which parents describe their motivations and experiences, are implicitly framed by particular assumptions about the inherent *value* of genetic connections. By suggesting either that more or fewer donor siblings (and their associated families) are either a good or a bad thing, value is implicitly being placed on genetic connection *per se*: that is, on a connection that is *purely* genetic with no necessary social element. Until one donor-conceived person, or their parents, seeks out a donor 'sibling', there is no social connection or relationship with that person or their family. Seeking out and creating that connection is an entirely voluntary act.[8]

How does that (potential) connection compare with the connections a person may have with distant and unknown members of their social family? I suggest that it is completely different in kind. Imagine, for example, your connection with a second cousin whom you have never met. You may not even know each other's name, but there *is* some kind of social connection between you, because at some point up the family tree there will be *existing* social connections that carry some emotional weight. Your mother may have known their mother or father well, growing up as first cousins. If not, your respective grandparents are siblings and have a whole lifetime of shared family experiences, good, bad or indifferent. Such 'vicarious' family connections are likely to matter if the intervening connections matter (and, conversely, *not* matter if the connections in

[7] The data in both sets of studies relate only to the voice of parents making contacts on behalf of their (mainly still young) children, and the reported experiences of their children. Millbank notes a lack of qualitative (as opposed to survey-based) data on the experiences of donor-conceived adults. She also suggests that the experiences of today's adults, who grew up under different regulatory regimes with no expectation of obtaining identifiable data about their donor or about any same donor offspring, may not be a good guide to how these connections are experienced by future generations.

[8] See, for example, the report in Chapter 8 of the mother who says: 'It is my *choice* to have a relationship. I could say it doesn't matter to me . . . I *chose* to give it significance'. (emphasis added)

between are unimportant or associated with negative emotions). So, for example, I may feel some degree of connection with my unknown second cousin because I love my granny, and I know she loves her nephew, who is the father of that cousin. With that sense of connection may also come a sense of (at least limited) responsibility: in the example above, I may feel it is right to offer hospitality to my unknown second cousin if she happens to be visiting my home town because she is 'family'. I would argue, however, that any such sense of responsibility derives not from the 'fact' of genetic connection with my second cousin, but from the intervening social connections that link the two of us together.

What does this say about the inherent value of genetic connections that have no pre-existing social element? The evidence presented to the Nuffield Council Working Party made very clear that people have diverse attitudes to the meaning of genetic connection: for some, the fact of a genetic link with another person is incredibly important; for some, it is a source of mild curiosity; and for some, genetic connection alone means nothing (Nuffield Council on Bioethics, 2013). The value to be placed on finding and creating relationships with 'donor siblings' simply cannot be assumed as an agreed starting point for the debate on offspring limits. For some people, the knowledge that there are donor siblings 'out there' whom they have not met will be a source of major regret; but for others it may be a matter of supreme indifference.

Just as it is important to identify the way that the debate around connections between same donor offspring is framed, it is similarly crucial to dig deeper into the *language* used to describe those connections. In cases where connections have been made by families whose children are still very young, some parents have reported that their children create an instant 'sibling-like' connection. But what is *meant* by a 'sibling-like' connection? Not all siblings get on with each other or play well together. Plenty of children, particularly of similar ages, appear to bond quickly and play together when they first meet: think, for example, of big multigenerational gatherings like weddings, where children tend quickly to find each other and head off to do something rather more interesting than hanging around the grown-ups.

It is quite easy to imagine how the positive relationships being formed between donor 'siblings', described in the surveys, might equally well be found in parallel situations where questions of genetic connection do not arise. One example might be that of a group of school or university friends who no longer live near each other, but still meet up regularly, and whose children hence get to know each other – perhaps through annual picnics or even a week's holiday away together. Another could be children linked through their mothers' ante-natal group: many first-time mothers, despite having little in common when they first meet, bond over their shared experience of childbirth, and give each other mutual support in the early months and years. Some of these relationships continue on indefinitely, creating a point of contact between their children who have known each other all their lives, and who are the same age to a matter of days. It seems plausible, at least, to advance the argument that the bond of sympathy reported both indirectly by parents of young donor-conceived children, and directly by donor-conceived adolescents and adults (Blyth, 2012; Jadva et al., 2010) might relate just as much, or more, to similarities of age and shared experience (including perhaps a sense of 'difference' from traditional families), as to shared genes.

Similarly, it is instructive to compare the reported experiences of the parents in the earlier chapter (Freeman, Jadva and Slutsky, Chapter 8) with respect to larger or smaller groups of donor sibling families, with other circumstances where families may come together. Some parents described a large group of donor siblings as being beneficial, as this enabled them to 'choose' which families to connect with; thus, implicitly discarding the prospect of relationships with the others without much anxiety at the loss of possible connections for their child. Others commented on the 'intimacy' of smaller groups. Such considerations could easily arise in all sorts of other social groupings: for example, where one set of parents meet other parents through their children's school or clubs, and form relationships that transcend the initial cause of their encounter with one another. Thus, while the fact of genetic connection might be one explanation lying behind how these relationships work (and it is clear that in many cases they *do* work), another plausible explanation could be that the 'donor in common' acts simply as a *trigger* for connection. That trigger for the initial encounter may then lead on to highly successful relationships where families and/or individuals 'click' with each other; or may result in little or no ongoing contact where that bond of sympathy is not found.

It is very important to emphasise that nothing in this analysis acts to undermine the *actual* value of such relationships, where formed, whether on a child-to-child or family-to-family basis. However, the extent to which genetic connection, as opposed to some kind of shared experience or trigger for connection, is the *necessary* basis for that successful relationship is at least open to question. Clearly, the extent to which these successful relationships are founded on, rather than triggered through, that genetic connection is highly relevant in terms of the extent to which regulators might be under an ethical obligation to influence such relationships, whether through limiting or promoting them.

Finally, in considering the potential harms of large 'sibling' groups, it is informative to look at the *language* used by both the children and parents in the reported studies. The use of the term 'sibling', or 'brother' or 'sister', was used by some families, but strongly resisted by others who took the view that these terms should be reserved for what were perceived to be quite different relationships. The popularity of the term 'cousin' to describe the connection between the children, by contrast, is striking, on a number of counts. First, it puts a certain amount of familial distance between the children: they are part of the 'family', but certainly not on a par with a full or social sibling, for example. Second, it suggests a degree of *choice* in terms of the level of intimacy: we may see some cousins every weekend, and others only every twenty years. Third, it raises very clearly the question of legitimate numbers. It is not so long ago in the UK that eight or ten children were a usual number in a family; and such large families still exist. If each parent is one of ten children, then the next generation may have up to eighteen sets of cousins, even leaving aside any re-marriage or step-families. This in turn brings the potential count of first cousins (let alone second cousins) in the hundreds rather than the tens.

Summing up on the harms

Where then does that leave the analysis of the potential harms arising out of large or unlimited groups of donor siblings? Looking first at the potential 'burden' of creating and maintaining contact with a large sibling group, it is clear that the extent to which this is a burden at all depends on the value placed on the genetic aspect of the connection. Where genetic connections are understood primarily as a trigger for contact, and any subsequent social relationships developed and maintained as a matter of mutual choice, then a wider choice of such relationship opportunities may not in itself be burdensome at all. On the other hand, if genetic connection is understood as creating an *inherent* obligation to cultivate a meaningful relationship, then it is easy to see how a large number of such relatively close genetic connections pose a potential psychological burden – particularly on donor conceived people themselves who, unlike their parents, had no choice about the situation in which they find themselves. And if a relationship with the *donor* is desired (either instead of, or alongside, relationships with donor siblings) then numbers do matter. It is clearly impossible for a donor to maintain more than a paper relationship with large numbers of donor offspring, even if he or she wishes to do so.

This shift from a focus on the possibility of relationships with donor siblings to that of the potential relationship with the donor himself or herself, serves to highlight a critical question in the analysis of whether there is an ethical imperative to control the number of same donor offspring.

This is the question of just *what* the connection between the donor and the donor-conceived person is, or ought to be.

The very clear underpinning assumption of regulation, both in the UK and elsewhere, is that a donor is *not* a parent. It is recognised (in some jurisdictions at least) that some donor-conceived people will feel a strong inclination for information about, and possible contact with, their donor. However, the fact that this information is only available (other than in 'known donor' cases) once the donor-conceived person reaches adulthood supports the regulatory position that the donor is not a 'parent'. The unease felt with the notion of a donor 'fathering' (and in this case the discussion is limited to sperm, rather than egg, donors) eighty or one hundred children seems at least partly to arise because, at least at the back of our minds, we are thinking of the donor as having some kind of 'parental' role or responsibility.[9]

And then, quite apart from what regulation intends us, or assumes us, to feel, there is the question of what people *actually* feel. Along with the question of the burdens or benefits of creating or maintaining relationships with donor siblings, there is the important further question of how donor-conceived people actually feel about the *concept* of those multiple donor siblings whether or not they know them. One donor-conceived person who gave evidence to the Nuffield Council Working Party felt strongly that it was dehumanising to be one of a hundred offspring of the same person: 'like cattle'.[10] If this were a wide-spread feeling (and we lack evidence on this point), then, like the fear of consanguineous relationships, it should be taken into account in terms of the psychological implications of donation for the people who result from it.

Implications for regulation

When considering what, if any, limits should be placed on the number of people who may be born with the help of one donor, it is not enough to identify the harms potentially associated with high, or no, limits. It is also necessary to explore, and justify, the *role* that is claimed for regulation. Is the role of regulation to prevent serious identifiable harms? Or to

[9] Note the findings reported in Almeling (2014) about the number of sperm donors who described themselves as 'fathers', in contrast with egg donors who do not see themselves as 'mothers'. It is arguable that these differences in self-description arise not because of any differences in terms of 'parental' feeling towards donor offspring, but because of an implicitly gendered understanding of these terms with respect to procreation and nurture: it is impossible to use the term 'mother' without also implying a nurturing role, while 'father' may be used both in that nurturing sense, but also simply to mean progenitor.

[10] Nuffield Council, Personal communication.

'hold the ring' between competing interests? Or to impose a particular normative stance on what it is to be a family, and what it means to share a genetic connection?

It is relatively uncontroversial to argue that regulation should aim to prevent serious identifiable harms. Many would also agree that regulators (whether state, professional or any other) should also attempt to strike a fair balance between any competing interests, although the *extent* to which intervention in the private lives of individuals to achieve this aim is regarded as acceptable will depend on a person's view on how intrusive the state should be. The third role – that of imposing a particular normative stance on the nature of families or the value of genetic connection – is at first sight highly controversial. However, it is critical to recognise that it is almost impossible for regulators to *avoid* this third role if they are to regulate at all. By taking an explicit stance on the issue to which the regulation relates (in this case, the maximum number of children, or number of families, who may be born as a result of one donor), the regulator also *implicitly* endorse particular values (in this case the moral significance to be placed on that connection between donor, recipients and donor-conceived people). It is very difficult indeed to regulate without some underpinning normative view about the broader context in which the regulated activity takes place. Thus, you cannot regulate with respect to the number of 'donor siblings' a person can have, in the absence of *some* normative assumption as to what a person's relationship with those 'siblings' ought to look like or indeed whether 'sibling' is an appropriate term at all.

The Nuffield Council report on information sharing in donor conception takes a view of the state as having a 'stewardship' role (Nuffield Council on Bioethics, 2013). Such a role is contrasted with a 'laissez faire' approach to regulation that leaves as much as possible to personal choice and negotiation between individuals, and a 'nanny' state, which would intervene directly to achieve particular outcomes that were deemed best for people. Instead, it is argued, a stewardship states seeks to be facilitative: to make it *possible* for people to do particular things if they wish to do so, without seeking to enforce those behaviours (at least in the absence of very strong justification). A stewardship approach potentially overlaps with a 'nudge' approach to public policy (Blumenthal-Barby and Burroughs, 2012) but need not. Thus, to take a public health example, a stewardship state might try to nudge people into adopting healthier diets through 'fat taxes', but it could also facilitate higher levels of physical activity by creating safe walking routes to schools or providing public sporting facilities without any attempt to nudge people into using them.

While a stewardship state is less intrusive than a nanny state, value judgments are still inevitably involved in determining what it is that the state should facilitate or promote. In some areas these judgements are relatively uncontroversial, such as in the physical activity examples cited above. In others, the underpinning normative judgements on which state action is based are clearly much more contested.

How might stewardship work with respect to donor conception? The Council's report suggests that, since the UK government has *already* explicitly endorsed the value judgment that it is right to encourage family creation through donor conception (both through the creation of a facilitative regulatory regime and the provision, at least to a limited degree, of services in the National Health Service (NHS)), then it should also take positive action to promote the welfare of people born as a result of donor-conception. At the same time, the Council's Working Party was concerned not to imply that that welfare could *only* be secured by information about genetic connections. Rather, it was argued that it should be a matter for each donor-conceived person to determine the value he or she placed on such connections.

The Working Party used this rationale to justify the existence of duties on the state both to retain a regulatory approach to donation that mandated identity-release donation, and to maintain accurate registers of donor information. While not all donor-conceived people want to find out about the donor when they reach adulthood, some do, and there is no way of knowing in advance who will and who won't. A stewardship state should thus ensure that information is available for those donor-conceived people who want it, while avoiding any implication that people 'ought' to want it. In coming to this conclusion, the Working Party also took into account the potential impact on both donors and recipients of abolishing anonymity and ensuring the collection and maintenance of donor information. A particular concern that arises repeatedly in this field is that of shortages of donor gametes. Had there been good evidence that mandating identity-release donation, or requiring minimum levels of personal information from donors, was genuinely the cause of shortages, there would have been a significant harm to potential parents unable to have children to balance against the benefit to those future donor-conceived people who might want information. The evidence available, however, suggested that difficulties in accessing donor gametes were much more complex, and that informational requirements being placed on donors were not a critical factor. It was thus much clearer what route a stewardship state should take with respect to mandating the collection of information about donors.

What might a similar analysis do with respect to limits on numbers of children born as a result of one person's donations? Those countries whose regulatory systems facilitate donor conception have, implicitly or explicitly, chosen to recognise donor conception as a legitimate means of creating a family. Alongside that normative stance should therefore run a concern for the welfare of the donor-conceived people born as a result of these policies, and for others directly affected. That would suggest both that action should be taken to ensure that donor-conceived people do not suffer from serious harm as a result of regulatory action (or lack thereof); *and* that the interests of all those concerned in donor conception should be taken into account, with the aim of achieving a regulatory stance that fairly balances all these interests.

The first part of this chapter focused on the possible harms of high, or no, limits on same donor offspring numbers. In brief, these can be summarised as: exacerbating fear of inadvertent consanguineous relationships (where the fear is real even if the actual risk is low); potentially contributing to a sense of dehumanisation (albeit with little evidence as to the scale of this concern); and the potential for the creation of too many families for 'real' relationships to be created either between same donor offspring, or between offspring and donor. The comparison with the number of cousins a person might have suggests that, even accepting (for the sake of argument) that genetic connections in the absence of any social relationship create 'family-like' connections, the harm of a large number of such connections is far from obvious. On the other hand, where social relationships are desired between donors and their donor-conceived offspring, then numbers *will* matter.

Having analysed these potential harms, and the justification for regulators to act where possible to promote welfare, we need to turn to the final part of the jigsaw, and consider what other interests might be at stake to which regulators should pay attention in seeking to 'hold the ring' in this field. In what ways, if any, might limits on same donor offspring affect others, whether positively or adversely? The main arguments put forward in favour of high, or no, limits on numbers of same donor offspring arise out of the value to be placed on 'reproductive autonomy', that is, the freedom to reproduce without interference by others. I suggest that any concern about interfering with the 'reproductive autonomy' of a *donor* can be dismissed very quickly. Being actively prevented from having your *own* children, at whose birth you acquire a set of legal and moral responsibilities, is a very serious matter. Parenthood is widely seen as a normal, and highly significant, part of a life trajectory. It is hard to see how the same can be said about having a limit placed on the number of times a person chooses to donate.[11]

[11] The same response might be made with respect to any claims of *financial* detriment to donors in jurisdictions that permit payment. While it is a serious matter to limit

For *prospective parents*, however, questions of reproductive autonomy are potentially very weighty indeed if the limits placed on the numbers of same donor offspring prevent them from receiving treatment, and hence being able to have a family at all. If this *were* the case, then prospective parents would have a very strong interest indeed in higher limits, and all the considerations relating to the potential, or perceived, harms of higher limits discussed above would need to be weighed against these countervailing harms.

This consideration returns us to the question touched on briefly above, as to the extent of 'shortages' in availability of gametes: that is, the mismatch between the availability of donor gametes and demand from prospective parents. However, while there are regular media stories relating to shortages of gametes, the Nuffield Council's Working Party concluded that the availability of donor gametes depended directly on the efforts taken by clinics to recruit donors: in short, that where the recruitment and treatment of donors was taken seriously, clinics were indeed able to meet the needs of prospective parents (Nuffield Council on Bioethics, 2013). Poor recruitment practices in many clinics may further be exacerbated by the commercial nature of many donation services, which have no incentives to co-operate with each other over access to gametes. In the UK context, a possible solution to these, essentially practical, challenges has recently been put forward with the creation of a new NHS-based sperm bank designed to offer an integrated recruitment, screening and banking centre to benefit prospective users across the whole UK (National Gamete Donation Trust, 2014). Moreover, while official statistics are sometimes difficult to interpret, it is clear that in both the UK and Australia, use of donated gametes falls short of existing regulatory limits on the number of families that may be created (Millbank, 2014).

The arguments for removing or increasing offspring limits based on concerns about shortages of donor gametes, do not, therefore, in practice, seem strong. Some might claim, however, that reproductive autonomy for prospective parents does not lie merely in simple access to donor sperm or eggs, but also in the prospect of having a *choice* of donors. Most of the parents taking part in Millbank's study of Australian families, for example, commented that they had little choice of local (sperm) donors, especially given that they had to bear in mind that their child might later choose to meet their donor (Millbank, 2014). With this in mind, they

a person's ability to earn a living, any active *entitlement* to earn that living through acting as a donor seems weak in the extreme when balanced against other interests at stake (whatever view you take on the permissibility of payment for donating eggs or sperm).

were concerned to choose a donor who 'seemed like a good person', one whose 'values were broadly in accord with their own', or indeed one that did not 'repulse' them (Millbank, 2014; see also Graham, 2014). Some recipient families in Millbank's study described having only one donor to 'choose' from, having excluded several others because of these kinds of concerns.

What value, then, should be ascribed to 'choice' for recipients? It is interesting to note that these questions seem to arise much more often in connection with sperm donation rather than in egg donation. Moving into the realms of speculation, might this be because very limited choice in egg donation has long been accepted as the norm, certainly in countries where strict limits have been placed on financial reward or compensation with respect to gamete donation? In other words, is it the case that, where choice is not routinely available, its absence is not perceived as a problem? Such a picture contrasts with that of the availability of a wide choice of donor sperm through international sperm banks, made possible because of the ease with which sperm may be frozen and transported between countries. The fact that an increasing number of the families being created through sperm donation are 'non-traditional' families (single mothers by choice and lesbian couples) may also be a factor in the increasing focus on 'choice', given that concerns about similarity of appearance with the infertile husband (the dominant point of concern in the era of anonymity) are inapplicable. All the single women participating in Graham's study found it a 'bizarre and surreal' experience to select a stranger to help create your child (Graham, 2014: 222). It is not a situation that arises in 'traditional' family creation.

A different angle on the question of choice is prompted by those who promote 'genius' or 'Nobel prize winner' sperm banks (Plotz, 2005). If certain donors are seen as particularly desirable, should more prospective parents be able to make use of their services? A considered analysis of the ethical questions at stake in such sperm banks (in particular in connection with concerns about so-called 'designer babies' or eugenic intentions) is beyond the scope of this chapter. However, these examples are helpful in distinguishing between what prospective parents might see as particularly *desirable* in a donor in the hope of their child's genetic inheritance (whether in terms of appearance, educational achievements, profession and so forth – and regardless of the scientific basis of such hopes), and what they might see as *necessary* for their child's welfare. The impact on parents of the introduction in some jurisdictions of identity-release donation should not be underestimated. Such (prospective) parents now know that the prospect of their child later making contact with the donor is a given: part of the 'package' of creating a family in this way.[12] I would therefore argue that, if the only choice of donor offered to prospective parents was someone with whom future contact would be genuinely troubling, then their reproductive autonomy would indeed be affected. The prospect of such future contact is simply not an issue that parents in 'traditional' families who are able to have their families without recourse to donor gametes have to worry about: it is a concern specific to those creating their families with donor gametes. On the other hand, most parents, however their families are formed, would like their children to be geniuses, or at least successful in their chosen field. The fact that there are many reasons why they cannot control how their children turn out does not mean that their reproductive autonomy has been compromised.

Thus, I would suggest that prospective parents' reproductive autonomy might indeed be affected if the limits on same donor offspring were so low, and hence choices were so restricted, that they were unable to find a single donor with whom they could contemplate future contact by their child without alarm. Given the existence of international sperm banks, quite apart from new public sector initiatives such as the NHS Sperm Bank mentioned above, it is, however, difficult to imagine this situation arising in connection with donor sperm (and, as noted above, it is striking that these concerns are rarely voiced with respect to donor eggs). While prospective parents might prefer a local donor, or a donor with particular professional or educational characteristics, they have not been *prevented* from reproducing as long as sperm is available from elsewhere from donors who seem like 'good people'.

Where then does all this leave us, or rather those tasked with regulating in this field? I have suggested that the aim of regulation should be to strike a fair balance between competing interests, while recognising that regulatory action in itself may exercise unintended normative influence, for example, with respect to the implied value to be accorded genetic connection in the absence of any social relationship. From the evidence we have at present, the current low regulatory limits do not appear to be harming any of those affected by donation. Indeed, there is little evidence of even those limits being routinely reached in the UK or Australia, although more commercially oriented sperm banks based in more permissive jurisdictions may indeed reach their own, self-imposed, limits of twenty or thirty families (Millbank, 2014). Some limit, though,

[12] Of course, as noted at the start of this chapter, parents may choose not to tell their child that they were conceived through the help of a donor. However, no parent can be confident that their child will *never* find out. Moreover, many more parents intend to tell than actually do: suggesting that disclosure is increasingly seen as the preferred option, even for those who in practice do not disclose.

provides a degree of reassurance to donor-conceived people regarding concerns about inadvertent consanguineous relationships, the original justification for creating a regulatory limit. In the absence of any strong countervailing interests in higher limits (such as would be found if limits were indeed an important factor controlling access to reproductive services), such reassurance offers justification for not jettisoning limits altogether.[13]

The more recent arguments put forward to justify limits, on the other hand, relating to the claimed importance of controlling the number of genetic connections 'out there', appear weak on closer analysis. In practice, families demonstrate how they 'choose' which connections to develop and maintain, very much as they do with other social (but not necessarily genetic) relationships. And even if we grant, for the sake of argument, that genetic connection outside social relationship may have inherent value, the language of 'cousins' which appears to be commonly used by donor-conceived families to describe same donor sibling relationships offers no steer to an acceptable maximum number.

So what numerical limit should be proposed? No statistical rationale was offered in the 1984 Warnock report for the original figure of ten suggested in the UK (see Freeman, Jadva and Slutsky, Chapter 8), and thirty years on there still exists little consensus on an appropriate model to adopt (HFEA, 2011). In the light of the arguments made above, that regulators implicitly endorse normative stances by choosing to regulate in particular ways, then there seems good reason *not* to recommend changes in the law in the absence of any new evidence with respect to these potential harms. Any decision to raise or lower limits in a particular jurisdiction, without evidence of specific harm, would inevitably send *some* form of message as to how people should or should not value a particular form of genetic connection. In the end, least harm may be done by retaining the *status quo* – without making any claim that that particular status quo has been reached through anything other than historic accident.

REFERENCES

Almeling, R. (2014). 'Defining connections: gender and perceptions of relatedness in egg and sperm donation', in Freeman, T., Graham, S., Ebtehaj, F.

[13] If, hypothetically, it were to be the case that limits were indeed limiting access to services, then the conclusions of HFEA (2011) would suggest that they could be 'greatly' increased with little actual impact on the risks of consanguineous relationships. Policy makers might then need to find other ways of providing appropriate reassurance: for example, through measures to ensure a wide geographical usage of sperm donations from one donor.

and Richards, M. (eds.), *Relatedness in Assisted Reproduction: Families, Origins and Identities*. Cambridge University Press.

Blumenthal-Barby, J.S. and Burroughs, H. (2012). 'Seeking better health care outcomes: the ethics of using the "nudge"'. *American Journal of Bioethics*, 12, 1–10.

Blyth, E. (2012). 'Genes r us? Making sense of genetic and non-genetic relationships following anonymous donor insemination'. *Reproductive BioMedicine Online*, 24, 719–26.

Graham, S. (2014). 'Stories of an absent father', in Freeman, T., Graham, S., Ebtehaj, F. and Richards, M. (eds.), *Relatedness in Assisted Reproduction: Families, Origins and Identities*. Cambridge University Press.

Human Fertilisation and Embryology Authority (HFEA) (2009). *Authority Paper: disclosure of donor codes to gamete and embryo recipients – evaluation and review of HFEA policy*. Available at www.hfea.gov.uk/docs/AM_Item_10_Jan09.pdf.

Human Fertilisation and Embryology Authority (HFEA) (2011). *Authority Paper: donation review – family limit*, and associated Annexes. Available at www.hfea.gov.uk/6516.html.

Jadva, V., Freeman, T., Kramer, W. and Golombok, S. (2010). 'Experiences of offspring searching for and contacting their donor siblings and donor'. *Reproductive BioMedicine Online*, 20, 523–32.

Millbank, J. (2014). 'Numerical limits in donor conception regimes: genetic links and "extended family" in the era of identity disclosure'. *Medical Law Review*, 22, 325–56.

National Gamete Donation Trust (2014). 'World's first national sperm bank launching in England: thousands affected by infertility to benefit', press release 24 July 2014. Available at www.ngdt.co.uk/press-releases.

Nuffield Council on Bioethics (2013). *Donor Conception: Ethical Aspects of Information Sharing*. London: Nuffield Council on Bioethics.

Plotz, D. (2005). *The Genius Factory: Unravelling the Mystery of the Nobel Prize Sperm Bank*. London: Simon & Schuster.

Readings, J., Blake, L., Casey, P., Jadva, V. and Golombok, S. (2011). 'Secrecy, disclosure and everything in-between: decisions of parents of children conceived by donor insemination, egg donation and surrogacy'. *Reproductive BioMedicine Online*, 22, 485–95.

Sälevaara, M., Suikkari, A.M. and Söderström-Anttila, V. (2013). 'Attitudes and disclosure decisions of Finnish parents with children conceived using donor sperm'. *Human Reproduction*, 28, 2746–54.

Saggar, A.K. and Bittles, A.H. (2008). 'Consanguinity and child health'. *Paediatrics and Child Health*, 18, 244–9.

Sheridan, E., Wright, J., Small, N., Corry, P.C. et al. (2013). 'Risk factors for congenital anomaly in a multiethnic birth cohort: an analysis of the Born in Bradford Study'. *Lancet*, 382, 1350–9. See also www.borninbradford.nhs.uk/.

Part III

Donors

Experiences, motivations and consent

10 Regulating the 'good' donor

The expectations and experiences of sperm donors in Denmark and Victoria, Australia

Susanna Graham, Sebastian Mohr and Kate Bourne

What makes a 'good' sperm donor?

The answer to this question clearly depends upon the perspective from which this judgment is made. A 'good' sperm donor from the view point of staff at a commercial sperm bank may well be different from the way in which a good donor is defined by a medical practitioner performing an intrauterine insemination (IUI), a woman seeking insemination with donor semen, a partner of a woman undergoing insemination, or indeed a donor-conceived individual. Not only is the construction of a good donor dependent upon the specific interests of certain stakeholders, but also the particular socio-cultural context in which semen is donated. With the aid of two case studies – an anthropologist's (SM's) account of the practices and donor experiences within commercial sperm banks in Denmark, and a counsellor's (KB's) interactions and interviews with past and current sperm donors in Victoria, Australia – this chapter will explore different modes of regulating the 'good' donor, as well as examine how donors themselves think about and experience this regulation. In this chapter, we use the term 'regulation' to encompass not only formal legislature and guidelines by regulatory authorities such as the Danish Health Authority or the Australian Reproductive Technology Accreditation Committee, but also the organisational practices of sperm banks, and the interactions between sperm bank staff and donors, through which sperm donors' compliance is enforced.

Changing landscapes of sperm donation – increasing visibility of the donor

In recent years, increasing emphasis has been placed upon donor-conceived individuals' 'right' to knowledge of, and information about, their conception. This shift has been reflected in changing organisational and legislative regulation of donor conception around the world.

Legislation for exclusive identity-release[1] donation systems, whereby children born through gamete donation can access donor-identifying information on reaching maturity, has been introduced in Sweden, the Netherlands, the UK, New Zealand, Austria, Norway, Iceland, Switzerland and the Australian states of Victoria, New South Wales and Western Australia (Daniels et al., 2005; Godman et al., 2006; Gottlieb, Lalos and Lindblad, 2000; Janssens et al., 2006; Glennon, Chapter 3, this volume). In Denmark, recipients of donor semen can choose between identity-release and anonymous sperm donors. In Germany, due to a lack of legislation, sperm donors have *de facto* always been non-anonymous, but donor-conceived individuals' right to access donor-identifying information has recently begun to be taken seriously following a court decision in 2013 (Lütticke, 2013). Thus, regulatory frameworks in these contexts are changing the conception of what being a 'good' sperm donor entails. In contexts with identity-release donation programmes, the good donor is now one who is accessible to his donor-conceived offspring.

Victoria, Australia, has been seen as particularly active in championing the interests of donor-conceived individuals. Legislation was first introduced in 1984[2] to enable donor-conceived people to access information about their donor. Although donor-conceived individuals have had the right to access identifying information about their donor once they are eighteen years since 1998,[3,4] doctors and clinics have been required to keep comprehensive records of donor treatment, and provide this to the Donor Register, since 1988. A central register managed by the Registry of Births, Deaths and Marriages contains information about all donors, donor-conceived individuals and their parents. All parties are able to apply for identifying or non-identifying information about those connected to them. The other party is contacted and asked to give consent before identifying information is released. A voluntary register also operates for: people to connect with genetic half-siblings; parents wanting to connect with other parents who have used the same donor; people who were donor-conceived prior to 1988 and individuals who are willing to provide information if the other party wants it (particularly donors) but don't necessarily want this information themselves. There is a limit on

[1] Also commonly known as open-identity donation.

[2] Infertility (Medical Procedures) Act 1984 Victoria.

[3] Infertility Treatment Act 1995.

[4] Donor conceived individuals have had the right to apply for identifying information about their donor since 1988. However, at this time the information would only be released upon consent of the donor. Following a change in legislation in 1998, only donors agreeing to be identifiable were accepted and further consent was not required to release this identifying information to adult offspring.

how many women can conceive from the same donor. The current limit is ten women including the donor's partner.[5]

In 2010, a State Inquiry in Victoria explored whether donor-conceived people should have access to identifying information regardless of when they were conceived. The report,[6] released in 2012, recommended that the Victorian Government introduce legislation to allow all donor-conceived people to obtain identifying information about their donors. It also recommended that donors should have the option of placing a contact veto if they did not wish to be contacted. The Victorian Government did not follow this recommendation and instead opted to introduce legislation enabling all donor-conceived people to apply for identifying information about their donor but with the proviso that the release of information would be contingent on the donor's consent.

In Denmark, there is no central register for sperm or egg donors. Despite calls for a central register to keep information regarding individuals born through donor insemination being voiced as early as 1953, no such register has ever been established (Lebech, 1980). Sperm banks and fertility clinics are responsible for storing identifying information about donors who have chosen to be identity-release donors, and donor-conceived individuals will thus have to contact sperm banks and fertility clinics directly in order to retrieve identifying information. Although identity-release donations were only legally introduced in late 2012, semen from donors who have agreed for identifying information to be released to donor-conceived offspring has been available from Danish sperm banks for some time. This peculiar circumstance was due to a loop-hole in Danish legislation. Prior to October 2012, the Danish fertilisation law (*Befrungtningsloven*) applied only to sperm banks and fertility clinics run by a physician. As the two largest sperm banks in Denmark are not run by physicians, they were able to offer semen from identity-release donors for home inseminations or for use in midwife-led fertility clinics.

In what has been dubbed 'the new Viking invasion' (Manzoor, 2012), Danish sperm banks export donor semen on a global scale. However, as figures released by the Danish Health Authority attest, most of these exports are to European countries (Sundhedsstyrelsen, 2014). All three sperm banks registered in Denmark are commercial and privately run. The two largest sperm banks, which are also the only ones exporting donor semen, have a combined yearly gross profit of about 7 million Euros or 9.5 million US Dollars (Proff.dk, 2014). Due to the lack of

[5] Assisted Reproductive Treatment Act 2008.

[6] Inquiry into Access by Donor-Conceived People to Information About Donors, Victorian Law Reform Committee: www.parliament.vic.gov.au/lawreform/article/1468.

a central register there are no official statistics regarding the number of sperm donors in Denmark. However, judging by the number of sperm donors listed on the Danish sperm banks' commercial sites, and one author's (SM) personal correspondence with the directors of these banks, the number of men actively donating semen in Denmark at any one time is anywhere between 200 and 400. Despite this, the number of men who are recruited by Danish sperm banks is much higher, since only about 10 per cent of all men who apply actually become sperm donors. Danish sperm donors receive compensation for each semen sample that passes quality assessments: donors receive between forty and eighty Euros per sample. General legislation administered through the European Union (EU) and its member states pertaining to sperm donation only exists for the procurement and handling of donor semen. There is currently no EU legislation regarding donor anonymity, access to donor-identifying information or family limits for use. It is thus the responsibility of sperm banks to meet the specific standards set by each of the countries to which donor semen is exported.

Yet the ways in which Danish legislation and sperm banks handle donor anonymity and donor-conceived individuals' access to donor-identifying information are also embedded in a larger context. The founding of the American based Donor Sibling Registry (DSR) and the private European initiative Scandinavia Seed Siblings – both registers for donor-siblings and gamete donors – impact upon the ways in which donor information is handled. Danish sperm donors who register with these web sites, and thus make information about themselves available to third parties may violate the contract they have signed with sperm banks and could potentially face legal action. Although demands for a central public register of gamete donors have surfaced recently, the ability of individuals born through donor insemination to access donor-identifying information currently still depends first and foremost upon parents' willingness to tell their children that they were donor-conceived, and second upon sperm banks' and fertility clinics' ability to provide the necessary information once donor-conceived individuals contact them.

In many contexts there has been a shift from non-disclosure and secrecy regarding donor conception towards increasing openness (Jadva et al., 2009). Alongside this increasing openness recipients' own constructs of a 'good' sperm donor have, in many cases, also changed: information and knowledge about the donor has increasingly been reported as important to some recipients of donor semen (Scheib, Riordan and Rubin, 2003). This seems to be particularly so for recipients who are choosing identity-release donors. Graham's (2014) study exploring how single women in the UK chose their sperm donor found that a good donor was constructed as a man donating for the 'right' reasons: a 'nice man' with whom a child could get in contact and meet in eighteen years' time. Of course, how recipients define a good donor may vary widely. Attributes deemed important in a sperm donor may depend upon factors such as a recipient's beliefs about (genetic) inheritance and the meaning attached to the role of a sperm donor, their intentions about disclosure, as well as their relationship status and sexuality. Eleven of the twenty-three single women in Graham's (2014) study imported sperm from identity-release donors registered at large Danish and American sperm banks so that they could access detailed information about their donor. For these women, a 'good' donor was constructed as someone they liked and 'knew' from their profile, and in turn, a 'father' they would be able to tell their child about. Rodino, Burton and Sanders (2011) report that single women place a higher value on biographical traits and good character when choosing a sperm donor when compared to partnered lesbian or heterosexual women. Similarly, Scheib, Riordan and Shaver (2000) found that information that enabled recipients to construct the donor as a 'nice' person was more important for single, rather than partnered, women. For other recipients, a 'good' donor may be merely one who physically resembles their partner. This does not seem to be the case only amongst heterosexual couples wishing to conceal the use of donor conception, since donor 'matching' has also been reported amongst lesbian couples (Jones, 2005; Mamo, 2005; Nordqvist, 2010). In this case the 'good' donor is one who, through physical resemblances with the non-biological social parent, is invisible in everyday life: even if the donor's importance is not negated in terms of a child's 'right' to access identifying information about him, the sperm donor will not be an everyday part of the family narrative.

The sperm donor's perspective – an invisible stakeholder

Despite the sperm donor becoming a more visible actor within the field of donor conception, this changing landscape of donation is not, in the most part, reflected in the academic literature. As a systematic review of the sperm donor literature concludes, 'It seems that the sperm donor as a person and as a stakeholder has been widely neglected in both medical and psychosocial research on this topic' (Van den Broeck et al., 2013: 49). Indeed, existing research predominantly consists of quantitative studies focusing upon donors' motivations and reactions to changes in legislation regarding donor anonymity. Motivation to donate has been reported as multifaceted, with 'primary' motivations including 'altruism' and 'financial incentive' and more 'secondary' motivations including procreation, the desire to pass on genes and investigate one's own fertility (Daniels et al., 2005; Ernst et al., 2007; Jadva et al., 2011; Riggs and Russel, 2011).

Recent survey-based research in Denmark supports such findings (Bay et al., 2014). However, it is important to note that asking sperm donors about their 'motivations' emphasises these men's role as mere providers of semen and as incentive-driven individuals, and it sets aside any questions regarding what it means to be a sperm donor or their expectations and experiences of donating their semen (Mohr, 2014a).

Emerging in-depth research on sperm donation (Almeling, 2011; Hammarberg, 2013; Mohr, 2010, 2011, 2014a,b,c, 2015; Mohr and Høyer, 2012) has begun to address these issues. Ethnographic research with Danish sperm donors has shown how the decision to donate one's semen goes beyond simple motivations such as 'financial incentive' and 'altruism' (Mohr, 2014a). Being a sperm donor entails entering a biomedical control regime, whereby men are required to discipline themselves and thus men are only likely to donate semen if they are able to integrate sperm donation into their own moral universe and ways of being a man (Mohr, 2014b). Likewise, research exploring egg and sperm banking in the United States has shown how gendered cultural norms and expectations shape the construction and experience of gamete donors (Almeling, 2011). When American sperm donors think of their contribution as merely 'another job', this is due to a cultural framework, reinforced by sperm bank staff, offering only certain pathways in which to construct and experience masculinity. However, in a commercial sperm bank setting a 'good' donor is also a marketable donor. Thus, these American sperm banks also require men to construct themselves as good donors from the perspective of potential recipients: Almeling reports how donors are encouraged to provide donor profiles indicating that they are 'real' persons motivated by more than just money.

Regulating the 'good' donor

Sperm banks engage in the making of the good donor while legislation frames these engagements. Through exploring the regulation of sperm donors, this section examines how the 'good' donor is constructed through donor–staff interaction at Danish sperm banks and via legislative changes in Victoria, Australia. In the first case study, we will see how the good sperm donor is constructed as someone who conforms to the regulative regime at Danish sperm banks, detailing how this is achieved through regulating men's gender roles and sexual practices. The second case study explores how legal changes have played a role in shifting constructions of the good donor in Victoria, Australia, with donors now expected to conform to ideals of what is 'best' for donor-conceived offspring. In contributing to the literature regarding the experiences of being a sperm donor, these case studies highlight how donors themselves think about and experience this regulation.

Regulating the 'good' donor through donor–staff interactions at Danish sperm banks

During fieldwork at a sperm bank in Denmark, one of the authors (SM) encountered the following incident: a man, who had been donating his semen for more than a year and whose semen quality always exceeded the sperm bank's requirements, had been caught lying about the time of abstinence in between ejaculations. The sperm bank requires a minimum of forty-eight hours abstinence before men are allowed to deliver a semen sample. This standard follows medical guidelines for good semen quality set in place to ensure that donors' semen samples will meet minimum quality requirements. Over a period of a few days, the donor had delivered multiple semen samples at the sperm bank's different locations. While being significantly lower than usual, his semen quality did not, however, fall under the sperm bank's minimum requirements. The staff discussed how to handle the situation. The donor-coordinator was convinced that the donor had lied and that he should be suspended due to his disrespectful behaviour. However, the laboratory manager at the sperm bank where the donor usually donated reminded everyone that this donor had a 'good profile' and therefore was valuable as a donor. After some discussion, the staff agreed that they would give the donor a warning but should the same thing happen again he would be dismissed as a donor.

Sperm banks need good donors. Without men willing to donate their semen once or twice a week, there would be no semen samples available to be sold and shipped to recipients. What does being a 'good' donor mean in this context? As the introductory field note portrays, making the good donor at Danish sperm banks relies on a regulative process entailing interaction between sperm donors and sperm bank staff. As part of this process, donors have to prove through their behaviour and conduct – for example, telling the truth about ejaculatory abstinence – that they are good donors. Different (medical) technologies (e.g. medical history questionnaires, semen quality tests, physical exams, chromosome tests), as well as sanctions (e.g. monetary compensation, warnings dismissal), are utilised to make sperm donors comply with this regulative process. This section focuses upon this regulative process.

The regulation of donors at Danish sperm banks follows certain guidelines and standards. As part of a transnational political regime, Denmark regulates the procurement and handling of human semen in accordance with European Union (EU) regulation. Danish sperm banks are required to follow EU directives and thus, with the objectives of security and quality control, must perform medical screening and evaluation to establish whether men are suitable donors. Yet, as Hoeyer's (2010) analysis of this regulative framework shows, the EU-directive also requires that donors enter a confessionary regime which invokes categories such as sexuality to mark certain groups as less eligible as donors than others. A similar implicit normative inscription also applies to how donor behaviour is regulated at Danish sperm banks (Mohr, 2010, 2011, 2015). Beyond adhering to the international and national regulatory statutes, sperm banks follow an implicit script when assessing potential donors. This script posits that the good donor is a responsible individual who does not disturb workflows at sperm banks (e.g. being on time for appointments, providing necessary information) and who is compliant with their organisational logic (delivering good quality semen samples in order to distribute them to recipients).

Following Akrich (1992), a script can be understood as inscriptions of cultural norms into technology and technological objects, which have performative effects in as far as they frame the (inter)actions of humans as well as the interactions of humans with technologies. In this sense, a script guides the selection of donor applicants at Danish sperm banks and materialises in artefacts such as the contract donors have to sign and the questionnaires they have to fill out. Far from being an all-determining framework, this script has a certain interpretative flexibility (Pinch and Bijker, 1984): it can, to a certain degree, be read differently in order to allow individual donors to ascribe meaning to it, and integrate it as part of his conduct as a good donor. Thus, regulating donor conduct and thereby making the good donor at Danish sperm banks is the application and negotiation of official guidelines and rules as well as implicit notions of what being a good donor entails. As seen in the field-note above, whether a man is considered a good donor will depend on his conduct with staff, his physical characteristics such as skin, eye and hair colour, as well as biomedical assessments of his body and semen. The significance placed on each of these factors will depend on both individual relations between staff members, as well as a sperm bank's more general considerations such as donor availability and recipients' requirements.

A central moment in which the regulatory script at sperm banks constitutes itself is the mandatory interview that all potential donors must attend. This interview is required by the Danish Health Authority's guidelines for donor screening and constitutes a measure to assess an applicant's personal and family medical history. However, it also represents an opportunity to determine an applicant's eligibility to become a donor in the sense of testing his willingness to comply. This objective is explained to donors at the beginning of these interviews. With phrases such as, 'The aim is to make sure that you don't have any hereditary diseases. We make sure that there is nothing wrong with you [at du ikke fejler noget]' or 'We want to make sure that you answered the questions correctly. And we want to assess if you can be a donor', sperm bank staff remind donor applicants that they are being scrutinised and that they must convince staff that they have the potential to be a good donor.

The individual interviews are all very similar. Most of the time, sperm bank staff use the medical and screening questionnaires, already completed by the donor candidates, to guide the interview. The information provided on these forms establishes a background upon which to assess whether men have the potential to be a good donor. During participant observation it became apparent that much of the interaction during these interviews stems from what is written on these forms. Sometimes without even looking up, staff would proceed to pose questions regarding recent sexual activity and sexual partners and interviewees would answer these questions while also looking at the forms. Checking answer boxes on the forms and orienting conversations towards these topics thus becomes part of the making of the good donor. The completed questionnaires, with answers by the applicants and comments by the 'responsible' staff, are proof that both donors and staff comply with the regulatory script.

Most of the interviews last between twenty-five minutes to an hour, depending on how 'difficult', as one donor coordinator put it, an applicant's medical history is and how many questions the donor candidate asks during the interview: 'I prefer that interviews last a little longer' one donor coordinator explained, 'since that is the only way of asking all the relevant questions and to get to know the donor candidates.' Getting to know the candidates is a self-proclaimed goal of Danish sperm banks: 'knowing' the donor enables sperm bank staff to assess whether or not they can trust the information donors have provided and thus also serves to reassure them that donors comply with the sperm bank's regulatory script.

Besides medical questionnaires, sperm banks also use an array of tests – blood tests, urine tests, semen quality tests – to guarantee compliance. Through these tests, the donors' bodies and their fluids serve as evidence for whether donors are telling the truth regarding their sexual practices, lifestyle and health habits. The following field note shows how sperm banks embed these kinds of tests as part of the regulatory script. Tests serve as measures that will potentially expose non-compliance and lead to subsequent sanctions:

The donor coordinator explains how semen quality is influenced by a variety of factors. Heat, diet, and physical activity would all have a big influence on whether a sample would pass the quality requirements or not. 'So don't come up here if you have been working out the day before' she tells the donor candidate and continues that his semen's quality would be tested every time when he delivers a sample. The donor candidate nods as if to signal that he understood. 'But you will only get an email from me, if your quality should not be good enough. So, no news is good news.' She then presents the prospect of an uncomfortable conversation about why the donor's semen quality is not good enough in case he receives four emails about samples that did not pass quality requirements. Making a grimace that signals anxiety, she tells the donor candidate: 'Let's do everything in order to avoid having this conversation. And don't come in under 48 hours [of abstinence]. It will be a waste of your and our time.

As this field note shows, the regulatory script at Danish sperm banks enforces donor compliance by an orchestration of donor behaviour, semen quality tests and sanctions. The donor coordinator explains to the applicant that good donor behaviour means disciplining one's body, by avoiding factors that reduce semen quality, and to adhere to the rules which the sperm bank sets, thereby guaranteeing a continuous supply of good quality semen samples. Tests are positioned as measures that expose potential non-compliance with these rules, and sanctions are used to tell donors that nothing else but compliance will be accepted. Donors are told not to waste their own time and the time of the staff at the sperm banks – if they do so, tests assessing semen quality will reveal their attempted betrayal and donors are threatened with questions about their sexual and masturbatory habits. The invocation of male shame is thereby a central disciplining measure: providing good quality semen is cast as the individual donor's responsibility, something he has to provide through having the right lifestyle and by adhering to the rules. His worth as a man and a donor are directly connected to his ability to deliver good quality semen. Failing to provide such good quality semen is thus a personal failure, a shameful experience that is sanctioned by an interrogating talk in which the intimate and private are scrutinised.

The introspection of the intimate and private was also a prevalent theme within interviews conducted with men donating their semen at Danish sperm banks. However, the necessity of being checked through questionnaires, medical tests, physical exams and personal interviews was hardly ever doubted by these men. Most of them regarded being tested as an additional benefit of being a sperm donor. August, single and in his early twenties, explained:

For me personally, the most important thing is that I get some compensation for this [donating semen], because I would have probably not been a sperm donor without some form of compensation. But beyond that, there are also other things which are important to me like for example that I can get my blood checked once in a while so that I don't have to go to my physician for that. That wouldn't have been a problem anyways, but this way I get my blood drawn regularly and I get checked by a physician, and I know that my sperm quality is alright. And if anything should happen then I also have a bank that stores my sperm. Normally people have to pay for that kind of thing. So, there are also advantages to that.

Moreover, the majority of donors expressed agreement with the screening logic of Danish sperm banks and held similar opinions to Thommy, a thirty-two-year-old sperm donor in a committed relationship with one child:

Well, of course they [the sperm banks] have to make sure that you don't have any flaws/defects [skavanker] somewhere on your body. So, that needs to be done. Of course they have to check whether what you say and what you write is correct, and so it won't help you that they find all sorts of things in your blood when you wrote that you are a virgin [laughing].

Nevertheless, a minority of donors also expressed being surprised at, and questioned the appropriateness and necessity of, some of the topics the sperm bank asked them about. Jeppe, nineteen years old and single, for example, questioned the meaning of certain inquiries about sexual partners:

One thing that surprised me was that I was asked whether I had sex with people from the Philippines or something like that [laughs a bit], well yes, they did ask that. I thought that it was almost a bit creepy that this was so nationalistic. [. . .] These kinds of things are puzzling, but then I thought: oh well, they probably have a good reason for asking this question. Actually, I did not mind the tests, I mean, you know that this will happen before you even apply [as a donor]. It's obvious that you will not be invited in at face value [på dit glatte ansigt].

Still others, like Noah, a twenty-five-year-old single student without children, voiced unease about being continuously physically examined for diseases and malformations:

[. . .] If you asked me, where I would draw the line, where I would not want to continue [as a sperm donor] any longer: I think if I had to go through one of those physical exams every time or every other time, that I would not be up for. [. . .] I do not mind getting my blood drawn and those kinds of things, that doesn't bother me, but those bodily visitations are a bit beyond my limits [grænseoverskridende].

Understood as a reflection of the extent to which donors at Danish sperm banks feel comfortable with the regulations in place, these donors' experiences could be interpreted as marking overall approval of, and compliance with, the regulatory script at Danish sperm banks, whilst at the same time highlighting that regulations of private and intimate matters do have the potential to cause unease and discomfort for individual donors. In the organisational context of Danish sperm banks, in which sexuality, and especially masturbation, are never talked about, while at the same time being a fundamental aspect of procuring donor semen, it seems questionable whether measures such as the threat of anxiety-laden conversations about male sexuality really are appropriate. Men who donate semen already find themselves in a situation in which they have to negotiate their gendered and sexual self-conceptions, or as Oliver, a twenty-seven-year-old single student with no children, who had just recently started to donate semen, put it:

> [. . .] Those people that I have told about it [donating semen] know very well to keep quiet about it. That is not something that they should talk about to anyone else, it is something rather private. In some way it seems ridiculous, but I feel a little bit ashamed about it, and I think that has to do with the fact that it involves me having to masturbate, even though it is natural to do, just as I also feel ashamed when I have to use a public toilet, and that it will smell when I used it. Everybody has to use the toilet but just the same you feel ashamed about it. And I feel a little bit the same in regards to this [donating semen], I know very well that it is something that we also do normally, but I just don't feel like that people should know that I go there and masturbate inside a room.

Regulating sperm donor conduct and behaviour is necessary. If donor conduct and donor–staff interactions were not scripted in accordance to a sperm banks' organisational logic, no donor semen would be available for use. However, as part of this process, men who donate their semen will unavoidably, amongst other things, have to confront their gendered and sexual self-conceptions, something that under certain circumstances might be difficult and influence men's well-being and their willingness to donate semen in the first place. Rather than alleviating men's anxieties in this regard, the regulatory script at Danish sperm banks utilises common assumptions about male sexuality, specifically masturbation, as taboo. The 'good' donor at Danish sperm banks is thus not simply the 'best' donor in regards to his sperm count or physical appearance. Nor is he only a responsible individual who keeps appointments and tells the truth about ejaculatory abstinence. The 'good' donor is someone who also keeps quiet about his sexual inhibitions and gender role concerns.

Regulating the 'good' donor through legislation changes in Victoria, Australia

Current practice in Victoria differs markedly from the Danish practice described. Whilst all sperm donors have a similar medical and genetic assessment in Victoria, there are additional legal requirements. The first guiding principle of the current Assisted Reproductive Treatment Act 2008 is: 'The welfare and interests of person's born or to be born as a result of treatment procedures are paramount.'[7]

The following account of changing donor practice, legislation and regulation draws heavily upon the narratives of men donating their semen prior to 1998 who participated in a consultation conducted by the Victorian Assisted Reproductive Treatment Authority (VARTA), in conjunction with researchers from Monash University.[8]

Pre-legislation

Donor conception practice has changed markedly in Victoria since it was first introduced. It is not known when donor insemination treatment first began but VARTA has had enquiries from people conceived as early as the 1940s. Initially there was no legislation regulating the industry. Doctors provided treatment in private practice and inseminations were carried out with fresh semen. The results and information about the donor were poorly recorded, as such information was not thought necessary.

One donor, Michael A, described donors as being 'Johnny-on-the-spot'. Given the need to have a donor who was geographically close to the site where patients were treated, he described having a beeper that was activated when he was required to donate semen, a source of some amusement amongst his peers. He did not recall having to sign any consent forms or documentation and described donating semen as 'harmless and praiseworthy'. He continued:

> It was simply a matter of providing the specimen. There would be no contact with us in the future from the program people, and certainly not from the recipient couple, and certainly not from the offspring . . . So we were absolutely certain, as we believed at the time, that this was no more than a specimen of biological material and with no downstream implications or complications that would flow from that.[9]

A good donor at this time was one who was readily accessible and willing to attend the clinic at short notice.

Freezing of semen became commonly practised in the early 1980s and subsequently donor insemination programmes were established at

7 Assisted Reproductive Treatment Act 2008 5(a) Victoria.

8 Consultation with donors who donated gametes in Victoria, Australia before 1998: Access by donor-conceived people to information about donors. Report to the Victorian Government, May 2013, www.varta.org.

9 Ibid., p. 60.

public hospitals (Johnson et al., 2012). They were usually young university students, often medical students, who were paid either nothing or a small amount of money (AU$5). A culture of secrecy surrounding donor conception prevailed, perhaps due to Australian statute law at that time whereby a sperm donor was considered to be the legal father (Leeton, 2013). Good sperm donors were therefore men recruited on the condition of anonymity. As one donor, who was donating at this time, described it:

> We had a valuable spare part that they needed; a critical spare part... And they were really keen to get people in.

Donors were asked to provide very little information about themselves and several of the donors described how there was no discussion about the implications of sperm donation, specifically the fact that their donation was going to create people.[10] One donor, when asking if he would ever know if there were any offspring resulting from his donation, was told, 'You will never know; it's completely anonymous. You will never know, even if there's a conception'.[11]

In this way a good donor was perceived by the clinic as someone who would remain invisible, had a good sperm count and was merely the provider of a biological substance: the missing ingredient. Reflecting societal norms at the time, there was little thought or consideration by the treating doctor to the needs of the people born as a result of the treatment.

Regulating donor practice – 1984 legislation and implications

Three separate Acts of Parliament have been introduced in Victoria since the time when these donors donated their semen, and thus clinic practice, including record keeping, recruitment practices and counselling of donors, has changed accordingly. Under the 1984 legislation,[12] donor-conceived people, parents and donors could apply for information from the Central Register. Identifying information could only be released with the consent of the other party. Donors had no rights or responsibilities towards the children born as the Status of Children (Amendment) Act[13] was also passed which recognised the infertile husband as the legal father. Donors could not be paid and only travelling expenses were

[10] Ibid., p. 62. [11] Ibid., p. 59.
[12] Infertility (Medical Procedures) Act 1984 Victoria.
[13] Status of Children (Amendment) Act 1984 Victoria.

compensated. There was a strict ten-family limit introduced to reduce the possibility of consanguinity occurring.

Donors were required to complete detailed consent forms and could also change their earlier consent if they later decided to withdraw from the programme. Prior to donating, mandatory counselling was provided for both donors and their spouses, providing information regarding donors' rights and responsibilities under the legislation and discussing the emotional implications of donating. One donor, Donald, described his experience of the donation process:

> What I was impressed about was that they gave me a certain amount of time when they were interviewing me to start with, and said, 'Well, what do you think any conceived children would want to know about you?' So I mean I gave them a bit of health history for the broader family, and I gave them a bit of background, historical background, saying the ancestors came from [overseas].[14]

More detailed information was collected from the donor and the outcomes of the donation were provided to the donor upon request. Good donors were no longer constructed as merely gamete providers paid for their services, but men who were motivated by altruism, prepared to provide medical and personal information about themselves in their profile, potentially open to providing more specific information to and possibly direct contact with the recipients, and with regard to whom perhaps their offspring and wives were comfortable with them donating. Sperm donors were now recognised as having rights and responsibilities in this process: it was acknowledged that donors may want to know more about the outcome of their donation and that donating may have implications for the donor's family.

Regulating donor practice – 1995 legislation and implications

The 1995 legislation[15] strengthened the right of donor-conceived peoples' access to information about their donor, reflecting increasingly broad acceptance of ARTs and donor conception (Kovacs et al., 2003). Offspring were now *entitled* to identifying information about their donor once they were eighteen. Indeed the guiding principle of the Act was that the welfare and interests of any person born was paramount.[16] The donor's spouse was also required to give written consent at the time of

[14] Consultation with donors who donated gametes in Victoria, Australia before 1998: Access by donor-conceived people to information about donors. Report to the Victorian Government, May 2013 www.varta.org.au, p. 62.

[15] Infertility Treatment Act 1995 Victoria. [16] Ibid., s5(1)(a).

donation and was able to retract this consent at a later date.[17] Written information about a donor's rights and responsibilities under the legislation was required to be provided. A Voluntary Register was established in addition to the Central Register previously set up under the 1984 Act. This Register could be used by donors, or their relatives and descendants to register information about themselves and apply voluntarily for information about a related party. In this way children of donors were able to register for information about genetic half-siblings. If other donor-conceived offspring of the same donor also registered they could be put in contact with each other.

Consent forms and written information supplied to the donor became even more comprehensive and detailed to reflect the legislative requirements. There was significant concern that donors would not donate under these conditions. Donor numbers have, however, remained steady,[18] although the characteristics of men willing to donate semen have changed. Clinics no longer recruited from universities and instead tried to attract older, more mature donors, who often had children of their own.

Contact with parents before donor-conceived children came of age was also possible under legislation and growing numbers of parents, particularly single mothers and same-sex mothers applied for information exchange or contact with their donor whilst their children were young. In keeping with the rhetoric of the 'rights' of donor-conceived individuals brought into play by the legislation, donors often consented to this early contact even though they were often expecting this to occur much later. One donor described his experience with linking with a family with two daughters who had been conceived with his donated sperm:

> I agreed to meet with this family on the basis that the daughter was interested in meeting me. I felt that the primary concern was the mental health and well-being of the child. That was my motivational factor to meet them.

A good donor consequently became a man who was prepared to provide private information and be open to the possibility of being contacted by recipient parents or their adult offspring. However, donors were counselled that they should in no way take on a parental role with this child. The donor's wife and children were also acknowledged as being affected by his donation as well as their possible wish to be in contact with the donor's offspring.

[17] If a donor formed a new partnership after donating, his new partner was also able to retract consent for the use of any remaining donor semen.

[18] See ITA and VARTA Annual Reports, www.varta.org.au.

Regulating donor practice – 2008 legislation and implications

The 2008 legislation[19] had fewer direct implications for donors. However, as changes to the birth certificates for donor-conceived people[20] will result in a legal incentive for parents to inform children they are donor-conceived, this is likely to result in more people knowing about their conception and hence more applications to the Donor Registers. The legislation also made it illegal to discriminate on the basis of sexuality or relationship status: single mothers and same-sex couples could now access donor treatment more easily. This caused a significant increase in the numbers of people having treatment with donor semen and created a shortage of supply.[21]

Clinics changed their recruitment to reflect these changes and better suit the needs of their patients. Homosexual donors were now encouraged to donate and in response to requests from patients for more detailed information, donor profiles became even more thorough, with more personal information about the donor provided, for example, motivation to donate, philosophy of life, message to the child, perhaps a childhood photo and permission to provide the first name of the donor. Clinics became more open to the use of recipient-recruited donors and men who would have previously been deemed unsuitable as donors due to a sub-optimal sperm count or quality were accepted for recipients willing to undergo IVF with ICSI.[22] The construction of a 'good' donor therefore expanded, no longer confined to an altruistically motivated fertile, heterosexual man who was prepared to be identifiable and altruistic: the donor now had to be open to donating to single and lesbian women, prepared to complete a lengthy personal profile and may also be gay or sub-fertile.

Current legislative issues

There has been ongoing debate within Victoria and lobbying from donor-conceived activists to further change legislation to allow identifying information to be released to offspring who had been conceived with semen from a donor who had previously donated anonymously, or with the

19 Assisted Reproductive Treatment Act 2008 (Victoria).

20 Children born after 2010 who apply for a birth certificate when adult will receive an addendum stating that more information is available. If this is requested they will be informed that their birth has been recorded on the Donor Register hence they are donor-conceived.

21 VARTA 2014. Annual Report. www.varta.org.au. Accessed 3 December 2015.

22 A treatment in which a sperm cell is micro-injected into the egg commonly used to treat male infertility.

understanding identifying information would be released only with his consent. The Parliamentary Law Reform Committee held a lengthy Inquiry and its final report recommended for this to be made possible.[23] Before introducing legislation the Victorian Government commissioned the Victorian Assisted Reproductive Treatment Authority (VARTA) to consult with donors who would potentially be affected by a possible change to legislation. Forty-two donors participated in the consultation. Approximately three quarters of these donors were open to providing some information about themselves, just under a half of all donors were prepared to provide identifying details, approximately a quarter of the donors were prepared to provide non-identifying information only and another quarter were not comfortable to provide any information (Hammarberg et al., 2014). Although these findings may not be representative of all sperm donors' views, these results go against commonly held assumptions that the majority of donors want to remain anonymous (Kirkman et al., 2014).[24]

What do donors really think?

The research indicated that donors' views do not necessarily fit with the clinic view of what makes a good donor and may also change over time. Some of the early donors did want to remain invisible and anonymous. However, many were open to providing information and to having contact with offspring who desired it, even though this was not envisaged at the time of their donation.

The VARTA Donor Consultation report[25] is rich with quotes from donors expressing their views about potential information release and the ways in which they see themselves in relation to the people they helped create. Donors who supported the release of identifying information often spoke with great sensitivity about the potential emotional needs of their offspring for 'genetic information' and said that they too had often wondered about their offspring and were curious to know more about them:

23 Law Reform Committee. *Inquiry into Access by Donor-Conceived People to Information about Donors.* Victoria, Australia: Parliament of Victoria 2012.

24 Indeed, the number of donors who are prepared to provide information to offspring can also be demonstrated by the numbers of donors who apply to the Voluntary Register. It has more donors making applications than recipient parents or donor-conceived people (although many offspring may not know of their origins and may not yet be old enough to apply). Current numbers of the Voluntary Register at 30 June 2013, include 188 donors, 83 donor-conceived people and 158 recipient parents.

25 Consultation with donors who donated gametes in Victoria, Australia before 1998: access by donor-conceived people to information about donors. Report to the Victorian Government, May 2013 www.varta.org.au.

Many times in my life I've looked at people walking around the streets as I pass in various places around the world, thinking, 'Could you be one of my children?' And in no way in the world am I able to contact them, because I signed away all rights. But should they ever wish to know about me, 'Here I am; come and see me.' (Bruce)[26]

Donors who were against providing information to their offspring thought that this was unethical and felt betrayed and cheated. Some were very concerned about the implications for themselves and their family and feared stalking or claims on their estate. A number of donors would not have donated if they had known this change were possible:

It . . . is a breach of a contract. I had an explicit undertaking when I entered it. For noble reasons I entered into those arrangements to help people. I did it on the basis of promises given, and now the proposition is that those promises be discarded. So I feel, firstly, betrayed, cheated. (Michael A.)[27]

The Victorian Government has taken a compromise position and recently introduced legislation that allows all donor-conceived people regardless of when they were conceived to apply for identifying information. However, this will only be provided with the consent of the donor. It will be interesting to further evaluate how these applications progress and follow what transpires when donors, offspring and recipient parents meet and whether this further changes the definition of a good donor for all concerned.

Future considerations – beyond regulation

The two case studies have illustrated how the sperm donor as a person and a stakeholder with his own interests remains largely invisible in the regulative and organisational contexts of sperm donation. Regulation, both formal, as in the case of legislation changes in Victoria, Australia, and informal, as illustrated in donor–staff interactions at Danish sperm banks, is involved in making the 'good' donor, as defined by other stakeholders – policy makers, sperm bank staff, recipients, as well as donor-conceived individuals. Donors are constructed as fulfilling a need and regulation ensures that they fulfil this need: the needs of donor-conceived offspring for information and possible contact with their donor in Victoria, Australia and the Danish sperm bank's requirement for a high quality semen sample to sell to recipients worldwide. The good donor thus serves first and foremost the needs and expectations of others. In Danish sperm banks, men's concerns regarding masturbation

[26] Ibid., p. 34. [27] Ibid., p. 42.

and the legitimacy of sperm donation are silenced. Their sexual practices are regulated through tests and sanctioning measures, yet the effects of these never openly discussed. Victorian regulatory policies have acknowledged the donor as a person embedded in a social network. He is able to access information about the outcome of his donations and has the right to apply for information regarding his donor-conceived offspring. However, according to the social and legislative context, donors are, in the main part, expected to 'wait in the wings' and be available if and when donor-conceived offspring want to make contact: as a person in their own right, sperm donors remain largely disregarded, their importance acknowledged primarily due to their requirement to be available to meet the needs of recipients and, those at the focus of legislative changes, donor-conceived individuals. Are there ways to be a good donor without submitting to these regulatory frameworks? Might it be easier for a man to meet his own expectations of a 'good' sperm donor by donating outside of a formally regulated donation programme?

In recent years, web-based connection sites have risen in popularity. In the UK, for example, more men are currently registered as donors on these sites than through the formally regulated system: 1656 men are currently registered as UK-based sperm donors on the connection site (Prideangel, 2014), compared to only 368 HFEA registered sperm donors in 2013 (HFEA, 2014).[28] Connection sites enable heterosexual couples, lesbian couples and single women wishing to conceive with donated semen to connect with, negotiate and arrange donation directly with men willing to donate. Due to operating outside of the UK's formal regulatory framework, such sites have, however, raised medical, ethical and social concerns. In the background to their public consultation on gamete donation, the UK's regulatory body overseeing assisted reproduction, the Human Fertilisation and Embryology Authority (HFEA), warned of the potential risks involved in using connection websites (HFEA, 2011), claiming they may exploit vulnerable women and, due to the lack of legal regulation and screening of potential donors, may expose recipients and their potential children to medical risks.

Indeed, media representations have equated these connection websites with the 'seedy, sinister side of the sperm trade' (John, 2010). However,

[28] Out of these 368 HFEA registered donors, only 209 were UK registrations (the other 169 were non-UK registrations from donors whose semen was imported from sperm banks abroad). Of course these figures only reflect the number of men who are accepted as clinic donors and we do not know how many of the 1656 men registered as sperm donors on Prideangel actually go on to donate their semen. However, from these figures it seems that web-based connection sites certainly seem to an attractive route of sperm donation for men in the UK.

might this form of donation actually be reassuring for sperm donors, enabling them to have more control over their donation than through a formally regulated system? Pennings (1995) has suggested that the removal of donor anonymity increases a donor's involvement and responsibility in the donation process, arguing that being identifiable could reinforce donors' request to allocate their gametes. The ability to choose who will receive their semen, and be the parent of their genetic offspring, may thus be one reason some men decide to donate through a connection website. Likewise, Raes, Ravelingien and Pennings (2013: 560) suggest that the shift towards identity-release donation focuses on the rights and interests of donor-conceived children and that 'policy-makers seem to overlook whether information exchange could also be of interest to the other parties involved, in particular the gamete donors'.

Legislation in Victoria, Australia has certainly taken steps in realising a donor's right to access information about their donor-conceived offspring. However, perhaps donors might want to negotiate information exchange and contact from the outset, negotiating a level of contact that suits both their, and the recipient's, desires. As part of one author's (SM's) research on Danish sperm donors, three men engaging in donation through privately organised connection sites were interviewed. One of these donors, Magnus, a man in his early forties and living with his life partner and her son, had previously been a donor at a Danish sperm bank. When asked about his decision to join privately organised connection sites, he described how the inability to access information regarding how many children were born through one's donations, as well as not being able to know whether one's semen is actually used for inseminations, had been crucial factors in his decision to donate privately. Magnus also valued the possibility of getting to know the recipients of his semen. He wanted to be told whether children were born as a result of his donation and, if so, to be informed of their wellbeing.

Thus connection sites could offer donors the possibility of embarking upon donation with a better understanding of what being a good donor will mean in that particular context. Without submitting themselves to the regulatory frameworks of legislation and policy, nor the regulatory script of a sperm bank, connection websites might allow men who want to donate their semen to define, and fulfil, their own particular expectations of what being a good donor entails.

Regardless of whether men donate their semen through a sperm bank with the expectation of anonymity, under a legally enforced identity-release programme, or indeed outside a formal regulatory framework, this chapter has shown that viewing sperm donors as a 'means to an end' is no longer feasible. Men who donate semen are themselves stakeholders and partners in donor conception and have their own perceptions and expectations of what being a 'good' donor entails. There is clearly no one perception of what makes a good sperm donor: the making of the good donor depends upon the particular socio-cultural context in which the donation occurs and the regulatory practices that shape the donation experience. However, in regulating donor conception, whether formally or informally, it is important to seek to establish the interests of all stakeholders. This includes not only the recipients of, and offspring conceived through, donor sperm, but also the men who donate their semen.

REFERENCES

Akrich, M. (1992). 'The de-scription of technological objects', in W.E. Bijker and J. Law (eds.), *Shaping Technology / Building Society: Studies in Sociotechnical Change*. Cambridge, MA: MIT Press.

Almeling, R. (2011). *Sex Cells: The Medical Market for Eggs and Sperm*. Berkley, CA: University of California Press.

Bay, B., Larsen, P., Kesmodel, U. and Ingerslev, H. (2014). 'Danish sperm donors across three decades: motivations and attitudes'. *Fertility and Sterility*, 101, 252–7.

Daniels, K., Blyth, E., Crashaw, M. and Curson, R. (2005). 'Previous semen donors and their views regarding the sharing of information with offspring'. *Human Reproduction*, 20, 1670–5.

Ernst, E., Ingerslev, H., Schou, O. and Stolenber, M. (2007). 'Attitudes among sperm donors in 1992 and 2002: A Danish questionnaire survey'. *Acta Obstetricia et Gynecologica Scandinavica*, 86, 327–33.

Godman, K., Sanders, K., Rosenberg, M. and Burton, P. (2006). 'Potential sperm donors', recipients', and their partners' opinions towards the release of identifying information in Western Australia'. *Human Reproduction*, 21, 3022–6.

Gottlieb, C., Lalos. O. and Lindblad, F. (2000). 'Disclosure of donor insemination to the child: the impact of Swedish legislation on couples' attitudes'. *Human Reproduction*, 15, 2052–6.

Graham, S. (2014). 'Stories of an absent "father": single women negotiating relatedness through donor profiles,' in T. Freeman, S. Graham, F. Ebtehaj and M. Richards (eds.), *Relatedness in Assisted Reproduction: Families, Origins and Identities*. Cambridge University Press.

Hammarberg, K., Johnson, L., Bourne, K., Fisher, J. et al. (2014). 'Proposed legislative change mandating retrospective release of identifying information: consultation with donors and Government response'. *Human Reproduction*. 29, 286–92.

HFEA (2011). 'The changing landscape of donation.' Available at www.hfea.gov.uk/docs/Factsheet-Changing_landscape_2011_02_11.pdf. Accessed 13 August 2014.

HFEA (2014). 'Number of new sperm donors registering in the UK'. FOI F-2014–00182, figures requested by S. Graham under the Freedom of Information Act on 30 June 2014.

Hoeyer, K. (2010). 'An anthropological analysis of European Union (EU) health governance as biopolitics: The case of the EU Cells and Tissue Directive'. *Social Science and Medicine*, 70, 1867–73.

Jadva, V., Freeman, T. Kramer, W., Golombok, S. (2009). 'The experiences of adolescents and adults conceived by sperm donation: comparisons by age of disclosure and family type'. *Human Reproduction*, 24, 1909–19.

Jadva, V., Freeman, T., Kramer, W. and Golombok, S. (2010). 'Experiences of offspring searching for and contacting their donor siblings and donor'. *Reproductive Biomedicine Online*, 20, 523–32.

Jadva, V., Freeman, T., Kramer, W. and Golombok, S. (2011). 'Sperm and oocyte donors' experiences of anonymous donation and subsequent contact with donor offspring'. *Human Reproduction*, 26, 638–46.

Janssens, P., Simmons, A., van Kooij, R., Blockzijl, E. et al. (2006). 'A new Dutch law regulating provision of identifying information of donors to offspring: background, consent and impact'. *Human Reproduction*, 21, 852–6.

John, E. (2010). 'Conceivable ideas: meet the modern sperm donor'. *The Observer*, 27th June 2010. Available at http://www.theguardian.com/lifeandstyle/2010/jun/27/jennie-withers-co-parents-fertility. Accessed 20 January 2014.

Jones, C. (2005). 'Looking like a family: negotiating bio-genetic continuity in British lesbian families using donor insemination'. *Sexualities*, 8, 221–37.

Kirkman, M., Bourne, K., Fisher, J., Johnson, L. et al. (2014). 'Gamete donors expectations and experiences of contact with their donor offspring'. *Human Reproduction*, 29, 731–8.

Kovacs, G., Morgan, G., Levine, M. and McCrann, J. (2003). 'Community attitudes to assisted reproductive technology: a 20 year trend'. *Medical Journal of Australia*, 179, 536–53.

Lebech, P.E. (1980). 'Present status of AID and sperm banks in Denmark,' in G. David and W.S. Price (eds.), *Human Artificial Insemination and Semen Preservation*. New York: Plenum Press.

Leeton, J. (2013). *The Test Tube Revolution: The Early History of IVF*. Clayton: Monash University Publishing.

Lütticke, M. (2013). 'No anonymity for sperm donors, court rules'. Deutsche Welle, 7 February 2013. Available at www.dw.de/no-anonymity-for-sperm-donors-court-rules/a-16582786. Accessed 13 August 2014.

Mamo, L. (2005). 'Biomedicalizing kinship: sperm banks and the creation of affinity ties'. *Science as Culture*, 14, 237–64.

Manzoor, S. (2012). 'Come inside: the world's biggest sperm bank'. *The Guardian*, 2 November 2012. Available at www.theguardian.com/society/2012/nov/02/worlds-biggest-sperm-bank-denmark. Accessed 13 August 2014.

Mohr, S. (2010). 'What does one wear to a sperm bank? Negotiations of sexuality in sperm donation'. *kuckuck.notizen zur alltagskultur*, 25, 36–42.

Mohr, S. (2011). 'On becoming a sperm donor: the analysis of masculinities in sperm donation,' in A. Biricik and J. Hearn (eds.), *GEXcel Work in Progress Report Volume XV: Proceedings from GEXcel Theme 9: Gendered Sexualed Transnationalisations, Deconstructing the Dominant: Transforming men, "centres" and knowledge/policy/practice*. Linköping: LiU-tryck.

Mohr, S. (2014a). 'Beyond motivation: on what it means to be a sperm donor in Denmark'. *Anthropology and Medicine*, 21, 162–73.
Mohr, S. (2014b). 'Containing sperm – managing legitimacy. Lust, disgust, and hybridity at Danish sperm banks'. *Journal of Contemporary Ethnography*, Online First Version, doi: 10.1177/0891241614558517
Mohr, S. (2015). 'Living kinship trouble: Danish sperm donors' narratives of relatedness'. *Medical Anthropology*, 34 (5), 470–84.
Mohr, S. and Høyer, K. (2012). 'Den gode sædcell . . . An antropologisk analyse af arbejdet med sædkvalitet'. *Kultur & Klasse*, 113, 45–61.
Nordqvist, P. (2010). 'Out of sight, out of mind: family resemblances in lesbian donor conception'. *Sociology*, 44, 1128–44.
Nuffield Council on Bioethics (2013). *Donor Conception: Ethical Aspects of Information Sharing*. London: Nuffield Council on Bioethics.
Pennings, G. (1995). 'Should donors have the right to decide who receives their gametes?' *Human Reproduction*, 10, 2736–40.
Pinch, T.J. and Bijker, W.E. (1984). 'The social construction of facts and artefacts: Or how the sociology of science and the sociology of technology might benefit each other'. *Social Studies of Science*, 14, 399–441.
Prideangel (2014). 'Search profiles'. Available at http://prideangel.com/searchprofiles.aspx?bsc=1&profId=0&ptId=3&fName=null&continentId=0&cntryId=2&cntyId=0. Accessed 20 January 2014.
Proff.dk (2014). '*Regnskabstal 2013*'. Available at www.proff.dk/. Accessed 2 July 2014.
Raes, I., Ravelingien, A. and Pennings, G. (2013). 'The right of the donor to information about children conceived from his or her gametes'. *Human Reproduction*, 28, 560–65.
Riggs, D. (2008). 'Lesbian mothers, gay sperm donors, and community: ensuring the well-being of children and families'. *Health Sociology Review*, 17, 226–34.
Riggs, D. (2009). 'The health and well-being implications of emotion work undertaken by gay sperm donors'. *Feminism and Psychology*, 19, 517–33.
Riggs, D. and Russel, L. (2011). Characteristics of men willing to act as sperm donors in the context of identity-release legislation'. *Human Reproduction*, 26, 266–72.
Rodino, I.S., Burton, P.J. and Sanders, K.A. (2011). 'Mating by proxy: a novel perspective to donor conception'. *Fertility and Sterility*, 96, 998–1001.
Scheib, J.E., Riordan, M. and Shaver, P. (2000). 'Choosing between anonymous and identity-release sperm donors: recipient and donor characteristics'. *Reproductive Technologies*, 10, 50–8.
Scheib, J., Riordan, M., and Rubin, S. (2003). 'Choosing identity-release sperm donors: the parents' perspective 13–18 years later'. *Human Reproduction*, 18, 1115–27.
Sundhedsstyrelsen (2014). *Humane væv og celler– årsrapport 2012*, Sundhedsstyrelsen, København.
Van den Broeck, U., Vandermeeren, M., Vanderschueren, D., Enzlin, P., Demyttenaere, K. and D'Hooghe, T. (2013). 'A systematic review of sperm donors: demographic characteristics, attitudes, motives and experiences of the process of sperm donation'. *Human Reproduction Update*, 19, 37–51.

Victorian Assisted Reproductive Treatment Authority (VARTA) (2013). 'Consultation with donors who donated gametes in Victoria, Australia before 1998: access by donor-conceived people to information about donors.' Report to The Victorian Government, May 2013. Available at www.varta.org.au/sites/default/files/public/2013%20Aug%20-%20Donor%20consultation%20full%20report.pdf. Accessed 18 January 2016.

Victorian Assisted Reproductive Treatment Authority (VARTA) (2014). Annual Report 2014. Available at www.varta.org.au/sites/default/files/VARTA%20Annual%20Report%202014_0.pdf. Accessed 18 January 2016.

LEGISLATION

AUSTRALIA

Assisted Reproductive Treatment Act 2008 5(a) Victoria.
Infertility (Medical Procedures) Act 1984 Victoria.
Infertility Treatment Act 1995 Victoria.
Status of Children (Amendment) Act 1984 Victoria.

11 Gamete donor motives, payment and child welfare

Stephen Wilkinson

Introduction

People's reasons for becoming gamete donors are many and varied. They include financial gain or other self-interest, directed or undirected altruism, feelings of empathy or solidarity, wanting one's 'genes to be passed on' to future generations or even wanting to find out about one's own fertility (see Graham, Mohr and Bourne, Chapter 10). Donor motives are of interest to at least some donor-conceived people. The Nuffield Council on Bioethics tells us that at its fact-finding meetings:

> . . . most donor-conceived adults present said that they would . . . like to know more . . . about the donor's motivation. (Nuffield Council on Bioethics, 2013: 67)

But, as the Nuffield Report also notes, finding out about donor motivation can have negative as well as positive effects on the wellbeing of donor-conceived people:

> . . . what a donor might see as an honest account of himself or herself, and their motivations for donating, might be a potential source of distress for a donor-conceived person: an example of where less, rather than more 'openness' might be ethically preferable. (Nuffield Council on Bioethics, 2013: 137)

This interest in donor motives raises important ethical questions. Are some donor motives, as is sometimes supposed, 'morally better' than others? And if some are better than others, should law and regulation react by seeking only to allow people with 'better' motives to donate?

These are huge and multi-faceted questions, not ones that can be addressed satisfactorily in a single chapter. This piece therefore confines itself to an analysis of one particular position: the suggestion that, for reasons related to the wellbeing of donor-conceived people, we should be concerned about those who donate mainly for financial motives, and that this concern should be reflected in the regulation of gamete donation (specifically by outlawing payment, or by restricting the levels and types of payment).

Similar ethical questions about payment and donor motives arise for both egg and sperm and, for this reason, the chapter makes no attempt to differentiate between the two. It should be noted however that, in practice, concerns about payment and donor motives arise more frequently and more powerfully in relation to sperm, partly perhaps because sperm donation is something that can, for obvious biological reasons, be done relatively 'casually' and in large quantities. Worries about donor motives are sometimes therefore linked to distinct ethical questions about donor offspring numbers, such as those explored in Chapter 8 by Freeman, Jadva and Slutsky and in Chapter 9 by Wright.

I note here for completeness that self-interest need not be financial or material. Directed unpaid gamete donation can be partly self-interested: for example, if a woman donates to her sister and has an interest in creating a nephew or niece, in creating cousins for her own children, or in seeing her sister's happiness. I also note that many people have mixed motives and that we cannot just assume that all egg sharers and paid gamete donors are acting purely, or even mainly, to gain personal advantage (e.g. some paid donors might give the money to charity and thereby be 'doubly altruistic').[1]

For the present though I shall focus on the 'central case' since this is what concerns most critics of paid gamete donation: the case in which someone donates mainly for financial rewards and where he or she wouldn't have donated but for the prospect of financial reward.

The position argued for in this chapter is that the ethical and regulatory stance towards donor motives should be largely determined by the practical question of whether or not regulating to screen out donors with 'the wrong' motives will cause (or worsen) gamete shortages. If it will not, then the child-welfare case for screening out such donors is strong since, other things being equal, it is better to create a future donor-conceived population with higher rather than lower levels of wellbeing. Furthermore, allowing or encouraging payment when it is not necessary to do so, is wasteful and may deprive people of the opportunity to participate in potentially socially valuable 'gifting' practices.[2] But if screening out donors with 'the wrong' motives will cause (or exacerbate) gamete shortages, then this policy response runs into potential difficulties as it involves deliberately reducing the size of the donor-conceived population as a solution to the problem of psychological distress. This

[1] Similar points have been made in the debate about financially compensating organ donors. See, for example, Wilkinson and Garrard (1996: 334–9) and Wilkinson (2003: 109–15).

[2] See Richard Titmuss' *The Gift Relationship: From Human Blood to Social Policy* (1972).

seems disproportionate and perhaps even perverse, for the very group that the measure seeks to protect could end up being 'regulated out of existence'.

My final introductory point concerns terminology: specifically the words 'donor' and 'donation'. There is a question about how widely these should be defined and, in particular, about whether 'paid donation' is a *type of* donation or should instead be called something else ('providing', 'selling', 'vending') and thereby *contrasted with* 'donation proper': that is, unpaid donation. There is some merit in each approach. Adopting the narrower definition (according to which 'paid donation' is not donation) is in line with many ordinary language conventions about the use of 'donation'; for we do often contrast *selling* goods and services with (e.g. charitably) *donating* our time or money. On the other hand, paid and unpaid 'donation' are sometimes hard to distinguish (e.g. when expenses and payments for time and inconvenience are involved) and so having a wider definition of 'donation' allows us to have a single term ('donation') without having to express a position on the point at which payments cross the line from reimbursement into reward or selling. Also, when gamete donation is the topic under discussion, there is an extra practical reason for sticking with a wide definition: the fact that the term 'donor-conceived person' is a widely accepted and used. And while there may be some important differences between those whose donors were paid and those who weren't, it will be at best confusing to have to have a different term for these two classes of persons. We could *in principle* talk about 'donor-conceived' and 'vendor-conceived' children, for example, but this would generate various problems. Foremost of these is that many of the people in question would not know into which category they fell and would therefore be forced to refer to themselves disjunctively as persons who were either 'donor' or 'vendor' conceived (or perhaps we would need to create an abbreviation like 'DVC people', for 'donor or vendor conceived people'). Another concern is that those who were 'vendor-conceived' might perceive this term as pejorative, given the negative attitude that some people have towards gamete selling. So for reasons of this kind, I will stick with the broader and more neutral definition of 'donation' in this chapter and will distinguish, within donation, between paid and unpaid donors.

The Origin View and its implications for gamete donation

To see why the question of gamete shortage is fundamental, it is necessary first to raise an issue that is well-known within the bioethics and philosophy literatures, but less so outside those domains: the non-identity problem (Parfit, 1984; Roberts and Wasserman, 2009; Wilkinson, 2010; Wrigley, 2006). It is necessary also to offer an account of how that problem applies in the case of gamete donation.

The non-identity problem arises because of what Parfit terms the Origin View. According to the Origin View:

> . . . each person has this distinctive necessary property: that of having grown from the particular pair of cells from which this person in fact grew. (Parfit, 1984: 352)

There is not space here to argue for the Origin View; I merely note for the present that it is widely regarded as plausible and that its supposed truth underpins a great deal of the ethics literature on the non-identity problem.[3] My main concern here then is exploring the *implications of* the Origin View, and more importantly of the non-identity problem, for certain aspects of gamete donation.

Crucially for the purposes of this chapter, the Origin View says that 'different egg' entails 'different child born', as does 'different sperm'. So, for example, if my parents had decided to use an egg donor instead of my mother's eggs, then (according to the Origin View) I would not have come to exist; a different child would have been created instead. Similarly, if they had decided to use a sperm donor, instead of my father's sperm, a different child would have been created and I would not exist. Thus when prospective parents (or their clinics) are choosing whether or not to use a gamete donor, and similarly when they are choosing between different candidate donors, they are (whether they realise it or not) choosing between different possible future people: choosing not merely what characteristics a child will have and who its biological parents will be, but which child, out of a number of distinct possible future children, will come to be born.

Before proceeding to look at the ethical implications of this, some initial clarificatory points need to be made.

First, the Origin View has no direct implications for questions of *parenthood*. In particular, there is nothing in the Origin View that commits

[3] For a critical discussion of the role of the Origin View, see Mackie's *How Things Might Have Been: Individuals, Kinds, and Essential Properties* (2006).

One additional complication is that, although the Origin View (combined with various biological facts about human reproduction) is capable of generating – and is arguably the most important source of – the non-identity problem, the non-identity problem can arise even if one rejects the Origin View. For simplicity's sake though the discussion here proceeds as if the Origin View were the only source of the problem. Nothing really hangs on this for the arguments presented in this chapter, since these are about the *implications of* the non-identity problem, rather than its origins. But it is worth keeping in mind that even those who reject the Origin View may have to grapple with the non-identity problem.

us to a biological or genetic account of who a child's 'real' parents are. The Origin View merely says that if my parents had decided to use a gamete donor, instead of their own gametes, then I would not have come to exist; a different child would exist instead. It does not however follow from this that that alternative donor-conceived child wouldn't have been as much my parents' 'real' child as I am, and the Origin View is just as compatible with social models of parenthood as it is with genetic or gestational ones.[4]

Second, the Origin View states a putative necessary condition, not a sufficient condition, for the identity of persons across possible worlds. It tells us that 'different egg' entails 'different child born', as does 'different sperm'. It does not though state that 'same gametes' *entails* 'same child born', and nor should it because of monozygotic twins, who provide us with many real-life examples of pairs of distinct people who originate from a single pair of gametes.

Third, as the twinning example illustrates, when discussing the Origin View and the non-identity problem, the term 'identity' is used to refer to numerical, as opposed to qualitative, identity. A and B are numerically identical if and only if A and B are the very same person (or, more generally, the very same thing). So, for example, *David Cameron* is numerically identical with *the man who became leader of the Conservative Party in 2005* who in turn is numerically identical with *the man who became British Prime Minister in 2010*. Identity in this 'numerical' sense can be contrasted with *qualitative identity*, also known as *exact similarly*. If Emma and Sophia are 'identical' monozygotic twins then they may well be almost *qualitatively* identical, meaning that they share (nearly) all of the same characteristics. But they are not numerically identical because they are two distinct people: Emma is not Sophia and Sophia is not Emma. Numerical identity is also quite distinct from ideas like cultural, national, political, sexual and social identity.

I have already suggested one way in which the Origin View is relevant to gamete donation. When prospective parents are deciding whether or not to use donor gametes, or deciding which gamete donor to use, they are (knowingly or otherwise) engaged in selective reproduction: choosing between numerically different possible future people.[5]

[4] See, for example, Archard and Benatar's (2010) *Procreation and Parenthood: The Ethics of Bearing and Rearing Children*.

[5] As is discussed in some detail below, some such choices are 'Same Number' (e.g. when prospective parents are choosing between different gamete donors) while others are 'Different Number'. 'Different Number' choices include cases in which the parents must choose between using donor gametes and not having a child at all, and those in

As well as its implications for individual prospective parents, the Origin View has implications at a policy level too, and so implications for governments, policymakers and regulators.

For example, the HFEA quite recently changed some of its policies on payments relating to gamete donation. Prior to 1 April 2012, the HFEA policy allowed reimbursement of reasonable expenses incurred within the UK but prohibited flat rate payments. At its 19 October 2011 meeting, the HFEA decided to move to something closer to a 'fixed rate' system. Both egg and sperm donors were to be offered a flat rate:

> ... which reasonably compensates them for any financial losses as well as recognising their time, commitment and dedication to helping others form a family. (HFEA, 2011: 4.4.3)

The amount decided upon was £750 per cycle of donation for egg donors and £35 per clinic visit for sperm donors. In most cases these amounts wholly replaced what would previously have been up to £250 in lost earnings plus reimbursement for out-of-pocket expenses. However, donors who 'incur excessive expenses', such as those from remote rural areas, can still claim additional amounts (above the £750) for such things as accommodation and travel. This provision cannot however be applied to donors from outside the UK because of fears that funding overseas travel costs could be an inducement (HFEA, 2011: 6.2.1.).

It is too soon to tell with any certainty what the effects of the HFEA policy change might be but it has been suggested that this more generous, or at least more straightforward, approach to remuneration has led to more British people becoming donors. The HFEA itself suggests in an October 2014 report that:

> The new policies, and perhaps the publicity surrounding them, may have had a positive impact on new donor registrations, if only temporarily for sperm donors. (HFEA, 2014: 22)

If that is the case (and we can assume this at least for the sake of argument, since this is just an illustrative example) then one consequence would be that, to some extent, the policy shift has changed who will donate and has therefore changed which children will come to exist. For example, maybe a few hundred additional donor-conceived children from British sperm donors exist now because of the 2012 policy-change. In many of these cases, the recipient parents would otherwise have gone abroad for treatment or would have imported gametes, if British

which they are choosing between using donor gametes and adoption (since adoption does not involve creating an extra person).

sperm had been unavailable.[6] So what the HFEA policy shift has done (at least in this 'thought experiment') is in effect to 'replace' a few hundred donor-conceived people from overseas donors with a few hundred donor-conceived people from British donors.

Similar thoughts apply to the policy of allowing 'egg sharing'. Egg sharing:

> . . . is where a woman receiving IVF treatment donates some of her eggs, for either treatment or research, at the same time as undergoing treatment herself. In return, the clinic can offer a significant reduction in the cost of her treatment. (HFEA, 2011)

UK policy is relatively permissive about egg sharing insofar as there is no limit on the value of benefits-in-kind offered for gametes. However, the only benefits-in-kind allowed are treatment services. Egg sharers then stand to gain the equivalent of many thousands of pounds worth of treatment services, far more in benefits-in-kind than the £750 in cash offered to egg donors not receiving treatment. As a result of this policy stance, egg sharing remains popular and more than 500 women registered as egg sharers in 2013 (HFEA, 2014: 17).

For the present purposes, the notable thing about this case is again that HFEA policy will at least partially determine which children come to exist. If, for example, the level of cash payments for egg donors and benefits-in-kind were equalised, as has been suggested by some critics, then presumably we would end up with fewer egg sharing donors and more paid donors not receiving treatment (Wilkinson, 2013). Or if egg sharing was banned altogether then perhaps this would lead to more women going overseas for eggs, or bringing overseas donors to this country. In any event, the policy on egg sharing will have a considerable impact on which eggs are used and therefore on which possible future children become actual children.

Finally, consider another recent example, the opening in October 2014 of the UK National Sperm Bank. This is an interesting and slightly different case as it is not about law or regulation as such and serves to remind us that other aspects of policy, such as decisions about service organisation and funding, or attempts to promote and support gamete donation through 'softer' means can have similar population-level effects. A BBC report on the opening of the sperm bank describes it as follows.

> A UK national sperm bank – charged with reversing a growing shortage of donor sperm – has started work in Birmingham. Fertility clinics have become

[6] 'British' here is shorthand for *resident in the UK*. It does not imply any particular ethnicity or nationality.

increasingly dependent on imported sperm giving rise to the so-called 'Viking babies' phenomenon. (Gallagher, 2014b)

If the BBC description of the situation is correct (and again let's assume that it is since this is just another illustrative example) then, as in the other cases described above, the decision to open a national sperm bank is very likely to be an instance of causing one group of possible future people to exist rather than another. For presumably a number, quite possibly a large number, of British couples who would otherwise have had a so-called 'Viking baby' will now instead have a child using British sperm. Thus, as well as possibly alleviating shortage (about which more later) the existence of the sperm bank will in effect cause a future population of 'Viking' babies to be replaced with an alternative set of numerically distinct babies (ones with predominantly British donors).

So, to conclude, when considering donor motives, payment and the welfare of the child, it is vitally important to keep in mind that many of the decisions made by prospective parents, by clinicians, and – most interestingly perhaps – by clinics, policymakers and regulators will affect which eggs and sperm come to be used and therefore will change who comes to exist.

For reasons explored in the next section, this point is vitally important to the ethics of gamete donation.

Harm and the non-identity problem

The ethical significance of the Origin View is that it generates what Parfit calls the non-identity problem. Parfit introduces the non-identity problem by reference to a number of cases, one of which concerns a fourteen-year-old girl who is deciding whether or not to have a child. He writes:

> This girl chose to have a child. Because she is so young, she gives the child a bad start in life. Though this will have bad effects throughout this child's life, his life will, predictably, be worth living. If this girl had waited for several years, she would have had a different child, to whom she would have given a better start in life. (Parfit, 1984: 359)

To elaborate slightly on Parfit's case, imagine that a fourteen-year-old girl (Amelia) is choosing between having a child now and having a child in ten years, when she will be twenty-four. Assuming that there is no embryo or gamete freezing involved, the child she has now (Oliver) will be a numerically different child from the one she will have if she waits (Jack). This follows from the Origin View combined with the fact that different gametes would be involved. Let's also stipulate, for simplicity's sake, that if she has Oliver then she will not have Jack and *vice versa*; that is, whatever happens there will be one and only one child.

Imagine first that Amelia has her child aged fourteen and Oliver is born. Because teenage pregnancy is challenging and disadvantageous in various ways, at least in our society, Oliver ends up with lower than average educational attainment, economic prospects and health. However, if Jack had been born instead ten years later he would (let's say) have had higher than average educational attainment, economic prospects and health. In short, Jack's anticipated levels of health and wellbeing would be much higher than Oliver's.

When Oliver is old enough to understand the circumstances of his conception, including the fact that Amelia could have waited to conceive but decided not to, he is distressed and cannot understand why she failed to give him the best possible start in life. What's more, he blames her for *harming* him, for deliberately, or at least knowingly, subjecting him to poor life prospects for no good reason. Amelia is sympathetic to Oliver's plight but does nonetheless set him right about one thing. It's true, she admits, that she could have waited and had a child some years later and that that child would probably have had a better start in life. However, that child would have been Jack (or some other child) not Oliver. So while clearly Oliver's life chances would have been better if he had been born into more favourable socio-economic circumstances, that was not one of the options available to Amelia when she was fourteen. Rather her choice was between having Oliver at fourteen and having a numerically different child, Jack, at twenty-four. For this reason, while Oliver might understandably be upset about his sub-optimal life prospects, provided that his life is 'worth living' (i.e. preferable to not being alive), he cannot claim to have been harmed by Amelia's decision not to delay pregnancy.

Now it may well be the case that *during his lifetime* Oliver is unjustly harmed by various things. For example, maybe, as a mother, Amelia didn't do everything that she could and should have done to help him, and maybe the government should have provided the family with better educational and social services to ameliorate the effects of its socio-economically disadvantageous position. These may well be valid harm-complaints. But what is much less likely to be justified is a harm-complaint regarding Amelia's *reproductive* decision (i.e. the initial decision to have a child at fourteen) because, as we have seen, any other decision would have resulted not in a better-off Oliver, but in Oliver's non-existence.

Does it follow from this that there is no reason for Amelia to delay pregnancy? No. All that follows directly from this is that, if there is a child-welfare rationale for delaying pregnancy, it is not that failing to do so will *harm* the child created (except perhaps in those very extreme cases in which the child's quality of life will be so appallingly low, and irredeemably so, that it would 'better off dead').[7] There may however be a different child-welfare rationale available in some cases; this is discussed in later sections.

It should also be noted that, in real-life policy debates, child-welfare is not the only consideration in play. For example, people may seek to justify public policies discouraging teenage pregnancy instead in terms of either cost saving (if it is the case that very young mothers generate more health and social care cost than other mothers) or in terms of other social issues (if, for example, it is claimed that the children of very young mothers are more inclined towards anti-social behaviour). And of course there is the welfare of the young mothers themselves to think of. However, given that the specific concern of this chapter is gamete donor motives and child-welfare, I will say nothing further about these other rationales.[8]

Payments to donors and harm to donor-conceived people

There is also concern that money detracts from the altruistic nature of donation and that non-altruistic donation may have a negative effect on the welfare of the future child, who may in fact feel that they were 'bought'. (HFEA, 2011: 13)

The above quotation – especially the suggestion that donor-conceived people may feel that they were 'bought' if they find out that their donors' motives were primarily financial – sums up very well the central concern of this chapter. The same papers quote a 'fertility patient and organisation supporting parents and would-be parents of donor-conceived children' which states that:

Donor-conceived people – half of whose genetic make-up is inherited from their donor – will inevitably speculate about the reason why their donor donated. Some will be disturbed by the thought that their donor may simply have donated for the money, a motivation that may be seen as disreputable. As one donor-conceived individual put it, 'to think that my donor might have been motivated by money and have no concern for my welfare makes me feel awful'. (HFEA, 2011: 78)

[7] I follow Buchanan et al. (2000) and many other scholars in distinguishing between cases in which a disease or condition, or in this case a set of adverse social circumstances, 'is so severe as to make the individual's life from that individual's perspective not worth living from those cases in which the harm is significant but still leaves the individual with a worthwhile life' (Buchanan et al., 2000: 224).

[8] I do however discuss some of these points in Stephen Wilkinson (2003). *Choosing Tomorrow's Children*, 99–107.

Consider also this extract from the Anonymous Us Project website.[9]

> I do not like it at all that I only exist because a graduate needed money to pay for his doctorate. Most donors would be decent enough to lie about their intentions, say they donate to help needy families, but my father was quite blatant. He told the complete truth on the donation forms, that he needed the money for a Ph.D. and that he wasn't donating to 'contribute to his fellow man'... one wonders how sick and twisted he had to have been in order to tell his future children quite plainly that he didn't want them and they only exist because he needed money for school.

Before proceeding to tackle directly the question of donor motives and harm to donor-conceived people, some important preliminary points must be noted. First, not *all* donor-conceived people feel this way about donor motives and financial reward; some may not care what their donors' motives were. Nonetheless, there does seem sufficient reason to warrant concern about the psychological impact that allowing payment would have on at least some donor-conceived people. Second, as is evident from the Anonymous Us quotation, as well as the question of what the donor's *actual* motives may or may not be, there is a whole other set of issues about what donors write on their donation papers, and about how and when this information is conveyed to donors. One possible view (for example) is that, for the sake of the welfare of the child, it would be better for donors to 'tell a story' (even one which is not wholly accurate) that the donor-conceived child will find more palatable than the bare truth that the donor simply needed the money. For simplicity's sake though, and because this is a topic that would merit its own chapter, I am going to leave this possibility to one side and will assume in what follows that the donors under discussion are ones who would (rightly or wrongly) give honest accounts of their motives in their donation papers – or that the donor-conceived children under consideration have some other way of finding out about the donor's motives.[10]

[9] The Anonymous Us Project describes itself as 'a safety zone for real and honest insights regarding third party reproduction (sperm & egg donation, and surrogacy)'. We aim to share the experiences of voluntary and involuntary participants in these new reproductive technologies, while preserving the dignity and privacy for story-tellers and their loved ones. All stories are contributed anonymously because '*anonymity in reproduction hides the truth, but anonymity in story-telling helps reveal the truth*'. See anonymousus.org/.

[10] I am not suggesting that this assumption is true of all or even most actual donors. Some donors will not give honest accounts, or any account at all. And of course some donor-conceived people will never find out about their biological origins because their social parents keep the information from them. This assumption then does limit the scope of the argument and its applicability to real-life cases. But it is an assumption that needs to be made because, without it, it is hard to see how the child-welfare argument against paying donors can work. For its central empirical premise is that many donor-conceived people are distressed *when they find out* that their donor was paid and so, in cases where

What then should we make of the fact that some donor-conceived people are angry, distressed, or psychologically scarred when they discover that their donors were acting primarily for financial gain. What implications does all this have for policy and practice? On a practical level, when dealing with people who exist now, we must do what we can to militate the negative effects of their receiving this information: for example, by encouraging recipient parents to provide it at the optimal time (even though there may never be a 'good' or 'easy' time), by providing contextual information and (where appropriate) counselling, and by encouraging and facilitating supportive social networks. But what about the more fundamental question of whether we should decommercialise gamete donation entirely in order to protect the interests of donor-conceived persons?

As has already been mentioned, my answer to this is that although decommercialisation of this sort may be justified (and justified on child-welfare grounds) in certain circumstances, this case for decommercialisation is not as straightforward as it might initially appear.

The underlying reason for this is that the position of those donor-conceived people who are distressed by the knowledge that their donor donated for money is not dissimilar – as far as *harm* is concerned – to that of Oliver, the boy brought into the world in adverse social circumstances by his fourteen-year-old mother. Imagine, for example, that Amelia is faced with a different decision. Should she have a child (Emily) using a paid sperm donor (Harry), given that Harry's sole reason for providing sperm is the money? Let's say that Amelia decides to go ahead and gives birth to Emily, having used Harry's sperm. When Emily finds out about her origins she reacts with anger and distress and accuses Amelia (and indeed Harry) of harming her. As in the case of Oliver, maybe Amelia has been an imperfect mother and harmed Emily *during her lifetime* by (for example) explaining her origins at the wrong time or in the wrong way. Similarly Harry may have done various things to harm Emily *during her lifetime*: not wanting contact perhaps. But then to differing degrees this sort of thing is true of all but the most saintly parents. However, again as was the case with Oliver, when it comes to the question of whether Amelia's *reproductive* decision (to have a child with a paid sperm donor v. not doing so) harmed Emily, the answer is almost certainly *no* (provided that Emily's life is not *so* bad that she would be 'better off dead'). For if we accept the Origin View, and on the assumption that Harry wouldn't have donated if it weren't for the money, then the only two possibilities

the donor-conceived person does not find out, the child-welfare argument does not engage (or at least not in this direct form).

for Emily were being a donor-conceived child originating from Harry's sperm, or not existing at all. And it is far from clear in those circumstances that Amelia and Harry have harmed Emily by causing her to exist.

Does it follow from this that Amelia's and Harry's decisions are beyond reproach? In the sections that follow, I shall argue that this very much depends upon the context in which they are made – and in particular on the question of gamete shortages, and more generally the question of what other options were available to Amelia at the time.

The Same Number Quality Claim

To start exploring what the *ethical* implications of all this might be, consider now the following thought experiment. The World Government must choose between two space colonisation projects: Mars or Venus. The Mars–Venus choice is thoroughly identity-affecting. If the Government opts for Mars, one set of people will go. If it opts for the Venus, a largely different set of people will go. Even if there is some overlap between the two initial groups, people's relationships and reproductive behaviour will diverge in the two different environments meaning that, by the time the second generation of space colonists is born, the two populations have diverged completely. The Mars–Venus choice is also a 'Same Number Choice', by which I mean that (as far as we can tell in advance) the same number of extra future people will be created in each scenario. There is however one known difference. While in the short-term, say the next one hundred years, the two colonies would be roughly equal in terms of their average quality of life, in the long-term, Mars will (owing to environmental degradation) become a much worse place to live than Venus. Hence, the Martian Colony would eventually contain much less wellbeing and much more misery than Venus would. Which colonisation project ought the World Government to choose? Surely (if all other things are equal) it should choose Venus even if, because the choice is thoroughly identity-affecting, no individual colonist will be harmed by the decision, whichever way it goes (Wilkinson, 2010: 90). Why should it choose Venus? Because of the plausibility of some sort of impersonal (non-person-affecting) welfare principle, such as what Parfit terms the Same Number Quality Claim:

> If in either of two possible outcomes the same number of people would ever live, it would be worse if those who live are worse off, or have a lower quality of life . . . (Parfit, 1984: 360)

The Same Number Quality Claim implies that when we are deciding between two (or more) possible future populations of equal size (and equal average life expectancy) then, other things being equal, we should prefer the one with higher average quality of life.[11]

'Populations' here includes populations of one. Thus when looking at Amelia's first decision (whether to give birth to Oliver at fourteen or to Jack at twenty-four), the Same Number Quality Claim says that (other things being equal) she should have waited and had Jack instead of Oliver. This then provides an answer to the question posed earlier: *does the fact that Amelia's decision to create Oliver does not harm him, does not make him worse-off than he would otherwise have been, mean that there is no reason for Amelia to delay pregnancy?* Not necessarily, for the Same Number Quality Claim is a possible reason. Since it is better (other things being equal) to create a child with more expected wellbeing than a child with less, we have some reason to prefer to create Jack.

The Same Number Quality Claim gives us a *putative* reason but is it a good reason? Should we believe the Same Number Quality Claim and, if so, why? One reason for accepting the Same Number Quality Claim is that an impartial preference for wellbeing (or for happiness or pleasure) and conversely a desire to avoid things that adversely affect wellbeing (pain and misery in all their various forms) seems constitutive of being a rational ethical decision-maker. Thus someone who was entirely indifferent to the wellbeing of others (even future others that he will never know) must be either irrational or unethical/non-ethical, some kind of moral psychopath perhaps. Similarly, it might be argued that, faced with something like the Mars–Venus choice, and knowing what we know about the likely future outcomes in each scenario, it would be simply perverse and irrational to opt for Mars. Why on Earth (so to speak) would anyone who is rational and cares about other sentient beings opt for Mars, the colonisation programme with *less* expected wellbeing?[12]

11 The 'other things being equal' clause is important because another variable here is the distribution of wellbeing. Many people would think it preferable, at least sometimes, to opt for a fairer and more equal possible future population even if this is not the one with the highest aggregate welfare levels. This egalitarian way of thinking is not however incompatible with the Same Number Quality Claim; it merely suggests that we need more than one moral principle when deciding which possible future population to create, and that sometimes considerations of distributive fairness need to be *weighed against* other considerations.

12 It should be noted at this point that the Same Number Quality Claim is not the only possible moral view of cases like the ones discussed and that some people have defended an alternative view of ethics, one which has been termed the Person-Affecting View. According to this view of ethics, as Parfit puts it (referring to a case which is in many respects like the Mars-Venus choice):

> ... *what is bad must be bad for someone.* On this view, there is no objection to our choice. Since it will be bad for no one, our choice cannot have a bad effect. The great lowering of the quality of life provides no moral reason ... (Parfit, 1984: 363).

Ethical and legal implications

What implications does this have for donor-conceived people and the question of payment and gamete donor motives? Earlier we looked at Amelia's second decision: whether or not to have a child (Emily) using a paid sperm donor (Harry) whose sole reason to donate is the money. If Amelia goes ahead (and does not take steps to prevent Emily from discovering Harry's motivations) then there is a good chance that Emily will be distressed and hurt when she finds out that Harry's sole motivation was financial. But because of the non-identity problem (i.e. because it's the case that, without Harry's financially-motivated donation, Emily wouldn't exist) it's also true that Amelia's decision is not *bad-for* Emily; it cannot harm Emily or make her worse-off. Now let's vary the case slightly. Imagine that Amelia has another option. She can either use Harry's paid donation to create Emily, or (perhaps by making an extra effort and travelling to a far-flung part of the country) she can source sperm instead from an altruistic donor (Jacob). If she uses Jacob's sperm then a different child, Isla, will be born instead of Emily. Should Amelia prefer to create Emily or Isla? The Same Number Quality Claim gives a reason to prefer Isla (just as it gives a reason to prefer Jack and to prefer Venus). If we grant that having a commercial gamete donor (on average) has a negative effect on the child's welfare (all other things being equal) Amelia should use an altruistic rather than a paid donor if this is practicable. For actualising a better-off possible future population (in this case a population of one) is morally preferable to actualising a worse-off possible future population.

Generalising from this, it looks as if there is a case for saying that unpaid donors are preferable to paid ones. The case is as follows.

First of all, a particular empirical premise must be accepted: that often, when donor-conceived people find out that their donors' motives were primarily financial, they are psychologically distressed or damaged, and seriously so. I make no attempt in this chapter to assess such claims; rather the point of the exercise is to ascertain *what would follow from* such claims ethically (and for regulation) *if* they turn out to be true.

On the Person-Affecting View, there is no (child-welfare based) ethical reason for Amelia to wait until she is twenty-four to have a child. Although Oliver's life will be much worse than Jack's would have been, creating Oliver is not *bad-for* anyone (since Oliver isn't harmed by being created), and so the choice between Oliver and Jack is (assuming all other things to be equal) morally neutral.

Against the Person-Affecting View, many people feel that intuitively it gives the wrong result in cases such as Amelia's choice between Oliver and Jack and the Mars–Venus choice and, in *Reasons and Persons*, Parfit (1984) spends a considerable amount of time discussing cases in which the Person-Affecting View looks to him to be implausible.

So what does follow from them?

As has already been noted, because of the non-identity problem, even donor-conceived people who find the idea of having come from a paid donor very upsetting are unlikely to be *harmed* by their parents' reproductive decision to use a paid donor, because the only alternative for them would have been non-existence. But such reproductive decisions may nonetheless result in donor-conceived offspring with lower levels of welfare than those that (probably) would have been enjoyed by an alternative set of possible future donor-conceived people: those who come from unpaid donors. Therefore since (according to the Same Number Quality Claim) we should, in general, create more rather than less wellbeing when faced with a choice between different possible future populations, we ought to opt for unpaid donors where a choice exists (assuming all other things to be equal).

This argument is about the ethics, the personal morality, of parents' reproductive decisions but can it also be applied to governments and regulators? Ought they too to prefer, or even to enforce, unpaid donation on this basis? How this question is answered depends on two things. First, what view in general do we take of state intervention and of interference with people's reproductive behaviour? And second, are we talking here about legal-regulatory restrictions, or about things like service organisation in the National Health Service (NHS)?[13]

Taking the first issue first, one well-known 'liberal' view of state restrictions on private behaviour (attributable to Mill) is that the only valid reason to restrict competent adults' liberties in law is to prevent harm to third parties (Mill, 2008). So because of the non-identity problem, which means that donor-conceived people themselves are very unlikely

[13] It is worth noting that European Law, specifically the European Union Tissues and Cells Directives, does prohibit, or at least limit, payment for human cells including gametes. Directive 2004/23/EC (March 2004) 'on setting standards of quality and safety for the donation, procurement, testing, processing preservation, storage and distribution of human tissues and cells' states that:

> As a matter of principle, tissue and cell application programmes should be founded on the philosophy of voluntary and unpaid donation, anonymity of both donor and recipient, altruism of the donor and solidarity between donor and recipient. (Preamble, s.8)

And that:

> Member States shall endeavour to ensure voluntary and unpaid donations of tissues and cells. (Article 12, s.1)

However:

> Donors may receive compensation, which is strictly limited to making good the expenses and inconveniences related to the donation. (Article 12, s.1)

to be harmed by the fact that their donors were paid, Millian liberals probably cannot support a prohibition on paid donation, or at least cannot do so for 'child protection' reasons. This is an interesting and important point as it shows that the earlier discussion of harm and the non-identity problem is not merely academic but that can have policy implications in certain particular areas, as least if one accepts political liberalism of this sort. However, liberals may nonetheless support state action to avoid harm occurring *during* children's lives: for example, if providing information to donor-conceived children in a certain way or at a certain time would be harmful to the child then there may be a case for state intervention to protect the child from such harms.

One response to this is of course to say that it just reveals a problem with that sort of political liberalism (e.g. an overly restrictive idea of the role of the state, or an insufficiently expansive conception of harm) and so all that we can conclude for now is that *if* one subscribes to a certain sort of political liberalism then, because of the non-identity problem, the case for prohibiting paid donation on child-welfare grounds seems weak.

I also asked earlier whether there might be a difference between questions of regulation and prohibition and questions relating to funding and service organisation. For example, we might ask whether, when setting up a publicly funded national sperm bank (and assuming for the sake of this example that a full-fledged commercial system in which donors are simply paid the market rate is a legal possibility), it should be organised with a view to ensuring that as many donors as possible are altruistic donors and, if so, whether child-welfare is a sound basis for doing this.

There are, it seems to me, at least two good (and closely related) reasons why, if faced with this choice, we should establish a purely altruistic sperm bank, rather than a commercialised one (and again this all proceeds on the assumption that (a) children from paid donors have lower average welfare levels than others and (b) that it is technically possible to establish an unpaid donation system that will deliver all the sperm we require). One reason is that the national health systems have a legitimate interest in the health and wellbeing of their populations, including future populations. The NHS Constitution for England, for example, says that the service exists 'to improve our health and wellbeing' (NHS, 2013: 2). Another is that national health systems have a legitimate interest in getting as much health and welfare gain as possible from any given unit of resource. Principle 6 of the NHS Constitution, for example, states that:

> The NHS is committed to providing best value for taxpayers' money and the most effective, fair and sustainable use of finite resources. (NHS, 2013: 3)

And so, if it is the case that a future population of donor-conceived children from altruistic donors will be better off than an alternative similarly sized one from paid donors, then (assuming that the health service costs are the same) creating the former will represent better value for money. For reasons of this kind, it is reasonable for national health systems (and other similar national organisations) to act on something like the Same Number Quality Claim and to organise services in ways that strongly encourage altruistic donation, or even which *de facto* rule out paid donation altogether. For rather different principles apply when deciding how to organise public services, as opposed to deciding which things should be legally prohibited or restricted.

So the main conclusions thus far are as follows:

(1) If it is true that the offspring of paid donors typically have lower levels of wellbeing than those of altruistic donors then, when they have a choice (and all other things being equal), prospective parents ought to select an altruistic donor in preference to a paid one. The basis for this however is not harm to the child but rather an impersonal ethical principle: the Same Number Quality Claim.

(2) Given the absence of harm, political liberals probably should not attempt however to translate this ethical requirement into law – although, as I have noted, not everyone is a political liberal and even most modern democracies are not entirely liberal in this strong Millian sense.

(3) If we accept the assumptions outlined in (1), then national health systems have good reason to facilitate and promote altruistic donation, rather than paid donation. This is because they have a legitimate interest in the wellbeing of future populations, and in maximising the benefit created by health service expenditure.

Conclusions (1) and (3) in particular are premised on parents, or on national health services, having a *choice between* paid and unpaid donation: that is, they refer to situations where payment is not a necessary means of getting the required gametes. But what about other situations, ones in which allowing or even encouraging paid donation is the only practical way of ensuring a sufficient supply of donor gametes? This question is the subject of the following section.

Financial incentives and gamete shortage

The non-identity problem arises because some choices which seem at first glance to concern a single determinate future person turn out to be identity-affecting: they 'affect the identities of future people, or *who* the people are who will live later' (Parfit, 1984: 355). Choices like Amelia's decision whether to use a paid or a different unpaid sperm donor, which initially seem like Same Person Choices (choices between two different sets of circumstance for the same person) turn out instead to be Different Person Choices (choices between two different possible future people).

As well as this distinction between Same Person and Different Person, a further distinction can be drawn, *within* Different Person Choice, between Same Number and Different Number Choice. As the name suggests, the distinction here is between cases in which we are choosing between two possible future populations *of the same size* and ones in which we are choosing between two possible future populations *of different sizes*. As Parfit puts it:

> Different Number choices affect both the number and the identities of future people. Same Number Choices affect the identities of future people, but not their number. Same People Choices affect neither. (Parfit, 1984: 356)

As before, 'population' here can refer to very small groups, such as a family's decision about how many children to have. Imagine, for example, that doctors have advised Charlie and Chloe that, if they conceive 'naturally' (i.e. through sexual intercourse) then, owing to a genetic condition, they are extremely likely to have twins, but that twinning can be avoided if they use IVF and PGD. Because of the Origin View, and the fact that different gametes will be involved in the two situations, this is a Different *Person* Choice. It is also a Different *Number* Choice because they must choose between creating one child (Child A) and (at least a strong likelihood of) creating twins (Child B and Child C).

Different Number Choices are, in one way at least, more complex and difficult than Same Number Choices; for we cannot rely on the Same Number Quality Claim to help us decide what to do. Imagine, for example, that Charlie and Chloe have to make the choice just described and that they know that, if Child A were to be born, he would have a very high level of welfare (let's say ninety on a quality of life scale of one to one hundred) whereas, if they were to have twins, their levels of welfare would be good but rather lower (let's say seventy-five each on the same scale). Ethically, from a child-welfare perspective, which option should Charlie and Chloe prefer? If they choose to have Child A then average wellbeing is maximised (at ninety); if they choose B and C then, while the average is lower (seventy-five), there is a higher aggregate (150). There are several competing answers to this question. One is that Charlie and Chloe should maximise the average expected level of child-welfare, in which case they should avoid having twins and go for Child A. A second is that they should maximise the aggregate and have the twins. A third is that both options are morally equal and/or that both are morally permissible. Each answer has its pros and cons but, before looking at these, let's see how all this applies to gamete donation and donor motives.

A good way into this is a real example. In June 2014, there were reports that the UK was 'facing a major sperm shortage' (Gallagher, 2014a). Let's allow for the sake of argument that that is the case. If it is, there are several possible responses (and what follows is not an exhaustive list). There might be more imported sperm, clinics might decide to accept poorer quality sperm, they might allow more donor offspring per man (if legally permitted) or they might (again if legally permitted) seek to attract more donors with higher payments. So now imagine a case in which the only effective way in which the clinic can deliver all the sperm that is required is the latter: paying donors more generously. Could that be an ethical option if it is known that the paid donors' offspring will have lower levels of wellbeing than those of unpaid donors?

What we have here is a choice like Charlie and Chloe's: a Different Number Choice. Imagine, for example, that if the clinic insists on accepting only altruistic donors then it will only be able to get thirty-five usable donations (when it needs one hundred) but that by paying £500 (way more than the present British level of £35) it can get more – well over one hundred donations – thus, as well as meeting otherwise unmet demand, giving prospective parents extra choice, and allowing there to be fewer offspring per donor. Is there a child-welfare objection to the clinic doing just that in these circumstances? (Of course there may be other ethical objections, such as concerns about the quality of the donors' consents, or about the commodification of the body, but these are the subject of other chapters and papers, not this one.)

This is a complex question but one thing we can say with certainty is that that the ethical position is nowhere near as clear or as straightforward as it was for the Same Number Choices discussed earlier.

One further distinction here is between situations in which the clinic's decision will be *wholly* identity-affecting and others in which there is a *partial overlap* between the two possible future situations. Think, for instance, about these two possible scenarios. In Scenario I, if no payment is offered there will be only thirty-five donations with thirty-five resultant children (set against a demand from patients of one hundred, so significant shortage). If alternatively payment *is* offered the 'original' thirty-five donations will still take place (and will still be unpaid) but *in addition* there will be an extra sixty-five paid donations (and an extra sixty-five children created), totalling one hundred (so no shortage). In Scenario II, if there is no payment there will be thirty-five donations with thirty-five resultant children (the same as Scenario I). But in Scenario II, if payment is offered then the original thirty-five unpaid donors will leave the programme but be replaced by a completely different set of one hundred paid donors (so again no shortage).

In Scenario I, the decision whether or not to allow payment comes down to this. Either the clinic can disallow payment, in which case only the 'original' thirty-five donations will happen; only the first thirty-five families on the list will get to have donor-conceived children with the other sixty-five remaining childless (if they don't already have children and aren't able or willing to adopt). Or the clinic can permit payment, in which case the 'original' thirty-five are unaffected and go ahead as normal but *as well as that* an additional sixty-five donor-conceived children will be created.

What should we make of the suggestion here that *for reasons relating to the welfare of the child* payment ought not to be permitted? Cases like this are quite unlike the Same Number cases discussed earlier. For to propose in these cases that payment should be restricted for the sake of the possible future children's welfare is in effect to say either that the world would be a better place without rather than with those sixty-five 'extra' children, or perhaps that those sixty-five 'extra' children would be better off not existing. And it is hard to see what reason there could be for supporting either claim. As for the suggestion that these children would be better off not existing, this *could* be true in cases where the psychological effects of finding out that one's donor was paid are so severe that they render life not worth living. There is no way of ruling this out *a priori* but the suggestion that the effects on average wellbeing are at that level of severity is a very strong claim indeed and one that would be hard to evidence. I do not deny here that these psychological effects can be very severe but are they really so severe (and in most cases, not just a few, since we are making a decision for a whole population here not just for those most adversely affected) that they make never having existed preferable to being alive?

An interesting parallel here is the debate about disability, quality of life and prenatal screening or preimplantation genetic diagnosis. In this context, many academics and people writing from a 'disability perspective' have been keen to point out, and rightly so, that even very severe mental or physical impairment and suffering is consistent with a 'life worth living' and therefore that we should be cautious about the proposal that, for reasons to do with their own wellbeing, possible future people with disabilities should be 'screened out of existence' (Albrecht and Devlieger, 1999; Buchanan et al., 2000; Shakespeare, 2013; Wilkinson, 2010). Similar thoughts might then apply to possible future people who come from paid donation. Whilst this group may have lower than average wellbeing, even if they do, this does not seem to be a sufficient reason to prevent them from existing at all (at least in these Different Number cases). We might also consider other parallels here such as with possible children who, if born at all, will be born into adverse socio-economic circumstances. There is every chance that such children will have lower than average levels of wellbeing but we don't generally think that, as a matter of law and regulation, only those who are relatively well-off financially should be allowed to have children. The reasoning here is the same. Whilst the children of people living in adverse socio-economic circumstances may, on average, have subnormal levels of wellbeing, most of them will still have lives worth living and therefore it would be irrational, perverse even, to prevent them from existing in the first place in order to protect them.

I conclude then that in cases like Scenario I, the child-welfare argument for not allowing paid donation is weak. But I should reiterate that the argument just presented applies only to Different Number Choices: cases in which the consequence of not allowing paid donation is a reduction in the total number of donor-conceived people. The position for Same Number Choices is different because, for those, the Same Number Quality Claim may give us an ethical reason to prefer to create (for example) one hundred children from unpaid donors, instead of one hundred children from paid donors.

What about Scenario II? Is that ethically the same as Scenario I? As I have said, the difference between the two is that, in Scenario II, the choice is between thirty-five unpaid donors and one hundred paid donors, rather than simply adding or not an extra sixty-five paid donors to a fixed group of thirty-five unpaid donors (who will donate whatever the clinic decides). If the average lifetime welfare level of the one hundred will be lower than that of the thirty-five then this case is more complex than Scenario I. This is because, although sixty-five more people with (let's assume) worthwhile lives are created if the decision to allow payment goes ahead, it might be objected that one consequence of this is that the thirty-five 'original' future children (those who would have been born following unpaid donation) are being 'replaced' by a different less well-off group of future children who come from paid donors. And this, it might be argued, is the opposite of what the Same Number Quality Claim demands.

This is one way of thinking about such cases, but to separate off the thirty-five seems artificial and unmotivated and it is probably better just to concede that the Same Number Quality Claim does not apply here because it is a Different Number Choice. This takes us into the realms of population ethics: a field which involves (amongst other things) a consideration of how to weigh the *size* of possible future populations against their *wellbeing*. As I suggested earlier when discussing Charlie and

Chloe's choice between a singleton and twins, there are several possible principles that we might deploy here.

One is to say that what matters is maximising the expected average level of child-welfare. If that is the preferred principle then it tells in favour here of the clinic banning payment and going with the thirty-five. Similarly it would tell in favour of Charlie and Chloe having just the one child (since it was suggested earlier that the only child would have higher levels of wellbeing than each twin). However, this principle is problematic because it seems that we can nearly always increase average wellbeing by being more selective and reducing the future population and it is a principle that would seem to push us towards quite draconian limits on reproduction, if it was enforced in law or even in the policies of health care providers. Even in this case the clinic might reason as follows:

Given our interest in maximising the average wellbeing of the children we create, rather than creating the 35 children, we will instead screen the recipient parents for socio-economic status, parenting ability, and anything else that might impact positively on health and wellbeing of the child and then only allow to be created the 5 children who have the very best chance of a very high quality of life, with the other 30 families remaining childless.

This might seem an absurd position but, if the focus is solely on average welfare, then such an approach is demanded. Therefore, we should reject this approach and not seek to maximise average welfare, or at least this cannot be our *sole* guiding principle.

Another option is to go for the maximisation of *aggregate* wellbeing. Based on this principle, the clinic may choose to use the one hundred paid donors instead of the thirty-five unpaid ones. The rationale for this would be that, unless the unpaid donor children have lives that are almost *three times better* than the lives of the paid donor children, the one hundred paid donor children will have more total wellbeing between them than the thirty-five unpaid donor children. This principle however is also problematic. One major problem with it is that can lead to what Parfit terms the Repugnant Conclusion. The Repugnant Conclusion is the view that when faced with a choice between creating (for example) a million extra people with lives only slightly better than not being alive (lives with positive but only very small amounts of wellbeing) and creating a much smaller number of extra people – let's say a thousand – with good lives, we should choose the former (unless, in this case, the smaller group will have lives which are more than a thousand times better) (Ryberg and Tannsjo, 2004).

A third option is to take the view that, in cases like this, both choices are equally good and/or that both are permissible. However, this third position too is problematic because it seems implausibly to commit us to not caring about, or at least to not having an ethical position on, important questions concerning future generations, such as climate change, the environment and even our own reproductive choices.

Returning now to the question of whether there is, in Scenario II, a defensible child-welfare oriented rationale for not allowing payment it again seems that there is not. Three possible principles for thinking about child-welfare in this case have just been considered. Two of those don't offer any reason whatever to prefer the thirty-five unpaid donors; the second tells us to go for the one hundred paid donors, while the third tells us to be morally indifferent. Only the first principle, the maximisation of average welfare, is a putative justification for preferring the thirty-five unpaid donors, but this principle itself looks highly problematic.

What are the implications of this for gamete donation, payment and gamete donor motives? The main conclusion of this section is that the question of whether prohibiting payment will cause shortage is crucial to the ethics of paying gamete donors. One obvious reason for this (not one discussed here) is that, when there is a threat of shortage, it is necessary to *weigh* the negative consequences of allowing payment (such as any ill effects on the donor-conceived population) against the positive consequences of allowing it (such as creating wanted donor-conceived children for families who need or desire them and who may otherwise be involuntarily childless). Whereas if there is no threat of shortage then there isn't an 'upside' to payment; there is no need to pay.[14] The point of this chapter though is more complex and, in one way, more fundamental. The central claim is that there is a huge difference ethically, in this domain, between Same Number and Different Number Choices. In cases where discouraging or prohibiting payment will not affect the size of the future donor-conceived population (e.g. by exacerbating shortage), then the choice between paid and unpaid systems is a Same Number Choice. And, if we grant that unpaid donor children will be better off on average than paid donor children, then it looks as if we have an 'impersonal' welfare reason to prefer an unpaid donation system. What underpins this is the Same Number Quality Claim. But where the absence of payment will cause shortages (where it will reduce the size of the future donor-conceived population) then the choice between paid and unpaid systems is a Different Number Choice. Some such situations will be like Scenario

[14] There may be reasons for paying other than the threat of shortage. One is to provide increased choice for recipients. In very commercialised systems in particular, payment could draw into the donor pool highly 'desirable' donors who might not otherwise donate; for example, in the United States, young attractive 'Ivy League' students can command more for their eggs and sperm than more 'average' donors.

I; it was suggested that, in such cases, there is clearly no defensible child-welfare rationale for not paying donors because the direct effect of not doing would be a reduction in the size of the donor-conceived population, and the non-existence of wanted children most of whom would, if born, have had worthwhile lives.[15] Situations like Scenario II are more complex and raise interesting and difficult questions in population ethics. But even in Scenario II it is difficult to come up with a plausible justification for preventing the above-mentioned wanted children who would, if born, have had worthwhile lives, from coming into existence.

Conclusions

What implications would (and should) there be for ethics and policy if we accept a particular empirical premise: the claim that, when donor-conceived people find out that their donors' motives were primarily financial, they are often psychologically distressed or damaged, and seriously so?

This chapter has argued that if this premise is true then, when they have a choice (and all other things being equal), prospective parents ought to use an altruistic donor in preference to a paid one. The basis for this however is not *harm* to the child created but rather an impersonal ethical principle: the Same Number Quality Claim. It is also important to note the 'when they have a choice' proviso; if paying is the only way in which prospective parents can procure suitable gametes, this may be acceptable.

Is this ethical requirement one that ought to be legally enforced? Not obviously so. Given the absence of harm, political liberals probably should not attempt to translate it into law – although, as I have noted, not everyone is a political liberal and even most modern democracies are not entirely liberal in this strong Millian sense. Public bodies may nonetheless have good reason to facilitate and promote altruistic, rather than paid, donation. This is because they have a legitimate interest in the wellbeing of future populations, and in maximising the benefit created by the deployment of health service resources.

Finally, and more controversially perhaps, it has been argued that the ethics of shortage situations (which are Different Number situations) may be quite different from that in non-shortage (Same Number) situations. If preventing payment to gamete donors will directly reduce the size of the donor-conceived population, arguments against payment which appeal

15 As has been noted, there are effects on existing people to consider too. For example, women whose best chance of having a child that is genetically and gestationally linked to them may be deprived of this opportunity if a ban on payment causes or exacerbates a shortage of donor sperm.

solely to interests of future donor-conceived people are likely to fail. For to propose that payment should be restricted in such circumstances for the sake of the possible future children's welfare implies either that the world would be a better place with fewer donor-conceived people, or that the children resulting from paid donation would not have lives not worth living (or both). Such implications are highly implausible and so child-welfare arguments for restricting payments to donors in shortage situations should be rejected.[16]

REFERENCES

Albrecht, G.L. and Devlieger, P.J. (1999). 'The disability paradox: high quality of life against all odds.' *Social Science and Medicine*, 48, 977–88.

Archard, D. and Benatar, D. (eds.) (2010). *Procreation and Parenthood: The Ethics of Bearing and Rearing Children*. Oxford University Press.

Buchanan, A., Brock, D., Daniels, N. and Wikler, D. (2000). *From Chance to Choice: Genetics and Justice*. Cambridge University Press. 224.

Gallagher, J. (2014a). 'UK facing 'major' sperm shortage'. 28 June. BBC News. Available at www.bbc.co.uk/news/health-28061263.

Gallagher, J. (2014b). 'UK Sperm Bank opens for business'. BBC News, 30 October. Available at www.bbc.co.uk/news/health-29815524.

Human Fertilisation and Embryology Authority (HFEA) (2011). *Authority Meeting Papers*, Paper 612, 19 October.

Human Fertilisation and Embryology Authority (HFEA) (2014). *Egg and Sperm Donation in the UK: 2012–13*. Available at www.hfea.gov.uk/docs/Egg_and_sperm_donation_in_the_UK_2012–2013.pdf. pp. 17, 22.

Mackie, P. (2006). *How Things Might Have Been: Individuals, Kinds, and Essential Properties*. Oxford University Press.

Mill, J.S. (2008). *On Liberty and Other Essays*. Oxford Paperbacks.

National Health Service (NHS) (2013). *The NHS Constitution for England*. p. 2. Available at www.nhs.uk/choiceintheNHS/Rightsandpledges/NHSConstitution/Documents/2013/the-nhs-constitution-for-england-2013.pdf.

Nuffield Council on Bioethics (2013). *Donor-conception: Ethical Aspects of Information Sharing*. p. 67. Available at www.nuffieldbioethics.org/wp-content/uploads/2014/06/Donor_conception_report_2013.pdf.

Parfit, D. (1984). *Reasons and Persons*. Oxford: Clarendon Press.

Roberts, M.A. and Wasserman, D.T. (eds.) (2009). *Harming Future Persons: Ethics, Genetics and the Non-Identity Problem*. Dordrecht: Springer.

Ryberg, J. and Tannsjo, T. (eds.) (2004). *The Repugnant Conclusion: Essays on Population Ethics*. Dordrecht: Kluwer Academic Publishers.

Shakespeare, T. (2013). *Disability Rights and Wrongs Revisited*. Abingdon: Routledge.

16 I would like to thank the following people for their helpful comments: John Appleby, Martin Richards, Rosamund Scott, Nicola Williams and everyone who contributed to the discussion of this chapter at our Cambridge workshop in April 2014.

Titmuss, R. (1972). *The Gift Relationship: From Human Blood to Social Policy*. New York: Vintage Books.

Wilkinson, S. (2003). *Bodies for Sale: Ethics and Exploitation in the Human Body Trade*. London: Routledge.

Wilkinson, S. (2010). *Choosing Tomorrow's Children: The Ethics of Selective Reproduction*. Oxford University Press.

Wilkinson, S. (2013). 'Is the HFEA's policy on compensating egg donors and egg sharers defensible?' *Medical Law Review*, 21, 173–212.

Wilkinson, S. and Garrard, E. (1996). 'Bodily Integrity and the Sale of Human Organs'. *Journal of Medical Ethics*, 22, 334–9.

Wrigley, A. (2006). 'Genetic Selection and Modal Harms'. *The Monist*, 89, 505–25.

LEGISLATION

EU

European Union Tissues and Cells Directive. Directive 2004/23/EC (March 2004).

12 Egg-sharing, motivation and consent

Ethical, legal and policy issues

Rosamund Scott

Introduction

The practice of egg-sharing, in which a woman may donate some of her eggs in exchange for benefits in kind, typically reduced-fee in vitro fertilisation (IVF) treatment, gives a woman who needs, wants and is unable to afford such treatment a very precious chance – namely that of having a genetically related child.[1] Drawing on relevant empirical evidence, in this chapter, I address a number of ethical, legal and policy questions about this practice. I first consider the significance and place of different kinds of reasons for donation. I then address the implications of this discussion for the quality and legal validity of consent to donation, referring again to the empirical evidence where helpful. I also reflect on a number of broader ethical issues, including the limited options a woman has when she may decide to donate, thus viewing her autonomy in a broader ethical context which includes the restricted availability of IVF treatment under the United Kingdom's National Health Service (NHS), coupled with the high costs of private treatment. I also touch on the question of to what extent either permitting, or not permitting, egg-sharing may benefit or harm a woman's interests. Finally, I turn to address the regulatory position, analysing aspects of current Human Fertilisation and Embryology Authority (HFEA) policy against the backdrop of the European Union Tissue and Cells Directive (EUTCD)[2] – which requires voluntary, unpaid and altruistic donation – and consider the extent to which the UK position is compliant with the Directive. With reference to terminology, I use 'egg-sharing' and 'donation in exchange for benefits in kind' interchangeably.

1 The Human Fertilisation and Embryology Authority (HFEA) defines egg-sharing as follows: 'Egg sharing involves a woman having fertility treatment and donating some of her eggs in return for benefits in kind in the form of discounted treatment services, usually a reduced treatment fee'. HFEA, 'Egg sharing schemes', www.hfea.gov.uk/1411.html.

2 Directive 2004/23/EC.

Reasons to donate eggs in exchange for benefits in kind: what the evidence does and does not tell us

In this section, I discuss key findings from some of the existing empirical evidence relating to the experience of benefits-in-kind egg donors. I discuss aspects of several papers that have been published based on survey evidence drawing principally quantitative conclusions; I also consider two qualitative studies based on interviews, in the context of egg donation for treatment and for research respectively. In addition, there are some facts from which relevant inferences may be drawn, including from overseas practices.

Several papers based on quantitative survey evidence have been published by Gurtin, Ahuja and Golombok (2012a, 2012b, 2012c). The authors obtained responses to questionnaires from forty-eight donors and thirty-eight recipients. In one, they report on the 'knowledge, motivations and concerns' of egg-share donors and recipients (Gurtin, Ahuja and Golombok, 2012c). As regards egg-share donors, a central conclusion is that 'most egg-share donors are motivated by the desire to have a baby, to obtain cheaper treatment, *and* to help another with whose plight they have empathy' (Gurtin, Ahuja and Golombok, 2012c: 192; emphasis in original). More specifically, the study found that for 87.2 per cent of donors the wish for a child was a 'key' motivator; that for 87.2 per cent of donors, an 'equally important' motivator was cheaper IVF; and that for 66.6 per cent of donors, there was also the wish to help another (Gurtin, Ahuja and Golombok, 2012c: 186).

Some free-text quotes give an indication of some donors' feelings, for example (interviewees' quotes in this section from Gurtin, Ahuja and Golombok, 2012c: 187–188):

> Egg sharing was the best option for me for two reasons. The first being that . . . I realized someone who could not even produce their own eggs would be suffering more than I. The second, it would also help with the costs of this treatment.

And, in another case: 'We made our decision 50–50 on altruism and financial support'. On the question of empathy with the situation of the recipient, one donor wrote: 'Egg-sharing seemed like a natural thing to do when we realised that there were many more people out there wanting to have a family like us, but were struggling in other ways that we could help with'. Another woman stated: 'I can empathise completely with my recipient . . . we both shared a longing to be a mother and I was more than happy to help another woman realise her dream of having a child'. With regard to the financial position of donors, while two donors said that 'although happy to help another, they would not have donated if they could have received treatment through the NHS', 'several others' noted their 'desire or happiness' to help others independently of their financial constraints: 'It felt right to share – I give blood, I am on the organ donor list and registered on the bone marrow register'. An egg donor using donor sperm wrote: 'Even prior to knowing about the egg-sharing programme I had discussed with my partner that I would like to 'give something back' and wanted to donate'. With regard to the last quote, the authors comment elsewhere in the paper on the high proportion of donors in lesbian relationships in this study (27.1 per cent) (Gurtin, Ahuja and Golombok, 2012c: 188), who wrote of the effect of their own need for donor sperm on their decision to donate. The authors also observe that, when asked about their financial position, 'significant numbers of donors indicated that they would have *considered* donating some of their eggs even if there was no benefit in kind (38.3%) and regardless of their ability to pay for treatment (54.3%)' (Gurtin, Ahuja and Golombok, 2012c: 189; my emphasis). This is a very interesting finding. Of course, we cannot know to what extent 'would have *considered*' would translate into actual donations, particularly if the possibility of benefits-in-kind egg donation had not been thought of before, for instance because there was no financial need to do so.

The authors also discuss the question of donors' options, noting that, 'contrary to concerns' only 6.5 per cent thought it was their only option (Gurtin, Ahuja and Golombok, 2012c). It would be very helpful to know more about this finding, particularly since the authors also note that '[t]he issue of treatment access was raised by several donors and recipients: women bemoaned their inability to receive treatment within the NHS and made a plea for the importance of funded fertility treatments' (Gurtin, Ahuja and Golombok, 2012c: 187).

An important question arising from the above findings concerns the relationship between the different motives, particularly whether any motive may be more dominant than another and, related to this, exactly what role may be played by any given one. Strictly based on the percentage figures above, the most important reason for donation was the desire to have a child (87.2 per cent), matched by the possibility of reduced-fee IVF (87.2 per cent), followed by the wish to help another (66.6 per cent). Overall, even though two thirds of donors said they wished to help another, and even though a number indicated that they 'they would have *considered* donating some of their eggs even if there was no benefit in kind (38.3%) and regardless of their ability to pay for treatment (54.3%)' (Gurtin, Ahuja and Golombok, 2012c: 189; my emphasis), it does not appear that we can say, based on this evidence, to what extent the wish to help another would *in fact* motivate donors *independently* of the financial issue. I return to the question of the *role* of this motivation below, following consideration of other empirical evidence.

Before turning to other evidence, we should note the authors' statements as to the limits of this evidence. In particular, they note 'the small sample size ($n = 86$) and the potential for bias within this sample' (Gurtin, Ahuja and Golombok, 2012c: 191), noting that respondents with stronger positive or negative views might have been more likely to participate; that they had 'a higher proportion of successful egg-sharers responding to the study than the clinical success rates for the same period indicate'; that recruitment was from only one clinic; and that, although respondents could 'complete open-ended items in their own words, these are not a substitute for face-to-face interviews, which would have allowed the researcher to explore emerging themes, to obtain much more detailed information, and to pursue any inconsistencies or topics of further interest' (Gurtin, Ahuja and Golombok, 2012c: 191). I refer to other aspects of Gurtin et al.'s evidence in the discussion of consent.

I now turn to a small-scale qualitative study conducted by Rapport by means of open-ended interviews using an 'interpretative phenomenological methodology' with eleven 'potential' egg-share donors (from one UK clinic) following initial consultations (Rapport, 2003). The particularly small scale of this study and the status of the interviewees as *potential* donors only should be noted at the outset. The interviewee data were analysed with reference to six key themes (namely egg-sharing, respectively, 'as' 'Context', 'Doubt', 'Coping', 'Exchange', 'Empathy' and 'Motherhood'). Here I note a few points in relation to several of these, selected for their relevance to the issue of motivation. I note some points particularly relevant to consent in the next section.

With reference to 'context', interviewees mentioned NHS waiting lists and concerns about how much time they still had left under their 'body clock' or before they were emotionally unable to continue with treatment. Treatments requiring the fewest number of 'personal compromises' were the first to be accepted (Rapport, 2003: 33). With regard to egg-sharing as 'exchange', Rapport observes that '[a]s a mutually beneficial exchange, the donation was akin to a pact between two women, and helping another woman was not to be underestimated . . . the notion arose in every interview and was . . . one of the most frequently discussed topics' (Rapport, 2003: 36). This appears to be consistent with aspects of Gurtin et al.'s evidence. However, Rapport suggests that the scheme was not necessarily seen as *equally* beneficial since donors saw themselves as giving more than they received, as in (following interviewee quotes from Rapport, 2003: 36): 'You cannot compare money to a life'. Rapport cites one instance in which the recipient was mentioned first and notes that in all other cases the donor was put first, as in '[s]o, mainly because obviously I want the treatment done and for someone else to be given the chance', or 'I get help for less money, and also there's somebody else out there'. Rapport notes that '[w]hen women were asked to describe what first attracted them to the scheme, they invariably mentioned that they saw egg sharing as an opportunity to have treatment without paying for it and being *also* able to help someone else' (Rapport, 2003: 36–37; my emphasis).

On the idea of egg sharing as 'empathy', Rapport states that '[t]hrough a heightened empathic concern, donors saw themselves as fulfilling a special task and, alongside their own desire to have a baby, this acted as a strong incentive to donate' (Rapport, 2003: 37). This could be seen as compatible with Gurtin et al.'s evidence. In this regard, Rapport observes that 'by associating with the recipient the donor was no longer alone', that helping another was seen as 'special', but that the women 'differed dramatically in the lengths to which they said they would go in order to assist the recipient' and that 'most interviewees described their own need as paramount', such as in '[t]he main thing is for us to have a child ourselves' (Rapport, 2003: 37). This evidence might be compatible with Gurtin et al.'s percentage figures regarding the different motives (for 87.2 per cent the desire for a child was a 'key motivator' and 66.6 per cent wished to help another.) Although 'there were times when the recipient was described as the more important of the two', as in 'If I could give her a baby and not have one myself I would do it because I know how it feels not to have a baby', such statements were 'invariably contradicted', as in 'I have only got one thing going for me, my eggs are OK. So I am willing to donate those eggs to get what I need' (Rapport, 2003: 37). With reference to egg sharing as 'motherhood', Rapport states that '[t]he need to experience motherhood was described as the *driving force* behind egg sharing' and that the wish to be a mother was 'forcefully and passionately' expressed (Rapport, 2003: 38; my emphasis). Of note, this can also be viewed as consistent with Gurtin et al.'s evidence that for 87.2 per cent of donors the desire for a child was the 'key motivator'.

Rapport's own conclusions with reference to her evidence are that we should question the role of altruism, given that egg sharing is 'very strongly based on co-dependency' (Rapport, 2003: 38). She suggests that although 'there was strong empathic concern and sympathy for another woman's plight, . . . it was personal desire complicated by a number of external factors [including waiting lists, shortage of NHS provision and the costs of private treatment] which drove their involvement' (Rapport, 2003: 39). Overall, she concludes that '[e]gg sharing is primarily a personal problem-solving device and, secondarily, a way of helping another woman have a baby; it is not, it would appear, an attempt to assuage an altruistic desire to give' (Rapport, 2003: 40). Thus, unlike Gurtin et al., Rapport draws a conclusion as regards the *primary* motivation for benefits-in-kind egg donation, arguing that this is clearly the recipient's own desire for a child. Although Rapport herself places the desire to help another as a secondary motivation, as I suggested earlier with reference to Gurtin et al., from this evidence we cannot say to what extent it was a *causally efficacious* motivation, particularly given the contextual factors noted relating to shortage of NHS provision, the passage of time and the cost of fertility treatment. What can other empirical evidence tell us about the question of the strength and causal role of different motivations?

The question of the effect of increased state funding of IVF treatment on donation rates has been discussed by Pennings and Devroey (2006) in the context of benefits-in-kind egg donation for the treatment of others in Belgium. On the question of reasons to donate, Pennings and Devroey's piece speaks directly to the question of the causative potency of different motivations because it refers to data both before and after Belgium introduced a policy providing for the costs of six cycles of IVF. On the relevant figures, they observe (Pennings and Devroey, 2006: 9, my emphases):[3]

> The data clearly indicate that there is a sharp drop (approximately 70%) in egg sharers after reimbursement was provided for the entire IVF cycle. A reduction was to be expected but these data show for the first time the impact of a cost reduction on the readiness of women to share their eggs. The data also show, contrary to the prediction of some, that full reimbursement of IVF does not bring egg sharing to a complete standstill (Rapport, 2003) . . . The data seem to confirm the fear that the *majority* of the women entering the egg-sharing scheme *are donating their oocytes because of restricted financial means* . . . .The conclusion that can be derived from the data is that *approximately two-thirds of the women who shared their eggs before full reimbursement of IVF were mainly motivated by the cost reduction.*

As Pennings and Devroey note, this contradicts the finding, for instance of Ahuja et al., that the main motivation for donation is the wish to help another (Ahuja et al., 1996, 2000).

These data provide very interesting insights into the question of the strength and role of different motivations for donation. They appear to indicate that only about one third of egg-share donors in Belgium during this time-period would donate without the fee reduction. Of note, this is

[3] For instance, in the last year before the change (2002), there were thirty-nine egg donors and in the first *full* year after it there were just twelve (2004), followed by ten the next year.

still a significant number. Thus, a reduction in IVF fees was a *causally necessary* condition for donation in 70 per cent of cases. Given, as Pennings and Devroey note (and as Gurtin et al.'s and Rapport's evidence shows), that both a woman's own needs *and* altruism may motivate (understood broadly at this point) benefits-in-kind egg sharing, those who did *not* donate after full reimbursement may include 'a group who shares oocytes purely for financial reasons and a group whose altruism or empathy is *not strong enough* to share after reimbursement is provided' (Pennings and Devroey, 2006: 9; my emphasis). In the latter group, altruism may make it *more likely* that a woman will donate but *only* when there is also a self-interested motivation (i.e., access to treatment is made possible because of a fee reduction or waiver).

The Belgian evidence shows that it is important to think carefully about the role that is actually played by empathy in donation decisions. For instance, one way in which we can think of empathy is in the sense that, given that one needs to do something (donate eggs) in order to attain something one very much wants (have the chance to have a genetically related child), one may, for instance, be *pleased* that the donation helps another (a woman who needs eggs). The fact that one is helping another may also help one *cope with* or somehow feel 'right' about what one is doing.[4] In this sense, empathy may well be cited as a 'reason', loosely understood, for the donation.

However, although one might feel empathy with others having fertility difficulties (Gurtin et al.'s evidence was that 66.6 per cent of women indeed do and Rapport observed that the notion of empathy arose in every interview and was one of the most frequently discussed topics), the key question is whether and, if so, to what extent that empathy actually has a *causally efficacious role* in one's donation, as Wilkinson has also discussed (Wilkinson, 2013). In this sense, in some cases empathy may have no causal role and in others it may have a causal role of varying degrees, sometimes being 'motivationally sufficient', to use Wilkinson's term (Wilkinson, 2013: 206), and sometimes not.

Of particular interest is the question whether that empathic concern is sufficiently strong to make one donate when free treatment is available. The Belgian evidence shows that for most women, in Belgium at least and during the period under discussion, the reason for donation in 70 per cent of cases – in the sense of the necessary cause – was access to reduced-fee treatment, presumably combined with the chance of having a genetically related child. Put another way, in 70 per cent of cases, by itself altruism was not a sufficiently strong causal factor. This seems a

[4] See the further discussion of Rapport's work below.

different position from one in which we conclude, as has been argued elsewhere, that altruism is very often a sufficiently causally efficacious motivation in egg-share schemes: 'In almost every case the donor egg sharer is attracted principally by the basic human desire for reciprocation but feels some recognition is entirely appropriate' (Ahuja et al., 2000: 104, citing Ahuja, Mostyn and Simons, 1997).

Thus, while all the empirical evidence discussed above indeed confirms that there are typically mixed motives and that, say, on Gurtin et al.'s figures, in 66.6 per cent of cases the desire to help another was present, it may be fair to say that empathy (or altruism),[5] by itself, is only a sufficiently causally efficacious motivation in a portion of the cases: on the Belgium figures, for instance, in 30 per cent of cases. That is still a significant number, particularly if the figure were at all generalisable, but it gives us important additional information regarding the *likely* role of empathy in egg donation arrangements in exchange for benefits in kind. With regard to the UK, we might reflect on the question of how many women undergoing either state-funded IVF or private treatment nevertheless choose to donate eggs and what conclusions might be drawn from this. (In this regard, Johnson has noted that there does *not* appear to be a pool of altruistic donors needing treatment (Johnson, 1999: 1915).) Now, the relevance of such evidence, if we could obtain it, would depend also on whether the women were asked to donate (most likely not), or whether they were aware of the egg shortage (to which questions of information from public campaigns would be relevant)[6] and in the light of such awareness simply thought to do so themselves. However, so far at least, we *do* know that in the UK the majority of egg donation has occurred in the context of benefits-in-kind egg donation arrangements (HFEA, 2012).[7] In other words, it would appear that, *generally*, women have *not* donated when they were simply seeking treatment for themselves which was either state-funded or for which they could pay. Of interest here, in its *Donation Review* of 2011, the HFEA noted that putting a cap on the fee reduction would likely reduce the number of benefits-in-kind donors (HFEA, 2011b).

Egg donation in exchange for reduced-fee IVF has also been discussed in the context of a collaboration between the Newcastle Fertility Clinic

[5] Clearly, I am not assuming these are the same.

[6] Of relevance here may be the intervention 'ladder' in the Nuffield Council on Bioethics Report, *Human Bodies: Donation for Medicine and Research* (Nuffield Council on Bioethics, 2011).

[7] The figures for 2010 are 57 per cent (776) for 'egg share' donors and 43 per cent (592) for non-patient donors. The information on 'egg share donors' does not state that these women are receiving benefits in kind. However, I presume that this is typically so.

and the Newcastle University stem cell research institute by Haimes, Taylor and Turkmendag (2012). I note some of their findings relating to motivation, which again speak to the question of the role of different motivations, in this section and I discuss their findings relating to consent and 'exploitation', a central concern of their paper, in the next. Haimes et al. interviewed twenty-nine women donating eggs for research at the Newcastle Fertility Centre along with twenty-one comparators (who donated eggs for others' treatment) and seventeen clinic staff; they also conducted a hermeneutic analysis of the transcripts (Haimes, Taylor and Turkmendag, 2012: 1203).[8] Generally, of the '19 analytic themes . . . identified . . . [c]entral to all . . . [was] the wish for a baby' (Haimes, Taylor and Turkmendag, 2012: 1203; my emphasis).[9] This is of course consistent with Gurtin et al.'s and Rapport's evidence and is to be expected when a woman undergoes IVF.

Of considerable interest, Haimes et al. note that before this reduced-fee scheme was introduced, researchers at Newcastle obtained HFEA approval to ask women whom it was thought would produce twelve or more eggs to donate two fresh eggs to somatic cell nuclear transfer ('SCNT') research, 'on the grounds that statistically this would not affect their pregnancy chances' (Haimes, Taylor and Turkmendag, 2012: 1200). There was a major problem, however, in that women 'proved reluctant' to donate eggs (Haimes, Taylor and Turkmendag, 2012: 1200). Haimes et al. had in fact interviewed these women previously and 'they had explained they could not contemplate giving eggs away before knowing if they were going to be of any use in their own attempts to have a baby' (Haimes, Taylor and Turkmendag, 2012: 1200). This is very interesting because it seems to indicate that, even if there had been some altruistic interest or intent on the part of these women, it did not have sufficient causative potency to make them risk compromising their own interests in having a child or children (about which I say more below). Accordingly, the researchers sought and obtained an HFEA license to operate a scheme in which women would receive a £1,500 reduction in IVF fees in exchange for donating half their eggs to research, arguing that this was akin to established egg sharing schemes (Haimes, Taylor and Turkmendag, 2012: 1201). Comparing the '12+' scheme with the scheme under consideration here, the authors state that '[t]he fact that they do provide eggs under the NESR [Newcastle egg sharing for

[8] See further the discussion in the paper.

[9] Note the five themes which were the most prominent: the interviewee's fertility story, money, the NESR [Newcastle egg sharing for research scheme], the interviewee's egg sharing story, and the juggling of considerations in deciding whether to provide eggs.

research scheme] is because the fees discount makes it significantly different from the 12+ . . . scheme', adding that 'it is notable that they highlight the increased chance of treatment that the reduced fees provide, rather than the discount itself' (Haimes, Taylor and Turkmendag, 2012: 1209). Of further interest is evidence which accords with that of Pennings and Deveroy above, to the effect that clinic staff advised that 'the local increase in NHS-funded IVF caused a decline in the number of volunteers for the NESR' (Haimes, Taylor and Turkmendag, 2012: 1209). While Haimes et al. discuss this in the context of consent, it is relevant also to the causal role, if any, of the motivation to donate for research (not a topic discussed at length in their paper). Haimes et al. also noted a 'very strong wish' for more NHS treatment and a preference for providing eggs *after* treatment (Haimes, Taylor and Turkmendag, 2012: 1208). Both of these preferences are of interest and relevance to this discussion of motivation and cause. Haimes et al. also noted the way eggs may be described as 'too precious to give away' (Haimes, Taylor and Turkmendag, 2012: 1209).

I now turn to consider the question of consent to donation.

Consent to donate eggs in exchange for benefits in kind: legal requirements and broader ethical issues

Background law

The consents involved in assisted reproduction treatment are governed by a mixture of common law and statute, namely the Human Fertilisation and Embryology (HFE) Act 1990, as amended by the Human Fertilisation and Embryology (HFE) Act 2008. When a couple seeks treatment the woman (or the one who is to carry the foetus in a same-sex relationship) is the patient (she will be subject to a certain drug regime and egg retrieval procedures) and she must consent to that treatment, the validity of which is assessed by the common law requirements of capacity, information as to nature and purpose and voluntariness.[10] The statutory provisions on consent require a couple's consent in writing for any of the stipulated purposes and compliance with these is a condition of a clinic's licence under section 12(1) of the amended 1990 Act.[11] I discuss relevant details of the common law and statutory position below.

[10] Regarding each of these elements, see respectively *Re M.B.* [1997] 8 *Med. L.R.* 217, *Chatterton* v. *Gerson* [1981] 1 All E.R. 257, *Re T (Adult: Refusal of Treatment)* [1992] 4 All E.R. 649.

[11] See also the HFEA *Code of Practice* (HFEA, 2015 [2009]), Licence conditions T57, R18.

The elements of consent

Capacity and information

All adults (those over 16) are presumed competent to consent to treatment and research in English law.[12] While it is theoretically possible that capacity could be negated, for instance as a result of the effects of the drugs used in IVF treatment (under the test in sections 2 and 3 of the Mental Capacity Act, 2005), this is unlikely and so I put the issue to one side.

To be informed about *treatment* sufficient for the legal notion of consent, a patient must be informed of its nature and purpose.[13] The HFE Act (as amended) imposes additional information requirements – relating to the 'implications requirements' – for the *donation* of eggs or embryos (to others or to research), requiring that (in text that must be read as applying to 'she'):[14]

Before a person gives consent . . .

(a) he must be given a suitable opportunity to receive proper counselling about the implications of taking the proposed steps, and

(b) he must be provided with such relevant information as is proper.

These requirements are duly interpreted in the HFEA's *Code of Practice* (HFEA 2015 [2009] paras 5.5–11, Box 12A, para 12.6), which also stipulates that centres 'should draw up separate agreements with the gamete provider and with recipient(s)' (para 12.13).

One of the 'implications' of benefits-in-kind egg donation is a reduction of 50 per cent in the number of eggs available to a woman seeking to become pregnant. In this regard, one of the women in Haimes et al.'s study observed (Haimes, Taylor and Turkmendag, 2012: 1206; cited as M18: 977–1029):

> I think it would be up to the person, as long as they're getting all the information and people [*sic*] saying to them 'you're going to be reducing your chances, you sharing your eggs'. As long as they are fully aware of that, I think the choice would be up to them.

Despite this, it is not clear that this is always fully understood, as a quote from Rapport's evidence shows: 'Well if I have had my share of the eggs, what I want, then if I can help somebody else, what is the problem, because they would go to waste' (Rapport, 2003: 35; interviewee 05). However, as I discuss below, the extent to which a woman has had 'her share' needs clarification.

12 Mental Capacity Act 2005, §1.

13 *Chatterton* v. *Gerson* [1981] 1 All E.R. 257.

14 Human Fertilisation and Embryology (HFE) Act 1990, as amended by the HFE Act 2008, Sched. 3, ¶ 3(1).

Voluntariness

The legal requirements

As noted above, consent to treatment or donation is only valid if voluntary. The little English case-law on point from treatment cases concerns a patient's will being overborne in some way. In the leading case of *Re T (Adult: Refusal of Treatment)* the Court of Appeal explored the notion of undue influence and the way it might negate voluntariness, analysing the effect of influence with reference to three factors: namely, the strength of will of the patient (for instance if tired or in pain s/he may be less able to resist); the relationship between the persuader and the patient; and the types of arguments used.[15] It is not easy to prove that voluntariness is negated by undue influence in the treatment context, as *U* v. *Centre for Reproductive Medicine* – a case from the assisted reproduction context – shows.[16]

Voluntariness may also be affected by factors beyond those such as 'undue influence'. For example, when the US President's Commission looked at this issue, it emphasised not just that treatment should not be coerced, but also that manipulation of information – through misrepresentation, fraud, or distortion – may affect voluntariness (President's Commission for the Study of Ethical Problems in Medicine and Biomedical and Behavioral Research, 1982: 66–8). Whilst the former examples imply intention, the latter may occur unintentionally. Although there are no English cases on point, these issues should be borne in mind.

Voluntariness and egg donation for benefits in kind: law and ethics

There are several points of possible relevance to voluntariness in the context of benefits-in-kind egg donation.

First, consider the following sections of the *Code*: 'Where relevant, the possibility of donating gametes for fertility treatment, mitochondrial donation or research should be raised before a potential donor's treatment cycle begins. Patients should not be put under pressure or unduly influenced to donate gametes or embryos' (HFEA 2015 [2009]: para 12.1). In part, this is clearly an implicit reference to the legal notion of undue influence discussed above. The *Code* also states: 'The gamete

[15] [1992] 4 All E.R. 649.

[16] [2002] E.W.C.A. Civ. 565. In this case, the Court of Appeal declined to find that a man who had changed his consent form so as to disallow posthumous use of his sperm, following discussions with a clinic nurse and who subsequently died, had been unduly influenced by her. The decision is respectfully criticised by Scott et al. (2012: 281–2).

provider should be given enough time to consider the implications of donating, before the donation is used' (HFEA, 2015 [2009]: para 12.9). In practice, however, there is little time available between egg collection and the use of eggs in the treatment of another, including by the creation of an embryo. It is a time which also has the potential to be highly emotional. For instance, a nurse who was interviewed in research that concerned donation of so-called 'spare' embryos to stem-cell research (as part of a collaborative research project in which I was engaged) observed (Scott et al., 2012: 277; Nurse 1, Site 3):[17]

> The patient's got to make their decision in a cold situation and not . . . with all the emotions going round their heads when they're at egg collection and they're full of hormones and they're full of expectations and anticipation and they've got a vision of this baby that's coming . . . that's not a time for decision making.

The implication is that it is very important that women are as sure as they can be *before* they start treatment that they are (sufficiently) content to donate eggs during the course of their treatment. It is also very important that they are fully aware of their right to change their mind up until the transfer of embryos created using their eggs to another woman's uterus.[18]

Second, there are a number of references to notions of 'vulnerability' and 'desperation' in the literature[19] and a few in the empirical evidence that are potentially relevant to the notion of voluntariness. Can it be argued that women have been induced to consent against their 'true wishes' by the significant fee reduction for treatment which they otherwise could not afford?[20]

Turning to the empirical evidence, there was only one quotation relevant to this in Gurtin et al.'s quantitative research papers, namely 'I think they are very lucky to have a mom/parents who were so desperate to have a child that they went through [*sic*] egg sharing process. I believe they must be very loved' (Gurtin, Ahuja and Golombok, 2012c: 1694). There is brief reference to 'desperation' in the section on 'coping' in Rapport's paper, in which she notes the idea of 'desperation' as one mechanism, for instance as in 'seeing egg sharing as the right way forward simply because you so desperately "want it to be"' (Rapport, 2003: 35; interviewee 02).[21]

There are also references to 'desperation' and 'vulnerability' in Haimes et al.'s work that often appear alongside the notion of 'exploitation', about

[17] See this paper for further discussion of this research.

[18] HFE Act 1990, as amended by the HFE Act 2008, Sched. 3, ¶ 4(1), (2).

[19] See, for example, the discussion in Wilkinson (2013: section III).

[20] See the discussion on point in ibid.

[21] There is also reference to '[a]ssociation', in the sense of likening egg sharing to other forms of donation (at 35). Rapport also reports that '[w]omen talked about being unable to cope if they searched their emotions too deeply' (Rapport, 2003: 35).

which the women were explicitly asked. Most strikingly, perhaps, one egg donor who had taken part previously in an egg sharing for treatment (EST) donation, 'described herself as having "baby madness" and would have done anything' (Haimes, Taylor and Turkmendag, 2012: 1204; cited as M17: 740–66):

At the time, it was all, 'that's good because I'll be helping someone' but thinking about it now, [EST] is quite exploitative really... the fact that I was going to have a child that was half mine out there in the world... I think maybe they are preying on people but I was probably quite happy to be preyed on if it meant that I was going to get the treatment.

Interestingly, interviewees 'regarded other volunteers as potentially vulnerable, emotionally and financially'. An egg donor said: 'I never felt like that' (Haimes, Taylor and Turkmendag, 2012: 1203; cited as M01: 850–903), although she and her husband said 'that would be the only objection I could think of... exploiting people who otherwise wouldn't be able to afford to do it' (Haimes, Taylor and Turkmendag, 2012: 1203–1204; cited as M01/M01P: 1079–1092). They also said (Haimes, Taylor and Turkmendag, 2012: 1204; cited as M01/M01P: 1979–2014, 2082–2106):

... regarding exploiting people and money... entrance criteria should not just be based on the medical side, it needs to weigh up desperation... it has to be people's emotional ability to cope... there's financial vulnerability and emotional vulnerability.

The women in Gurtin et al.'s study were also explicitly asked about whether they felt they were being 'exploited'. Gurtin et al. report that (Gurtin, Ahuja and Golombok, 2012b: 706):

... 87.5% of donors and 75.7% of recipients expressed disagreement or strong disagreement with the statement 'Egg-sharing is exploitative', with only 4.2% and 5.4%, respectively, expressing agreement. Even among unsuccessful egg sharers, only 12.5% agreed with this statement.

As Gurtin et al. conclude, rightly, '[t]hese data indicate that egg sharers *themselves* do not generally feel that they are being exploited' (Gurtin, Ahuja and Golombok, 2012b: 706; my emphasis).[22] Further, Haimes et al., summarising their evidence with reference particularly to the notion of exploitation, observe (Haimes, Taylor and Turkmendag, 2012: 1208):

[C]oncerns about exploitation are not uppermost in women's accounts of their experiences of the NESR. Most grounds for acknowledging the potential of the

[22] Note, however, that '[s]uccessful women were significantly more likely than unsuccessful women to disagree or strongly disagree with the statement that "Egg-sharing schemes exploit women" (92.5% versus 62.5%, respectively...)' (Gurtin et al., 2012b: 704).

NESR to be exploitative are dismissed and other grounds are cited for rejecting the charge outright. . . . the charge is rejected as interviewees position the NESR within a landscape of fertility treatment where private fees are high, helping somebody else's treatment has serious, lifelong, consequences and global markets are alienating and untrustworthy. In such a terrain, the NESR seems a reasonable alternative. Interviewees did not enter the NESR naively but with a sense of what they regarded as acceptable and unacceptable. Those who rejected the charge of exploitation outright did so on the grounds that they had to take the initiative, there was no coercion, they felt well informed, they were gaining the chance of more treatment and they were helping research.

Once again, the implication would seem to be that the *women*, at least, felt both that they were not being exploited and that they were giving valid consent. Of course, the perception of egg-sharers as to whether or not they are being exploited does not necessarily determine the question of whether they are, since they might not realise this themselves; however, I do not have the scope here to engage in a substantive discussion of theories of exploitation (to which Haimes et al. helpfully attend, given the central focus of their paper).

A woman who had already had several cycles of IVF and later decided not to go ahead stated (Haimes, Taylor and Turkmendag, 2012: 1206; cited as M11: 795–818; my emphasis):

I don't believe it at all personally because it was full choice . . . it was just a leaflet I had seen, it wasn't pushed or anything, it was just informative . . . If someone's desperate and they can't afford a full cycle they may decide to do that, when they don't really want to, but that's still their choice. The *centre's* not forcing them.

This brings out an interesting point, which is that the *clinic* is very unlikely to be *unduly* influencing a woman's choice and it would be extraordinary if it forced her to donate. This may go some way to explaining the strong feeling in those asked that they were not being 'exploited'.

However, the position may be more complicated than that. For instance, another woman said (Haimes, Taylor and Turkmendag, 2012: 1207; cited as M29: 872–918; my emphases):

Nobody's getting exploited, if they didn't want to do it they wouldn't do it, but some people are so *desperate* for a family. Four and half thousand pounds is a *lot of money* . . . you've got to give people a chance . . . the *NHS waiting list* is five years and they're on about putting it to seven.

This interviewee seems to be saying that although she thinks that women are not being exploited, nevertheless they may be desperate (in the light of their wish to have a child) given the shortage of NHS provision and the high cost of private treatment. The question that arises is whether it is possible to give valid, especially voluntary, consent when the available options constrain one's autonomy to such a degree.

It has been argued by Wilkinson that these two factors – namely, that NHS funding may not be adequate (or consistent or fair) and that fertility clinics' prices may be 'too high' – which he describes as 'contingent structural features', coupled with the issues of possible 'desperation' and 'vulnerability', give us reason to be concerned about the 'quality' of consents in the case of benefits-in-kind egg donors (Wilkinson, 2013: 200). We can link these points with the Belgian evidence of the very significant drop in donation rates after free treatment was introduced and our knowledge that (at least in that case) 70 per cent of women would *not* donate if they did not 'have to' (given their very strong wish for a child). It would be rather puzzling not to be concerned about this, though I discuss below the question of the possible balance between benefits and harms. Does the fact that 70 per cent of women (at least based on the Belgian evidence, and perhaps also implied in Rapport) would not donate if they did not 'have to' mean that their consent is involuntary, either ethically or legally speaking?

As we have seen, the law has a rather stringent approach to establishing invalidity of consent, such that it is hard to establish undue influence and rebut a presumption that free will has prevailed. Further, since its focus is rather narrowly on the parties to hand, which in this case would be the woman, possibly her partner, and the clinic, questions of the effect on voluntariness of the constraints of NHS funding or the cost of private treatment would likely be thought too remote. Accordingly, provided the woman has capacity and the information elements for donation are appropriately covered (which is a very important issue in its own right), I suggest it will be hard to maintain that consent to donate eggs in exchange for reduced-fee IVF is legally invalid.[23]

Moreover, and importantly, it is not clear that it would be helpful to establish this, because then (assuming ongoing financial constraints) such women may be unable to take part in such schemes, thus depriving them of the clearly highly valued chance of a genetically related child conceived in this way. This would be a very real harm. So although, following Wilkinson's line of argument, we can say that the women who are affected by a shortage of NHS provision and high private fees may have been unjustly deprived of options, arguably the law is right to accept their consents. This is an important conclusion. This is not at odds with Wilkinson's argument, since he notes that, ethically speaking, sometimes it is right to accept people's consents for this reason (Wilkinson, 2013: 197). However, we should note that such consents are being given, and accepted, in circumstances of significantly constrained autonomy, namely

[23] Compare the discussion in Scott et al. (2012), regarding flaws in the process of consent to the donation of so-called 'spare' fresh embryos to research.

the choice between *no* chance of one or more genetically related children on the one hand, or of one or more in exchange for the donation of half a woman's eggs on the other. Viewed in one way, neither of these choices might be thought to be fully autonomous, for instance if the relevant conception of autonomy is one that encompasses the ability to choose between an 'adequate' range of options (as for instance Joseph Raz has argued (Raz, 1986: 373 and following discussion)) and the option of benefits-in-kind donation is not thought to be 'adequate'.

The literature suggests awareness of the limited options open to benefits-in-kind egg donors. For instance, Gurtin et al. comment in the closing stages of one article (Gurtin, Ahuja and Golombok, 2012a: 192; my emphasis):

> Within the *broader context* of donor egg shortages, as well as cutbacks to health services which have led to reduced NHS provision of IVF in some areas of the UK, egg-sharing presents a means for more women to access IVF while simultaneously providing more donor eggs.

Further, Johnson states that 'anecdotal evidence from personal testimonies by paid egg sharers as well as the very low incidence of unpaid egg donation by the infertile, both suggest that recourse to paid egg sharing would be a last resort if a true choice between the two treatment options were available' (Johnson, 1999: 1915, 1913). Haimes et al. note that 'although interviewees regard the decision to provide eggs under the NESR to be freely made, these are not necessarily decisions made under *circumstances wholly of their own choosing*' (Haimes, Taylor and Turkmendag, 2012: 1209; my emphasis). The question of options is also discussed by Blyth, in the context of a discussion of responses to a 1998 HFEA *Consultation on the Implementation of Withdrawal of Payments to Donors*, who notes that given limited NHS provision (and egg shortages) 'several respondents commented that egg sharing represented the *only* means by which some people might access treatment' (Blyth, 2002: 3256; emphasis in original).[24]

On the question of options, one point from the Haimes et al.'s evidence (touched on in their summary above) concerns the distinction between donating for research and donating for the treatment of another. On this, Haimes et al. observe (Haimes, Taylor and Turkmendag, 2012: 1204; cited as M01: 850–903):

> For some, providing eggs for research was preferable and less exploitative than providing eggs for the treatment of others. For example: '[S]haring for treatment for other people . . . could be classed as more exploitative because of what the

[24] This was the HFEA's *Consultation on the Implementation of Withdrawal of Payments to Donors* (1998).

consequences are, the emotional things. [The NESR] is a lot easier to get your head around, even though [EST] is free to you'.

We do not know how many women might feel this way, but it is worth noting the very significant differences between the two options, and the possibility that at least *some* improvement may be made to the range of limited options if women were to have the choice. Haimes et al. note that there *was* a choice at the Newcastle clinic and that most women chose to donate for research, not another woman's treatment. By contrast, Gurtin et al. found that only '27.7% of donors said that they would have considered donating eggs to research rather than to another woman' (Gurtin, Ahuja and Golombok, 2012a: 189). Presumably, the nature of the sample in each case may have something to do with these differences.

Harms and benefits

I have suggested that if we were to hold that there cannot be valid legal consent to donate eggs as part of an egg donation in exchange for benefits-in-kind arrangement, this could be very harmful to women, given the available options. I now turn to note some of the factors that may be relevant to an assessment of the ways in which and the extent to which the practice of egg-sharing could benefit or harm a woman's interests.

On the one hand, as touched on above, as compared with the alternative in which a woman does *not* need to donate eggs in order to obtain treatment, there is always a *potential* detriment to a woman where she 'loses' the opportunity to have half of her own eggs fertilised in order to create a richer pool of embryos from which those thought to have the best chance of live birth can be selected, and the remainder frozen for possible future use. Where she did not need to donate eggs, she might seek to use one or more of these frozen embryos either in the event that her first cycle fails or where further children are sought following a live birth.[25] However, if she has no (or fewer) frozen embryos, she will either certainly (or possibly) have to undergo a further fresh stimulation cycle. Where this occurs at least several months following the birth of one child, she will necessarily be older and her fertility may have declined to some degree. Moreover, with developments in egg- and embryo-freezing, coupled with policy developments relating to single embryo transfer (SET), there are now *more* negative effects from egg donation than previously and thus greater potential for damage to a woman's (and her partner's) fertility interests since there will *always* be fewer eggs or embryos to

[25] This is discussed in detail in Scott et al. (2012).

freeze as a result of donating eggs.[26] These issues should all be addressed comprehensively at the information stage. As noted earlier, however, it is not clear that this is always the case.

On the other hand, and very importantly, this scenario needs to be compared with the one in which a woman is not eligible for NHS-funded treatment and cannot afford to pay for private treatment: in such a case, she cannot use *any* of her eggs to try to become pregnant unless she donates half of them as part of a benefits-in-kind donation agreement.

Another key area for consideration concerns the emotional aspects of this kind of donation. The donation may result in the birth of a child to someone else, who may well seek the donor out (in a way that could of course go very well) in the future. To such a child the donor may be as related, genetically at least, as to a child to which she had given birth, but there would only be the possibility of any social relationship when the child can access identifying information at eighteen under UK law.[27]

There is only space to note a few aspects of the conflicting empirical evidence on point. Turning first to Rapport's interviews with potential donors, she observes that 'doubts suffused the interviews' and included doubts about: whether the donor would feel differently twenty years later; the parenting skills of the recipient; the various possible future meetings between different parties; as one interviewee put it, 'whether you would be doing this if you had money for private treatment'; and, as Rapport describes it, 'lack of control over the consequences of one's actions [which] frightened the women' (Rapport, 2003: 34), as, for example, in the statement 'It's going somewhere and you don't know where' (Rapport, 2003: 34 (text box); interviewee 04). Rapport suggests that the interviewees were 'incapable of talking about eggs in any other than uncertain or ambivalent terms' (Rapport, 2003: 34), and began to dissociate from the donation, using such expressions as '[n]ot a life form' (Rapport, 2003: 34; interviewee 06) or '[n]ot a person . . . you are giving it before it is a human being' (Rapport, 2003: 34; interviewee 07), '[l]ittle tadpoles' (Rapport, 2003: 34; interviewee 09). Overall, she suggests that

26 Compare McMillan and Hope (2003: 584), who suggest that there is 'virtually no extra risk'. The position in Ahuja et al. (2000: 104), that freezing should be seen as a 'bonus' was, in my view, never sustainable and is clearly not so now. As Ahuja et al. also note: 'The key advantage of shared egg donation is that no third party takes risks for the benefit of the recipient because the donor requires drugs and an operation for her own needs' (Ahuja, Mostyn and Simons, 1997: 2845). It is clearly right that, as compared with non-patient donors, egg-share donors are already certainly going through *one* cycle of assisted reproductive treatment; if they successfully give birth as a result of that cycle, and have no desire to have another child (or have one or more frozen embryos from that cycle which they successfully use in a subsequent cycle), they will not need to undergo another treatment cycle.

27 HFE Act 1990, as amended by the HFE Act 2008, § 31ZA(4).

'[t]hese feelings made them appear at best slightly discomforted and at worst extremely uncomfortable' (Rapport, 2003: 35). With reference to egg sharing as 'coping', Rapport notes what she describes as interviewees' 'coping mechanisms', such as alluding to the '[d]ispensability' and '[o]verabundance' of eggs (Rapport, 2003: 35; interviewee 05).

By contrast, Gurtin et al.'s study paints a much more 'positive' picture. For instance (Gurtin, Ahuja and Golombok, 2012c: 1694):

> Of the 30 donors who responded to the open-ended question enquiring about their feelings towards any potential children born using their eggs, the most popular sentiments that were expressed were those of curiosity and those of general goodwill (by eight donors each) . . . Five donors wrote about the recipient, their family and their sense that the child/children would be much loved by them . . . Of the remaining eight donors, three mentioned that they would be interested to meet the child/children one day; two expressed affection and one pride. All of these responses were positive.

However, there were also three responses that Gurtin et al. suggest could be described 'either as ambivalent or negative' (Gurtin, Ahuja and Golombok, 2012c: 1694):

> One wrote 'It's a strange feeling of love for a child that you will have no say over'; another said she felt strange and sad at the thought that 'there may be a child with my genes (perhaps who looks like my own child, etc.?) whom I won't ever know'; and one donor who knew that her recipient conceived but did not carry the child to term wrote 'When I found out that she had a miscarriage, I needed to mourn the loss of the/my child'.

To give a flavour of the evidence more generally, Gurtin et al. note that:

> [T]here were few significant differences between successful and unsuccessful egg-share donors regarding their feelings about their recipient, any potential children that may have been born through their donation and the potential for contact with such children in the future.

They also suggest that, '[t]aken overall, the data on donors' and recipient's feelings paints a portrait of goodwill in both directions' (Gurtin, Ahuja and Golombok, 2012c: 1697). Only five of the forty donors were unsuccessful and of these 'none . . . expressed negative feelings regarding their recipients' conception, and three explicitly reported positive feelings (although one noted that she was "upset" at first)' (Gurtin, Ahuja and Golombok, 2012c: 1698). More generally, regarding successful benefits-in-kind donors (Gurtin, Ahuja and Golombok, 2012b: 704):

> [T]he great majority of those who had children felt that the overall impact of egg-sharing on their lives had been 'very or quite positive' (94.3%), almost all were glad to have taken part (94.4%) and none (0%) expressed regret. If they

could make the decision again with the benefit of hindsight, 94.4% would still take part in egg-sharing.

Turning to the views of unsuccessful benefits-in-kind donors (Gurtin, Ahuja and Golombok, 2012b: 704):

> Over half (56.3%) rated the experience of egg-sharing and its impact on their life as either very positive or quite positive and three-quarters (75.0%) were glad to have taken part. However, unlike the successful egg sharers, a small minority (9.4%) of unsuccessful egg sharers expressed regret regarding taking part in the scheme and 62.5% stated that if they could make the decision again with the benefit of hindsight, they would still take part in egg-sharing, compared with 94.4% of successful egg sharers.

Of note, the number of donors in this study who were unsuccessful was small. It seems likely that it could well be difficult for a woman who has not been able have a child herself to know that another woman was successfully able to do so following the donation of her egg. It will be particularly important to know how the feelings of such women may develop over time.

Clearly, then, more empirical evidence is needed. However, we can at least draw some very preliminary conclusions on the balance of benefit and harm. Of particular note, the existing conflicting evidence just discussed must be set in the context of the already-reduced options that such a woman has, specifically the hardly voluntary alternative of no chance of a much-wanted genetically related child or children. On balance, then, at least until there is an increase in NHS funding, it seems likely that the practice is more beneficial than harmful, since it gives a woman a highly valued chance that she probably would not otherwise have; moreover, the 'cost' of donating half of her eggs from a given cycle has to be compared with an alternative in which there is no chance to use *any* of her eggs. Accordingly, ethically speaking, the HFEA has been correct to permit the practice. But is the HFEA right to think that its policy complies with the EUTCD?

Motivation and consent: the legal and HFEA policy position relating to benefits-in-kind egg donation

The EUTCD

The 'legal parameters' (HFEA, 2011b: para 1.2) of donation are governed by the EUTCD. Paragraph 18 states:[28]

[28] Directive 2004/23/EC, para 18.

As a matter of principle, tissue and cell application programmes should be founded on the philosophy of voluntary and unpaid donation . . . [and] altruism of the donor and solidarity between donor and recipient.

The HFEA states in its *Donation Review* papers of 2011 that '[t]he Directive delegates power to the HFEA, as the UK Competent Authority, to decide how UK donors are compensated' (HFEA, 2011b: para 1.1). I presume that this is an interpretation of Article 12(1), which states:[29]

Member States shall endeavour to ensure *voluntary and unpaid* donations of tissues and cells. Donors may receive compensation, which is *strictly limited to making good the expenses and inconveniences related to the donation.* In *that case,* Member States define the conditions under which compensation may be granted.

Given the conjunction of the first and second sentences of Article 12(1), it is not clear that there is in fact that much scope to 'define the conditions' for the granting of compensation. Further, on the question of implementation, Article 4 states:[30]

1. Member States shall designate the competent authority or authorities responsible for *implementing the requirements* of this Directive.
2. This Directive shall not prevent a Member State from maintaining or introducing *more stringent* protective measures, *provided that they comply* with the provisions of the Treaty.

Thus, I note that the Directive allows for the possibility of the introduction or maintenance of more stringent measures, providing that they comply with the Directive but not, perhaps unsurprisingly, for less stringent ones.

Are benefits-in-kind egg donation schemes compliant with the EUTCD requirements noted above?

The HFEA interpretation and policy

I turn first to the notion of 'unpaid' donation and the Directive's guidance on 'compensation'.

The HFEA (2011b: para 1.2; emphases in original) states:

We have been advised that the concept of *'compensation'* under EUTCD is sufficiently broad to encompass egg sharing schemes. Factors that support such an interpretation include the fact that egg sharing arrangements serve to promote an over-arching objective of the EUTCD by increasing the availability of human cells and tissues for donation and fostering *'solidarity between donor and recipient'.*

[29] Ibid., Art. 12(2), my emphases.

[30] Ibid., Art. 4(1), (2), my emphases.

It would be helpful to have more detail about this advice, in the absence of which it is hard fairly to assess this approach. However, it is not clear that the notion of 'compensation', which the Directive itself states should be 'strictly limited to making good the expenses related to the donation',[31] can necessarily be further explicated with reference to the supposed policy objectives of the Directive (on which I say more below). By contrast, with reference to the Directive's requirement, in Article 12(1), that compensation be 'strictly limited to making good the expenses and inconveniences related to the donation', it could well be plausible to suggest that a reduction in fees for an egg donor can be seen as 'a recognition that a part of her treatment involves an egg donation and, as such, should not be chargeable to her', as the HFEA suggests in the *SEED Report* of 2005 (para 6.13), presumably in response to the EUTCD of 2004 (HFEA, 2005).[32] Of course, strictly speaking, the same course of 'treatment' is *also* treatment for the donor for the purposes of assisting her to become pregnant and, arguably, typically *primarily* so, based on the discussion of the nature and causal efficacy of different motivations in the section entitled 'Reasons to donate eggs in exchange for benefits in kind: what the evidence does and does not tell us', above. A woman will, however, donate half of the eggs from that same course of treatment and the fee reduction could be seen as 'making good' the 'inconveniences'. (On the question of compensation, note also the HFEA's relatively recently adopted position on compensation for non-patient donors, whereby non-patient donors can now receive £750 which, according to the HFEA (2011b: para 4.3), 'reasonably compensates them for any financial losses as well as recognizing their time, commitment and dedication to helping others form a family'.[33])

Further, it is not clear that an 'over-arching objective of the EUTCD' has been correctly identified simply as 'increasing the availability of human cells and tissues for donation'. Whilst Paragraph 3 of the Directive notes that '[a]s there is a need to ensure the availability of tissues and cells for medical treatments, Member States should promote the donation of tissues and cells . . . ', Paragraph 18 states that 'Member States are urged to take steps to encourage a strong *public and non-profit* sector involvement in the provision of tissue and cell application services . . . ';

[31] Ibid., Art. 12(1)).

[32] Blyth and Golding (2008: 467) suggest that this was 'anticipating implementation' of the EUTCD.

[33] The HFEA noted that Spain compensates in the region of this figure (HFEA, 2011b: para 1.7). For discussion comparing the HFEA's policies on benefits-in-kind donation and compensated non-patient donation, see Wilkinson (2013). For discussion of what the HFEA's 'Ethical Principle of Altruism' (HFEA, 2011b: para 5.1) could mean, see Wilkinson (2011).

moreover, the final section of Article 12(2) states that 'Member States shall endeavour to ensure that the procurement of tissues and cells as such is carried out on a *non-profit* basis'.[34] So, it is not entirely clear to what extent the objective, to use the HFEA's phrase, of 'increasing the availability of human cells and tissues for donation' can fairly be cited as a relevant policy objective in the context of *private* sector egg donation in exchange for benefits in kind. The HFEA does not mention the 'public and non-profit sector' point. The Belgian evidence shows that *public* sector benefits-in-kind egg donation, while it exists, is very limited and so, indeed, the Directive might well seek further to promote such donation. But that is a different matter.

The second 'over-arching objective' to which the HFEA refers is that of '*fostering* "solidarity between donor and recipient"' (HFEA, 2011b: para 1.2; my emphasis). However, if we look again at the EUTCD, we see that it makes no mention of 'fostering' solidarity. As noted above, the Directive says that '[a]s a matter of principle, tissue and cell application programmes should be *founded on* the philosophy of voluntary and unpaid donation . . . [and] altruism of the donor and solidarity between donor and recipient'.[35] There are two potentially important differences between this and what the HFEA says. First, the Directive mentions altruism and the HFEA does not at this juncture. Second, the Directive refers to 'programmes' being 'founded on . . . altruism of the donor and solidarity between donor and recipient', whilst the HFEA refers to 'fostering "solidarity between donor and recipient"'. As the following discussion tries to show, it is not clear that these are the same thing, although it could be argued that 'fostering' is nevertheless compatible with this 'philosophy'.

Turning first to the notion of 'founded on', on one plausible interpretation, this could be said to mean something akin to 'based on', in the sense that altruism and solidarity are the 'driving' factors or motivations for donation. In this sense, 'founded on' would be seen as implying a *necessary* causal role for altruism and solidarity. This takes us back to the discussion of the role of different motivations for donation in the section entitled 'Reasons to donate eggs in exchange for benefits in kind: what the evidence does and does not tell us', above. As we saw above, the existing empirical evidence on point indeed shows that altruism and solidarity may be motivations of donors, but it also shows that these may only be causally efficacious in a (significant) minority of cases (at least on the Belgian evidence (evidence that the HFEA (2011b: para 4.3)

[34] Directive 2004/23/EC, para 18 and Art. 12(2), my emphases.
[35] Ibid., para 18, my emphasis.

itself notes)), and by implication also in the United Kingdom given the lower levels of donation beyond the benefits-in-kind donation context. Of course, it might be argued that 'founded on' also encompasses donations in which the presence of altruism or solidarity makes it *more* likely that a woman will donate her eggs as part of a benefits-in-kind egg donation arrangement.[36] However, this might also be thought to be something of a stretch which is not really true to the 'spirit' of the Directive. Of relevance to this discussion is also the point that the HFEA does not itself mention 'altruism' at this juncture.

I turn next to the notion of 'fostering', which I have suggested is not the same as 'founded on'. It seems plausible to suggest that benefits-in-kind egg donation arrangements may 'foster' solidarity,[37] in the sense that they give an opportunity for women (both donor and recipient) to feel and act on empathy for one another. Earlier, I cited aspects of the empirical evidence that would support this (evidence noted by the HFEA itself and present also in the HFEA's own evidence) (HFEA, 2011b: para 4.3, 116). Arguably, the term 'fostering' implies something like 'creating', 'promoting' or 'encouraging'. Indeed, the HFEA itself states that 'egg sharing *creates* a sense of reciprocity and solidarity between sharer and recipient, who are helping each other to address each other's infertility' (HFEA, 2011b: para 3.2, para 4.6; my emphasis). Once again, I also note that the HFEA does not mention the other Directive requirement of 'altruism' at this juncture.

On the one hand, then, it seems right to say that 'fostering' and 'founded on' are not the same. On the other, 'fostering' solidarity or altruism is, other things being equal, an ethically desirable goal and one that may be compatible with the EUTCD 'philosophy of tissue and cell application programmes . . . [being] . . . *founded on* . . . altruism of the donor and solidarity between donor and recipient'.[38] For instance, put very simply, we could say that when we successfully encourage altruism and solidarity we then generate donations that are based on or founded on solidarity and altruism. However, reflecting on the empirical evidence

36 I note that Pennings and Deveroy suggest that '[i]t can be argued that a system of donation is morally acceptable if donors are at least partially motivated by empathy and the desire to help others. For this group, the incentive of discounted or free treatment services gives the *extra push* to make them donate' (Pennings and Devroey, 2006: 9; my emphasis). It is not clear, however, that we can necessarily conclude that it is not, rather, the other way around in some cases, such that the possibility of altruism constitutes the 'extra push'.

37 As Wilkinson (2013: 203) notes, a recent 'working definition' of solidarity has been given by Prainsack and Buyx: '. . . solidarity signifies shared practices reflecting a collective commitment to carry "costs" (financial, social, emotional or otherwise)' (Prainsack and Buyx, 2011).

38 Directive 2004/23/EC, para 18, my emphasis.

that we have, it is important to recall that it seems fair to conclude that altruism and solidarity generally seem *not* to be motivationally sufficient (to use Wilkinson's phrase). Rather, donation is typically motivated (in the sense of a necessary cause) by the need to access reduced-fee treatment. In this sense, the donation might be said to be *founded on that need*, even though donors may well *also* feel empathy with their recipient. It might still be argued that that is compatible with the Directive, but the difference should be noted.

More generally with regard to the HFEA's policy approach to benefits-in-kind donation, I note that it appears to have made some statements that are both inconsistent and not clearly supportable, including with reference to its own evidence. In its *Donating Sperm and Eggs: A Review of the HFEA's Sperm and Egg Donation Policies 2011*, the HFEA (2011a: Annex A, *Facts Sheets Stimulus Used within the Forums and Interviews*, 250–1) states:

> Little is known about what motivates people to donate sperm or eggs, but what is known suggests that . . . some donors want to help a friend, family member or stranger to have a family . . . *most egg sharers would not donate if there were no incentive to do so* . . . many egg sharers want to both help themselves and to help someone else. Certainly in relation to egg donation the benefits in kind are part of the reason why people donate, but *a main motivator appears to be a desire to help others*. Outcomes of a survey we carried out with UK fertility clinics and interviews with some sperm and egg donors support this.

It is not clear that the two emphasised passages are consistent with each other unless, that is, we downgrade the meaning of 'main' in the second passage or emphasise the 'a' which precedes it. Based on my discussion in the section entitled 'Reasons to donate eggs in exchange for benefits in kind: what the evidence does and does not tell us' of evidence which the HFEA also considered (HFEA, 2011a: Annex E, *Literature Review*), it is also not clear that the Authority can fairly make the second statement (and I note that the two illustrative quotations provided by the HFEA also do not clearly support this second statement).[39] Indeed, this latter statement, namely that 'a main motivator appears to be a desire to help others' (unless this is meant to mean something quite different from, say, '*the* main motivator . . . ') in any event appears inconsistent with aspects of the HFEA's evidence, for instance from its Report on the Clinic Meetings, amongst its 2011 *Donation Review* papers, to the effect that 'most

[39] Thus, the HFEA observes: 'Comments from clinicians included: "*I don't think that most donors are doing it for the money but we would probably get more donors if they felt valued and the reimbursement was more proportionate.*" And "*The amount is part of the whole jigsaw of what encourages a donor to donate*"' (HFEA, 2011a: 12; emphases in original).

did agree that if fertility treatment was fully funded by the NHS, the number of women choosing to egg share would decline significantly' (HFEA, 2011b: Annex K, *Report on the Clinic Meetings*, 265). Indeed, this in fact supports the first emphasised statement above, namely that 'most egg sharers would not donate if there were no incentive to do so'.

To be fair to the HFEA overall, it does acknowledge that the existing empirical evidence is limited and has typically 'involved low numbers'; as noted earlier, it also cites the Belgian evidence (HFEA, 2011b: para 4.3).

As for the other relevant requirement of the EUTCD – the notion of voluntariness – I have argued that benefits-in-kind egg donation may well be voluntary as regards the law's rather narrow requirements for the purposes of the legal notion of consent. For this reason, I suggest that the HFEA was right to conclude, in its 2005 *SEED Report*, and as recalled by the Authority in 2011, that 'there was little evidence that egg sharers' judgment was distorted by a promise of free treatment' (HFEA, 2011b: para 4.2), at least from a legal standpoint. Although I also argued above, compatible for instance with Wilkinson's arguments, that ethically speaking such consents are being given in circumstances of highly constrained autonomy, significantly, given the apparent balance of benefit and harm, I suggest that the HFEA was right to conclude that 'the potential harms of egg sharing were not likely or significant enough to justify prohibiting the practice' (HFEA, 2011b: para 4.2; 2008: para 6.14).

Overall, as regards the EUTCD, we have reason to question the extent to which benefits-in-kind egg donation schemes (which are necessarily in the private sector) are in accordance with the 'spirit' of the Directive. However, to be fair to the HFEA, the letter of the Directive is not that clear, given uncertainties in phrases such as '[a]s a matter of principle' and 'founded on'. Nevertheless, until there is greater NHS funding of IVF treatment I also conclude that, ethically speaking, the HFEA is right to continue to permit the practice in a regulated form and that, for this reason, the various possible 'stretches' in the HFEA's attempt to reconcile the practice with the terms of the Directive may be less problematic than they might otherwise be. In some ways, the ethics of the HFEA's current position seem nicely captured by an excerpt from its Patients Focus Group Report, amongst its 2011 *Donation Review* papers (HFEA, 2011b: Annex H, *Patients Focus Group Report*, 193; emphases in original):

> The group expressed mixed feelings on egg sharing. On the one hand people felt that women may share their eggs because they feel like they have no other

choice: – *'I think it's quite sad egg sharing, you're having to give away something that you desperately want yourself.'* At the same time, the group did feel that egg sharing gives women an option that they wouldn't otherwise have: – *'It does have its advantages – you could think of it as enabling her [the egg sharer] to have cycle* [sic] *that she wouldn't be able to do.'*

Conclusions

The empirical evidence that we have so far on egg donation in exchange for benefits in kind is of great value. However, it is also contradictory in various ways and limited. It is clear that more evidence is needed. On the basis of the limited evidence that we have, some of which indeed presents a 'positive' picture of the practice of benefits-in-kind egg donation,[40] I have drawn the following preliminary conclusions.

First, while motivations for donation are mixed and feelings of altruism, empathy, solidarity, or reciprocity are typically present, financial compensation in the form of relief, in whole or in part, of IVF treatment fees may well be causally necessary for egg donation in the majority of cases, though a significant minority may still be prepared to donate.

Second, given the law's rather narrow approach particularly to the issue of voluntariness, it seems right to conclude that women can give valid legal consent to be egg-share donors. Despite this, ethically speaking we still have reason to worry about the quality of the consent, or at least the circumstances in which it is given, as others have argued. Thus, we should take note of the situation of significantly constrained autonomy in which a woman who very much wants to have a child – and may well feel 'desperate' and be 'vulnerable' – has to make such a choice, given the involuntary nature of the alternative in which she has no chance of a genetically related child due to the limited nature of NHS funding and the high cost of private treatment. However, and very importantly, if a woman can only access treatment that she very much needs and wants by donating half her eggs from a given cycle, then the chance that this gives her of having a genetically related child appears to be a very significant benefit. Moreover, particularly if she is successful in her attempt to have a child, it is also one that may well outweigh the possible harms.

Accordingly, until there is greater NHS funding of IVF treatment, it appears right, ethically speaking, that the HFEA permits and regulates the practice; moreover, it could be very harmful to ban it. As has been shown, however, it is not so clear whether, or to what extent, the practice

40 See generally the papers by Gurtin et al. (2012a, 2012b, 2012c).

is in accord with the EUTCD. While in the short term the HFEA's current possibly rather stretched interpretation has the merit of legitimising the practice, in the longer term this might be seen as reinforcing the status quo and thus reducing the pressure on the NHS further to fund IVF. It also reduces the pressure, of course, on the question of how to address the shortage of eggs, which is another hugely important topic in its own right.[41]

REFERENCES

Ahuja, K.K., Simons, E.G., Fiamanya, W., Dalton, M. et al. (1996). 'Egg-sharing in assisted conception: ethical and practical considerations'. *Human Reproduction*, 11, 1126–31.

Ahuja, K.K., Mostyn, B.J. and Simons, E.G. (1997). 'Egg sharing and egg donation: attitudes of British egg donors and recipients'. *Human Reproduction*, 12, 2845–52.

Ahuja, K.K., Simons, E.G., Rimington, M.R., Nair, S. et al. (2000). 'One hundred and three concurrent IVF successes for donors and recipients who shared eggs: ethical and practical benefits of egg sharing to society'. *Reproductive BioMedicine Online*, 1, 101–5.

Blyth, E. (2002). 'Subsidized IVF: the development of "egg sharing" in the United Kingdom'. *Human Reproduction*, 17, 3254–9.

Blyth, E. and Golding, B. (2008). 'Egg sharing: a practical and ethical option in IVF?', *Expert Review of Obstetrics and Gynecology*, 3, 465–73.

Gurtin, Z.B., Ahuja, K.K. and Golombok, S. (2012a). 'Egg-share donors' and recipients' knowledge, motivation and concerns: clinical and policy implications'. *Clinical Ethics*, 7, 183–92.

Gurtin, Z.B., Ahuja, K.K. and Golombok, S. (2012b). 'Egg-sharing, consent and exploitation: examining donors' and recipients' circumstances and retrospective reflections'. *Reproductive BioMedicine Online*, 24, 698–708.

Gurtin, Z.B., Ahuja, K.K. and Golombok, S. (2012c). 'Emotional and relational aspects of egg-sharing: egg-share donors' and recipients' feelings about each other, each others' treatment outcome and any resulting children'. *Human Reproduction*, 27, 1690–701.

[41] Of interest, in its October 2014 report *Egg and Sperm Donation in the UK: 2012–13*, with regard to its 2011 amendments to compensation policy discussed above, the HFEA reported that 'three quarters of survey respondents said that following the new donation policies, the number of women expressing an interest to donate eggs had increased and around half reported an increase in actual donations. This perception is reflected in the figures from our Register. In 2013, there were 1,103 new egg donor registrations, an increase on 2012 when there were 1,005 and 2011 when there were 815' (at 13). It also reported that 'In 2013, 533 patients registered as egg sharers, a decrease on 2012 and 2011 figures when there were 629 and 708, respectively' (at 17). It has been beyond my scope to address the question of the possible effect, if any, of egg-sharing in exchange for benefits in kind on levels of altruistic donation; or to consider the question of the possible benefits to clinics themselves of this practice, which brings in two groups of patients (both egg-sharers and egg recipients); or to consider the way clinics set the relevant fees for egg recipients.

Haimes, E., Taylor, K. and Turkmendag, I. (2012). 'Eggs, ethics and exploitation? Investigating women's experiences of an egg sharing scheme'. *Sociology of Health and Illness*, 34, 1199–214.

Human Fertilisation and Embryology Authority (HFEA) (1998). *Consultation on the Implementation of Withdrawal of Payments to Donors*. London: HFEA.

Human Fertilisation and Embryology Authority (HFEA) (2005). *SEED Report: A Report on the Human Fertilisation and Embryology Authority's Review of Sperm, Egg, and Embryo Donation in the United Kingdom*. London: HFEA.

Human Fertilisation and Embryology Authority (HFEA) (2011a). *Donating Sperm and Eggs: A Review of the HFEA's Sperm and Egg Donation Policies 2011*. London: HFEA.

Human Fertilisation and Embryology Authority (HFEA) (2011b). *Donation Review: Compensation of Donors and Benefits in Kind*. London: HFEA.

Human Fertilisation and Embryology Authority (HFEA) (2012). 'Egg share donors and non-patient egg donors'. Available at www.hfea.gov.uk/3412.html.

Human Fertilisation and Embryology Authority (HFEA) (2014). *Egg and Sperm Donation in the UK: 2012–13*. Available at www.hfea.gov.uk/9386.html.

Human Fertilisation and Embryology Authority (HFEA) (2015 [2009]). *Code of Practice*, 8th edn. London: HFEA.

Johnson, M.H. (1999). 'The medical ethics of paid egg sharing in the UK'. *Human Reproduction*, 14, 1912–8.

McMillan, J. and Hope, T. (2003). 'Gametes, money, and egg sharing'. *The Lancet*, 362, 584.

Nuffield Council on Bioethics (2011). *Human Bodies: Donation for Medicine and Research*. London: Nuffield Council on Bioethics.

Pennings, G. and Devroey, P. (2006). 'Subsidized in-vitro fertilization treatment and the effect on the number of egg sharers'. *Reproductive BioMedicine*, 13, 8–10.

Prainsack, B. and Buyx, A. (2011). *Solidarity: Reflections on an Emerging Concept in Bioethics*. London: Nuffield Council on Bioethics.

President's Commission for the Study of Ethical Problems in Medicine and Biomedical and Behavioral Research (1982). *Making Healthcare Decisions: The Ethical and Legal Implications of Informed Consent in the Patient-Practitioner Relationship*, Vol. 1. Washington, DC: US Government Printing Office.

Rapport, F. (2003). 'Exploring the beliefs and experiences of potential egg share donors'. *Journal of Advanced Nursing*, 43, 28–42.

Raz, J. (1986). *The Morality of Freedom*. Oxford: Clarendon Press.

Scott, R., Williams, C., Ehrich, K. and Farsides, B. (2012). 'Donation of "spare" fresh or frozen embryos to research: who decides that an embryo is "spare" and how can we enhance the quality and protect the validity of consent?'. *Medical Law Review*, 20(2), 255–303.

Wilkinson, S. (2011). 'Ethical principles and the HFEA donation review'. *BioNews* 632. Available at www.bionews.org.uk/page_111532.asp.

Wilkinson, S. (2013). 'Is the HFEA's policy on compensating egg donors and egg sharers defensible?'. *Medical Law Review*, 21, 173–212.

CASES

UK

Chatterton v. *Gerson* [1981] 1 All E.R. 257.
Re M.B. [1997] 8 *Med. L.R.* 217.
Re T (Adult: Refusal of Treatment) [1992] 4 All E.R. 649.
U v. *Centre for Reproductive Medicine* [2002] E.W.C.A. Civ. 565.

EU LEGISLATION

Directive 2004/23/EC of the European Parliament and of the Council of 31 March 2004 on setting standards of quality and safety for the donation, procurement, testing, processing, preservation, storage and distribution of human tissues and cells.

UK LEGISLATION

Human Fertilisation and Embryology (HFE) Act 1990, as amended by the Human Fertilisation and Embryology (HFE) Act 2008.
Mental Capacity Act 2005.

Part IV

Information about donors

The interests at stake

13 Thoughts and feelings about the donor

A family perspective

Lucy Blake, Elena Ilioi and Susan Golombok

Introduction

In this chapter we examine what is known about the thoughts, feelings and experiences of individuals who are aware that they were conceived by sperm or egg donation. What kind of information would they like to have about their donor? And what questions do they have about them? We also explore how parents feel about the donor and the possibility that their child may wish to contact them in the future. The experiences of families in which donors are anonymous, open-identity and known, are examined, as are similarities and differences between families headed by heterosexual couples, lesbian couples and single mothers. Empirical data on families in which children are aware of their origins is in many ways limited. Therefore, we also turn to the adoption literature in order to examine trends and patterns that may have relevance to families created by gamete donation. The more that we know about how such families experience and perceive their options regarding contacting the donor, the better informed policy makers and practitioners will be to offer appropriate guidance and support.

Openness in families created by gamete donation: the UK context

The question of whether it is in children's best interests to be told that they were conceived using donated sperm, eggs or embryos has incited a great deal of debate. The current consensus in the UK is that it is generally best for parents to tell their children that they were conceived using donated gametes, and to begin this process when children are very young, ideally when they begin to show an interest in where babies come from and how they were made (Nuffield Council on Bioethics, 2013). This advice is driven by a belief that there is little or no reason *not to* share this information with children, and that donor conception needn't be a difficult issue for parents or for children if it has been discussed with children from an early age.

The rate of disclosure in the UK is indeed rising. Studies of sperm donation and egg donation families the 1980s and 1990s found that very few parents had told their children of their donor origins (see Golombok et al., 1996). More recently, a study of families in which children were born in the new millennium found that of the thirty-six donor insemination families who took part when children were aged seven, 28 per cent of parents had started the process of disclosure, and of thirty-two egg donation families, 41 per cent of parents had started the disclosure process (Readings et al., 2011). Families headed by lesbian couples or single women tend to be more inclined towards disclosure (see Vanfraussen, 2001); their use of sperm donation is more visible, as parents typically have to explain the arrival of the child in the absence of a male parent.

In the UK, there has been a shift from anonymous donation to open-identity donation. Children born through assisted reproduction involving donated sperm, egg or embryos, from April 2005 onwards, are entitled to identifying information about their donor(s) upon reaching age eighteen. This includes the donor's date of birth, name and last known address. Children conceived using donated gametes are also entitled to non-identifying information about their donor at age sixteen, including: physical description, year and country of birth, ethnicity, number and gender of children, marital status and medical history at the time of donation (HFEA, 2009). In addition to this information, donor-conceived individuals are entitled to find out the number, sex and date of birth of the donor's (donor-conceived) children, and may also have the opportunity to access identifying information, provided that the donor's children consent (HFEA, 2009).

Rates of disclosure may be higher in families created using an open-identity donor than in families with an anonymous donor. Under the anonymity system, some parents chose not to disclose as they did not want their child to feel frustrated by the absence of information, identifiable or otherwise, about the donor (Cook et al., 1995). Parents who conceived in the open-identity system will not face this predicament (in theory, at least). Although it is also possible that the fact that the donor is open-identity may lead parents to choose not to disclose, for example, if they are concerned that the child may wish to contact and/or meet the donor in the future. For other parents, the distinction between having used an anonymous or open-identity donor may have little bearing on their decisions regarding disclosure.

There are other factors that may be contributing to the increasing rate of disclosure. As opposed to parents who conceived two decades ago, parents can now access books, general guidance and academic papers on this subject with relative ease. As guidance and social scripts become increasingly available, disclosure may seem as though it is a more feasible task, therefore parents may feel more comfortable in doing so. Parents are also now typically advised by fertility counsellors to disclose and to do so when children are in early childhood (HFEA, 2009). Broader cultural factors may also influence parents' disclosure decisions. Individuals and couples who wish to start their families using donated gametes are now doing so in a time and culture in which transparency is revered, and discussion of genes and genetic connection is prevalent (Freeman et al., 2014; Nuffield Council on Bioethics, 2013).

Although we recognise that the trends of open-identity donation and rising rates of disclosure are not universal, in this chapter we will move on from the debate as to whether disclosure is in the child's best interests. We shall examine what is known about donor conception families in which donor-conceived individuals are aware of their origins, from both the perspective of the child and the parents. The different kinds of donation will be considered throughout the chapter: anonymous, open-identity and known, and the fragility and ambiguities within and between these different categories will be explored. Openness in families created by reproductive donation is a relatively recent trend, therefore there is great deal that we do not know. Fewer studies have focused on egg donation families compared to sperm donation families, and thus far few data have been obtained from fathers or children. Research with embryo donation families is particularly scarce, and has therefore been excluded from this chapter. Due to the limited nature of research on families in which donor-conceived children are aware of their origins, we turn to the adoption literature in an attempt to foresee patterns and trends that might have relevance to families created by gamete donation.

Anonymous donation

Most of the empirical research that has explored the experiences of parents and children has obtained data from families in which parents conceived their children using an anonymous sperm donor. This is therefore the type of donation that we know most about. However, over time this category has become increasingly fragile. In the UK, sperm and egg donors who originally gave their donation anonymously (pre-2005) can now re-register as an open-identity donor. Parents and children can also search for their donor relations through websites such as the Donor Sibling Registry, which has approximately 40,000 members since its creation in 2000 (Donor Sibling Registry, 2014). DNA testing services are also giving donor-conceived children and their parents the opportunity potentially to make contact with the child's donor relations (Motluk,

2005). The reality that the children and parents in these families face might therefore be different from the one that they had imagined. The experiences of children and parents in these families are examined below.

The child's perspective

Children growing up in sperm donation and egg donation families who are told about their donor conception at a young age (typically before the age of seven) have been found to react either neutrally or positively to this information (Blake et al., 2010; Mac Dougall et al., 2007). Studies from New Zealand and Sweden, where early disclosure has been widely recommended for many years, corroborate these findings and indicate that children's responses to their conception story are typically that of curiosity (Lindblad et al., 2000; Rumball and Adair, 1999). Along with curiosity, some parents describe their children's reaction to disclosure as amused or pleased (Blake et al., 2010, 2013a; Lycett et al., 2004).

Although it is difficult to discern how much children understand about their conception and how they feel about the donor, young children often describe their egg or sperm donor as being kind or nice (Blake et al., 2010; Blake et al., 2013b; Lycett et al., 2004). We do not know whether the children in these families understand that their donor is anonymous, and we know nothing about how and when this understanding starts to develop. In a study of lesbian-mother families, approximately half of the children showed curiosity about their sperm donor (Vanfraussen, Ponjaert-Kristoffersen and Brewaeys, 2003). Similarly, studies have found approximately 50 per cent of children in families of heterosexual couples to be curious about their sperm donor (Linblad, Gottleib and Lalos, 2000; Rumball and Adair, 1999).

Donor-conceived individuals in single-mother households have been found to feel more positively about their donor origins than those in families of heterosexual couples (Beeson, Jennings and Kramer, 2011). This may be for a number of reasons. For example, children's feelings about their donor origins do not impact upon existing family relationships as there is no father in the family home as there is in the families of heterosexual couples (Blake et al., 2013b).

While disclosure in early childhood does not appear to have a negative effect on children's psychological well-being or family relationships, some who find out about their donor conception later in life report feeling deceived by their parents, and that this caused them severe psychological harm (Blyth et al., 2012; Franz and Allen, 2001; Lorbach, 2003; Rushbrooke and Whipp, 2000; Turner and Coyle, 2000). Negative feelings towards their conception seem to be especially strong when disclosure occurs accidentally or from a third party, with those who discovered that they were conceived with donated sperm later in life describing that they both want and need to know about their genetic origins (Turner and Coyle, 2000). Some of the adults in this study described feeling unwanted and abandoned by the donor, and in the absence of any information about him, had created images or fantasies of who he might be and what he might be like. It is important to note that these studies have typically recruited participants from online support groups and/or donor linking websites; therefore, it is unsurprising that participants report feeling upset and angry or that these adults are interested in their donor relations. Studies which recruit participants in other ways (e.g. systematically, through fertility clinics) may produce findings which are more representative of donor conceived population as a whole.

The parents' perspective

Parents who started their families using an anonymous sperm donor think about the donor in complex and ambivalent ways. In families headed by heterosexual couples and lesbian mothers, parents are generally dismissive of the donor's significance in their family life and family relationships, whilst also being curious about the donor and the traits he might have passed on to their children (Grace, Daniels and Gillett, 2008; Vanfraussen, 2001; Wyverkens et al., 2013). Parents' feelings have been found to range from wanting to thank the donor, to hoping that they will never meet him and being fearful that their child may consider him to be a parent (Kirkman, 2004). When children are in infancy, it may be easier for parents to conceptualise the donor as a depersonalised sperm provider, but as the child grows older and develops a more unique personality and appearance, parents may be more likely to wonder about the donor as a person (Hertz, 2002; Vanfraussen, 2001). Of the qualitative studies that have examined parents' thoughts and feelings about the donor, there is a consensus that the donor exists on the margins of parents' minds, and that 'regardless of efforts to erase the donor, he keeps appearing' (Grace, Daniels and Gillett, 2008).

Parents are now able to search for and potentially find their child's donor and donor siblings through websites such as the Donor Sibling Registry. An online survey of 791 parents who were recruited from this registry found that those parents in fatherless families (i.e. those headed by lesbian couples and single women) were more likely than those from father-present families to be searching for the donor. Parents who were searching for the donor were typically doing so as a means of gathering and providing information about him to give to their child, most often driven by a desire to help enhance their child's sense of identity (Freeman et al., 2009). Parents who were searching for the donor were therefore doing so out of a desire to gain more information, rather than to develop and build a familial relationship with him.

Although some parents are interested in searching for the child's donor, a greater number of parents were found to be searching for their child's donor (half) siblings (Freeman et al., 2009). Parents with only one child were more likely to search for their child's donor siblings than were parents who had more than one child. Parents who were searching for their child's donor siblings were often doing so in the hope of making a meaningful connection with them (Scheib and Ruby, 2008). For parents, establishing relationships with their child's donor siblings seem safer and less complex than establishing a relationship with the donor. It might also be that the donor themselves cannot be traced and that donor siblings are the only donor relations for whom parents have an opportunity for contact or perhaps to meet. The studies mentioned above have typically obtained data from parents through online surveys, which are helpful in providing an initial overview in these new areas of exploration. Future research would benefit from utilising methods that are more suitable for exploring how parents perceive and conceptualise meaningful connections and draw the boundaries of family.

Open-identity donation

In the UK, individuals who were conceived after 2005 using an open-identity donor will have the opportunity to obtain identifying information about their donor (providing they have been told about their donor conception), in 2023. The shift from donor anonymity to open-identity donation has not only occurred in the UK, but also in Sweden, Austria, Switzerland, the Netherlands, New Zealand and the Australian State of Victoria, and is becoming increasingly common in the United States (Scheib and Cushing, 2007). How do the children and parents in these families feel about the donor and about potentially contacting him or her in the future? And for what reasons might they want to do so?

The child's perspective

Little is known about the thoughts and feelings of people conceived using an open-identity donor. An American study collected questionnaire data from twenty-nine adolescents growing up in families of heterosexual couples, lesbian couples and single women, all of whom had known about their donor conception since childhood (Scheib, Riordan and Rubin,

2005). The adolescents in this study felt comfortable with their donor origins, and felt that disclosure did not negatively impact upon their relationship with their parents. Some reported that knowing about their conception had a positive influence in their lives, making them feel very loved and wanted. Others reported that their conception did not affect their life and that what mattered to them was the way they were brought up.

Most of the adolescents in the study were curious to know more about their sperm donor and what they had in common with him. Some wanted information about their donor for medical or ancestral reasons, and others were curious for answers to questions such as 'What's he like?' While these adolescents were curious about their donor, only 10 per cent of the participants identified the donor as an important person in their lives, with more adolescents in single mother couples reporting that they cared about the donor compared to adolescents being raised by heterosexual and lesbian couples. Adolescents in single-parent families were also more positive about the donor, and more likely to refer to him as 'dad'.

Across household types, most of the adolescents planned to seek identifying information about the donor when they were able to (at age eighteen) although 40 per cent reported that they would request this information later or were unsure when they would request the information. Of those adolescents who wanted a relationship with their donor, most seem to want a friendly relationship. Only a minority (6.9 per cent) wanted a father–child relationship with him and none reported wanting money from him. All of the adolescents were also interested in finding out more about, and meeting, their donor siblings.

There are numerous questions and concerns that have not yet been addressed by the theoretical or empirical literature on open-identity donation. For example, how will donor offspring who have grown up with the knowledge that they were conceived using an open-identity donor feel if they discover at age eighteen that their donor is in fact deceased or has moved abroad and cannot be traced? What if their donor can be traced but refuses to have any form of contact? Or what if upon being traced, donor-conceived offspring learn that their donor is in fact from another country or culture, and might not speak their language? Regulators and policy makers need to acknowledge and address this issue given that the number of donors in UK clinics who registered with an overseas address is rising each year. It is also unknown whether the consequences of late or accidental disclosure are similar for those conceived with anonymous and open-identity donors. It could be that under these circumstances, the potential to contact the donor will have a buffering effect, allowing donor-conceived offspring to feel more in control and less frustrated about their donor conception, but this has not yet been examined.

The parents' perspective

In addition to knowing little about donor-offspring in families created by open-identity donation, we know little of how parents think and feel about open-identity donors. In an American, questionnaire-based study of parents in forty-five households, most parents reported feeling positive about their choice of an open-identity sperm donor (Scheib, 2003). Single mothers were more likely than parents in heterosexual or lesbian couples to report that the donor was a significant person in their lives. Some parents reported having concerns, wondering whether they had made the right choice of donor, and whether the donor would meet their child's expectations or try to make parental claims. As for the fact that their child will have the opportunity to contact the donor, the majority expected that their son or daughter would want to do so in the future.

In-depth, qualitative research is required to shed light on parents' thoughts and feelings about the donor in these families. Parents' concerns might be of a more practical nature (e.g. hoping that their child is not disappointed if they were to contact the donor), compared to the thoughts and feelings of parents who conceived using an anonymous donor. Researchers who have studied parents' perceptions of anonymous donors have noted that the policy of donor anonymity at the time of conception might have created an image of donors as being disinterested in the results of their donation (Grace, Daniels and Gillett, 2008). How the policy of open-identity donation may affect parents' thoughts and feelings about the donor has yet to be examined. Unlike those who conceived with an anonymous donor who cannot be traced, parents who conceived using an open-identity donor may contact and potentially meet the donor in the future. Their thoughts and feelings about the donor are therefore likely to change, as they will have new information and experiences to draw on. We are just beginning to learn how meetings between donor relations are perceived and experienced by donor offspring and their parents (Freeman, Jadva and Slutsky, Chapter 8).

Known donors

Parents may have decided to start their families using the gametes of a family member, friend or a more distant 'other' who is known to them in some way. Unlike anonymous and open-identity donation, parents who conceived using the eggs or sperm of a family member have a past and likely ongoing relationship with the donor. We know little about families in which parents have used intra-family sperm donation, and in families in which parents have conceived using intra-family egg donation the rate of disclosure has been found to be low (Jadva et al., 2011; Laruelle et al., 2011). We therefore know little about the thoughts and feelings of parents or children in these families. As with families in which children were conceived with anonymous or open-identity donors, there is a risk that children may discover their donor origins inadvertently (e.g. through overhearing a conversation between those who are aware of the intra-family donation). In these families, issues surrounding disclosure may be particularly complex (Vayena and Golombok, 2012). If, for example, an individual was conceived through sister-to-sister donation, they may be learning that their aunt is in fact their genetic mother, and that their cousins are their half-brothers or half-sisters.

We also know little about the experiences and perceptions of parents who conceived by asking a friend or acquaintance to act as an egg or a sperm donor or by finding a donor through contact websites such as Prideangel (2014). A qualitative study of lesbian mothers who conceived outside a clinical setting found that some couples chose to conduct and maintain their relationship with the sperm donor at arms-length, typically arranging donation in a way that allowed the identity of the couple to remain unknown to the donor (Nordqvist, 2011). This 'arms-length' approach may protect couples in cases where they have concerns that the donor may wish to take on or establish a parenting role in the future, even though they do not wish to do so at the present time. For other individuals and couples, building a relationship of trust with one another may be important and the prospective parents and donor may develop a friendship or familial relationship. Single mothers who used a known donors have been described as gatekeepers, determining the role and significance of the donor in the family, authoring and editing the story that they tell their children about how their family came into being (Hertz and Ferguson, 1997). Compared to single women who conceived using an anonymous sperm donor, known donors often appreciate and know the child from a distance, and the relationship of the child with the donor may well change over time (Hertz, 2002). No research to date has examined the thoughts, feelings and experiences of the children in these families.

Adoptive families: thoughts, feelings and experiences of birth relatives

As noted throughout this chapter, empirical data on families created using reproductive donation is limited in many ways and therefore it can be helpful to turn to the adoption literature. Adoption has generally had a similar history to that of sperm donation (in Wales and England in particular), in that the roots of both were originally characterised by confidentiality, anonymity and secrecy, that has gradually subsided over time. A number of research questions in the field of adoption are pertinent to families created by gamete donation in which children are aware of their donor origins. Specifically, who is most likely to want to search for information about their birth families and potentially meet, and why? What kind of information are they looking for? What are the outcomes of searching? And how are relationships with birth-relatives maintained?

There is great variation within adoptive families, ranging from those which are structurally closed (in which there is no exchange of information between the adoptive family and the birth family), to those which are structurally open (in which the adoptive family has identifying information about the birth family and in some cases have contact with one another). Similarities could be drawn with gamete donation families in which the donor is anonymous and cannot be traced (a structurally 'closed' family in which there is no exchanging of new information) and those in which the donor is open-identity or known (which has the potential to be a structurally 'open' family, in which new information could be exchanged and contact may be made between the family and the child's donor relations). In the United States, Grotevant et al. (2007) found that adolescents and their mothers in structurally open arrangements had greater levels of satisfaction than those in structurally closed arrangements. However, the authors cautioned against a 'one-size-fits-all' approach, and recommended that all parties involved in open arrangements (adoptive parents, the child and birth-parents) retain flexibility when thinking about the future, as feelings may change during the 'dance' of arriving at a mutually agreeable level of contact. This advice could perhaps be of great relevance and utility to parents of children born through gamete donation, regardless of whether they conceived using an anonymous, open-identity or known donor.

Where individuals have been adopted in infancy, and have little or no knowledge or memory of their birth family, they may be curious to find out information about them and potentially contact them. In a comprehensive review of the literature, Muller and Perry (2001) estimated that in countries in which adopted individuals can access their birth certificates, approximately 50 per cent will at some point in their life search for their birth-parents. This review also concludes that fantasies around birth-relatives typically revolve around the birth mother whereas the birth father remains a more 'shadowy' figure. Most studies have found women to be more curious about their birth parents, and more likely to search for them, than men. As Muller and Perry (2001) explain, some have suggested that this difference is driven by women's experience of pregnancy and child-birth, heightening their awareness of generational ties. This is in line with the findings of research on inheritance of disease in families, in which women have typically been found to be the 'genetic housekeepers' of the family, as they are the most likely to initiate contact with genetic clinics, collect information from family members, seek counselling and opt for genetic testing (Richards, 1996). Initial studies on the searching behaviour of parents and offspring in families created by donor insemination have found women to be the most likely to do so (Freeman et al., 2009; Hewitt, 2002; Jadva et al., 2010). Also worth noting that as with studies on adoption, the majority of participants in these studies have been female.

Of adopted adults who search for their birth parents, most tend to do so in their late twenties to thirties, which for most is precipitated by a major life event such as a marriage, death of an adoptive parent or pregnancy (Muller and Perry, 2001). Thus, it may be expected that donor offspring may not want to access identifying information about the donor at age eighteen, but instead may do so later in life in accordance with reaching certain milestones, such as marriage or parenthood.

Of those adopted individuals who search for their birth-parents, most have been found to be psychologically well-adjusted and to have conducted their search in the context of positive family functioning (Wrobel, Grotevant and McRoy, 2004). On the other hand, compared to those who do not search for their birth-parents, those who search have been found to have more negative adoption experiences and to experience greater identity problems (Muller and Perry, 2001). A longitudinal study conducted in the Netherlands revealed that in childhood, before beginning their search, those who went on to search for their birth-parents had higher levels of behavioural problems compared to those who did not go on to search (Tieman, van Der Ende and Verhulst, 2008). Problems may therefore not be caused by the search itself, but rather are present before the search begins. Regarding gamete donation, one might expect those children who are experiencing psychological difficulties to be the most likely to want to search for their donor relations. However, studies have found children in donor insemination and egg donation families to be psychologically well-adjusted and no different to their naturally conceived peers (see Golombok et al., 2006, 2011; Shelton et al., 2009). Therefore, it is possible that the percentage of donor offspring who search for their donor relations might be lower compared to adopted individuals who search for their birth parents.

Numerous factors have been found to influence adopted individuals' levels of interest in their origins and their searching behaviours. In a study examining the searching behaviour of international adoptees, those searching for birth relatives in countries in which searching was logistically and practically challenging had a greater preoccupation with their biological origins compared to those who faced fewer barriers in doing so. In terms of families created by donor insemination and egg donation, perhaps those who experience the greatest barriers in finding their donors (i.e. those conceived using anonymous donors in clinics in which there are no medical records) may have a greater preoccupation with their donor origins compared to those who can access information about the donor with relative ease.

There is consensus in the literature that adopted individuals who search for their birth parents are doing so out of curiosity, or a desire to gain knowledge about their birth parents (Muller and Perry, 2001). Other motivations include a desire to tell their birth-parents that they are happy and well, or wanting to find out more about the reasons why they were placed for adoption. The vast majority of adopted individuals are not searching in order to establish a parent–child relationship with their birth-parents. Whereas some adopted individuals want factual information about their birth parents (such as background or medical information), others want to contact them, or to meet them. If these findings were also true of donor-conceived individuals, it is possible that for some, non-identifying information about the donor would satisfy their curiosity, but that for others who wanted to contact or meet their donor, or ask them questions as to why they donated, identifying information would be desirable.

Although the large body of adoption literature can be useful for thinking about reproductive donation, it is important to remember that there are differences between the two. In families created by donor conception, there is no disruption of the family as children are raised by their parents from birth. These children have therefore not been relinquished by their birth parents, and were wanted by their parents, who have gone to great lengths to have a child. Parents and children in adoptive and donor conception families may also differ in how they perceive and define their family. In the United States, the adoptive kinship network is typically conceptualised as having the child in the centre of a family system that includes the adoptive parents, siblings and extended family and the child's birth parents, siblings and extended family, whether these individuals are known to one another or not (Grotevant and McRoy, 1998; Grotevant, 2007). Grotevant (1999) emphasises the importance of collaborative involvement between the adoptive family and the birth family as forming the basis of the child's emotional well-being, and an integral aspect of adoption-related communication. Whether donor conception families can or should be conceptualised in a similar way is debatable. Historically donor conception families were considered as nuclear families, but with disclosure and open-identity donation increasing, the walls that were once built between donors and recipient families are beginning to crumble (Richards, Pennings and Appleby, 2012; Smart and Nordqvist, 2013). Therefore, parents and children in donor conception families may well consider the donor and their donor relations to be a part of their kinship network. The question of how family is conceptualised in those created by donor conception is perhaps best answered by the parents and the children themselves, and may well differ within and between different family types (donor insemination and egg donation), different cultures and countries, different family structures (those headed by heterosexual couples, lesbian mothers and single women) and within the family itself.

Many of the intricacies and ambiguities that have emerged in research on searching in adoptive families may be relevant to those working in the field of gamete donation. Muller and Perry (2001) caution against using a simple dichotomy of 'searchers' versus 'non-searchers', recognising that even though adopted individuals may not be searching for their birth relatives they may still be interested in their roots. For example, adopted individuals may not want to express an interest in searching for their birth-parents because they want to avoid hurting their adoptive parents' feelings, or because they do not yet feel ready to do so (Wrobel et al., 2013). It is also important to note that studies that rely on volunteer or opportunistic samples may not be representative of the general population of adoptive families, or the population of adopted individuals who search. These suggestions and recommendations are just as relevant when thinking about the searching of donor-conceived offspring and their parents.

Conclusions

In the UK and a number of other countries, rates of disclosure are rising and open-identity donation has replaced donor anonymity. An increasing number of donor offspring and their parents are searching for, and making contact with, their donor relations online through websites such as the Donor Sibling Registry, as well as using online forums, blogs and social media platforms, in order to make contact with one another and communicate with the donor conception community more generally. In light of some of these trends and shifts, we have focused on those families in which offspring are aware of their donor origins to examine the understandings, experiences and reflections of children and their parents.

In families created using anonymous donors there is an absence of information about the donor, therefore donor offspring and their parents think imaginative and creatively about the donor, imagining him or her in different ways at different times. It appears that the donor exists on the margins of parents' and children's minds, occasionally drifting to the fore. Although we have little empirical data on which to draw, it seems that for those who conceived using an open-identity donor, parents and children may have more practical concerns and curiosities about the donor and what he or she is like and what it would be like if they were to ever meet. As with anonymous donation, the donor appears to exist on the periphery of parents' and children's minds, rather than being a central or significant figure in family life. Comparisons between different family structures indicate that the donor may be a more important figure for parents and children in families of single mothers compared to families headed by heterosexual or lesbian couples, which is perhaps unsurprising due to the absence of a second parent in these families. It is also important to emphasise that the majority of studies in this field have focused on families created using donated sperm. We know little about how parents and children think and feel about egg donors (be they anonymous, open-identity or known) and this lack of data should be acknowledged by policy makers and regulators in the field. It is tempting to infer that findings from donor insemination families are just as relevant to egg donation families, but this may not be the case.

The experiences of children have been found to differ according to the nature of disclosure, that is, how and when they discovered that they were donor conceived, with those finding out later in life typically feeling greater frustration. It could be that these family process variables have a greater impact on how children and parents feel about the donor than the category of donation used (anonymous, open-identity or known), but there is a long way to go in terms of empirical research before conclusions such as this can be drawn with any kind of accuracy or certainty.

The adoption literature tells a similar story to what we know of families of gamete donation so far. It seems that for most donor offspring (and adopted adolescents alike), there is a natural, normative curiosity about their origins, which may, for some, result in searching behaviours of varying degrees. Searching for donor relations or birth-parents is mostly driven by a desire to know what their birth-parents are like, and perhaps to gain certain kinds of information about them. The vast majority do not do so out of a desire to establish a parent–child relationship with them. This may be comforting for parents who may be concerned about their child's level of interest in their origins. Ultimately, the more that is known about families in which donor-conceived offspring are aware of their donor origins, the better able practitioners will be to offer appropriate guidance and support for those who search for or obtain identifying information about their donors, as well as those who do not.

REFERENCES

Beeson, D. R., Jennings, P. K. and Kramer, W. (2011). 'Offspring searching for their sperm donors: how family type shapes the process'. *Human Reproduction*, 26, 2415–24.

Blake, L., Casey, P., Jadva, V. and Golombok, S. (2013a). '"I Was Quite Amazed": donor conception and parent–child relationships from the child's perspective'. *Children and Society*, 28, 425–37.

Blake, L., Casey, P., Readings, J., Jadva, V. et al. (2010). '"Daddy ran out of tadpoles": how parents tell their children that they are donor conceived, and what their 7-year-olds understand'. *Human Reproduction*, 25, 2527–34.

Blake, L., Zadeh, S., Statham, H. and Freeman, T. (2013b). 'Families created by assisted reproduction: children's perspectives', in T. Freeman, S. Graham, F. Ebtehaj and M. Richards (eds.), *Relatedness in Assisted Reproduction: Families, Origins and Identities*. Cambridge University Press.

Blyth, E., Crawshaw, M., Frith, L. and Jones, C. (2012). 'Donor-conceived people' s views and experiences of their genetic origins: A critical analysis of the research evidence'. *Journal of Law and Medicine*, 19, 769–89.

Cook, R., Golombok, S., Bish, A. and Murray, C. (1995). 'Disclosure of donor insemination: parental attitudes'. *American Journal of Orthopsychiatry*, 65, 549–59.

Donor Sibling Registry (2014). 'The Donor Sibling Registry. Educating, connecting and supporting donor families'. Available at www.donorsibling registry.com/index.php. Accessed 20 February 2014.

Franz, S. and Allen, D. (eds.) (2001). *The Offspring Speak: An International Conference of Donor Offspring. A Report to Health Canada*. Toronto: Infertility Network.

Freeman, T., Jadva, V., Kramer, W. and Golombok, S. (2009). 'Gamete donation: parents' experiences of searching for their child's donor siblings and donor'. *Human Reproduction*, 24, 505–16.

Freeman, F., Graham, S., Ebtehaj, F. and Richards, M. (eds.) (2014). *Relatedness in Assisted Reproduction: Families, Origins and Identities*. Cambridge University Press.

Golombok, S., Brewaeys, A., Cook, R., Giavazzi, M. T. et al. (1996). 'The European study of assisted reproduction families: Family functioning and child development'. *Human Reproduction*, 11, 2324–31.

Golombok, S., Murray, C., Jadva, V., Lycett, E. et al. (2006). 'Non-genetic and non-gestational parenthood: consequences for parent–child relationships and the psychological well-being of mothers, fathers and children at age 3'. *Human Reproduction*, 21, 1918–24.

Golombok, S., Readings, J., Blake, L., Casey, P. et al. (2011). 'Children conceived by gamete donation: psychological adjustment and mother–child relationships at age 7'. *Journal of Family Psychology*, 25, 230–9.

Grace, V. M., Daniels, K. and Gillett, W. (2008). 'The donor, the father, and the imaginary constitution of the family: parents' constructions in the case of donor insemination'. *Social Science and Medicine*, 66, 301–14.

Grotevant, H. D. (1999). 'Adoptive identity development: New kinship patterns, new issues', in A. L. Rygvold, M. M. Dalen and B. Saetersdal (eds.), *Mine–Yours–Ours- and Theirs: Adoption, Changing Kinship, and Family Patterns.* University of Oslo Press.

Grotevant, H. D. (2007). 'Openness in adoption: Re-thinking "family" in the US', in M. C. Inhorn (ed.), *Reproductive Techniques: Gender, Technology, and Biopolitics in the New Millennium.* New York: Bergshaw Books.

Grotevant, H. D. and McRoy, R. G. (1998). *Openness in Adoption. Exploring Family Connections.* London: Sage Publications.

Grotevant, H. D., Wrobel, G. M., Von Korff, L., Skinner, B. et al. (2007). 'Many faces of openness in adoption: perspectives of adopted adolescents and their parents'. *Adoption Quarterly*, 10, 79–101.

Hertz, R. (2002). 'The father as an idea: a challenge to kinship boundaries by single mothers.' *Symbolic Interaction*, 25, 1–31.

Hertz, R. and Ferguson, F. I. T. (1997). 'Kinship strategies and self-sufficiency among single mothers by choice: Post modern family ties'. *Qualitative Sociology*, 20, 187–209.

Hewitt, G. (2002). 'Missing links: identity issues of donor conceived people'. *Journal of Fertility Counselling*, 9, 14–20.

Human Fertilisationand Embryology Authority website (HFEA) (2009). *Code of Practice*, 8th edn. London, England. Available at www.hfea.gov.uk/docs/Code_of_Practice_8_-_October_2013.PDF. Accessed 26 February 2014.

Jadva, V., Casey, P., Readings, J., Blake, L. et al. (2011). 'A longitudinal study of recipients' views and experiences of intra-family egg donation'. *Human Reproduction*, 26, 2777–82.

Jadva, V., Freeman, T., Kramer, W. and Golombok, S. (2010). 'Experiences of offspring searching for and contacting their donor siblings and donor'. *Reproductive Biomedicine Online*, 20, 523–32.

Kirkman, M. (2004). 'Saviours and satyrs: ambivalence in narrative meanings of sperm provision'. *Culture, Health and Sexuality*, 6, 319–34.

Laruelle, C., Place, I., Demeestere, I., Englert, Y. et al. (2011). 'Anonymity and secrecy options of recipient couples and donors, and ethnic origin influence in three types of oocyte donation'. *Human Reproduction*, 26, 382–90.

Linblad, F., Gottleib, C. and Lalos, O. (2000). 'To tell or not to tell – what parents think about telling their children that they were born following donor insemination'. *Journal of Psychosomatic Obstetrics and Gynecology*, 21, 193–203.

Lorbach, C. (2003). *Experiences of Donor Conception: Parents Offspring and Donors Through the Years.* London: Jessica Kingsley Publisher.

Lycett, E., Daniels, K., Curson, R., Chir, B. et al. (2004). 'Offspring created as a result of donor insemaintion: a study of family relationships, child adjustment, and disclosure.' *Fertility and Sterility*, 82, 172–9.

Mac Dougall, K., Becker, G., Scheib, J. and Nachtigall, R. (2007). 'Strategies for disclosure: how parents approach telling their children that they were conceived with donor gametes'. *Fertility and Sterility*, 87, 524–32.

Motluk, A. (2005). 'Anonymous sperm donor traced on internet'. *New Scientist*. Available at www.newscientist.com/article/mg18825244.200-anonymous-sperm-donor-traced-on-internet.html. Accessed 21 October 2013.

Muller, U. and Perry, B. (2001). 'Adopted persons' search for and contact with their birth parents: Who searches and why?' *Adoption Quarterly*, 4, 5–37.

Nordqvist, P. (2011). '"Dealing with sperm": comparing lesbians' clinical and non-clinical donor conception processes'. *Sociology of Health and Illness*, 33, 114–29.

Nuffield Council on Bioethics (2013). *Donor Conception: Ethical Aspects of Information Sharing*. London: Nuffield Council on Bioethics.

Prideangel (2014). Prideangel. Available at www.prideangel.com/. Accessed 26 February 2014.

Readings, J., Blake, L., Casey, P., Jadva, V. et al. (2011). 'Secrecy, disclosure and everything in-between: decisions of parents of children conceived by donor insemination, egg donation and surrogacy'. *Reproductive BioMedicine Online*, 22, 485–95.

Richards, M. (1996). 'Families, kinship and genetics', in M. Richards and T. Marteau (eds.), *The Troubled Helix*. Cambridge University Press.

Richards, M., Pennings, G. and Appleby, J. B. (2012). 'Introduction', in *Reproductive Donation: Practice, Policy and Bioethics*. Cambridge University Press.

Rumball, A. and Adair, V. (1999). 'Telling the story: parents' scripts for donor offspring'. *Human Reproduction*, 14, 1392–9.

Rushbrooke, R. and Whipp, C. (2000). 'Speaking for Ourselves. Report from 'What About Me?' The Child of ART. In *Comment on Reproductive Ethics (CORE)*. Royal Society, London.

Scheib, J. E. (2003). 'Choosing identity-release sperm donors: the parents' perspective 13–18 years later'. *Human Reproduction*, 18, 1115–27.

Scheib, J. E. and Cushing, R. A. (2007). 'Open-identity donor insemination in the United States: is it on the rise?' *Fertility and Sterility*, 88, 231–2.

Scheib, J. E., Riordan, M. and Rubin, S. (2005). 'Adolescents with open-identity sperm donors: reports from 12–17 year olds'. *Human Reproduction*, 20, 239–52.

Scheib, J. E. and Ruby, A. (2008). 'Contact among families who share the same sperm donor'. *Fertility and Sterility*, 90, 33–43.

Shelton, K. H., Boivin, J., Hay, D., van Den Bree, M. B. M. et al. (2009). 'Examining differences in psychological adjustment problems among children conceived by assisted reproductive technologies'. *International Journal of Behavioral Development*, 33, 385–92.

Smart, C. and Nordqvist, P. (2013). '*Relative Strangers: Key messages*'. Available at www.manchester.ac.uk/morgancentre/research/relative-strangers. Accessed 26 February 2013.

Tieman, W., van Der Ende, J. and Verhulst, F. C. (2008). 'Young adult international adoptees' search for birth parents'. *Journal of Family Psychology*, 22, 678–87.

Turner, A. J. and Coyle, A. (2000). 'What does it mean to be a donor offspring? The identity experiences of adults conceived by donor insemination and the implications for counselling and therapy'. *Human Reproduction*, 15, 2041–51.

Vanfraussen, K. (2001). 'An attempt to reconstruct children's donor concept: a comparison between children's and lesbian parents' attitudes towards donor anonymity'. *Human Reproduction*, 16, 2019–25.

Vanfraussen, K., Ponjaert-Kristoffersen, I. and Brewaeys, A. (2003). 'Family functioning in lesbian families created by donor insemination'. *American Journal of Orthopsychiatry*, 73, 78–90.

Vayena, E. and Golombok, S. (2012). 'Challenges in intra-family donation', in M. Richards, G. Pennings and J. B. Appleby (eds.), *Reproductive Donation: Practice, Policy and Bioethics*. Cambridge University Press.

Wrobel, G. M., Grotevant, H. D. and McRoy, R. G. (2004). 'Adolescent search for birthparents: who moves forward?' *Journal of Adolescent Research*, 19, 132–51.

Wrobel, G. M., Grotevant, H. D., Samek, D. R. and Korff, L. V. (2013). 'Adoptees' curiosity and information-seeking about birth parents in emerging adulthood: Context, motivation, and behavior'. *International Journal of Behavioral Development*, 37, 441–50.

Wyverkens, E., Ravelingien, A., H, V. P., Provoost, V., Raes, I. et al. (2013). 'Adolescent Search for Birthparents: Who Moves Forward?' *Journal of Adolescent Research*, 19, 132–51.

UK LEGISLATION

The Human Fertilisationand Embryology Act (2004) (Disclosure of Donor Insemination Regulations).

The Human Fertilisationand Embryology Act (1990), as amended (2008).

14 'Choosing' a donor

Parents' perspectives on current and future donor information provision in clinically assisted reproduction

Sophie Zadeh, Susan Imrie and Andrea M. Braverman

The use of donor gametes in assisted reproduction clearly raises critical, practical and ethical questions about the provision of donor information. How much information about donors is deemed sufficient for recipients, and by whom? This chapter addresses this issue from the perspective of recipients themselves. It presents the views of individuals and couples who have undergone fertility treatment with donor gametes in a clinical setting. The chapter reviews current and cross-cultural research on the information needs of recipients of donor sperm and donor eggs, reflects upon how these needs may vary both within and between family types, and evaluates the extent to which the existing regulation of donor information adequately meets the needs of recipients in the UK in particular. This chapter offers a crucial contribution to debates about the moral significance and ethical implications of donor selection and donor information (see Farsides, Chapter 16).

Historical and current context

Initially, recipients of donor gametes in the UK were not legally entitled to identifying information about the donor(s) used to help them conceive (Human Fertilisation and Embryology Act 1990, as amended (2008)). However, changes to regulations in 2004[1] now permit persons conceived through gamete donation – at or after the age of eighteen – to access identifying information about donors registered after 1 April 2005.[2] Such policy changes regarding donor anonymity – now in effect in both the UK and in other parts of Europe – have provided the basis for research on donor information provision. As such, much of this work has focussed on donor type, and has questioned whether recipients would

[1] Human Fertilisation and Embryology Authority (Disclosure of Donor Information) Regulations 2004.

[2] The changes to regulation allowed clinics a transitional period (1 April 2005–31 March 2006) in which they could continue to treat patients using gametes donated anonymously by donors who had registered before March 2005.

prefer an anonymous donor, or one who can be identified (often termed an identity-release donor). Although this research is useful in establishing recipient perspectives on current regulation, it is less useful in understanding the specific information recipients receive, or indeed the information recipients *would like* to receive about the donor(s) involved in their path to parenthood.

Beyond legislation, the cultural climate of assisted reproduction has also changed in other ways. New information technologies have not only shaped the context in which donor information can be received, with extensive donor catalogues – including photographs, voice and video recordings (Pennings, 2000) – appearing online, but have also enabled the circumvention of legislation in ways previously impossible. Individuals may, for example, now identify their legally anonymous donor through the internet (Freeman et al., 2009), and others may use online fertility forums, which allow patients to discuss their treatment with others, in order to circumvent the legal limits imposed on the amount of donor information available to them. This may be particularly problematic in cases of egg-sharing, where it is likely that the egg-sharer and recipient will receive treatment at the same clinic at a similar time.[3] More directly, potential recipients of donor eggs or sperm may opt to use one of several online organisations designed to facilitate assisted conception outside of the clinical context by introducing potential donors and recipients to one another.[4] Others may undergo cross-border reproductive care in order to circumvent regulation regarding anonymity and identity-release donation at home (Culley et al., 2011).

While the issue of donor information is of clear significance to assisted reproduction in the technological age, it is perhaps especially relevant to contemporary debates about whether or not children should be told about their donor conception, and specifically, the gamete donor(s)

[3] This concern was raised by one woman who had donated eggs in an egg-sharing arrangement to fund her IVF treatment, interviewed as part of the ER families study (see footnote 6). During a treatment cycle, she had seen a message on an online forum from a woman who was receiving treatment at the same time and was encouraging her donor to make contact through the site. Enough information about the donor's physical characteristics and the time of treatment was available for the woman to identify herself as the donor.

[4] There has been no systematic research investigating prospective parents' motivations for using such services, rather than conceiving at a clinic. It may be the case that the regulated information provided about donors in the clinical context is deemed insufficient. Indeed, although this chapter focusses upon the clinical provision of donor information, the existing literature on both egg and sperm donation indicates that some individuals or couples may decide to use a donor who is known to them, specifically because of a desire to have extensive information about the donor, and, in some cases, because of a desire for their child to have a relationship with the donor (Brewaeys et al., 2005; Chabot and Ames, 2004; Greenfeld and Klock, 2004; Hertz, 2006; Hudson and Culley, 2014).

involved. Although historically, prospective parents were advised by clinicians not to tell their children about their use of donor sperm, the sharing of this information is now widely recommended – for recipients of both sperm and egg donation – in both policy and practice (HFEA Code of Practice, 2013; Nuffield Council on Bioethics, 2013). While this recommendation may have an impact upon the sort of information sought by parents about the donor, research on this issue is limited. The question of whether or not information provided in the clinical context is sufficient for recipients of donor gametes – and particularly those who wish to tell their children about the person(s) involved in their conception – is one of many that this chapter therefore seeks to address.

What information do recipients have about the donor?

Sperm donation

The amount of information available about sperm donors varies both within and between countries. In the UK, recipients of donor sperm from a licensed clinic are entitled to non-identifying information about the donor at the time of treatment, and the Human Fertilisation and Embryology Authority (HFEA) currently advises that clinics encourage donors to provide 'as much information as possible' (HFEA Code of Practice, 2013). The standard information form invites donors to include biographical information about themselves, including their occupation, interests and religion, a goodwill message to any children conceived as a result of their donation, and a 'pen sketch', including additional, handwritten information. Once a child is born, recipients are entitled to access all non-identifying information about the donor, as well as information about the number, sex and year of birth of any other children born as a result of his donation (HFEA Code of Practice, 2013).

In other countries, the situation varies. In Australia, for example, there are no national guidelines on how donor information should be stored or released (Rodino, Burton and Sanders, 2011a). In France, all donations are anonymous, and must be made by men who are already fathers (Kalampalikis et al., 2012). In the United States, there is no national legislation regarding donor information, but the number of clinics offering identity-release donation seems to be increasing (Scheib and Cushing, 2007). Some states are beginning to consider statutes on this issue, and in the State of Washington, a law that requires donors to be identity-release unless they choose to opt out has recently come into force. Despite these cross-cultural differences, little is known about how much information recipients in these different contexts actually have. No research has yet attempted to address the relationship between recipients' knowledge and the regulatory framework within which they undergo treatment (Broderick and Walker, 1995), although some interesting questions have been raised regarding the rationale behind providing particular donor information in different regulatory contexts (see Graham, Mohr and Bourne, Chapter 10), and about the relationship between donor information and the commercialisation of assisted reproduction in the United States in particular (Almeling, 2011; Johnson, 2013).

Existing research on the experiences of individuals and couples who have used donor sperm within a UK clinic has indicated that despite regulation, the amount of information recipients have varies widely. Participants in a study of one and two-parent donor insemination (DI) families by the University of Cambridge's Centre for Family Research were asked about the donor information they received both at the time of, and after, treatment.[5] The majority of participants indicated that they had some non-identifying information about the donor. Often this included information about the donor's physical appearance (height, hair and eye colour), ethnic background, education, occupation, interests and occasionally, blood group. For some participants, this information was supplemented by a goodwill message and a pen sketch. Some participants had contacted the HFEA for further information about the donor after having given birth.

> I've managed to get loads more from the HFEA, but this was nothing to do with [clinic]. They didn't even tell me that was available . . . I realised I could apply to get more, so now I've got really a lot . . . also this really lovely pen sketch . . . so I'm pleased that I was able to do that. (Single mother, DI family)

Applications to the HFEA for further information were described exclusively by single mothers in the study and, in general, mothers in two-parent families were less likely to readily discuss the information they had about the donor with researchers. In some cases, however, both single and coupled mothers reported that they were unable to recall the information about the donor provided to them by the clinic.

> I never wrote any of it down. I think they had dark brown hair but I can't, I won't swear on it. Cos after so many tries, they did so many different donors and I think I'm probably getting muddled up . . . (Single mother, DI family)

[5] The findings presented throughout this chapter are based on semi-structured interviews with forty-eight single heterosexual mothers and eighteen mothers who are either married or in long-term heterosexual partnerships, all of whom had a child between 2003 and 2009. This study is referred to as the 'DI families study' in this chapter.

While it is possible that participants who reported not being able to remember details about the donor were unwilling to share this information with researchers, it is also possible that they did not retain this information because they did not deem it to be important, and/or because they did not want to think about it. Participants' lack of engagement with donor information appeared to be tied to their thoughts and feelings about the relative impact of 'nature' and 'nurture' upon children in general, and the heritability of certain specific traits. One coupled mother, for example, discussed how she had read but not retained information provided by the clinic about the donor's personality, explaining that her child 'will get the personality of the people she's brought up with . . . as opposed to what's in her DNA.'

The deliberate disengagement with donor information also seemed to be a means by which some recipients minimised the donor's role specifically in the process of conception. This was mostly, but not exclusively, found to be the case for some of the coupled mothers interviewed.

> We had slightly mixed feelings, I suppose, because on the one hand . . . you want as much information as you can to make a good choice, but then on the other hand it almost felt like we didn't want to know – to think of him too much as a person, because, in a way we were thinking of this more as a medical procedure than anything else . . . [like] you want to know that your surgeon's qualified, but you don't necessarily want to know whether he plays golf at weekends or not . . . it doesn't seem relevant. (Coupled mother, DI family)

Following from research conducted in the United States (Becker, 2000), and on different family types (Ehrensaft, 2008; Hertz, 2006), it therefore seems that the amount of information recipients have or can recall about the donor may be tied to their feelings about the donor's involvement as either a symbolic or physical presence in their families. Relatedly, a small number of the single mothers who took part in the Cambridge study opted to import sperm from an overseas donor about whom they were able to access extensive information, including a photograph. Like the single women in Graham's (2014) research, importing sperm from overseas enabled mothers to feel not only that they were accessing information about the donor's sperm, and so his 'DNA', but also information about the donor as a person they might be able to get along with, were they ever to meet him.

Of those mothers who used a donor from a UK clinic, several described the way in which undergoing fertility treatment with donor gametes within the UK inevitably resulted in having much less information about the donor than would be accessible in the United States. At the same time, several study participants seemed to have inferred information about the donor from the fact of donation itself. This was particularly true of post-2005 recipients of donor sperm; some mothers suggested that donors who willingly donate knowing that identifying information will be released to donor offspring must be well-intentioned. This was the case for both coupled and single mothers.

> Yeah, just that he was a nice person, and things like that really, but then he would be a nice person hopefully doing that anyway. (Coupled mother, DI family)

However, the fact of having used an identity-release donor did not always lead participants to feel that they had additional donor information. In fact, several of the mothers interviewed expressed some uncertainty about whether or not the donor would be identifiable in the future. Some mothers referred to the donor as anonymous, although they had conceived after legislative changes had come into force, and subsequently sought to clarify this issue with researchers. Others described a misunderstanding in which they had initially believed that the donor would be identity-release, and had later found out that this would not be the case. This was particularly true of mothers who conceived in 2005, suggesting that miscommunication about donor status may have been more common immediately following the change in the law than in more recent years.

> I'm really worried . . . but there's absolutely nothing I can do. I'm worried about [child], how she's gonna turn out, cos as soon as all of that happened I went on the internet and read . . . and it was like an explosion . . . Like I'd disturbed a hornet's nest of information that I wasn't aware of, of how people can react to having a white, blank page . . . (Single mother, DI family)

Egg donation

As is the case with sperm donation, the amount of information available about egg donors varies greatly between countries. In France, for example, as with sperm donation, all egg donation must be anonymous and altruistic (Bujan, Le Lannou and Kunstmann, 2012). In Australia, however, egg donation is altruistic and no national guidelines exist on whether donation should be anonymous or identity-release, although several States have legislated to prohibit anonymous donation (Johnson, Bourne and Hammarberg, 2012), and many clinics actively encourage patients to find their own donors (Boulos, Kerridge and Waldby, 2010). There are similarly no national guidelines on the amount – or type – of donor information to be provided to egg recipients in the United States; individual states vary as to whether or not identity-release egg donation is mandated (Johnson, 2013). Recipients using anonymous or identity-release egg donation in the United States frequently receive detailed information about their donor, including physical characteristics, medical and reproductive history, and information about the donor's personality (The Ethics Committee of the American Society for Reproductive Medicine, 2013), with the majority of agencies and clinics also providing adult or child photographs of the donor (Johnson, 2013). A survey of members of the Donor Sibling Registry who had used egg donation to conceive – of whom 61 per cent were American recipients – found that nearly 60 per cent of respondents knew their donor's year of birth and the number and ages of the donor's siblings, and approximately half of respondents had received information about the donor's health, fertility history, country of birth and educational institution, as well as a child or adult photo of the donor, and a personal statement (Blyth, Kramer and Schneider, 2013). Similarly, a survey of anonymous egg recipients in the US found that over 80 per cent of respondents knew the donor's age, ethnicity, reason for donating, education, medical history, blood type, number of children and physical characteristics (height, weight, hair and eye colour). Around three-quarters knew the donor's profession, and approximately half had information about her religion and hobbies (Greenfeld and Klock, 2004; Klock and Greenfeld, 2004).

There is no systematic research examining the donor information provided to UK identity-release egg recipients. The few studies conducted suggest that recipients are given basic information (donor's age, eye and hair colour, weight and height), and that there is little scope for choice, given the shortage of egg donors in this context (Stuart-Smith, Smith and Scott, 2012). Preliminary findings from a study of two-parent heterosexual egg recipient (ER) families by the University of Cambridge's Centre for Family Research indicate a similar trend.[6] Couples generally reported being provided with basic information about the donor's physical characteristics, indicating that the information received by egg recipient couples may be more limited than the information provided to recipients of donor sperm in the UK. However, like recipients of identity-release sperm, many egg recipients were unsure about the information they had about the donor, both because they did not consider there to be much variation between donor profiles, and because they were unable to recall the information they had been given at the time of treatment.

[6] The findings presented form part of a study based on semi-structured interviews with forty-three women who had had a child through identity-release egg donation, and thirty-three of their partners. Interviews were carried out between October 2013 and July 2014. This study is referred to as the 'ER families study' in this chapter.

The profiles seemed to be similar. Ok, I get the impression she was slightly shorter than [partner] but uh, I might be wrong in that, cos, you know, we had three different donor profiles coming through and it was only the third one we went with. So yeah, I'm a little confused as to exactly what they were, but, you know, they were all much of a muchness. (Coupled father, ER family)

Given the preliminary nature of these findings, it is not yet clear that UK recipients of donor eggs – in a similar vein to some recipients of donor sperm – attribute little significance to information about the donor, and if this might be because they similarly seek to minimise the donor's role in their families.

Which donor information is most important to recipients?

Sperm donation

Although little is known about recipients' thoughts and feelings about the significance of specific donor information, it seems that couples and individuals currently seeking or undergoing treatment with donor sperm may be more interested in the appearance, character traits and educational level of the donor than those who conceived with donor sperm in earlier decades (van Berkel et al., 1999). The few studies to have investigated the information needs of recipients seem to suggest that there may also be some variation between recipients in different family types. Research from both the Netherlands and the United States has indicated that heterosexual couples may regard identifying information about the donor as less important than their single and female same-sex couple counterparts, and may be less likely to actively choose an identity-release donor (Brewaeys et al., 2005; Godman et al., 2006; Scheib, Riordan and Rubin, 2003). In contrast, the majority of mothers in the UK DI families study highlighted the importance of identifying information about the donor, irrespective of family type. Most often, recipients viewed this information as of potential importance to their child, and in some cases, mothers described feeling differently about the significance of this information following childbirth.

I think before when I was [undergoing treatment] I would have thought, ooh it would be better to be anonymous, but then I thought oh well it doesn't matter, and then when I thought about it, I think no. I think it's really important because . . . if she ever wants to know, which, you know, she may do . . . you know she'll have some detail about it, but I think it's really important that she has that option. (Single mother, DI family)

Research has also indicated some differences in the level of importance attributed to particular donor characteristics by individuals in different family types. One study, for example, found that single women rated donor age, occupation, interests and feelings about contact as more important on average than partnered heterosexual and lesbian women, and anecdotal evidence has suggested that single women may have more questions about, and higher expectations of, their donor's characteristics in general (Rodino, Burton and Sanders, 2011b). Another study, however, found no differences between the mean scores of recipient groups in rankings of donor information, with the donor's health, name and photograph ranked as highly important by single women and partnered heterosexual and lesbian women (Rodino, Burton and Saunders, 2011a). Findings from in-depth, ethnographic research in the United States suggest that recipients of donor sperm in heterosexual partnerships may be particularly likely to request information about the physical appearance of prospective donors, ultimately matching these characteristics to those of the infertile partner, so that they may present 'as if' donor sperm has not been used (Becker, 2000). Such findings have been echoed in research on heterosexual couples in Poland (Bielawska-Batorowicz, 1994), and authors have noted practices of 'donor matching' in the United States, including matching to a photograph (Pennings, 2000).[7]

In keeping with these findings, the majority of coupled mothers in the DI families study stressed the importance of using a donor whose characteristics were either 'like [their male partner]' or 'like us':

> It was quite important that there was some physical likeness, because otherwise it . . . it's quite apparent as your child is growing up that they're not . . . so I think we asked things like . . . it was skin tone and eye colour, so we tried to keep it similar to me or to [partner]. (Coupled mother, DI family)

Several mothers also discussed the ways in which the process of matching donor-to-partner characteristics was encouraged and facilitated by clinic staff.[8] The role of the clinic in reproducing narratives of genetic heritability – particularly with regards to race – has been discussed elsewhere (Quiroga, 2007). For both single and coupled mothers in the DI families

[7] Readers may also be familiar with Precision Donor, a US-based company launched in 2011, which uses 3D facial recognition software to match donors to recipients' photographs (of themselves, the infertile member of the couple (where present), or another person). Research has yet to explore the extent to which recipients may engage with such services.

[8] This finding is of particular interest given the history of assisted reproduction, in which it was previously believed to be more important to match the donor to the partner on the basis of 'capabilities and aptitudes', and much too difficult 'to match the colouring and build of donor and sterile husband at all precisely' (Jackson, 1957).

study, the need for the ethnic background of the donor to match either the infertile partner or the mother herself was most often described as 'obvious', a finding echoed in Nordqvist's (2012) research on female same-sex couples using donor sperm.[9] Other studies have also highlighted how recipients of donor sperm incorporate the 'genetic information' provided by the clinic into their own understandings of the relationship between 'nature' and 'nurture' as they imagine social and genetic connections with their future children (Mamo, 2005). This emphasis on the 'genetic knowledge' participants may bring to the clinic is reinforced by research on British South Asian recipients of donor gametes, for whom information about a donor's religious beliefs was found to be significant (Hudson and Culley, 2014).

The importance of similarity between donors and family members is also apparent in the narratives of single women using donor sperm. In Graham's (2014) study, the majority of women interviewed described choosing a donor on the basis that he should share physical characteristics with both themselves and their family; a means by which children would feel a sense of 'belonging' to their families, and mothers would avoid questions from other people about their child's father. This finding was echoed in the DI families study; as one single mother suggested, sharing physical characteristics with the donor increased 'the chance of [child] looking, you know, more like she was mine'. At the same time, mothers in one-parent families acknowledged that matching the physical characteristics of the donor to themselves and/or to their wider family was unlike the experience they might have had if they had conceived naturally. In so doing, they appeared to invoke a representation of the 'traditional' family (Zadeh, Freeman and Golombok, 2013).

> I think somebody had said to me it's quite good to go for similar colourings . . . but then when I thought about it afterwards, if you met somebody, they wouldn't be your colouring anyway, and none of my boyfriends probably have been, so, um, I think I just heard it [and] I went for that really . . . (Single mother, DI family)

Single mothers were also more likely than their coupled counterparts to suggest that they wanted to match the donor to themselves and/or to their families on non-visible traits, such as intelligence (inferred from a donor's educational level) and interests, although other research has indicated that some heterosexual couple recipients also do this (Becker, Butler

[9] Like ethnic background, mothers also described the 'obvious' need for a donor who did not have any heritable diseases. Although they rarely detailed what these diseases might be, they most often suggested that using donor sperm from a clinic meant that the donor was of course healthy.

and Nachtigall, 2005). Rather than attempting to maximise 'competitive' traits, a claim sometimes made about this cohort (Pennings, 2000), here, mothers in one-parent families again invoked an image of 'traditional', heterosexual reproduction. One mother, for example, reported that 'it was very important to me that I knew what their educational level was, because I wouldn't choose to have a child with a thicko'.

Other single recipients, however, described their decision to use a particular donor as based upon the fact that his characteristics were entirely unlike their own. This was especially the case for height and interests, and was explained by mothers as a means by which they could 'balance out' their own traits, reinforcing the idea that the importance attributed to particular donor characteristics is based upon recipients' beliefs about inheritance (Mamo, 2005). At the same time, it is worth noting that some recipients in the DI families study described how their beliefs about what constitutes 'genetic information', and their desire to know certain aspects of this information, changed after childbirth.

> Sometimes [child] does things, and I think I wonder. You know that little thought creeps into your head. You sometimes think, I wonder if that's . . . that's come from via his donor. Um, that genetic inheritance . . . At the time, no, [the information] didn't bother me in the slightest. [I] wasn't interested. (Coupled mother, DI family)

In addition to recipients' needs changing over time, it was also clear from participants' reports that some mothers increasingly felt that information about the donor may be important to their *children's* thoughts and feelings – not only about the donor, but also about themselves. Donor information was described by one single mother, for example, as the means by which her child could 'understand that side of her genetic self'.

> I wrote to the clinic a couple of times, and said: Can I ask you some questions a little kid might want to know? So I – and can you say thank you to him for me, so they did, eventually. And he replied with the answers, so I know his favourite food is pasta. His favourite things at school. You know, his favourite colour, things like that. So I told those to the kids. (Coupled mother, DI family)

Related to this was an interest in information concerning the donor's personality traits; in particular, recipients often suggested that it was important that the donor was a 'nice', 'kind' person. Although some mothers assumed this to be the case, given the fact that the donor had chosen to make a donation, others were interested in the information provided by the donor in his pen sketch. This was especially true of some mothers in one-parent families.

He did write a lovely... small section about himself that was to be given when she was born... I thought that was really nice... Cos he'd obviously clearly thought about it, as opposed to being on the university round and just like here's your 400 quid. No, that's quite an endearing quality about somebody I think. (Single mother, DI family)

The importance of the donor's reason for donating has also been found in other research on single recipients of donor sperm in the UK (Graham, 2014) and in research with female same-sex couples in the United States (Chabot and Ames, 2004; Mamo, 2005). Significantly, in addition to this information being accessed from the donor's pen sketch, both single and coupled mothers in the DI families study frequently described how further information about the donor's personality had been gleaned from conversations with staff at the fertility clinic. Indeed, in some cases, these staff impressions were critical to recipients' donor choice, a finding that also emerged from Mamo's (2005) research.

The donor nurse mentioned this guy that had been in that day... [he was] the opposite of what I was going to go for, but she just said he's so nice, he's got such a lovely personality... and then she said to me he's gorgeous looking! As well as being really lovely, I was like sold! I'll take it! (Single mother, DI family)

For many participants, the fact that somebody had met the donor and thought him to be a 'nice' or 'kind' individual was highly significant. By adding what one participant described as 'meat on the bones', this additional information seemed to be a source of comfort, allowing recipients to differentially envisage what one described as the 'ghost-like' figure of the sperm donor, about whom they would otherwise have only a paper profile. It is also clear that this personal information was seen as crucial to recipients who decided to tell their child about the use of a sperm donor; a somewhat unsurprising finding, given that the 'kind man' discourse is also used in the children's literature on gamete donation (Blake et al., 2014).

Egg donation

The majority of research into egg recipients' choice of donor has focussed on couples' choice of anonymous, identity-release or known donation. Once this initial decision has been made, much less is known about how recipients then choose between individual donors. Few studies have addressed this question, but those that have suggest some cross-cultural variation with regard to the donor characteristics prioritised by recipients. It is also possible that these decisions may be influenced to an as-yet-unknown extent by the type of egg donation available to recipients in each country, their expectations about the amount of information available, and country-specific practical restraints, such as the availability of donors and/or the length of waiting lists.[10]

One study of anonymous egg recipients in the United States found that the donor's medical history was rated as most important, followed by ethnicity and intelligence (Lindheim and Sauer, 1998). Another survey of US recipients found that the three most important characteristics influencing donor choice for both men and women were appearance, health and intelligence, with appearance being rated as valuable to recipients either because of the donor's attractiveness, or because of how much she resembled the female member of the couple, or both (Greenfeld and Klock, 2004; Klock and Greenfeld, 2004). A minority of respondents also listed donor availability, blood type and proven fertility as important factors (Klock and Greenfeld, 2004). One study found that recipients' donor preferences changed after consultation with mental health professionals and nurses at the clinic. Post-consultation, recipients reported that education and ethnic background were less important, and that the donor's willingness to have future contact was more important (Braverman et al., 2010). However, a more recent study found that recipients' preferences had changed over the preceding five-year period, with an increasing number of recipients showing a preference for donors with good health, athletic ability and high intelligence (Flores et al., 2014). Another study found that recipients felt less strongly about their donor's characteristics after childbirth, although health remained the most important factor (Braverman et al., 2011).

Australian egg recipients rated knowledge of the donor's name (78 per cent), reason for donating (56 per cent), health (39 per cent) and family (39 per cent) as most important (Rodino, Burton and Saunders, 2011a). Information about the donor's hobbies, religion, education and age was not considered a priority by any respondent. It has been suggested that egg recipients may regard knowledge of the donor's reasons for donating as important information for future offspring, and that knowledge of the (altruistic) reasons for donation may enable recipients to construct a birth narrative that is sensitive to their child's needs (Nuffield Council on Bioethics, 2013; Rodino, Burton and Saunders, 2011a; Stuart-Smith, Smith and Scott, 2012).

With regard to concerns about the donor, both women and men in Klock and Greenfeld's (2004) study were most concerned about

[10] For a discussion of the ethical, legal and policy issues raised by the practice of egg-sharing as a means to increase numbers of egg donors and reduce waiting times for treatment for egg recipients, see Scott, Chapter 12.

the donor's genetic and medical background, followed by the donor's intelligence. Concerns about the donor's physical resemblance were rated significantly higher by women than men. Conversely, a study of Finnish anonymous egg recipients (who had received information about the donor's ethnic background, age, height, eye and hair colour) found that the majority had few or no concerns about the donor's characteristics in terms of physical resemblance, personality traits or intelligence, and concerns about the donor's physical resemblance were not significantly higher for women than men (Söderström-Anttila, Sälevaara and Suikkari, 2010).

The only qualitative study to consider egg recipients' views on information provision at different stages of the process (both pre- and post-treatment) found wide variation in the extent to which women in the UK were concerned with the screening and 'matching' process (Stuart-Smith, Smith and Scott, 2012). Several recipients stated that they did not want to know too much about the donor, for fear of being disappointed if treatment failed, and others seemed to resist this information as it may have made the need for a donor more perceptible and potentially more painful. In this study, however, several recipients had information about their donor's motivation for donating, and one recipient who had initially expressed a preference for very little donor information later decided to pursue treatment in the United States in order to have more comprehensive information about the donor, and to feel that she could 'trust' her.

Preliminary findings from the ER families study suggest that recipient couples may have some concerns about 'matching' the donor's physical characteristics to the recipient. However, recipients also explained that they assumed that the clinic would be responsible for this process. As one recipient reported, 'the clinic filters them so that they'll offer you somebody who they think physically has similar characteristics to you'. However, several mothers reported having rejected potential donors on the basis of age, believing that by prioritising the age of the donor they would maximise their chances of the treatment being successful.

> If I remember rightly they sent me some details of a lady in her late thirties and I just said 'no she's too old', and they then went back and started looking for someone a lot younger. I'm not sure, I think (child's) donor was just 27, 28, something like that . . . and she had to be younger otherwise it wasn't going to be successful in the long run. (Coupled mother, ER family)

However, for many couples, information provided about the donor was less important than the fact that they had reached the top of the clinic's waiting list and could therefore pursue treatment. Recipients seemed acutely aware that the pool of available donors and the time frame in which they could have treatment were both limited.

I think I just saw the two [profiles] in the end. Yeah, cos by the time they've found somebody, the months are going by and you're getting that much older that you can't pick and choose and be that fussy. (Coupled mother, ER family)

This view was also echoed by those who emphasised that the particular characteristics of the donor were less important than the wish for their treatment to have a successful outcome.

As long as the eggs were good quality then you don't really mind about are they blonde, are they dark, are they red hair? Or whatever it's not – you know, at the end of the day you just want to have your baby. (Coupled father, ER family)

Given that most of the participants in this study had undergone multiple treatment cycles, and in some cases, had pursued treatment with more than one donor, it is perhaps unsurprising that many emphasised the importance of successful treatment, rather than specific donor information.

Is there any other information recipients would have liked about the donor?

Sperm donation

To date, no research has been published on recipients' desires for additional donor information in the case of sperm donation. In the DI families study, recipients were explicitly asked if there was any other information about the donor they would have liked. For some mothers, this question was clearly difficult to answer. Many responded that they had never considered the issue before, suggesting that the context in which information is provided may be critical in shaping recipients' expectations about donor information, and may be central to the ways in which they conceptualise the donor.

I didn't know what to ask to be honest really. You know, I had spoken to nobody, nobody about this. I was just trying to work it all out myself. (Single mother, DI family)

For other participants in the study, the fact of having used a sperm donor – whom they had not met, but had been matched with by clinic staff – inevitably rendered this person unknowable, a finding also echoed elsewhere (Graham, 2014). Although mothers mostly did not describe a desire to meet the donor, some suggested that not having met him meant that their knowledge about him was inevitably limited.

It doesn't matter how much stuff you read about someone on a piece of paper, you can never know what they're like, really, unless you met them, and you're not gonna meet them. (Single mother, DI family)

Others were more specific about the pieces of information they perceived as missing about the donor. For example, one mother described how she wanted to know about the donor's feelings regarding contact in the future in order to safeguard her children from potential upset. Others described that they would have liked to know more about the donor's personality.

I'd like to know things like, the sort of thing if you're meeting someone for the first time and you sat down and had a cup of coffee with them, what would you ask them? You know. What are your likes, dislikes, what's important to your values, that kind of thing. Um, but I don't think you're ever gonna get enough, if I'm honest, because it's anonymous. (Single mother, DI family)

Some mothers wanted information about the donor that they knew the clinic advised donors to provide, such as a goodwill message or pen sketch. Others wanted information that they knew other recipients of donor sperm had about *their* donors, such as the reason for donation. Like the mothers who were unsure how to respond to questions concerning additional information, these mothers seemed to similarly measure the level and standard of information they received within the existing context of gamete donation, rather than in terms of the infinite information they could potentially have about the donor.

Some single mothers suggested that it would have been preferable to see a photograph of the donor, and/or to know his name. This was mainly described in terms of being of benefit to their children, for whom conceptualising the donor without these pieces of information was perceived to be difficult, a finding also true of research in the United States (Hertz, 2006). Mothers in both one and two-parent families also suggested that they would have liked to know more about their donor's medical history. This was particularly the case for mothers whose children had experienced some sort of health difficulty, and clearly relates to the idea that recipients' information needs may change over time, particularly in relation to their child's development.

Egg donation

Several studies have found that many egg recipients state that they do not want additional information about the donor, both in cases in which recipients had only basic information about their donor (Söderström-Anttila, Sälevaara and Suikkari, 2010), and when they had more detailed information (Klock and Greenfeld, 2004). Those who would have liked additional information prioritised having more details about the donor's family and medical history, and expressed a desire to see a photograph of the donor (Greenfeld and Klock, 2004). Only women stated an interest in knowing more about why the donor had donated (Klock and Greenfeld, 2004). A study of pregnant anonymous egg recipients highlighted recipients' concerns about the importance of, and access to, genetic information about the donor as it changes over time (Hershberger, 2007). In the United States, where egg banking is growing rapidly as an option, information is increasingly offered to recipients as an incentive for choosing one bank over another. However, it remains to be seen whether or not egg banks begin to resemble sperm banks in the United States – both in terms of the amount of information that is offered to recipients, and in terms of the information most desired by recipients using these services.

The only study to survey European recipient couples found that 48 per cent of Finnish recipients of anonymous eggs did not want to receive any information about the donor. Others were interested in the donor's age, profession, physical appearance, hobbies and place of residence (Söderström-Anttila et al., 1998). Stuart-Smith, Smith and Scott's (2012) in-depth qualitative study of 11 UK egg recipients found that one recipient wanted more information about the donor's medical history, and two wanted more information about the donor's intelligence, personality and sense of humour.

In contrast to UK identity-release sperm recipients, preliminary findings from the ER families study suggest that in general, coupled recipients were content with the amount of information they had about the donor. Lack of interest in additional information was explained as a means of preserving the anonymity of both donors and recipients.

> I don't, wouldn't really want too much. I would never want to walk down the street and 'oh I wonder if it's that person?' I, if they'd said to me 'do you want their name and address?' I probably would have said no. (Coupled father, ER family)

In line with Hershberger's (2007) findings, several participants also mentioned the importance of access to evolving genetic information when asked if there was anything else they would like to know about their donor.

> If they were to suffer with a genetic illness in the future, whether that would be passed to us, you know, sometimes things get skipped generations. Just, just so we will know what signs to look for if there is a health issue, and that when you take [child] to the doctors and they ask about the family history and we go, 'well we don't know'. (Coupled father, ER family)

There was also some uncertainty about which medical conditions clinics screened donors for, leading to a desire amongst some recipients for more detailed medical information.[11] One recipient also suggested that the clinic had responded to an enquiry about whether further donor information was available by emphasising the role of environmental factors in child development, a response with which she remained unsatisfied.

It's interesting because the first time at [clinic] I asked the consultant about, did they look at the educational background of the donors, and he said, 'no that's got nothing to do with it'. He said, 'it's all to do with the way the child's brought up'. And I've sat and thought about that over the – over the years after that, and I think that's a big part of it is the way the child's – the child's development and things go afterwards . . . I think he's got a point but . . . maybe, maybe there ought to be a little more information on – on someone like that, something to do with their occupation perhaps. (Coupled mother, ER family)

As has been noted with recipients of donor sperm, several small, qualitative studies have suggested that egg recipients' concerns about the amount of donor information available to them may also change over time, particularly amongst families intending to disclose the egg donation to their children (Blyth, Langridge and Harris, 2010; Stuart-Smith, Smith and Scott, 2012). Researchers have suggested that the wish to have more donor information may assume greater prominence as children age, and that parents may become increasingly aware of the inadequacy of the information they have. However, given that the majority of research in this area has been conducted at a single time-point with small sample sizes, these findings should be considered with caution. Furthermore, it is also not yet known whether this suggested change in satisfaction with the amount of donor information available would also be seen in families who do not intend to disclose the use of donor eggs to their child.

Conclusion

Current research on donor information thus presents a complex picture. It is clear that the amount of information recipients have about sperm and egg donors varies not only according to the regulatory context in which they access fertility treatment – and the degree of commercialisation of gamete donation within that context – but also by the extent to which they are motivated to receive or retain such information. It is also

[11] This finding is worth considering in relation to recent findings that clinical practitioners believe the medical information collected from gamete donors to be extensive, and that it provides sufficient reassurance to recipients with regard to the risk of genetically inherited illnesses (Nuffield Council on Bioethics, 2013).

apparent that the type of information recipients deem most important about sperm and egg donors is at least in part governed by the regulatory framework within which they access treatment, with the majority of recipients either seemingly satisfied with the amount of information they have about their donor, desiring further information which falls within existing regulatory parameters, or acknowledging that access to further information is not possible. In general, it is clear that the majority of information about both egg and sperm donors that is deemed by recipients to be important is information about characteristics both perceived by them, and generally described by the clinical sector, as inheritable. For both coupled and single recipients of donor sperm, and couples receiving donated eggs, the perceived need to 'match' between donor and recipient(s) is marked. At the same time, it seems that there may be some differences between coupled and single recipients of donor sperm with regards to how much information is requested or required. Although differences between egg recipients in different family types are not yet known,[12] the existing literature from the United States suggests that there may be some within-couple variation, along gendered lines. In all cases, it is clear that the needs of recipients may change over time, and in concert with a changing recognition of their children's need for information, both about the donor, and about themselves. In line with the recent recommendations of the Nuffield report on donor conception (Nuffield Council on Bioethics, 2013), this chapter therefore highlights the limitations of adopting a 'one-off' approach to donor information gathering – as is currently the case in the UK – and the problems of assuming a 'one-size-fits-all' position vis-a-vis individual recipients' needs regarding this information.

While this discussion has demonstrated that there may be much variability in recipients' perspectives, it is also evident that the question of what constitutes appropriate donor information provision may be differentially conceived by other stakeholders, such as donors themselves (see Graham, Mohr and Bourne, Chapter 10).[13] Similarly, the possibility that different clinics – ostensibly operating under a single regulatory framework – may differentially apply national guidelines should not be overlooked. However, given gamete shortages, and the related

[12] Nothing is known, for example, about the information needs of male same-sex couples forming their families through egg donation and surrogacy. The existing research on this recipient group seems to suggest that the use of assisted reproduction is felt by some such couples to provide them with extensive medical information about the person(s) involved in their child's conception, and is therefore preferable to other methods of family formation, such as adoption (Lev, 2006).

[13] The issue of equity in donor-recipient relations with regards to donor information provision is not one which this chapter can suitably address (see Farsides, Chapter 16).

finding that UK recipients often experience delays to treatment, it is also possible that online resources – in which both donors and recipients have access to information about one another – will be increasingly used by recipients in their search for a donor. It is also possible that the use of these resources will become more common, given that the contemporary climate of assisted reproduction is characterised by commercial practice.[14] How recipients using *these* resources – rather than the clinic – will reflect upon donor information specifically, and how their choices will change the terrain of assisted reproduction in general, remains to be seen.

REFERENCES

Almeling, R. (2011). *Sex Cells: The Medical Market for Eggs and Sperm*. Berkeley: University of California Press.

Becker, G. (2000). *The Elusive Embryo: How Women and Men Approach New Reproductive Technologies*. London: University of California Press.

Becker, G., Butler, A. and Nachtigall, R.D. (2005). 'Resemblance talk: a challenge for parents whose children were conceived with donor gametes in the US'. *Social Science and Medicine*, 61, 1300–9.

Bielawska-Batorowicz, E. (1994). 'Artificial insemination by donor – an investigation of recipient couples' viewpoints'. *Journal of Reproductive and Infant Psychology*, 12, 123–36.

Blake, L., Zadeh, S., Statham, H. and Freeman, T. (2014). 'Families created by assisted reproduction: children's perspectives', in T. Freeman, S. Graham, F. Ebtehaj and M. Richards (eds.), *Relatedness in Assisted Reproduction: Families, Origins and Identities*. Cambridge University Press.

Blyth, E., Langridge, D. and Harris, R. (2010). 'Family building in donor conception: parents' experiences of sharing information'. *Journal of Reproductive and Infant Psychology*, 28, 116–27.

Blyth, E., Kramer, W. and Schneider, J. (2013). 'Perspectives, experiences, and choices of parents of children conceived following oocyte donation'. *Reproductive Biomedicine Online*, 26, 179–88.

Boulos, M., Kerridge, I. and Waldby, C. (2010). 'Reciprocity in the donation of reproductive oocytes', in M. Nash (ed.), *Reframing Reproduction: Conceiving Gendered Experiences*. Basingstoke: Palgrave Macmillan.

Braverman, A.M., Taylor, D., Galen, B., Nicholson, R. and Scott R.T. (2010). 'Does mental health and nursing counselling influence ovum donor recipients' preferences for their donors?' *Fertility and Sterility*, 94, S67.

Braverman A.M., Galen, B., Taylor, D. and Scott, R.T. (2011). 'Do ovum donor recipient preferences change over time?' *Fertility and Sterility*, 96, S10.

Brewaeys, M., de Bruyn, J.K., Louwe, L.A. and Helmerhorst, F.M. (2005). 'Anonymous or identity-registered sperm donors? A study of Dutch recipients' choices'. *Human Reproduction*, 20, 820–4.

[14] Online searches reveal an increasing number of forums and groups where potential donors and recipients meet to discuss uncompensated donation.

Broderick, P. and Walker, I. (1995). 'Information access and donated gametes: how much do we know about who wants to know?' *Human Reproduction*, 10, 3338–41.

Bujan, L., Le Lannou, D. and Kunstmann, J-M. (2012). 'Anonymat du don de gamètes'. *Gynécologie Obstétrique & Fertilité*, 40, 8–15.

Chabot, J.M. and Ames, B.D. (2004). 'It wasn't "let's get pregnant and go do it": decision making in lesbian couples planning motherhood via donor insemination'. *Family Relations*, 53, 348–56

Culley, L., Hudson, N., Rapport, F., Blyth, E., Norton, W. and Pacey, A.A. (2011). 'Crossing borders for fertility treatment: motivations, destinations and outcomes of UK fertility travellers'. *Human Reproduction*, 26, 2373–81.

Ehrensaft, D. (2008). 'Just Molly and me, and donor makes three: lesbian motherhood in the age of assisted reproductive technology'. *Journal of Lesbian Studies*, 12, 161–78.

Flores, H., Lee, J., Rodriguez-Purata, J., Witkin, G. et al. (2014). 'Beauty, brains or health: trends in ovum recipient preferences'. *Journal of Women's Health*, 23, 830–3.

Freeman, T., Jadva, V., Kramer, W. and Golombok, S. (2009). 'Gamete donation: parents' experiences of searching for their child's donor siblings and donor'. *Human Reproduction*, 24, 505–16.

Godman, K.M., Sanders, K., Rosenberg, M. and Burton, P. (2006). 'Potential sperm donors', recipients' and their partners' opinions towards the release of identifying information in Western Australia'. *Human Reproduction*, 21, 3022–6.

Graham, S. (2014). 'Stories of an absent "father": Single women negotiating relatedness through donor profiles', in T. Freeman, S. Graham, F. Ebtehaj and M. Richards (eds.), *Relatedness in Assisted Reproduction: Families, Origins and Identities*. Cambridge University Press.

Greenfeld, D. and Klock, S.C. (2004). 'Disclosure decisions among known and anonymous oocyte donation recipients'. *Fertility and Sterility*, 81, 1565–71.

Hershberger, P.E. (2007). 'Pregnant, donor oocyte recipient women describe their lived experience of establishing the "family lexicon"', *Journal of Obstetric, Gynecologic and Neonatal Nursing*, 18, 1–7.

Hertz, R. (2006). *Single by Chance, Mothers by Choice*. Oxford University Press.

HFEA Code of Practice, 8th edn (2013). Available at www.hfea.gov.uk/docs/Code_of_Practice_8_-_October_2013.pdf. Accessed 28 February 2014.

Hudson, N. and Culley, L. (2014). 'Beginnings and belonging: third party assisted conception, ethnicity and relatedness in British South Asian communities', in T. Freeman, S. Graham, F. Ebtehaj and M. Richards (eds.), *Relatedness in Assisted Reproduction: Families, Origins and Identities*. Cambridge University Press.

Jackson, M. (1957). 'Artificial insemination (donor)'. *The Eugenics Review*, 48, 203–9.

Johnson, K.M. (2013). 'Making families: Organizational boundary work in US egg and sperm donation'. *Social Science and Medicine*, 99, 64–71.

Johnson, L., Bourne, K. and Hammarberg, K. (2012). 'Donor conception legislation in Victoria, Australia: the "Time to Tell" campaign, donor-linking and implications for clinical practice'. *Journal of Law and Medicine*, 19, 803–19.

Kalampalikis, N., Haas, V., Fieulaine, N., Doumergue, M. and Deschamps, G. (2012). 'Giving or giving back: New psychosocial insights from sperm donors in France'. *Psychology, Health and Medicine*, 1–9.

Klock, S.C. and Greenfeld, D.A. (2004). 'Parents' knowledge about the donors and their attitudes toward disclosure in oocyte donation'. *Human Reproduction*, 19, 1575–9.

Lev, A.I. (2006). 'Gay dads: Choosing surrogacy'. *Lesbian and Gay Psychology Review*, 7, 72–6.

Lindheim, S.R. and Sauer, M.V. (1998). 'Expectations of recipient couples awaiting an anonymous oocyte donor match'. *Journal of Assisted Reproduction and Genetics*, 15, 444–6.

Mamo, L. (2005). 'Biomedicalizing kinship: Sperm banks and the creation of affinity-ties'. *Science as Culture*, 14, 237–64.

Nordqvist, P. (2012). '"I don't want us to stand out more than we already do": Lesbian couples negotiating family connections in donor conception'. *Sexualities*, 15, 644–61.

Nuffield Council on Bioethics (2013). *Donor Conception: Ethical Aspects of Information Sharing*. London: Nuffield Council on Bioethics.

Pennings, G. (2000). 'The right to choose your donor: a step towards commercialisation or a step towards empowering the patient?' *Human Reproduction*, 15, 508–14.

Quiroga, S.S. (2007). 'Blood is thicker than water: policing donor information and the reproduction of whiteness'. *Hypatia*, 22, 143–61.

Rodino, I.S., Burton, P.J. and Sanders, K.A. (2011a). 'Donor information considered important to donors, recipients and offspring: an Australian perspective'. *Reproductive Biomedicine Online*, 22, 303–11.

Rodino, I.S., Burton, P.J. and Sanders, K.A. (2011b). 'Mating by proxy: a novel perspective to donor conception'. *Fertility and Sterility*, 96, 998–1001.

Scheib, J.S., Riordan, M. and Rubin, S. (2003). 'Choosing identity-release sperm donors: The parents' perspective 13–18 years later'. *Human Reproduction*, 18, 1115–27.

Scheib, J.E. and Cushing, R.A. (2007). 'Open-identity donor insemination in the United States: Is it on the rise?' *Fertility and Sterility*, 88, 231–2.

Söderström-Anttila, V., Sajaniemi, N., Tiitinen, A. and Hovatta, O. (1998). 'Health and development of children born after oocyte donation compared with that of those born after in-vitro fertilization, and parents' attitudes regarding secrecy'. *Human Reproduction*, 13, 2009–15.

Söderström-Anttila, V., Sälevaara, M. and Suikkari, A.M. (2010). Increasing openness in oocyte donation families regarding disclosure over 15 years. *Human Reproduction*, 25, 2535–42.

Stuart-Smith, S.J., Smith, J.A. and Scott, E.J. (2012). 'To know or not to know Dilemmas for women receiving unknown oocyte donation. *Human Reproduction*, 27, 2067–75.

The Ethics Committee of the American Society for Reproductive Medicine (2013). 'Informing offspring of their conception by gamete or embryo donation: a committee opinion'. *Fertility and Sterility*, 100, 45–9.

Van Berkel, D., van der Veen, L., Kimmel, I. and te Velde, E. (1999). 'Differences in the attitudes of couples whose children were conceived through artificial insemination by donor in 1980 and in 1996'. *Fertility and Sterility*, 71, 226–31.

Zadeh, S., Freeman, T. and Golombok, S. (2013). 'Ambivalent identities of single women using sperm donation'. *Revue Internationale de Psychologie Sociale / International Review of Social Psychology*, 26, 97–123.

LEGISLATION

UK

Human Fertilisation and Embryology Act (1990), as amended (2008).

15 Regulating the provision of donor information to donor-conceived children
Is there room for improvement?

John B. Appleby

Introduction

One of the most contentious debates in the field of reproductive donation is centred on the question of what information donor-conceived (DC) persons should have about their gamete (sperm and egg) or embryo donors.[1] On the one hand, if regulators provide too little information about donors there is a risk that they will frustrate a range of possible interests held by DC persons. On the other hand, if regulators agree to provide too much information about donors they risk, for example, alienating donors as a result of violating their privacy interests. Furthermore, questions also exist about how and when donor information should be provided.

This chapter attempts to clarify and respond to this regulatory debate by discussing the two main categories of donor information that can be provided to DC persons: non-identifying information and identifying information. The following questions are asked in relation to each category of information: (1) what can the available evidence tell us, if anything, about the information that DC persons want and why regulators should (or should not) provide it; and (2) is donor information being provided effectively or is there room for regulators to make improvements? The discussion that follows from these questions is generally framed in this chapter according to the context of UK regulation; however, comparative examples are drawn from international contexts and the issues at the heart of this discussion are relevant to regulatory contexts beyond the borders of the UK.

In response to the above questions, it is argued that while UK regulators appear to provide non-identifying donor information to DC persons in reasonable quantities and in an effective manner, the same cannot necessarily be said about how regulators currently provide identifying donor

[1] From here onward the term 'DC' will generally refer to any person conceived via donated sperm, egg or embryo.

information. In contrast, the right amount of identifying information appears to be provided to DC persons by regulators, but the process by which this information is provided appears to be fundamentally flawed. Therefore a recommendation is made for regulators in the UK to allow the release of identifying donor information to parents from the outset of the DC child's life, rather than maintain the status quo of restricting the release of such information until DC persons may request it at the age of eighteen. According to this recommendation, parents should be in control of how and when (if ever) identifying donor information is released to their DC children. The early release of identifying donor information to parents would ensure that this information is more likely to be accurate and more likely to be in the interests of children, which appears to be more in line with the regulatory spirit of requiring open-identity donation in the first instance.[2] It is important to acknowledge that the interests of parents and their offspring are often intertwined; however, the discussion in this chapter is primarily focused on how changes to the provision of donor information could be made to better satisfy the interests of DC persons.[3] To begin, a brief summary is provided of the main types of gamete donors that typically exist and the information they provide for DC persons.

Types of donors and what donor-conceived persons can find out about them

The information that DC persons can find out about their donors typically depends on the type of donor that their parents used. For this reason, much of the debate about what kind of information DC persons should have about their donor, is rooted in a related debate: what types of donors should regulators permit? Generally speaking, there are three types of donors: 'anonymous', 'open-identity' and 'known'. The donor types are described in this instance according to the regulations set out under the Human Fertilisation and Embryology Act (HFE Act) 1990, as amended (2008).

[2] In this chapter, the term 'disclosure' refers to the process of informing children that they were donor-conceived. Someone has been disclosed to once they understand that they were donor conceived. The question of whether or not parents should disclose to their DC children is separate (although related) from the arguments put forward in this chapter. Instead, this chapter starts from the basic position that some DC children have been disclosed to or will be disclosed to, and it is these DC persons that are the focus of the chapter.

[3] This chapter does take into account the interests of parents, but for a more detailed discussion of parents' interests and perspectives on the provision of donor information, see Zadeh, Imrie and Braverman, Chapter 14.

Individuals conceived with anonymous donations may have access to a range of non-identifying information about their donors. For example, in the UK, at the age of sixteen, donor-conceived children can contact the Human Fertilisation and Embryology Authority (HFEA) to find out non-identifying information about their donors (HFE Act 1990, as amended (2008): §31ZA). This information includes: a physical description (i.e. weight, hair colour, eye colour and height); their ethnicity; the year and country of their birth; if they had any children at the time of donation and possibly additional information, such as a pen portrait and their reasons for donating (HFEA, 2011).[4] However, the HFEA also explains that although the above donor information may be available to some DC persons conceived with donations made between 1 April 1991 and 1 April 2005, donors may not have provided all of this information to clinics in every case (HFEA, 2011).[5]

Those individuals who were conceived using an open-identity donor will likely receive similar information to that of someone who was conceived with an anonymous donation (as outlined above). However, someone conceived with an open-identity donor will also be able to access identifying information about their donor. Persons conceived with donations made after 1 April 2005 are eligible to request identifying information about their donors from the HFEA when they turn eighteen (HFEA, 2004; HFE Act, 1990, as amended (2008)).[6] The identifying donor information that is available from the HFEA includes: name and last known address (HFEA, 2012a). Also, some additional non-identifying information is also made available by the HFEA about open-identity donors, including: the gender of their children if they have any at the time of the donation; marital status; medical history and possibly a goodwill message to the children conceived with the donation.

'Known' gamete donors are a third group of donors that exist. These donors might be friends, family members or anyone who is known (identifiable) to the prospective parents. What distinguishes known donation from open-identity donation is that the parents know the identity (often

[4] A pen portrait can also simply be referred to as a 'description of yourself'. There are typically no limits with respect to the kinds of information that can be provided in pen portraits; however, if they are being requested for anonymous donation, then any description provided would need to exclude identifying information.

[5] In contrast, the United States has no legally binding requirements for fertility clinics to provide any particular pieces of information about donors (including anonymous donors) to DC children or their parents. Nevertheless, many US fertility clinics provide parents and children conceived with anonymous donations with similar amounts of information to that which the HFEA has aimed to provide to UK children conceived with anonymous donors (see Glennon, Chapter 3).

[6] The use and market demand for open-identity donation has also increased in the United States (see Glennon, Chapter 3).

very well) of the donor and therefore have access to a potentially broader range of information about them from the outset of their agreement to donate. Furthermore, if parents disclose to their children, the children will have additional information about their donors which may be of interest to them. However, if a known donor is used, parents in the UK do not have a legal obligation (as in all cases of donor conception) to disclose to their children; thus, donors of this type will always be known to parents, but (as with all forms of gamete and embryo donation) will not necessarily be known by their DC children.

The provision of non-identifying donor information to donor-conceived persons

In the regulatory context of reproductive donation, non-identifying donor information often represents a baseline or common-currency of information that DC persons can likely expect to receive about their donors; or at least this is often the case in most countries (e.g. UK, Belgium and Denmark) where donation is regulated and some information is collected from donors and made available to DC persons. As outlined above, in the UK the HFEA makes a range of non-identifiable information available to DC persons when they reach the age of sixteen.[7] In addition, at any time parents can apply to the HFEA to receive all of the non-identifying information on record about their DC child's donor (HFEA, 2012b). According to the HFEA website, '[t]his is because parents are seen as guardians of their children's interests and are in the best position to pass information on to their children at an age when they can understand it' (HFEA, 2012b). Therefore, DC persons could potentially have access to a range of non-identifying information about their donor from an early age if their parents wished to make it available to them.

What is known about the kinds of non-identifying donor information that DC persons wish to be provided with? There is only a very limited amount of empirical evidence available that sheds light on which pieces of this information are important to DC persons (see Blake, Ilioi and Golombok, Chapter 13) and the majority of this evidence is drawn from the context of sperm donation. A recent report by the Nuffield Council on Bioethics (2013) reviewed evidence on the preferences of DC persons towards having different kinds of information about their donors. The report's findings suggest that there is a plurality of views among DC

[7] However, the HFEA only began keeping records of birth in licensed clinics from August 1, 1991. Therefore, the HFEA cannot guarantee the provision of any information about donors from before that time.

persons about which pieces of non-identifying donor information matter to them. For example, some DC persons place more value on having physical and medical information about their donors. Meanwhile, other DC persons appear to value information about the donors' families and their motivations for donating. Given the limited evidence that is available (especially from the context of egg and embryo donation), it is difficult to argue that either too much or too little non-identifying donor information is currently being collected in the UK by licensed clinics and subsequently being made available by the HFEA to DC persons.[8]

There will inevitably be some additional pieces of non-identifying information that some DC persons may want to have, but which are not currently requested from donors by clinics. For instance, there is a small amount of qualitative evidence which suggests that some DC persons wish that UK regulators would expand the categories of information that would be mandatory for clinics to collect about donors (Nuffield Council on Bioethics, 2013). Some of the additional categories of information that were suggested include the donor's financial status, sexual orientation, hobbies and motivations for donation (Nuffield Council on Bioethics, 2013: 66). While pieces of donor information such as these may be important to some DC persons, it is not clear that donors should be required to provide them. Any proposal to increase the amount of information that donors are required to provide would likely need to be based on a robust foundation of empirical evidence.[9] However, at this time insufficient evidence exists to motivate any policy change towards making additional donor information available to DC persons. Instead, the breadth of information aggregated from donors could potentially be increased in a more straightforward way: clinics could do more to encourage and help donors voluntarily provide additional information about themselves (e.g. in a pen portrait) at the time of donation. By gathering as much information as donors are willing to provide, clinics could increase their chances of satisfying the varying preferences future DC persons might have about knowing a range of different facts about their donors.

In fact, the provision of non-identifying donor information to DC persons appears to be relatively uncontroversial. There is little evidence to

[8] Given the overall shortage of evidence on this topic, it would also be difficult to say whether or not too much or too little non-identifying donor information was being offered to DC persons in most countries, beyond the UK.

[9] If we assume that policy makers are generally interested in serving the interests of DC persons, then the above requirements for empirical evidence (with respect to motivating policy change) would need to demonstrate that offering DC persons addition pieces of donor information would be important for the sake of their interests.

suggest that there is much discontent among DC persons, DC parents or donors about the amount of this information that is currently provided in the UK. Similarly, there appear to be few issues with the way this non-identifying information is provided to DC persons (as well as their parents).[10] In contrast, I now turn to the provision of identifying donor information to DC persons, which is more problematic in several respects.

The provision of identifying donor information to donor-conceived persons

As explained earlier, in addition to the provision of non-identifying information, some countries[11] such as the UK, now require that identifying information about donors be made available to DC persons at the age of eighteen; however, the provision of such information remains controversial. Some (Wincott and Crawshaw, 2006) argue that children have a right to such information and that it is generally in their interests to have it. Others are of the view that such regulations infringe on the privacy of donors (and their families) (as discussed by Pennings, 2012), that it possibly reduces the number of potential donors, and that DC persons probably do not really need to have identifying information about their donors anyway. The challenge is making sense of these conflicting views in order to determine the most coherent way of regulating the provision of donor information.

What can the available empirical evidence tell us about the interests that DC children have in obtaining identifiable information about their donors? As Blake, Ilioi and Golombok have explained in Chapter 13, there is only limited evidence on the views held by DC persons about accessing identifying information about their donors in the future and much of this evidence is about sperm donor-conceived persons. At this point in time it is also impossible to know how many DC persons conceived after 1 April 2005 in the UK will likely want to contact their donors when they turn eighteen (this will not be until at least 2023). However, the evidence[12] that is currently available indicates that there

[10] Here I am only referring to DC persons who have been disclosed to. Of course, it remains possible that DC persons would like more information, but at this point in time research is scarce with respect to this particular topic.

[11] Other examples of countries include: Switzerland, Sweden, Austria, the Netherlands, the Australian State of Victoria and New Zealand. See Blake, Ilioi and Golombok, Chapter 13.

[12] This evidence consists of some quantitative studies and small qualitative studies (primarily about sperm donation), as well as relevant observations from adoption research. For full details, see Blake, Ilioi and Golombok, Chapter 13.

are at least some DC persons who are curious about the identities of their donors and will want to access identifying information about them in the future. What follows is a short summary of some of the key points from the relevant evidence presented and discussed by Blake, Ilioi and Golombok in Chapter 13.

Much of the available evidence can be drawn from a small US study ($n = 29$) by Scheib, Riordan, and Rubin (2005) of adolescents conceived with open-identity sperm donors. This study found that most children were interested in finding out the identities of their donors when they reached eighteen. Many children wanted to learn more about their open-identity donors, for reasons such as: discovering what they had in common; learning medical related information about the donor; finding out about their ancestry; general curiosity; wanting to form a friendly relationship or father–child relationship and discovering information about and potentially meeting any donor siblings they had. These findings are not necessarily surprising, as Blake, Ilioi and Golombok (Chapter 13) point out that the adoption literature does show similar patterns of adopted children who express an interest in finding out the identities of their biological parents and who also have a desire to potentially meet them as well.

There is also limited evidence to suggest that parents have an interest in using open-identity donors. Some evidence suggests that parents may be more likely to disclose to their child if they have an identifiable donor (either known or open-identity) as opposed to an anonymous donor. As Blake, Ilioi and Golombok (Chapter 13) have explained, a study by Scheib (2003) ($n = 45$) on families with open-identity sperm donors reports that most parents felt positive about their donor choice. Scheib's (2003) study also reported that DC children in these families would likely want to contact the donor in the future. For example, a website called the Donor Sibling Registry, based in the United States, exists to help connect DC persons with donors and donor siblings. The website has an approximate membership of 40,000 parents and DC children (see Blake, Ilioi and Golombok, Chapter 13). The presence of such high membership numbers (many members are from lesbian or single mother families) since the website's establishment in 2000 suggest that there is a considerable level of interest among children conceived by anonymous donation and their parents, to identify and learn more about donors.[13]

In addition, some studies have shown that the use of open-identity donors may reduce the risk of DC persons suffering psycho-social harms

[13] It should also be noted that there are certainly plenty of DC persons out there who have no interest in their donor and who never will have any interest in their donor.

(e.g. stress, anxiety and distrust in others) as a result of late or accidental disclosure (Blake, Ilioi and Golombok, Chapter 13; Turner and Coyle, 2000).[14] However, there is also a possibility that DC persons could suffer psycho-social harms (e.g. sadness, disappointment and rejection) as a consequence of any negative experiences they may have when making contact with donors. Nevertheless, as emphasised in Chapter 13 by Blake, Ilioi and Golombok, the current consensus is that disclosure to DC persons at an early age is usually in the interests of children. This is a position held by both the HFEA (2014b) and the Nuffield Council on Bioethics (2013). Evidence discussed by Blake, Ilioi and Golombok (Chapter 13) indicates that parents who use anonymous donors may be less likely to disclose to children in order to save their children from the frustration of not having identifying information about their donors; thus, these DC persons would be at risk of accidental disclosure and possibly suffering any psycho-social harms that could follow-on from such an incident. Therefore, the use of open-identity donors and the availability of identifying donor information to DC persons appears to also be advantageous because it increases the likelihood of disclosure and further minimises the possibility of psycho-social risks to the welfare of DC persons.

Having outlined the available evidence, what can be said about the way in which regulators in the UK, for example, go about providing identifying information about donors to DC persons and their families? To begin, the UK's regulatory shift from requiring the provision of (only) non-identifying to identifying information about donors from April 2005 onward appears to be rooted in the desire to protect the interests of DC persons. Several events in particular are reported to have contributed to this change of law. The first is that the British Association of Social Worker's Project Group on Assisted Reproduction (Progar) and the Children's Society had campaigned for DC children to be given access to identifying information about their donors, in the same way that adopted children at that time already had access to identifying information about their biological parents (Nuffield Council on Bioethics, 2013: 22; Wincott and Crawshaw, 2006). This campaigning helped to trigger the UK Department of Health's 'Donor Information Consultation: Providing information about gamete or embryo donors' (2001). The consultation sought '. . . the views of the public and professionals as to whether, and to what extent, information about people who have donated sperm, eggs or embryos should be given to offspring born as the result of those donations' (Department of Health, 2001: 1).

[14] 'Late' in this instance refers to disclosure after early adolescence.

While the Department of Health consultation was taking place, a case was brought to the courts by a DC child (EM) and a DC adult (Joanna Rose). Both Rose and EM were conceived prior to the establishment of the HFEA and the HFE Act 1990, and argued under the Human Rights Act 1998 (HRA, 1998) that they had a right according to Article 8 of the European Convention on Human Rights (ECHR) to non-identifiable information about their donor (*Rose* v. *Secretary of State for Health*, 2002). Article 8 states that: 'Everyone has the right to respect for his private and family life, his home and his correspondence' (ECHR, 1950, as amended in 2009). The resulting judgement for the case found that Article 8 was engaged and that a case could be made under the Human Rights Act 1998 to contest whether or not donors have the right to maintain their anonymity (Nuffield Council on Bioethics, 2013; *Rose* v. *Secretary of State for Health*, 2002).

Both the Rose case and the 'Donor Information Consultation' contributed to the Department of Health proposing a change to regulations which ended donor anonymity and ensured that DC persons would be provided with identifying information about donors in the future. As a consequence, new HFEA regulations were approved in 2004 and came into effect on April 1, 2005 (HFEA, 2004).[15] Importantly, all of the above events illustrate that the desire to protect the interests of DC persons was one of the central motivations behind the Department of Health reforming the HFE Act 1990 to require that identifying information be made available to DC persons. In addition, the empirical evidence outlined above appears to support the UK's use of open-identity donors to protect the interests of DC persons. However, some important questions remain about the use of open-identity donation and whether or not there is room for improvement in the way that Parliament makes identifying information about donors available to DC persons.

Some of the most common criticisms of open-identity donation are that it has resulted in a decrease of donors in the UK and that it violates the privacy rights of donors and their families (Turkmendag, Dingwall, and Murphy, 2008). The first criticism can be rejected based on the statistical evidence that the HFEA makes available about donor numbers. While some previously anonymous donors may not have been interested in continuing to donate in the UK as open-identity donors after April 2005, the figures suggest that the numbers of new (identifiable) donors actually grew in the years following the removal of anonymity (HFEA, 2014a). The second criticism that the removal of anonymity violates

[15] The HFE Act 1990 was later amended in 2008 to include the regulatory changes that were adopted in 2004.

the privacy rights of donors can also be rejected. This criticism is not valid because the removal of anonymity in the UK was not retroactive and therefore any donors who provide gametes or embryos after 1 April 2005, must as a legal condition of their donation, consent to the potential release of their identifying information to DC persons. If a potential donor feels that the release of their identity to future DC persons would be a violation of their privacy, then they can choose not to donate.[16] While these criticisms often dominate the debate about using open-identity donation, more pressing questions exist about whether or not identifying donor information is being properly kept up-to-date by the HFEA and why identifying information is only made available to DC persons at the age of eighteen?

UK regulators introduced open-identity donation because it was seen to be in the interests of DC persons to be able to find out accurate and identifiable information about their donors, and to have the means to possibly make contact with them at some point in time. However, as the law stands, DC persons do not enjoy any benefits of having identifiable donor information until they are eighteen years old. This means that identifying donor information is inaccessible to DC persons for the duration of their childhood and during this time they are treated the same way as a DC person with an anonymous donor. One would therefore imagine that Parliament has decided that there are good reasons for withholding identifiable donor information from DC persons until adulthood.

One reason for withholding identifying information about donors until DC children turn eighteen is so that these DC children do not disrupt the stability and functioning of their DC families as a result of trying to make contact with their donors. The root of this policy appears to be found in long-standing adoption laws from across the UK. Since 1975, at the age of eighteen, adopted children in England and Wales have been able to request copies of their birth certificates[17] (Adoption Act, 1976; Adoption and Children Act, 2002; Children Act, 1975; Children Act, 1989).[18] Similarly, since 1987, adopted children in Northern Ireland have been able to request their birth certificates (The Adoption (Northern Ireland)

[16] It is beyond the scope of this chapter to debate whether or not the removal of donor anonymity violates a more general overarching interest (which some may feel is a right) held by some persons to be able to donate without revealing their identity.

[17] For an extensive history of the role and significance of the birth certificate in England, see Higgs' (2011) book titled *Identifying the English: a History of Personal Identification 1500 to the Present.*

[18] However, under section 60 of the Adoption and Children Act 2002, it is possible for the High Court to veto this request if it is felt that there are reasonable grounds not to allow an adopted person to receive their birth certificate. One such reason could be that it would be harmful to the original family who put the child up for adoption.

Order, 1987), and Scotland has allowed adopted children to request their birth certificates from the age of sixteen since the introduction of the Adoption of Children (Scotland) Act 1930 (this act was amended and later repealed, and the current law is the Adoption and Children (Scotland) Act, 2007). Policies limiting adopted children's access to their birth certificates until a later age (i.e. sixteen or eighteen years old) were typically put in place to ensure that the identities of biological parents were kept secret. UK law has attempted to maintain a period of secrecy during the early years of the adoptive child's life because, historically – and especially in the 1960s – there was a desire to encourage the permanence of families with adopted children by minimising any chance of disruption that could be caused by the adopted child searching for his or her biological parents (at least during the formative years of the child's development) (Bainham, 2005). In this era (e.g. the 1960s and 1970s), experts working in adoption also believed that by around the age of eighteen, adopted persons would probably be mature enough to psychologically and socially cope with making contact with their birth parents (Baran and Pannor, 1993; Carp, 2000).

Based on the research that has taken place since the 1960s, we now know that best practices in adoption, as in donor conception, recommend disclosure of adoption to children at an early age (see Blake, Ilioi and Golombok, Chapter 13). Adoption law has not changed to allow access to birth certificates earlier in the child's life, but it is now more common for families to disclose at an early age and to keep their adopted children in touch or aware of their biological parents when possible. When new UK regulations were put in place in 2004 (HFEA, 2004) to abolish anonymity and to allow DC children access to identifying information about their donors at the age of eighteen, it brought the law in line (to some extent) with current adoption law (Wincott and Crawshaw, 2006). However, bringing the amended HFE Act 1990 in line with adoption law appears to have imported and perpetuated a vestige of outdated thinking about children's welfare – namely that allowing DC children to find out identifying information on their donors prior to the age of eighteen, could have a negative impact on the functioning of families.[19]

[19] As a consequence of this discussion, the question does arise about whether or not adoption law (such as the Adoption and Children Act, 2002) should also be amended to improve the legal rights that adopted children and their adoptive parents, have to access birth records. However, the socio-legal context of adoption is in many ways different from the socio-legal context of assisted reproduction (e.g. unlike adoption, babies born through gamete donation are typically raised by the same family that they were born into) and it is beyond the scope of this chapter to investigate and engage

Some might argue that it is important to withhold identifying donor information from parents so that it is not passed on to their DC children, because early contact (by DC children) with donors (i.e. before the child reaches the age of eighteen) may be problematic.[20] One could imagine how it might be different and in many ways more complicated for a DC person to make contact with their donor at the age of ten rather than the age of eighteen (or even sixteen). For example, it could be traumatic for a DC person (especially at a young age) to go about contacting and meeting a donor, or the information could be a lot for DC persons to deal with; however, it is only reasonable to expect that a child's parents would help them to manage their expectations and actions, in relation to the donor's information, and would oversee any contact with donors. Parents would also need to ensure that their children were given appropriate counselling and support. In short, the parents of DC children should take age-appropriate actions to protect and assist their children through the experience of making contact with donors, much in the same way that parents would normally be expected to help their children engage and cope with any sensitive social situation. Once these practical measures are recognised and put in place by parents, it appears that it would be reasonably safe and responsible for DC persons younger than eighteen years old to be allowed to make contact with donors. After all, it is important to remember that known donors are currently allowed under UK law and DC persons often make contact with known donors with the assistance and oversight of their parents. Moreover, nobody ever claimed that making contact with a donor from the age of eighteen onward would be easy for DC persons either, and adequate counselling and support should be given to DC individuals seeking contact at this age (and beyond) as well. If an open-identity donor takes issue with the idea of their donor offspring getting in touch with them, then they should probably never have become a donor in the first instance.

There is no clear benefit to the UK's policy (or those like it internationally) of not releasing identifying donor information until DC children are eighteen. Instead, it would be best if the UK amended the HFE Act 1990,

in debates about revising adoption law. Nevertheless, it is worth keeping in mind that although it has become customary for many adoption agencies to facilitate contact and information sharing between birth parents, adoptive parents and adopted children (often before the child is eighteen years old), these are not practices in which adoption agencies are required by law to engage (Bainham, 2005). Adoption agencies typically engage in such practices because they are understood to be in the interests of adopted children. For a detailed and critical discussion of the law related to information sharing in the context of UK adoption, please see Bainham (2005).

20 This worry was also discussed by the Nuffield Council on Bioethics (2013).

as amended (2008) so that identifying information was made accessible to DC[21] persons and their parents in the same way that non-identifying information is currently made available: at the age of sixteen DC persons should be able to request identifying details about their donors from the HFEA and DC parents should be able to request identifying information about donors from the outset of the child's life. This change would ensure that parents maintain control over when their DC children find out identifying information about their donors. In other words, children could find out identifying information about their donors via their parents, but only if their parents wished to disclose. Similar systems of information release are already set up in places such as the Australian State of Victoria, where parents are currently able to place requests to the state for identifiable information about their child's donor (Freeman et al., 2014). It would be surprising if the HFEA disagreed with a proposal along these lines, because after all, as I pointed out earlier, the HFEA website clearly states: '. . . parents are seen as guardians of their children's interests and are in the best position to pass information on to their children at an age when they can understand it' (HFEA, 2012b).

Two of the main benefits of making identifying donor information available to parents from the outset of DC children's lives are: (1) this information will be left in the control of parents to use and share with their DC children as and when they see fit; and (2) this information will be made accessible to parents at a time when the information is most likely to still be up-to-date and accurate (rather than being released after almost two decades, as the law currently stands).

By giving parents control over the management and release of identifying donor information to their children, the regulators are likely to further benefit the interests of those children. For some parents and DC persons, it may be valuable to be able to contact donors and potentially keep in touch before DC persons reach the age of eighteen. In fact, some parents may feel it is important to have identifying information because they want to try and arrange for their children to meet their donors and they may also wish to find out about and meet the donors' children or other donor siblings (see Freeman, Jadva, and Slutsky, Chapter 8). Of course, donor siblings and donors are under no legal obligation in the UK to acknowledge or accommodate any attempts by DC persons or their parents to make contact with them. Meanwhile, other parents may feel that it is important to have access to identifying information about donors early in children's lives so that they can respond to questions the

21 To be clear, again, this generally refers to anyone conceived with sperm, eggs or an embryo.

children might have about what the donor's name is or where they are from, for example. Early access to identifying information about donors may help to ensure that some DC persons do not have to experience the frustration of not being able to find out basic facts about their donor up until they are eighteen years of age.

One objection to this proposal might be that it will further deter prospective parents from having DC offspring in the UK if they do not wish for their offspring to find out their donor's identity. For example, one fear might be that this proposed regulatory change could drive more prospective parents abroad so that they can access anonymously donated gametes or embryos. It might also discourage intra-familial donation in the UK, particularly in instances where family members are uncomfortable with the idea that DC persons may discover that they (the family members) are the donors. However, this objection is misplaced because the proposed regulatory changes would still allow parents to choose not to disclose if they wished and DC persons would only have legal access to identifying information about their donors two years earlier than they are at present under the amended HFE Act 1990. In other words, if prospective parents would feel uncomfortable with the idea of having DC children in the UK under the proposal put forward in this chapter, they would almost definitely have the same reservations under the current laws in place in the UK. The proposal put forward in this chapter would not make prospective parents of DC persons any worse off with respect to their offspring being at risk of discovering the identity of their donors.

The purpose of open-identity donation is to make identifying information about donors available to DC persons; however, this may amount to nothing more than an empty promise if the information that is provided by the HFEA is not up-to-date or accurate. Currently, the HFEA does not have a reliable system of keeping donor information up to date and DC persons cannot be sure that the information that they will be able to receive at eighteen is accurate. At this point in time clinics rely on donors to voluntarily offer updates to the information that they initially provided at the time of donation. Over the course of eighteen years it is quite possible that a donor's address or name may change. It is also possible that DC persons could wait eighteen years only to find that their donor is deceased (Blake, Ilioi and Golombok, Chapter 13). The easiest and most reliable way of getting accurate identifying information about donors to DC persons is to make it accessible to parents from the outset of the child's life. This approach would mean that clinics could continue to encourage donors to update the information that is kept on record about them by the HFEA, but the HFEA would not need to overhaul their system of information collection to ensure that all details on record were up to date. Instead, it would ultimately be left up to parents, donors and DC children to make further negotiations about what information, if any, is shared between them. Unless these reforms are made to the way identifying information is provided to parents and DC children, the current UK system of providing identifying donor information will continue to undermine the interests of the DC persons that the law is meant to protect.

Conclusion

This chapter has explored and discussed several central questions in the debate about how regulators should go about providing information about donors to DC persons. When it comes to the provision of non-identifying donor information it appears that the UK's HFE Act 1990, as amended (2008) generally results in DC persons and their parents receiving the information they want to know about their donors. There is little evidence to suggest that the way the UK regulates the timing or amount of non-identifying donor information that is provided to DC persons should be changed. However, the way the UK regulates the provision of identifying donor information should be treated as a different matter.

The empirical evidence discussed in this chapter and the chapter of Blake, Ilioi and Golombok (Chapter 13) suggests that making identifying information about donors available to DC persons is in the interests of at least some DC persons. The availability of such information may increase the likelihood that some parents will disclose to their children, which is seen by many as being in the interests of children. For example, there is a chance that some DC persons could suffer psycho-social harms if they are disclosed to but cannot subsequently access any identifying information about their donor. Also, it appears that the UK's HFE Act 1990 was originally amended to allow the provision of identifying information to DC persons because such changes were seen to be in children's interests. Common criticisms that the removal of donor anonymity would increase donor shortages or be problematic for families, have been rejected or remain unfounded according to the empirical evidence that is available. It is argued instead that the main problem with the UK's current method of regulating the provision of donor information is that it is only released to DC persons at the age of eighteen. A review of some of the legal history leading up to this change suggests that the idea of only releasing donor information to DC persons at the age of eighteen was likely imported from outdated adoption laws (Baran and Pannor, 1993; Carp,

2000) which have similar provisions that restrict the age at which adopted persons can access copies of their birth certificates. A further problem with the way the HFEA withholds identifying information for eighteen years after the DC child's birth is that the information held on record by the HFEA may very well be out of date by the time is it accessed. This chapter has therefore recommended that Parliament should amend the HFE Act 1990, as amended (2008) to allow DC persons to request identifying donor information at the age of sixteen, in addition to the non-identifying donor information they can currently request at this age. It is also recommended that the amended HFE Act should be amended so that identifying donor information is released to the parents of DC persons, upon request, from the outset of their children's lives. This way parents can be in control of managing (e.g. updating the information, using it to contact donors or potentially making contact with donor siblings) and sharing this valuable donor information with their children at the time that they feel is right. In the words of the HFEA, parents are typically best placed to make judgements about how and when donor information is made available to their children. If the HFEA relinquishes control of identifying donor information to parents, then regulators will likely be doing what is in the interests of DC children, which after all, was the main purpose behind making such information available to DC persons in the first place.[22]

REFERENCES

Bainham, A. (2005). *Children – The Modern Law,* 3rd edn. Bristol: Jordan Publishing.

Baran, A. and Pannor, R. (1993). *Lethal Secrets: The Psychology of Donor Insemination.* New York: Amistad.

Carp, E.W. (2000). *Family Matters: Secrecy and Disclosure in the History of Adoption.* Cambridge, MA: Harvard University Press.

Department of Health (2001). Donor information consultation: providing information about gamete or embryo donors. Available at www.webarchive.nationalarchives.gov.uk/20040112155434/www.doh.gov.uk:80/gametedonors/gametedonorconsult.pdf. Accessed 15 August 2014, pp. 1–17.

Freeman, T., Bourne, K., Jadva, V. and Smith, S. (2014). 'Making connections: contact between sperm donor relations', in T. Freeman, S. Graham, F. Ebtehaj and M. Richards (eds.), *Relatedness in Assisted Reproduction: Families, Origins and Identities.* Cambridge University Press.

Higgs, E. (2011). *Identifying the English: A History of Personal Identification 1500 to the Present.* London: Continuum.

[22] I am very grateful to the following people for their helpful comments on versions of this chapter: Rosamund Scott, Hallvard Lillehammer, Susan Golombok, Martin Richards and Stephen Wilkinson.

Human Fertilisation and Embryology Authority (HFEA) (2011). 'If you were conceived between 1 April 1991 and 1 April 2005'. Available at www.hfea.gov.uk/5525.html. Accessed 21 January 2014.

Human Fertilisation and Embryology Authority (HFEA) (2012a). 'If you were conceived after 1 April 2005'. Available at www.hfea.gov.uk/5526.html. Accessed 21 January 2014.

Human Fertilisation and Embryology Authority (HFEA) (2012b). 'What you can find out about your child's donor or donor-conceived genetic siblings'. Available at www.hfea.gov.uk/118.html. Accessed 12 August 2014.

Human Fertilisation and Embryology Authority (HFEA) (2013). 'New donor registrations'. Available at www.hfea.gov.uk/3411.html. Accessed 21 January 2014.

Human Fertilisation and Embryology Authority (HFEA) (2014a). 'Egg and sperm donation in the UK: 2012–2013'. Available at www.hfea.gov.uk/docs/Egg_and_sperm_donation_in_the_UK_2012–2013.pdf. Accessed 4 November 2014.

Human Fertilisation and Embryology Authority (HFEA) (2014b). 'Chapter 20: donor assisted conception', in *Code of Practice*, 8th edn. Available at www.hfea.gov.uk/496.html. Accessed 11 January 2015.

Nuffield Council on Bioethics (2013). *Donor Conception: Ethical Aspects of Information Sharing*. London: Nuffield Council on Bioethics.

Pennings, G. (2012). 'How to kill gamete donation: retrospective legislation and donor anonymity'. *Human Reproduction*, 27, 2881–5.

Scheib, J.E. (2003). 'Choosing identity-release sperm donors: the parents' perspective 13–18 years later'. *Human Reproduction*, 18, 1115–27.

Scheib, J.E., Riordan, M. and Rubin, S. (2005). 'Adolescents with open-identity sperm donors: reports from 12–17 year olds'. *Human Reproduction*, 20, 239–52.

Turkmendag, I., Dingwall, R. and Murphy, T. (2008). 'The removal of donor anonymity in the UK: the silencing of claims by would-be parents'. *International Journal of Law, Policy and the Family*, 22, 283–310.

Turner, A.J. and Coyle, A. (2000). 'What does it mean to be a donor offspring? The identity experiences of adults conceived by donor insemination and the implications for counselling and therapy'. *Human Reproduction*, 15, 2041–51.

Wincott, E. and Crawshaw, M.A. (2006). 'From a social issue to policy: social work's advocacy for the rights of donor conceived people to genetic origins information in the United Kingdom'. *Social Work in Health Care*, 43, 53–72.

LEGISLATION

EU

European Convention on Human Rights (ECHR) 1950, as amended in 2009.

UK

Adoption Act 1976.

Adoption of Children (Scotland) Act 1930.

Adoption and Children (Scotland) Act 2007.
Adoption and Children Act 2002.
The Adoption (Northern Ireland) Order 1987.
Children Act 1975.
Children Act 1989.
Children Act 2004.
Human Fertilisation and Embryology Act 1990 (HFE Act, 1990).
Human Fertilisation and Embryology (HFE) Act 1990, as amended (2008).
Human Fertilisation and Embryology Authority (Disclosure of Donor Information) Regulations 2004/1511 (HFEA, 2004).
Human Rights Act 1998 (HRA, 1998).

CASES

Rose v. *Secretary of State for Health* (2002) EWHC 1593.

16 The informational needs of prospective parents
An ethical perspective

Bobbie Farsides

People sometimes describe choosing the person with whom to create a child in terms suggestive of an intuitive non-cognitive experience – 'I just felt she was the one', 'it just felt right' and 'my ovaries were singing'. However, mating at first sight is rare, and sub-consciously at least some sifting or selecting will usually have taken place, either as a relationship develops, or as someone who wants a child outside a relationship looks for a suitable person with whom to procreate. Things can become complicated if having settled into a relationship a couple decide to have a child and are then unable to do so. Similarly if someone decides to parent independently, or if having found their same-sex life partner, biology determines that having a child will necessarily involve a donor procreation becomes more challenging. In these cases, prospective parents could be heading towards becoming recipient parents (as their parenthood could be dependent upon them receiving a donation from another party). It is this sub-group of parents that will be the focus of this chapter.

Setting the scene

Involving third parties in creating a pregnancy places an individual or couple in a different landscape to those who can reproduce without assistance. This is further complicated if donor sperm and/or eggs are required. In the UK, the Human Fertilisation and Embryology Authority (HFEA) has recently acknowledged the need for better guidance and support for those considering conception using donated sperm and/or eggs, and the Lifecycle campaign was launched with the aim of improving the donation process. Key to this initiative is the provision of clear information to all parties, be they donors or recipients.[1]

Requiring assistance in securing a pregnancy means many prospective parents enter an overtly regulated and medicalised environment, the

[1] For details of the Lifecycle initiative and to access the resources created, see www.hfea.gov.uk/8350.html (HFEA, 2014a).

world of the clinic. Despite recent amendments, the Human Fertilisation and Embryology Act 1990, as amended (2008)[2] still requires scrutiny of those involved in creating an assisted pregnancy to ensure that the safety and the welfare of the child born is appropriately considered. As such would-be parents seeking assistance will have to adhere to the practices of the providers they approach, who will in turn be bound by law and professional guidance.

Within the publicly funded health sector choice of donor is rarely discussed in outward facing literature, due in part to the relative scarcity of donors and the need to manage expectations. For those seeking infertility treatment through privately funded clinics the landscape is changing with commercial sperm banks advertising 'easy to use online catalogues' of donors which the prospective recipient is told 'enable you to select a donor based on characteristics that matter to you' and come complete with 'staff impressions' to help you make that all important decision (see also Graham, Mohr and Bourne, Chapter 10).

In recent years, more opportunity has arisen for potential parents to avoid this regulated environment, leading one eminent scholar to describe the current reproductive landscape as akin to the Wild West of old (Jackson, 2013). Prospective parents can now access donors who place their details on unregulated internet based sites, or the would-be parents can 'advertise' their need for a donor on such platforms.

The fact that medically, legally and ethically other parties will have a role in determining how and if a pregnancy is established introduces an element of complexity rarely experienced by those who can procreate unassisted, for whom a pregnancy may remain a completely private matter until well established.

Those requiring assistance may find their choices restricted by financial considerations or by scarcity of donated gametes. Despite NICE (National Institute for Care Excellence) recommendations regarding provision of in vitro fertilisation (IVF) within the UK National Health Service (NHS) many couples and individuals will not qualify for assistance, or they will not become pregnant during the treatment cycles provided by the NHS service (NICE, 2013). This means that they could face substantial financial burdens in their pursuit of a child, particularly if they require egg donation within the context of privately provided IVF.

Regarding scarcity, the shortage of donated eggs and sperm is well recognised and despite recent measures such as the establishment of a British National Sperm Bank in October 2014 (Gallagher, 2014) and

[2] For an up to date account of the Human Fertilisation and Embryology Act 1990 (as amended 2008) and accompanying guidance, see www.hfea.gov.uk/5473.html.

the higher remuneration for egg donors, easy access to donated gametes through secure and official routes cannot be guaranteed (HFEA, 2014b). This problem could be exacerbated if the prospective parent/s is a member of a community with particularly low levels of sperm and egg donation.

Whilst it is important to acknowledge this complexity and the issues that arise as a result, this chapter is not concerned with whether or not it is right (or indeed possible) to pursue donor conception in the various circumstances in which the need arises. Rather it looks at some of the responsibilities one takes on as a prospective parent when the birth of a child is dependent upon a donor. Particularly, the responsibilities one might have to choose 'the right donor'. To explore this issue fully we may need to put aside some of the practical constraints already alluded to and assume for the sake of argument that individuals have the opportunity to exercise choice regarding a donor in a meaningful way. If so, we can then ask what they should consider as their criteria for choosing, and what they will need others to do/provide in order to support that choice. We may also need to explore the difficult possibility that in the absence of an opportunity to secure the 'right donor' the responsible decision might be to forgo the possibility of having a child.

The need to choose a 'good donor'

It is uncontroversial to claim that most people will want to choose a 'good donor' in order to ensure that a successful pregnancy ensues and that as far as possible 'the sort of child they would like' is born. However, given the different ways in which people might define their perfect child it is unlikely that one type of donor will suit all potential recipients. What people want is to some degree unpredictable. As a bookish individual with no appreciation of competitive sport, I might consider the ideal donor as someone who mirrors my preferences, or conversely I might look for someone who appears to counter or compensates for my characteristics and leanings. As an individual who is shall we say on the short side I might consider height an advantage in a way that my much taller sibling might not, or I might want to further my 'small is beautiful' campaign by raising a diminutive child with confidence and high self-esteem. Beyond a certain limited range what we choose in terms of the child we wish to create is subjective and as a result unpredictable.

It is likely that the universally acknowledged characteristics of a good donor are minimal, and may have more to do with the absence of harmful or unacceptable features than with a necessarily culturally and individually specific list of qualities. To put it another way, given our most commonly shared assumptions about what it takes to create a child with a chance of a good life there may be core features that are needed to secure a 'good donation'. It is surely inconceivable that anyone would look for a donor who displayed morally abhorrent behaviour or whose health was such that their life had no quality. What is less clear is how an individual would balance a variety of features and experiences to come up with the right donor profile for them. One could imagine the challenge of weighing something such as a slightly shady past against impressive current achievements and robust good health, or how a recipient might feel conflicted when offered a donor who is kind, clever and also obese.

It is probably helpful to explore the idea of what would make a donor 'good enough' before proceeding to consider what makes a donor the right donor for an individual or a couple. Although disputed, the distinction between a 'need' and a 'want' which is often engaged within health-related discourse could prove useful here. In general terms, the idea is that if you have a goal in sight (e.g. creating a healthy child) there are certain things one has to have in place in order to achieve this goal. If what you are aiming for is recognised as a basic component of a good life then it might be the case that society will accept a moral obligation to provide those things, or at least to not prevent access to them. At the most basic level we can think of food, shelter, education, but in the context of procreation we go further and protect a woman's claims to such things as reasonable working arrangements, free medications and health checks, etc. and in some cases medical assistance to secure a pregnancy (Cribb and Owens, 2010; Wiggins, 1998).

At the same time there are many things that we would want, in an ideal world, which we can reasonably be expected to live without. Whilst a society might be commended for giving people the means to get what they want, we worry when that is at the expense of others getting what they need to survive. So, meeting essential needs will usually trump satisfying less basic wants particularly when the benefits to be gained by meeting the need can be objectively validated. If in turn we accept that a 'need' more effectively grounds a claim or entitlement than a 'want', then we can go on to argue that a well-founded need will give rise more readily to an obligation or duty on the part of another to meet that need.

In this chapter, I shall explore the experience of identifying the right donor by considering the question of what information a recipient parent might require to make an appropriate choice. We know that the issue of information is of immense importance to parties engaged in and affected by donor conception. What is less straightforward is establishing what prospective recipient parents really *need* to know in order to choose a good donor, irrespective of what they might *want* to know in order to feel that they have chosen the best donor for them.

Returning to the idea of objectivity, it might be possible to argue that some basic informational needs can be identified and generalised across different cases. The question is how useful such a list would be in helping specific parents feel that they had made the right choice of donor.

Ensuring a donor is 'good enough'

At the most basic level there are things we need to know about a donor and things that need to happen in order to ensure that the statistical chance of having the child that is wanted is high. On the other hand there are things that a recipient might want or like to know about a donor that the system in which they are operating feels no obligation to provide.

If we attempt to establish what a person *needs* as opposed to what they might *want* when identifying a donor, we must acknowledge that this will in turn have implications for how a donation is set up and proceeds. A particular account of what a recipient needs to know about a donor could affect the terms upon which donors are recruited, what the donor is required to undergo in terms of screening and testing, and what information they may be asked to provide about themselves beyond their basic medical history. Similarly on the recipient side the informational strategy of the different types of provider might be the thing that determines where they as prospective parents go to access the eggs or sperm they require. If the clinic is focused on satisfying basic needs rather than meeting specific wants the unregulated environment may exert a strong pull.

I will argue here that there are some basic informational needs that it is a recipient parent's responsibility to consider and a donor's responsibility to provide. Ensuring that such information is available would therefore become a core activity of any individual or organisation involved in arranging a donation. However, I will also argue that information that goes beyond what is needed to make an appropriate choice of a 'good enough donor' may not have to be provided.

In the publicly funded and regulated environment of an NHS clinic thorough health checks, basic psychological screening, simple physical descriptions and the provision of more personal information through the use of good will messages and pen portraits, etc. which are designed to 'show the person behind the donation' (Lifecycle, 2014)[3] allow

[3] Lifecycle (2014). Information for current egg and sperm donors is available at www.hfea.gov.uk/docs/Lifecycle_-_Info_for_current_egg_and_sperm_donors_v1.pdf.

prospective parents (and subsequently donor conceived children) to receive information deemed essential to the process. Choice is limited by scarcity of donors and information is bounded by confidentiality and anonymity requirements, but the clinic will have ensured that certain features of a good enough donor have been checked for before the recipient becomes aware of any particular donor's profile. At some level the clinic exercises more choice than the recipient parents, screening out those considered not to be good enough, leaving the prospective recipients the choice of those who do meet the standard of what is needed to be a good enough donor. In line with the limited purpose of offering a range of good enough donors the information provided is limited to that which would allow a good match in the most basic sense of sound health profile, similar physical appearance, ethnicity, vague sense of shared interests, etc.

As has already been mentioned many prospective recipients either choose or feel forced to turn to the privately funded reproductive medicine sector to create the child they hope for.

Some will even go abroad to avail themselves of a more highly developed market driven sector where sperm or eggs become a marketable commodity, and where intermediary providers have an interest in supplying information beyond that which will ensure that the donation meets a safe minimum standard. Indeed, the provision of detailed information allows egg and sperm providers (the term donor no longer really does the definitional work) to price their commodities according to market forces.

Stories circulate of US donor agencies pricing the eggs of individual providers according to factors such as their educational abilities, sporting prowess and/or physical appearance. The advertisements produced by US egg and sperm 'agencies' cast prospective parents more in the role of a consumer than of a grateful recipient of donation, and the information provided could make it possible to choose a donor on criteria unavailable in a less market driven system, this is despite the American Society of Reproductive Medicine guidelines prohibiting the linking of compensation to donor personal characteristics (ASRM, 2007).

A Hastings Center report established a 'strong positive relationship between SAT scores and compensation' and concluded that:

> This relationship strongly suggests that donor agencies and couples are placing more value on oocytes donated by women with higher SAT scores, which would violate the ASRM guidelines which state that 'To avoid putting a price on human gametes or selectively valuing particular human traits, compensation should not vary according to the planned use of the oocytes (e.g. research or clinical care), the number or quality of oocytes retrieved, the outcome of prior donation cycles, or the donor's ethnic or other personal characteristics'. (Levine, 2010)

Increasingly however there are also those who eschew 'the clinic' in the first instance, be that at home or abroad, and choose instead to follow less regulated routes. Such is the rise of interest in such routes that the HFEA, whilst clearly stating that 'Our advice is simple. Only use a licensed clinic' (HFEA, 2014e) is at the same time attempting to ensure that those choosing to work outside the regulated environment are well informed both clinically and legally. These individuals and couples might work via personal connections or through an online matching site where they will be faced with more and different choices, and where they may well have access to much more information than in the clinic. Having said this, the prospective parents who use a matching site or personal introduction/connection may be denied the up-front reassurance that the donor is 'good enough'. This is not an insurmountable problem, as it is open to a donor and recipient to join the more formal route to donation and avail of a regulated clinic's screening and counselling services *after* having been matched.

It is clear then that choices are made to a greater and lesser extent in a number of different settings. What I wish to explore is the extent to which prospective parents need information about donors to make a good choice on three levels:

1. A choice that facilitates their preferred parenting model;
2. A choice that will secure the health and well-being of the future child and
3. A choice that will allow both recipient parents and future children to see the donor as the right sort of person to play the prescribed role in their lives.

I will go on to consider how having particular informational needs might determine which route the prospective parents want to follow in order to arrange and secure a donation. In so doing I will reflect upon the growing popularity of informal/unregulated routes to donation and ask whether there might be a need for registered clinics to reconsider their policies regarding information provision in response to the apparent popularity of this route to parenthood.

The good donor as the right sort of parent

In an established relationship where procreation can proceed unassisted we might choose our mate and then 'see what type of child comes along'. For recipient parents the issue could be importantly different in that they may judge and choose the donor primarily in terms of the type of child they want *and* the type of parent they want the donor to be. A 'good donor' will hopefully allow them to have a 'good child' which will mean something specific to a particular parent or parents and will vary in terms of how specifically that is defined. The second issue is rather different in that 'the right donor' for a particular recipient or recipients will in part rest upon how the donor may or may not fit into the recipient's plans for parenting.

One could argue that people in modern western societies think on a number of different levels when choosing a 'mate' (meant here as the person with whom to procreate). First, they may see a 'partner' becoming a 'mate' as a form of progression in a relationship, an acknowledgement that as a couple and/or as individuals they have reached a certain stage in their life and/or relationship where new positional duties and obligations can be shared. On the other hand, accepting a particular person as a 'mate' may be based less on their personal characteristics and the existing relationship with them than it is prompted by a certain sense of urgency or an overwhelming desire to have a child that trumps or maybe even obscures other considerations.

Many people when deciding to have children will in their own interest (and in the interest of the future child) look for a mate ready to commit to a long term emotional investment in any future child, a commitment which would hopefully survive even the break-down of the parents' relationship with one another. Of course this need not necessarily be the case, and particularly in a situation of urgency an individual or a couple may compromise on longer term goals in order to ensure a timely pregnancy.

It is interesting to consider whether things look the same when considering the selection of a donor as opposed to the choice of a mate. Clearly for some a good donor will be one who is willing and able to fulfil an active parenting role, but for others the good donor might be specifically characterised as someone who is ready to accept a very limited role as a biological as opposed to social parent (see also Zadeh, Imrie and Braverman, Chapter 14). More than ever in the twenty-first century families are constructed in ways unconstrained by previous models, and the recipient parent may choose very consciously to construct their family in a manner that depends upon the donor accepting a pre-specified account of their parenting role.

As we know donor conception supports several different models of parenting and in the background are a variety of life situations and relationships any of which might result in the need for intervention and donation. For example:

1. Heterosexual couple requiring sperm or egg due to infertility;
2. Same-sex couple requiring sperm or egg and/or surrogate and
3. Single woman requiring sperm or sperm and egg.

For each of these scenarios the parties involved could have complementary shared views on the appropriate role of the donor once a child is born, but on occasion this issue could quite quickly be revealed as a source of disagreement and potential conflict. Similarly, the views of recipient parents might be in tune with the politically constructed accounts of 'appropriate donor conception' or they might challenge officially adopted norms in relation to issues such as openness and transparency.

Given the variety of ways in which families are now constructed and function it would probably be wise for *all* potential parents to rehearse with their mates the type of parents they hope to be. As some will come to discover, fundamental disagreements on issues such as religious affiliation, schooling, medical treatment, punishment, etc. might be difficult to accommodate within a relationship, but few if any of us have the foresight to consider such issues during the transition from partner to mate.

Those seeking an anonymous donor through formal routes will have very little information upon which to base assumptions about a donor's view on such matters. This is not necessarily a problem if there is very little expectation that the donor will be involved in such decision making in future. However, the donor will potentially be such a presence with the part they play in future being dependent upon the choices of the future child and the responses of the donor. The recipient parent has little power to manage this, particularly once their child reaches eighteen, other than the power to withhold information about the nature of the child's conception from the outset.

This is a big issue beyond the scope of this chapter. Suffice to say whilst certain approaches might be seen as good practice in recipient parenting – for example, being open about donor conception from an early age – there has been a reluctance to impose requirements upon families relying instead on trust.[4]

For the sake of argument let us assume that the gold standard approach involves openness about donor conception. When choosing a donor, recipients will also be making a choice about how (if at all) that individual

[4] Nuffield Council on Bioethics Report titled 'Donor Conception: Ethical Aspects of Information Sharing' (2013) states: 'The evidence points to the conclusion that it will usually be better for children to be told, by their parents and at an early age, that they are donor-conceived. However, every family is different and there can be no hard and fast rules'. See more at www.nuffieldbioethics.org/report/donor-conception-2/knowledge-donor-conception-access-donor-information/#sthash.1bl6DxUk.dpuf.
Also The American Society for Reproductive Medicine (ASRM) Ethics Committee report states, 'While ultimately the choice of the recipient parents, disclosure to the donor-conceived persons of the use of donor gametes or embryos in their conception is strongly encouraged' (ASRM, 2013). Available at www.asrm.org/uploadedFiles/ASRM_Content/News_and_Publications/Ethics_Committee_Reports_and_Statements/informing_offspring_donation.pdf.

will be involved in the life (and possibly the parenting) of their future child. For some recipients, it will be important that the donor is seen as extraneous to the parenting relationship, which may in turn lead them to prefer that the donor remains anonymous and largely featureless, allowing for the construction of a narrative which is about donating and creating (maybe also gifting) as opposed to parenting. Others whilst feeling that biological parenting is distinct from social parenting, might nonetheless welcome the involvement of the donor in the child's life either from the outset or when their identity can be revealed later on in the child's life.

This suggests that despite the existence of activist bodies and highly vocal individuals who advocate strongly for particular ways of doing things in the context of donor conception, perspectives can differ particularly around the issue of openness and information. For prospective parents, one important element of the good donor profile will be the extent to which the donor could be relied upon to fit their preferred model of involvement and parenting, and to co-operate with a model that prioritises openness or non-disclosure, involvement or non-involvement irrespective of whether either is the right or wrong way of doing things.

It is also important to recognise at this stage that a child will be created who will come to have interests in the matter of her parenting as yet unknown and not entirely predictable. Research into the views, preferences and experiences of donor conceived people can inform our thinking, but it will not necessarily provide a ready-made account of how a particular child will respond to her parents' parenting choices. However, we could argue that it is always advisable for a parent to have a good account of why they chose to create a child and parent in the way that they did. In the case of donor conception, we could add to this the responsibility to prepare the child for understanding and accepting the way in which their conception may have been different. However, it does not mean that the recipient parents are then in sole charge of how the child chooses to negotiate that difference. Clearly openness will provide the broadest range of possibilities for the child, and therefore one could argue that a parent who wishes to do the best by their child has a responsibility to access and be prepared to share the information a child might need in future.

To sum up so far, in seeking assistance through the donation of sperm and/or eggs one is necessarily involving another individual in the biological parenting process. It is less clear what may be initially intended in terms of including the donor in social parenting terms. It is however clear that what *should* happen in terms of social parenting within a particular family is to some extent dependent upon the future wishes of the child not yet born. It is therefore important to consider how open a future you wish to create around this issue, and this in turn will determine the route you follow to donation and your approach to information sharing after the birth of a child. As in the case of any advance decision, there is the problem of the decisions holding good over time (in this case around twenty years) and change of circumstance (e.g. a donor having children with a partner). However, it is important to recognise that certain choices at this early stage will exclude the possibility of other choices later on. The goal should be a fair contract between provider and recipient which clearly indicates the options for future interactions with a child born. The law now sets the minimal terms of this arrangement within the regulated environment but as suggested many children will be born outside this framework.

The good donor as healthy donor

Having highlighted the issue of future involvement and parenting it is worth briefly returning to the core issue of being a 'good donor' this time as it relates to the health and wellbeing of a child born as a result of donation.

The need for a 'healthy donation'

Very few people would dispute the claim that it is of interest to establish the good health of someone with whom you hope to conceive a child. In practice however, health considerations may not trump other important matters. We know for instance that some people choose to have children even when they know their own or their partner's life will be foreshortened by illness, and the law now supports widows in accessing their dead husbands' sperm and recording them as a resulting child's father as long as appropriate consent is in place.[5] A Canadian study recently reported that 73.5 per cent of men and 61.8 per cent of women within the 498 studied agreed to leave their cryopreserved embryos to their partners for reproductive use in the event of their death (Côté et al., 2014). Just as an individual might choose to parent alone, the compromised health of a co-parent may not prevent (and may even lead to) an individual deciding to have a child. Where the health of the donor becomes of vital importance is in relation to the health of the child to be born.

Some philosophers place a very strong moral imperative on conceiving the 'best possible child' (Harris, 2001; Savulescu, 2001; Savulescu and

[5] See HFEA Chair's Letter, CH(03)06, 15 September 2003: www.hfea.gov.uk/2684.html (Leather, 2003).

Kahane, 2009). A parent would therefore be seen as negligent if they did not establish the health of their donor, and use that information to avoid harm to any child born. In fact taken to its extreme the enhancement model might require you to prefer an anonymous healthy donor over and above a much loved long-term partner who could pass on a genetically inherited disease.

If a donor is unknown to the recipient, the question arises as to how to manage health related information within the donation system. As previously mentioned, the recipient parent who goes down the regulated clinic route can be confident that the donated sperm or eggs they receive have been screened and tested for a range of serious conditions. Screening for serious diseases through family history, blood tests, etc., and in time no doubt genetic profiling, should mean that the 'big problems' that we should worry about have been removed. At the same time responsible donor matching sites advise those choosing an identified donor to avail of the screening available through registered clinics once a match has been made (HFEA, 2014d).[6]

As we become more aware of the impact of general health related features upon children born clinics could decide to screen out certain potential donors. So, for example, were evidence to grow about paternal age being a significant factor in relation to the health of children born, clinics could choose to impose stricter limits on the age of donors, thereby removing the choice/responsibility to pay due regard to this factor from recipients. At present in the UK donations are ideally sought from men aged between 18 and 41 and the HFEA states that 'centres should normally observe the relevant donor age limit'. However, they go on to state on their website that 'due to less substantial evidence on age limits for sperm donors, centres can assess the possible effect of a donor's age on a case by case basis'.

Deciding what counts as a 'serious' health problem is a definitional problem not restricted to this area of health care provision. For example, within the context of termination of pregnancy relevant bodies have consistently avoided putting prescriptive content to the term 'serious' foetal anomaly, and in the field of pre-implantation genetic diagnosis professionals have struggled to decide whether certain conditions are 'serious enough' to justify intervention (Williams et al., 2007).

It would be wrong to consider that clinics can do all the work in this regard as a recipient will need to establish what counts as serious for

[6] Standards of practice for regulated clinics are set out in the Code of Practice accompanying the Human Fertilisation and Embryology (HFE) Act 1990, as amended (2008) the key principles of which are set out at www.hfea.gov.uk/184.html (HFEA, 2014d).

them and their family, and how proximate a health risk needs to be to 'count'. For some recipients, the standard screening procedures will be sufficient guarantee of a healthy enough donor, with the fact that a clinic has a robust system in place being enough to ensure that all health related concerns have been met. An interesting issue could arise within the privately funded sector if recipients requested particular tests over and above the standard offered, either because of potential risks resulting from their own genetic profiles or because of a specific health related concern not generally deemed to be high risk and/or serious.

Having selected a potential donor, recipients could identify a matter of particular concern which the clinic has effectively defined as an 'allowable health risk'. So, for example, a recipient might be interested to know whether the donor experiences a range of mild reactions to common allergens such as cat fur, tree pollen or certain foods either because of the environment they live in or because of the profile of the recipient parent. It is not necessarily clear however that they would be morally entitled to this information and if they would have been wronged if it were not provided.

Essentially we need to decide at what stage we accept that health issues are 'non-material' and therefore not significant enough to investigate and report and/or test for if requested. One could argue that a problem such as mild allergy would be obvious to those who know one another well, but would rarely if ever be the make or break issue in terms of having a child together. Given that this is so, we might allow it to fall outside the formal exchange of information between donor, clinic and recipient.

The preceding example probably sounds relatively trivial and unimportant but other examples will be more challenging. Consider instead a six foot tall athletic man with a creative job and a good degree from a top university who comes forward as a sperm donor and reveals that congenital deafness means he is 50 per cent deaf in one ear.

When deciding what should happen here we can consider a range of options which are more or less permissive in their approach:

1. The offer of donation could be refused by the clinic (or even a matching site) with the health issue being seen as unacceptable in a good enough donor;
2. The donation could be accepted, the health problem recorded but not passed on to prospective recipients;
3. The donation could be accepted and the health problem shared with prospective recipients and
4. The donation could be accepted, the health problem shared with prospective recipients *and* the donor be asked (directly or indirectly) to provide information about how he has dealt with the issue and the impact it has had on his life.

Option 2 must clearly be rejected, especially if we think there is any way of defending Option 1 which would imply a degree of seriousness which goes beyond an acceptable threshold. If the health related risk is considered allowable but significant the information clearly needs to be shared. Option 4 is the nearest approximation to a choice made in ordinary life, but Option 3 at least provides the basis for some level of balancing of considerations. Option 3 provides the medical diagnosis which would then need to be judged against the available information, whereas Option 4 goes further and asks more of the donor.

It is important to acknowledge that within the regulated environment these options will be required to 'fit' with the regulatory framework within which choices are made. In the case of the UK, the Human Fertilisation and Embryology Act requires that 'A donor must not be selected because they are known *to* have a particular gene, chromosome or mitochondrial abnormality that, if inherited by any child born as a result of the donation, may result in that child having or developing a serious physical or mental disability'. This takes us back to the previous discussion of seriousness and suggests a strong prohibition upon deliberately selecting in a serious disability (although the issue of where to access the definition of such remains problematic). Having said this, the guidance goes on to state that such donors (i.e. those capable of passing on genetically inherited disabilities) will not be completely ruled out rather:

> Potential donors that are known to have a gene, chromosome or mitochondrion abnormality involving a significant risk that a person with the abnormality will have or develop:
> a. a serious physical or mental disability,
> b. a serious illness or
> c. any other serious medical condition must not be *preferred* to those that are not known to have such an abnormality (HFEA, 2014c).[7]

It could be argued that engaging the donor in an open discussion of their disability is valuable because a 'fault' or difficulty could be transformed into a strength or virtue by the information relating to how the person has dealt with the challenge. The question then arises as to whether the recipient parent is entitled to such information and/or the donor is required to present it. One could argue that if a donor is accepted despite an obvious health related problem the clinic should have assessed the impact of that problem on the individual's life and the information they have gathered should be shared. However, collecting such information is clearly going to require a commitment that goes beyond the sharing of a medical history to instead capture the biographical impact of the medical

[7] HFEA Licence Conditions T55. Available at www.hfea.gov.uk/498.html (HFEA, 2014c).

facts. This information might in turn be used by the potential recipients to speculate on the 'type of person' he is.

In some ways this echoes an age-old discussion on the form, content and use of the medical history and invites us to say that for the donor the health related issues *they* will consider important are those that have had an impact upon their life. For the recipient parents, the information will be all about the future health of a child created. However, it would be wrong to suggest that the donor should have no interest in the health of a future child, and it is at least possible that they might need to consider that it would be inappropriate to pass on a disability that they acknowledge as having had a negative impact upon their life.

Whilst a thorough examination of this issue would be a chapter in itself, it is nonetheless important to reach some sort of conclusion about what health related information is needed by recipient families and how that information should be collected, recorded and shared.

It has been argued that in both regulated and unregulated environments when considering the health of a donor the guiding principle should be the welfare of the future child. As such clinics will have a primary responsibility to screen and select potential donors and manage relevant information, and donor matching sites should work to encourage recipients and donors to avail of the services offered.

Whilst serious health risks should be eliminated by careful selection (or rejection) of donors, health related information may still be relevant to recipients if it falls below the threshold of 'seriousness' that is agreed. In these cases, the 'meaning' of the condition or complaint for the individual donor might need to be captured and passed on to potential recipients in narrative form.

Whether operating in a regulated or unregulated environment recipients will have a responsibility to establish, assess and balance health based considerations against other factors to decide if and when they make a donor unsuitable. However, their ability to access the information required may differ across settings.

The good donor as the right sort of person

Research conducted with young women regarding egg donation suggested the power of the concept of 'the right sort of person acting for the right sort of reasons' in this context (Butcher, 2012; see also Graham, Mohr and Bourne, Chapter 10). A recipient may want to choose their donor in a manner not dissimilar to the choice they make when choosing a friend or partner. The information provided may or may not facilitate this process, and when deciding what is *needed* as opposed to wanted it is important to remember that the goals of the selection are very specific – the creation of a child and the acceptance of a person as someone who may feature in that child's life at some point in the future.

As previously stated the requirements of any particular recipients will vary, although research and anecdotal evidence can give us some sense of what physical features and traits and levels of achievement might be considered desirable at a cultural level (Furnham, Salem and Lester, 2014).

The interesting ethical landscape is this. Within a publicly funded system, the informational needs of recipients will be recognised and met as far as possible, but financial and other resource constraints, combined (in some domains) with the reliance on scarce altruistic donors, will mean that information provision will be restricted to what can be achieved realistically within the system, and what is expected of donors will be bounded by their status as donor rather than paid provider.

In the unregulated environment of the donor matching sites information is the most commercially exploitable good available. Systems and processes vary, but essentially the sites are financially supported by potential recipients 'buying' more detailed information as they progress on the way to choosing a donor. In a private market based system such as that in the United States where donors can be paid for the service they provide, information can and does become part of the package, and donors have an interest in selling themselves through the information they provide.

The donor who sells their egg and sperm within a commercial environment could plausibly acquire a contractual obligation to provide extensive information, the tone and content of which will be directed towards 'selling' them to prospective recipients. This does not exclude the possibility of altruism, nor does it exclude the possibility of the 'offer' being the morally significant moment, but it does allow for those who have no altruistic concern for recipients or future children to participate. If motivation to donate is an important consideration for them in judging the donor to be 'the right sort of person' some recipients may reject the paid donor as 'the wrong sort of donor' and may choose not to enter the arena in which they operate.

It is possible that the altruistic donor within the non-market system might most readily conform to the idea of the 'right sort of person' for most recipient parents due to the absence of payment and the inferred beneficent motivations. They may also have the least interest in 'selling themselves' as donors as their altruism lies in making the offer and going through with the banked donation. The donor may have no independent free standing interest in being chosen, although they would presumably be pleased to hear that their altruism had assisted others in achieving their wishes.

Having said this it would be unrealistic to assume that donors within the regulated system are always and only motivated by pure altruism (if there is such a thing), nor should they necessarily be judged if this is the case. It is possible that some donors very actively will want to be successful in helping others to create children not only to help the recipient parents but also to be a part of creating children in the world who may or may not want to become part of their life in the future.

Whilst it is risky to oversimplify the donors' motivations within the regulated system, the available evidence does suggest that altruism is a very strong factor in studies of motivation (Bay et al., 2014). It is even more difficult to generalise about the donor who registers on a matching site or makes an informal arrangement unmediated by any organisation. A quick survey of sites reveals that there is no 'average donor' who can be simply described or defined in terms of their motivation and intentions. Donors might have a very personal interest in procreating (or indeed super-procreating), they might wish to actively co-parent, or they may want to support and facilitate particular models of parenting such as same sex couples or single women. The donor is as much of a chooser as the recipient, and each party has to trust that the information exchange they 'buy in to' reflects 'the type of person the donor is, their health, and very importantly (going back to section 1) the type of donation they intend.

The interesting thing is that once again the choices that recipient parents want to make will have an impact upon the route they follow to securing a donor/gamete provider.

It would appear to be the case that the system within which a donation is made *may* tell you something of the motives and intentions of the person donating, but the issue is complex and it is important not to make assumptions and/or generalisations. It is possible that the donor about whom one can learn the least is the donor who has donated within the system that relies on altruistic donation. Some recipients will believe that this in itself speaks well of the donor. The donor about whom we can find out the most may have entered the private market driven sphere where the information they provide will help them to sell themselves to recipients. Somewhere in the middle lies the matching site donor whose motivations may be mixed, but who will by virtue of the route they have chosen appear to favour a negotiated and bespoke approach to information provision and exchange and subsequent donation. Finally, the private arrangement between friends or relatives ensures that the recipient is well aware of the 'type of person' the donor is and in a strong position to explore any health issues, etc., but, the donor will clearly be in the strongest position to shape and maintain their subsequent place in the parenting process of any child born making it a difficult option for those who want the donor to fade from view.

In this chapter, I have suggested that information must be seen as a means to a very particular end in the context of donor conception. The primary end is the creation of a child within the context of a parenting set up that will promote the best interests and welfare of that child.

Whilst the donor may not be a parent in the accepted sense of the word (although that option is available), they will be a presence in the child's life. A recipient has a responsibility therefore to establish the expectations they will have of a donor in relation to any children born. As such they will need to consider how the information available within the regulated and non-regulated frameworks within which they could choose to operate open up or close down options.

If we work with the assumption that donor conception is a response to infertility/childlessness, we can assume that the aim is not to create a 'perfect child' but rather a child healthy enough to survive, thrive and enjoy life. We can further assume that a huge motivating factor behind the whole transaction is the recipients' parents' wish to be parents. If we remain committed to a liberal regime which allows recipient parents to work with an informational model of their choice, that is disclosing or not their child's conception, we must allow for the fact that some will seek a donor who does not wish or need to be part of their child's life, and this priority might have significant impact upon how they proceed. However, these parents still have a responsibility to ensure that they secure the information needed to give their child the possibility of an open future. Information will need to be provided and shared to this end, with relevant parties taking responsibility for deciding what should and should not exclude a possible matching of donor and recipient on health and other grounds.

Conclusion

Clearly many people feel that it is important that donor conception is openly discussed, recorded and owned by those who seek it out. Donor conceived children and adults are seen by many to have a clear right to know and understand their origins. A part of the narrative that will emerge in the context of growing openness and normalisation of donor conception is each family's story of 'how and why I/we chose your donor'.

The recipient parent(s) will be the established presence in the child's life and may want to be able to reassure the child that the donor was chosen in some true sense, and that the choice was made in the interests of the future child. For some parents the honest account might have to include their express choice to keep the donor in the background, for others the donor will be (or become) a visible presence in the child or young adult's life. In explaining the choices they made recipient parents will refer to the information they sought and the way in which what they needed *and* wanted to know determined the route they took to secure a pregnancy. In being able to tell this story the recipient parents provide their own version of the age old story or 'how I met your mother/father' and one must hope that a careful and timely telling of any of the versions explored in this chapter could help to secure the good life they would have always hoped to provide the child in question.

In a sense we come full circle, the recipient parent for whom information has been so important becomes the person responsible for passing that information on. One must hope and work towards ensuring that they feel equipped to provide their children with what they claim they need at that point.

For this to be possible there has to be some level of information available about 'the type of person' the donor is, but this information only justifies the choice made when combined with the specific manner in which the recipient has characterised and worked towards securing the welfare of their future child. Parenting styles differ and this will be as true for donor conceived families as any other, recipients may not be able to access all the information they would like but similarly it is important not to be too prescriptive in terms of what they should know. What we can ensure is that they are given what they need to feel as if they can explain why they chose the donor they did. For some it will be a 'they jumped off the page moment', for others it will be a painstaking and detailed matching process.

REFERENCES

American Society for Reproductive Medicine Ethics Committee (ASRM) (2007). 'Financial compensation of oocyte donors'. *Fertility and Sterility*, 88, 305–9.

American Society for Reproductive Medicine Ethics Committee (ASRM) (2013). 'Informing offspring of their conception by gamete or embryo donation: a committee opinion'. *Fertility and Sterility*, 100, 45–9.

Bay, B., Larsen, P.B., Schiøler Kesmodel, U. and Ingerslev, H.J. (2014). 'Danish sperm donors across three decades: motivations and attitudes'. *Fertility and Sterility*, 101, 252–7.

Butcher, F. (2012). *Selling your eggs: an empirical study of young women's views on the ethics of financial compensation for egg donation.* Unpublished dissertation. Brighton and Sussex Medical School, University of Sussex, UK.

Côté, S., Affdal, A.O., Kadoch, I.J., Hamet, P. and Ravitsky, V. (2014). 'Posthumous reproduction with surplus in vitro fertilization embryos: a study exploring users' choices'. *Fertility and Sterility*, 102, 1410–5.

Cribb, A. and Owens, J. (2010). 'Whatever suits you: unpicking personalization for the NHS'. *Journal of Evaluation in Clinical Practice*, 16, 310–4.

Furnham, A., Salem, N. and Lester, D. (2014). 'Selecting egg and sperm donors: the role of age, social class, ethnicity, height and personality'. *Psychology*, 5, 220–9.

Gallagher, J. (2014). 'UK national sperm bank opens for business'. *BBC*. Available at www.bbc.co.uk/news/health-29815524.

Harris, J. (2001). 'One principle and three fallacies of disability studies'. *Journal of Medical Ethics*, 27, 383–7.

Human Fertilisation and Embryology Authority (HFEA) (2014a). Lifecycle. Available at www.hfea.gov.uk/8350.html.

Human Fertilisation and Embryology Authority (HFEA) (2014b). 'Chapter 13: Payment for donors'. *Code of Practice,* 8th edn. Available at www.hfea.gov.uk/500.html#guidanceSection4582.

Human Fertilisation and Embryology Authority (HFEA) (2014c). 'Chapter 11: Donor recruitment, assessment, and screening'. Code of Practice, *8th edn.* Available at www.hfea.gov.uk/498.html.

Human Fertilisation and Embryology Authority (HFEA) (2014d). 'Principles'. Code of Practice, *8th edn.* Available at www.hfea.gov.uk/184.html.

Human Fertilisation and Embryology Authority (HFEA) (2014e). 'Using donated sperm in your treatment'. Available at www.hfea.gov.uk/79.html.

Jackson, E. (2013). 'The internet is a dangerous wild west of DIY-assisted conception'. *The Guardian*, Monday 29 April.

Leather, S. (2003). 'Urgent: posthumous conception – consent requirements for birth registration'. HFEA Chair's Letter, CH(03)06. 15 September. Available at www.hfea.gov.uk/2684.html.

Levine, A.D. (2010). 'Self-regulation, compensation, and the ethical recruitment of oocyte donors'. *Hastings Center Report*, 40, 25–36.

Lifecycle (2014). 'Information for current egg and sperm donors'. Available at www.hfea.gov.uk/docs/Lifecycle_Info_for_current_egg_and_sperm_donors_v1.pdf.

National Institute for Health and Care Excellence (NICE) (2013). 'NICE guidance fertility: assessment and treatment for people with fertility problems'. NICE guidelines [CG156]. Available at www.nice.org.uk/guidance/cg156.

Nuffield Council on Bioethics (2013). *Donor Conception: Ethical Aspects of Information Sharing.* London: Nuffield Council on Bioethics.

Savulescu, J. (2001). 'Procreative beneficence: why we should select the best children'. *Bioethics*, 15, 413–26.

Savulescu J. and Kahane G. (2009). 'The moral obligation to create children with the best chance of the best life'. *Bioethics*, 23, 274–90.

Wiggins, D. (1998). *Needs, Values, Truth*. Oxford: Clarendon Press.
Williams, C., Ehrich, K., Farsides, B. and Scott, R. (2007). 'Facilitating choice, framing choice: staff views on widening the scope of pre-implantation genetic diagnosis in the UK'. *Social Science and Medicine*, 65, 1094–105.

UK LEGISLATION

Human Fertilisation and Embryology Act 1990, as amended (2008).

Index

Lightning Source UK Ltd.
Milton Keynes UK
UKOW06n0743030416

271408UK00004B/102/P

9 781107 090965